The End of Intelligent Writing

The End
of
Intelligent Writing

Literary Politics in America

Richard Kostelanetz

Sheed and Ward, Inc.
Subsidiary of Universal Press Syndicate

To Ethel & Jacques Cory
Progenitors of Scrutiny

ISBN— 0-8362 — 0554-5
Library of Congress Card Number 73-9098

Ten years of my life have been consumed in correspondence and litigation about my book *Dubliners:* it was rejected by 40 publishers; three times set up, and once burnt. It cost me about 3,000 francs in postage, fees, train and boat fare, for I was in correspondence with 110 newspapers, 7 solicitors, 3 societies, 40 publishers and seven men of letters about it. All refused to aid me, except Mr. Ezra Pound. In the end it was published, in 1914, word for word as I wrote it in 1905. My novel [*Portrait of the Artist as a Young Man*] was refused by every publisher in London to whom it was offered—refused (as Mr. Pound informed me) with offensive comments. When a review did decide to publish it, it was impossible to find in the United Kingdom a printer to print it.—James Joyce, in a letter (10 July, 1917).

Table of Contents

EPIGRAPHS
TO THE BOOK

When cultural life is dominated by people with similar backgrounds and outlook and similarly trained sensibilities—when there is indeed a cultural establishment—the limits of the range of taste tend to become rigid; . . . the obstacle in the path of non-members of the establishment is not a conspiracy to exclude them. It is simply a lack of understanding, often even a lack of perception that there is something to be understood. . . . Establishment members, like people generally, recognize most easily what they have been trained to expect and to evaluate. Even when dimly perceived, the ability of outsiders is too uncomfortable to recognize. No one likes to be forced to reexamine his whole outlook, the premises and precepts that have governed his conduct and his rationalizations throughout his life—least of all when the articulation of these premises and precepts has been his life work and has gained him his intellectual and material position.—Ernest van den Haag, *The Jewish Mystique* (1969).

Significant writers today are not trying to change the world abstractly but *concretely,* naming names, quoting money prices, deals, what so-and-so had for lunch and what his cardiogram says, committing themselves totally to a specific piece in every conceivable sense so that a result can *issue* from the union of art and journalism.—Seymour Krim, *Shake It for the World, Smartass* (1970).

The answer does seem to be that the academic world, like other worlds, is run by the politicians, and sensitively scrupulous people tend to leave politics to other people, while people with genuine work to do certainly have no time as well as no taste for committee-rigging and the associated techniques. And then of course there are the forces of native stupidity reinforced by that blind hostility to criticism, reform, new ideas and superior ability which is human as well as academic nature.—Q. D. Leavis, "Academic Case-History" (1943).

Epigraphs to the Book

A lot of lip service has been paid to the ideas in [my book], but they haven't changed anything in the real world. . . . I still hope that things will be done better; but if they ever are, I don't flatter myself that my book will have done much to accomplish it, except perhaps to have given some people a little more confidence in forcing changes. The book may make it a little harder for the 'experts' to tell them they're wrong. I'm looking forward to the next generation. If my book has any effect, it will be on the young. Certainly not on people who hold power at present. It won't have the slightest effect on them.— Jane Jacobs, "Social Uses of Power" (1969).

One cannot be seriously interested in literature and remain purely literary in interests—F. R. Leavis, *Education and the University* (1943).

Knowledge that is not communicated has a way of turning the mind sour, of being obscured, and finally of being forgotten.—C. Wright Mills, "The Social Role of the Intellectual" (1944).

One has to face the fact that literature isn't, of necessity, permanent.—Cyril Connolly, in an interview (1971).

Preface

The title of this book announces its argument, which holds that a panoply of growing forces and festering symptoms forecast the likely end of "intelligent writing" or "literature" as we have known those traditions. The reason for this crisis is not that such writing is no longer produced—quite the contrary is true—or that it is not read—also untrue—but that the channels of communication between intelligent writer and intelligent reader have become clogged and corrupted. Since this polemic differs from the other literary essays in taking its perspective from the future—the young and the new—the book's opening half explains how this predicament came about. It focuses upon the intermediary agencies that lie between writers and readers—between writers and print on the one hand, and between print media and readers on the other; for one theme reiterated in the following pages holds that the institutions of writing, which feed the channels of communication, determine not only what is published, but also what is promoted and recognized. This power in turn affects what is read by selecting what one is advised to read or what is available to be read, at a time when educated Americans still get most of their information and opinion from print.

As the institutions of writing are run not by machines but by people, this book begins with a general consideration of literary politics in America. The opening chapters endeavor to ascertain not only who, what, and when—the questions of literary history—but also who else, what else, why, and how. The latter considerations inevitably raise specific questions that would normally go unasked: Why do certain tendencies dominate, while others seem unduly neglected? How does "recognition" develop? Why do the activities of some writers seem collusive? What is "literary power" and how is it exercised? Who lacks it and why? How are they thus handicapped? Since the print media have previously considered these issues *verboten*, merely raising them constitutes a radical activity not unlike comparable investigations of economic disparities in the larger society.

By regarding literary individuals as members of larger constellations, some of which are more explicit than others, literary-political analysis confronts such anomalies as why the reputations of certain "leading" writers should seem so much larger than their ostensible achievements—say, Norman Podhoretz's or Allen Tate's, Archibald MacLeish's or Robert Creeley's—or why one talented writer becomes a star, while another of apparently comparable quality (or even style) remains a bit player. Of the numerous "poetic realists" who emerged around 1960, why should Philip Roth and John Updike have become literary household words, while other novelists of comparable quality, such as Walter N. Miller, Jr. (*Canticle for Leibowitz,* 1959), Robert Phelps (*Heroes and Orators,* 1958), and Paule Marshall (*Brown Girl, Brownstones,* 1959) remain neglected. Equally unknown are Mitchell Goodman, Alfred Grossman, Arno Karlen, Alan Marcus, Clancy Segal, Richard Yates, and Curtis Zahn, all of whom published their initial works of fiction around 1960. Faced with discrepancies like these, the literary historian customarily offers the answer of "critical opinion"; but let me suggest that a writer's place in that shifting hierarchy of publicized ratings ultimately reflects literary-politicking, precisely because the opinion-makers are entwined in the literary-political process. Explanations of such disparities must therefore take historical forms, showing in verifiable detail how individual endeavors reflect collective aspirations (and vice versa) and how literary-political threads underlie years of superficially miscellaneous activity, for it is the purpose of such examinations to penetrate beneath the chaotic surface and raise into consciousness what might otherwise remain hidden. Analysis of this sort constitutes not a sociology of literature, to draw a crucial distinction, but a sociology of literary reputations or literary history.

A further assumption is that the efforts of a lone writer, like those of an individual voter, count for naught until his lot is allied with that of others. Though individual works and careers have an existence apart from literary-political history, it will become clear, in the following chapters, that much literary art and literary life reflect, to various degrees, the demands of professional business. "We do not in fact know who are our greatest living novelists," the literary historian Jay B. Hubbell has remarked, "and I doubt whether we can even identify them by polling any number of editors, critics and authors." That is true, to be sure, partly because such surveys will probably reflect the literary politics of the time (and perhaps the pollsters). At its best, then, literary-political analysis brings concept and rigor to what might otherwise be dismissed as "gossip" precisely because such analysis talks about groups—both formal institutions and informal alliances welded together by varying degrees of cohesiveness. The principal deceit of literary politics is the establishment of a system of taste upon non-esthetic criteria. For this reason, literary-political analysis usually proceeds apart from critical judgment, instead identifying factors other than intrinsic quality as contributing to literary eminence. Therefore, how one or another critic values a particular work is less important than the place of that work (and criticism supportive of it) in larger patterns that signify the presence of a "movement." Rather than conjecture about the motives of complex people, such analysis also prefers to let scrupulously marshalled facts suggest their own conclusions. One pitfall of this approach—not only here but also in Harold Cruse's otherwise exemplary *The Crisis of the Negro Intellectual* (1967)—is an excess of petty intellectual history of figures who are, for the while at least, thought to be culturally eminent.

Literary politics, like politics in general, also affects what is written, though its power over the individual writer is ultimately less decisive simply because writing itself is a fundamentally private transaction between an isolated mind and a piece of paper. The act of setting words to paper is done in nearly ideal freedom, epitomizing the qualities of independence and integrity that are subsequently compromised by the processes (and politics) of public communication. Indeed, since the phrase "literary politics" incorporates a contradiction in purist terms, the necessary length and detail of the following discussion is itself symptomatic of the current malaise. Out of small problems, by contrast, come short books.

The prime social reality behind literature is, of course, publishing, which supports the auxiliary domains of book-reviewing and bookselling; and though publishers customarily blame the neglect of important works upon the "illiterate public," my contention is that the literary industry, rather than the populace, is primarily responsible for the imminent death of intelligent writing. The villains lie not outside but within the publishing system, in the shapes—not only—of restrictive policies but deleterious attitudes; so that foisting blame upon "the public" (which is in no position to talk back) represents an evasion of both responsibility and truth. It is statistically known that, despite the impact of television, more Americans are buying good books and magazines than ever before, and that more good works are sold, especially to young people, who are also more likely to read them. What Dwight Macdonald noted a dozen years ago is true today: "So far, our Renaissance, unlike the original one, has been passive—a matter of consuming, rather than creating." However, the reasons why certain manuscripts are published (while others are neglected) reflect narrowly concerned business priorities; and why one high-quality book or magazine (and not another) is purchased and read has less to do with personal taste than the degree of merchandising effort.

It should be clear by now that this critique deals with the fortunes of Literature rather than cookbooks, comic books, trade manuals, and the like; and the adjective "sub-literate" is used to characterize works and writers (and at times an audience) that are at best journalistic—accessible, simplistic, transient, stylistically derivative, superficial, and unashamedly faddish. In this respect, both the daily newspaper and the underground press, both *Time* and nearly all of *The Whole Earth Catalog* are sub-literate; so are television programs and rock music. Literature, by contrast, is simply that writing which is appreciated long after its first publication, as well as that writing which emerges from distinctly "literary" traditions. "Intelligent writing" particularly includes poetry and fiction, and also criticism that is more substantial and considered than glib reviewing, and, to a lesser extent, other serious non-fiction expository forms that inhabit a realm between special knowledge and the general interests of the educated public. (The predicament of American theater and, by extension, American playwrighting constitutes another terrain, deserving its own detailed study.) In generalizing about literature, I frequently use such terms as "radical" and "conservative," "innovative" and "conventional," for although precise definitions would take another book, my practical assumption is that most of us roughly know the meaning of these discriminations. Nonetheless, this critique deals less with differences in taste, though they are worth noting, than larger issues of literary classes and collective fate.

The End of Intelligent Writing is, in many passages, also a personal book about the literary universe as I have discovered it. Although everyone this side of egomania naturally hesitates to generalize from his own observations, I think that experience in several worlds of writing, both critical and creative, has given me some of the perspective and comparative criteria prerequisite to objective scrutiny. Perhaps because my work has been various, I have managed to meet American writers of all classes—young and old, poets and novelists, critics and playwrights, professionals and amateurs. Conversation has frequently enabled me to discover what they are doing or wanted to do, what their professional experience was like, and what problems they faced in realizing their aims. Especially if they were equally young, I noticed that their sense of the writing world, as well as professional obstacles, resembled my own; if they were similarly experimental, in their sense of either writing style or personal activity, then our accounts were often identical. For that reason, most of my generalizations about "young writers" or "new writing" are also true for me, and vice versa. (If not at least personally true, then such generalizations would be dubious.) This is, quite frankly, a book I would prefer not to have written—or not to have found enough compelling reasons to write.

It is obvious that in a state-supported literary society such as Soviet Russia, certain writers and styles are disseminated to the exclusion of others; yet too many of us remain oblivious to similar forces and pressures shaping the public life of American writing today. The pervasive neglect of whole classes of literature suggests the possible existence of a "conspiracy"; but since American publishing is scarcely of a single piece, the causes, as well as the explanation, must be more various, elaborate, and complex. It is illegal, by analogy, to exclude blacks or to conspire to exclude them; yet it is also clear that certain areas of American society are lily-white. The most sophisticated explanation of this incongruity would probably show how what might seem the result of a "conspiracy" was actually caused by a confluence of attitudes, historical precedents, and initially independent discriminations, all of which combine to function

with conspiratorial effectiveness. It is also true that one definition of a "conspiracy" is that all parties act toward a common
goal, whether by design or by inadvertent cooperation that is
only retrospectively apparent. By this criterion, a "conspiracy"
can be more implicit than explicit. However, since "conspiracy
theories" are so disreputable nowadays, one would sooner be
caught clutching Confederate money.

This essay repeats criticisms made by me in periodicals and
conversations over the past decade, when they were heard or
read by an angry but ineffectual few. Only in 1970 did I realize
that if my complete critique were written and then published in
permanent form, we could have more leverage in dealing with
adversity. The first few chapters came so quickly that I saw the
end in sight, and so I submitted those early drafts to some of
my previous publishers. All of them refused it. Junior editors at
several other firms sponsored the manuscript, only to find their
chiefs refusing them. Parts appeared prominently in literary
journals, some of whose editors asked, with more generosity
than I could accept, to print the entire book out of personal
funds. A prominent bookseller wanted to found a publishing
imprint with *The End of Intelligent Writing* as his initial book,
but he was unable to get appropriate backing. One young
editor-in-chief said he wanted to publish the book, but then
seemed unable to deliver the promised contract. Perhaps the
manuscript was more "threatening" than even I envisioned it to
be, since its own history with publishers was illustrating one of
my theses. However, proof-by-suppression was not the kind of
convincing I initially had in mind. No, no, not at all.

I began to realize more immediately, and viscerally, the real
costs of non-publication, not only for myself, but for others.
While suffering, on one hand, from a growing fear that more
than two years of persistent effort would be wasted, I found, on
the other, that people seeing one chapter in a periodical would
ask about the others, trying to piece the book together from its
fragments, that more people wrote me about these essays than
anything else I had recently published, and that booksellers had
repeated requests for the whole book (from those who had read
these parts). Or, when asked my sense of "American culture," I
would launch into an analysis that would prompt me to cry,
"This is all explained in greater, more definitive detail, in a
book you unfortunately can't get." I made so many xeroxes,

for so many reasons, that I began to consider self-publication as a cheaper solution to the problems of private communication. The most disheartening conclusion was that nobody would publish a comprehensive critique of the channels of literary communication.

My interest in *de facto* censorship was fed by the appearance of George Orwell's recently uncovered essay on the difficulties he encountered in finding a publisher for his classic *Animal Farm.* After noting that "extremely centralized" newspapers frequently censor controversial material, he continued: "The same kind of veiled censorship also operates in books and periodicals.... Anyone who challenges the prevailing orthodoxy finds himself silenced with surprising effectiveness. A genuinely unfashionable opinion is almost never given a fair hearing." What Orwell exposed was not the familiar kind of censorship that occurs after publication, but the more subtle and less visible blockage that publishers exercise among themselves, largely on their own initiative. "The sinister fact about literary censorship in England," Orwell wrote, "is that it is largely voluntary. Unpopular ideas can be silenced, and inconvenient facts kept dark, without the need for any official ban." He attributed this insidious censorship to British publishers' fear of "public opinion," but it became clear, in his experience, that those few publishers possibly interested in his kind of books were afraid not of the amorphous public or even the government. What they primarily feared was *the disapproval of each other,* which is to say the gossip circle in which they immediately moved.

One suggestion frequently made in the following pages is that writers are obliged to expose the crisis, and that is precisely what I have done. I have named names where possible, preserving anonymities largely when revealing privileged information and/or threatened with a libel suit (which is worth a rich man's while, though not a poor defendant's time and money); and for that reason, I have favored published sources wherever possible. Rather than clutter the manuscript with footnotes, I have identified these sources in the book's bibliography. In general, my criticisms are directed at kinds of behavior, rather than specific individuals, because the decapitation of some stuffed heads will be less consequential than truly comprehensive change in the literary climate. As an anarchist, I tend to regard individuals as the victims of circumstance, rather than the reverse.

In the course of drafting the text, I was frequently asked "to go easy" on one or another individual or institution, for some reason or other (or warned that a certain powerhouse "won't like what you say about him"); but the text alone should make it clear that I have scrupulously avoided such compromises. C. Wright Mills reportedly observed of the responses to his classic *White Collar* (1951) that white-collar readers tended to agree heartily with his critiques of everything except their own particular profession whose self-image still commanded their loyalty; and I suspect that the following pages might well produce a comparable pattern of reactions. The first reader radicalized by this book was myself, and that may account for the burst of outrage; but both the book and its author, after all, remained enmeshed in the real world it describes.

Certain parts, points, and phrases of this book draw upon essays published before—in *Hudson Review, The San Francisco Book Review, December, Chicago Review, Panache, Michigan Quarterly Review, Unmuzzled Ox, Quadrant, Kontexts, Denver Quarterly, Margins, Open Letter, Stations Three, Voyages, American PEN, Surfiction* (Swallow, 1973), and elsewhere. I am grateful not only to the editors of these publications for permission to reprint here, but also to those friends who supported the book in innumerable letters, corrected drafts, gave good advice, threw parties, or typed the final version. Among those taking particular trouble were Nicholas and Joan Acocella, Jane Augustine, Anne M. Barry, Regina N. Cohen, Curt Johnson, Susan R. Harris, Henry and Joan Korn, Susanna Opper, and Ted Wilentz. It should be known that James F. Andrews, the new president of Sheed & Ward, saw that this book and his publishing designs complemented each other; that Philip Nobile, as Sheed & Ward's executive editor, has been both a generous intermediary and a tough scrutinizer; and that their associates, especially W. Conger Beasley, Jr., have helped speed the manuscript into print. The history documented in these pages stopped with the date at the bottom of the page.

Richard Kostelanetz
New York, New York
January 1, 1973.

PART I

Locating American Literary "Establishments"

I

Literature generally, but literary criticism in particular, has always been an area in which social forces assume symbolic guise, and work out—or at least exemplify—conflicts taking place in the contemporary, or, rather usually the just past, wider arena of society. —Kenneth Rexroth, *The Alternative Society* (1970).

Given this sort of group, I think I may disregard the claim of propriety and say quite plainly that, so far as I know, there was never so much talent, knowledge and character accidentally brought together at one American place at one time. —Allen Tate, "The Fugitive 1922-1925" (1942).

[Bellow's] appearance as the first Jewish-American novelist to stand at the center of American literature is flanked by a host of matching successes on other levels of culture and subculture. What Saul Bellow is for highbrow literature, Salinger is for upper middlebrow, Irwin Shaw is for middle middle-brow and Herman Wouk for lower middlebrow. . . . The acceptance of Bellow as the leading novelist of his generation must be paired off with the appearance of Marjorie Morningstar on the front cover of *Time*. On all levels, the Jew is in the process of being mythicized into the representative American. —Leslie A. Fiedler, "Saul Bellow" (1957).

Literary politics in America differs from European in lacking a single self-perpetuating establishment, customarily located in the capital city and closely linked to the major publishing

1

houses and reviewing media. Washington, D.C., the political capital, has never had a flourishing community of writers, let alone a first-rank university or even, until recently, an important literary magazine. Boston-Harvard, in the late nineteenth century, provided perhaps the closest semblance of this European model, claiming as local residents nearly all the writers important at the time along with several major publishers. Its dominance disintegrated after World War I, however, as the center of cultural business subsequently gravitated to New York where the keystones of several other communications industries also resided. American literary inspiration, on the other hand, has remained comparatively plural and mobile in its social origins, the best writers living and working, as well as coming from, almost everywhere in these states.

The realities of pluralism and mobility hardly prevent, however, various kinds of exclusive organization and collusion. Even assertedly independent Americans invariably look for reasons, or excuses, to band together. As a result, this country has witnessed the rise of not one cultural establishment but a proliferation of them, one hardly in touch with most of the others, each with its own set of chiefs, assistant chiefs, molls, henchmen, and lackeys. Usually formed by writers about thirty in age, a literary lobby is united not only by personal friendship and fairly similar artistic attitudes but also, and most important, by a sense of collective fortune. Therefore, the professional help that individuals render each other is based upon a sense of mutually entwined professional investment. Every literary establishment also needs, to be sure, a foundation of cultivated talent and several likable writers, as well as intellectual issues and artworks capable of persuasion or winning admiration, for these are the crucial prerequisites for competing in the cultural marketplace. However, with the increasing influence of its articulated positions and the greater prosperity of its membership, such qualities as artistic biases and critical standards are, to varying degrees, compromised by aspirations for continuing personal and collective success.

What defines each modern American literary constellation are the common social origins of its members, be that inclusive factor geographic, academic, racial, ethnic, or sexual. What usually reveals the existence of such a tribe is an articulate claim

2

for the specialness of this common sociological factor coupled with a noticeable penchant for touting each other's works, whether published or not, and appearing by name in each other's "criticism," if not their poetry, fiction—and eventually—their memoirs as well. The threads that stitch a cabal together are necessarily informal, because the mere existence of dues, say, or membership cards (or, worse, legal incorporation) would automatically inspire outraged protests. Therefore, the alliances binding a sociologically-defined constellation of individuals are often more implicit and possibly tenuous than explicit, except, of course, when, as often happens, the allied writers are legally married to each other. These establishments are *not* "conspiracies" but chains of interpersonal relationship based upon common sentiment and mutual interest whose links can be mobilized at times to function in rather aggressive, if not apparently conspiratorial, ways.

It must first be understood that such minority-identifying terms as "San Francisco," "beat," "Southern," "academic," "New York," "Jewish," are ultimately not stylistic descriptions or even genuine critical categories; for each epithet is a literary-political "front" for an entire group—its badge of membership, so to speak. The crucial fact is that the term "Southern writers" encompasses considerably less than all Southern-born novelists, and only a few American-Jewish intellectuals have been known as "Jewish writers." Nor have all the consequential poets who were ever resident at Black Mountain College marched under the banner of "Black Mountain Poets" (the distinguished exceptions including M. C. Richards, Jonathan Williams, John Cage, and R. Buckminster Fuller). The writers claiming these titles were and are, in fact, members of small cliques within a larger sociological category, for the number of writers needed to form a cohesive literary-political machine is, as we shall see, amazingly few.

In practice, nonetheless, it is primarily by such fronting epithets that American literary groups have been publicly known. This custom explains why native writers are frequently identified by their minority affiliations even if the reality of their personal lives contradicts their professed identity on the writing scene. That is, just as most "Jewish writers" have been non-observant, a few even anglicizing their names, so do most

3

major "Southern writers" now live and teach in the North, while Black Mountain College went defunct nearly two decades ago! It was H. Richard Niebuhr's penetrating insight, in *The Social Sources of Denominationalism* (1929), that many Protestant sects in America serve as fronts for sociological differences—racial, ethnic, geographical—rather than doctrinal disputes; and many classifications in American literature are similarly deceptive, actually defining not esthetic issues of personal culture but literary-political allegiances.

The practice of minority-identification also accounts for why reviewers and other lesser critics tend not only to discuss whole groups together and then regard particular works as inseparable from such collective background, but also to portray individual writers within each minority as competing primarily with one another. That is, "Southern" or "Jewish" novelists are first of all compared with other "Southern" or "Jewish" writers rather than with novelists in general, thereby creating, in the eyes of criticism, a *de facto* minor league with its own exclusively segregated hierarchies. The critical advocacy of such a socially hermetic system, or the recognition of its existence, is a sure surface index of a clique. Collective terms also function to inspire serious interest in works that would otherwise be beneath critical notice, imploring the literate audience to pay attention to Author X simply because he is Southern or Jewish. Thus his writing, no matter how inconsequential, is regarded as contributing to, or commenting upon, a larger, critically-certified enterprise (and vice versa).

The mere reiteration of key commitments (or godfathers), especially in response to challenges, can serve to curb the idiosyncratic waywardness of allied writers and thus revive otherwise slackening allegiances. Precisely by such processes do intellectual issues, individual reputations, and collective interest coalesce into a barreling snowball, where one dimension cannot be separated from the other two and all have an influence upon professional behavior. The exigencies of literary politics can supersede the predilections of individual taste, instilling loyalties that can overcome personal antipathies; so that even if an allied author or his work is currently disliked, both it and he will be prominently noticed and probably praised. Endeavors of this sort enabled certain twentieth-century Americans to overcome the precedents of public neglect and professional isolation that had plagued some of their most accomplished predecessors (e.g., Whitman, Poe, and Melville). It should be noted, however, that the audience whose favor they solicited was, until quite recently, a shockingly minuscule percentage of the total U. S. population. Not all modern American writers have been coterie-linked, no doubt, though most were; but more crucial is the fact that such categories have come to inform our historical understanding of both general literary developments and the reputations of individual writers.

In their internal structure, these literary establishments resemble an onion with a center consisting of major theorists and organizers, surrounded by successive layers of imaginative writers, critics, editors, and publicists with various degrees of allegiance to the core. Individuals within an onion are continually redefining the proximity of their relationship to the center, so that Southern-born novelists are, say, "Southern writers" to idiosyncratic degrees. "The word 'establishment' does not refer to a formal organization," notes the sociologist Ernest Van den Haag. "There is no acknowledged hierarchy, visible or secret, no lines of authority fixed by explicit rules, no bureaucracy, regulations, instructions, or formalities." Membership on the outer layers is often transient, as some writers are able gracefully to switch primary allegiances or even to belong to two onions simultaneously. Instances of overlapping include both Allen Ginsberg and Clark Coolidge, two otherwise dissimilar poets, who have been grouped with both "New York Poets" and "San Francisco Poets," even though both men now live primarily in separate upstate New York hamlets.

Just as all groups of any pretension compete with one another in the larger free market of publishers, professional prizes, and common readers, so each also claims to represent the "mainstream" of American literary culture or its most viable current trend. This deception is best achieved by trying, whenever possible, to represent *all* American literature with just their parochial part. When Donald Allen and Robert Creeley, for instance, were commissioned by British Penguin to do *The New Writing in the U.S.A.* (1967), nearly everyone included in their selection belonged to one (or more) of three closely allied cabals—the San Francisco "beats" (Allen's entourage), the Black

5

Mountain Poets (Creeley's), or the "New York School" (a common ally). Such exclusivity, especially when masquerading under an encompassing banner ("in the U. S. A."), also denies the fundamental pluralism of American culture by suggesting that literary energies might be concentrated in only one or a few places.

For various practical purposes, such as apportioning the available spoils (e.g., inclusion in the Creeley-Allen anthology), groups occasionally collaborate with each other and yet preserve their own literary-political identities; and these associations-between-associations are often prolonged (like that between the San Francisco "beats" and Black Mountain). In the end, the existence of such a multiple competition makes most American literary reputations (especially those lacking a foundation in an acknowledged classic work) the product of extended literary politicking.

Every group sets as its prime literary-political goal the professional success of its members. As the primary means to this end is the promotion of characteristic enthusiasms and fraternal reputations, the first sign of possible prosperity is an increasing non-coterie taste for these writers and their enthusiasms. As a general rule, it is essential that writers' works be likeable. That these might also be disliked is meaningless, for only enthusiasm counts in building an artistic reputation; success makes prior detractors seem philistine and silly. (Indeed, nothing in art can be prominently hated unless it is also liked by someone else, and what is passionately hated usually embodies a crucially divisive issue. What counts at this point in a minority's career is the persuasiveness of the art and its advocates.) In the evolution of an establishment, collective success begins when the group's stars earn recognition outside their immediate sphere (where acclaim had previously been guaranteed), when its pet "ideology" gains increasing acceptance, when its academic colleagues are chosen as professors in the major universities, when editorial associates become moguls in New York publishing and reviewing media, and so forth.

At this optimal point in collective development, writers who have been identified with the group can individually capitalize upon its prestige. Eminence also creates an inviting image of a particular kind of literary gent, and that myth in turn might

6

capture the developing sensibilities of aspiring young writers and perhaps influence their literary juvenilia. The most prominent young authors are invariably those who fulfill a current establishment's concept of literary personality and existence; thus do old groups compete through their younger agents. (The question of whether John Updike is "better" than Philip Roth involves more than esthetics.)

Even superlative literary enthusiasms are doomed to remain regional until they become established in literary New York from where they are in turn disseminated over nation-wide publicity channels. Therefore, a literary clique must try to infiltrate these media of publishing and reviewing — if not with core operators, then at least with sympathizers on the perimeters of the onion, or by recruiting the loyalty of people already empowered within these hierarchies. For these reasons alone, some of its associates must necessarily come to New York. "Because there was no city in the South where writers may gather, write and live, and no Southern publisher to print their books," Allen Tate once noted, "the Southern writer, of my generation at least, went to New York." Absence of a loyal New York publisher has, by contrast, severely limited the Black Mountain writer's national exposure. Within Manhattan reside representatives of not one but several literary establishments, only a few of which, however, have their literary-political base or origins there. This partially explains why, as C. P. Snow once observed, in New York, unlike London, "Distinguished literary figures show a cheerful unawareness of each other's existence." Among the symptoms of collective decline are intrinsic repetition, a lessening of output, the absence of auspicious new names, and demise of magazines, the disappearance of outside support, and the disintegration of alliances.

II.

I would call the Fugitives an intensive and historical group as opposed to the eclectic and cosmopolitan groups that flourished in the East. There was a sort of unity of feeling, of which we were then not very aware, which came out of — to give it a name — a common historical myth.

Allen Tate, "The Fugitive 1922-1925" (1942)

Prior to World War I, "American Literature" was largely the creation of WASP New Englanders who wrote the most influential books, plus the primary scholarship about the books. They consistently equated all U.S. cultural history with just the achievements of their kind and rarely looked beyond their immediate milieu. (Houghton Mifflin, a Boston company, held many of the New Englanders' copyrights and also published the most popular textbooks and anthologies.) Prior to the twentieth century, major writers from New York like Herman Melville and Walt Whitman were likely to be neglected simply because they lived and worked outside what was then regarded as the cultural mainstream; and not until the twenties were many new literary publishers founded in New York, mostly by recent graduates of Columbia College. As late as the twenties, nearly all of the important writers and literary moguls were Anglo-Saxon in background, Protestant in religious origins, Ivy League in education, wealthy by inheritance, and New York-Boston-Paris in residence. Not every well-known figure had every one of these credentials, to be sure, but most of them had more than less. "Literature was regarded as an effeminate upper class affair, open chiefly to men with a Harvard education," Malcolm Cowley observed, some years afterwards. "They expressed and represented only one stratum of American society. Their morals and manners, their virtues and limitations were those of prosperous people living near the Atlantic Seaboard."

In more recent times, however, the Northeastern WASP establishment has become just another literary minority still centered in Cambridge, Massachusetts, and based on those same social roots. Though much less dominant than before, it remains both continually active and generally immune to appeals by subsequent powerful groups. Its critical traditions, whose style it is rarely to penetrate beneath the literary surface, run from Van Wyck Brooks and F. O. Matthiessen through such similarly superficial Harvard-educated critics and reviewers as Cowley himself, Granville Hicks, John Mason Brown, Arthur Mizener, and George Plimpton; and its allied magazines include *The Atlantic Monthly*, especially, and *The New Yorker,* as well as *Paris Review* (particularly at its beginnings) and *Harper's* (prior to 1967)—the first three titles geographically circumscribing its cultural world. The magazines of Time, Inc. were its most loyal employer, in a continuing tradition of "Time-Life" intellectuals. This group's last very prominent poet was probably Archibald MacLeish, who graduated from Yale and then Harvard Law School, or maybe Conrad Aiken. Its recent poetic luminaries include such Harvard alumni as Robert Fitzgerald, who inherited MacLeish's Boylston Chair in "Rhetoric," Richard Wilbur, Donald Hall, and Adrienne Rich, along with L. E. Sissman and Peter Davison, Arthur Freeman, and Robert Dawson of the youngest generation. (Such Harvard alumni as Norman Mailer, William S. Burroughs, William Melvin Kelly, R. Buckminster Fuller, John Ashbery, John Hawkes, William Gaddis, Kenneth Koch, Frank O'Hara, Charles Olson, and Peter Viereck are, for various sociological or esthetic reasons, unfavored; and none of *them*, indicatively, has lived much in the Cambridge area.) This old-boy network was responsible for successfully reviving the declining reputation of Henry James and has since persistently championed such Harvard-educated WASP novelists as James Gould Cozzens and John Updike, in addition to such Yalies as Louis Auchincloss and Peter Matthiessen, in spite of steadily declining energies and influence, especially outside its New England turf.

The subsequent social history of modern American literature traces the ascendancy and decline of other groups. The next to dominate the literary marketplace were Southern writers whose movement originated at Vanderbilt University in the middle twenties and became coherent by the early thirties, its "front" name changing from "Fugitives" to the more sociological and, thus, more effective, "Agrarians." (Fugitives, Tate once explained, were fleeing from something; Agrarians were returning.) This group spread slowly outward through other Southern universities and finally into the North, reaching the pinnacle of America's literary mountain. It had a core of writers and ideologists; a set of social ideals formulated in an early collective manifesto—*I'll Take My Stand* (1930)—and extended in later writings; characteristic styles of both literary criticism and historical erudition; common themes and interests; a hierarchy of reputations, both critical and creative; a network of magazines sympathetic to one another, with overlapping lists of editors, contributing editors, contributors, reviewers—magazines in which the star critics were frequently quoted, both in the essays

9

and in the ads, and their contributions featured over those by a supporting cast; its efforts to make writers of similar backgrounds (e.g., Ransom, Tate, Warren, Faulkner) into masters and prophets of the age; its reinterpretation of the intellectual and literary traditions to emphasize (and often resurrect) appropriate predecessors for themselves; decided penchants for mentioning each other in the same breath with the greatest figures of Western literature and for measuring both earlier or contemporary writers against either the Agrarian ideology or literary values derived from that ideology; a self-generated myth of its own achievement as comparable to, as Tate wrote in 1935, "the outburst of poetic genius at the end of the sixteenth century when commercial England had already begun to crush feudal England"—a sociological circumstance similar, in Tate's mythology, to the modern South; and finally entrenched connections in New York reviewing media and publishing which culminated respectively in both featured notices and textbooks propagating its ideology and reputations among the literate young.

As the Agrarian movement succeeded, its critics became established as professors at first-rank universities, most of them in the heart of the Northern enemy's geographical territory (where their incomes increased while their literary talents atrophied); their textbooks became best-sellers; their essays and poems were frequently anthologized; the most-touted novelist (though not an original or close member of the group, as well as a Mississippi resident to his death) got the Nobel Prize; its chiefs became judges on fellowship committees and members of the National Institute of Arts and Letters (America's most august repository of literary-political pressure); their former students won lesser prizes and recognitions; its younger men honored their elders in print and with book dedications (both Randall Jarrell and Robert Lowell selecting Allen Tate for their opening works). Alliances were made in the forties with an emerging Catholic minority (influenced by the presence here of the French philosophers Etienne Gilson and Jacques Maritain), whose native members included Morton Dauwen Zabel, Wallace Fowlie, Robert Fitzgerald, Marshall McLuhan, W. K. Wimsatt, abetted by such fresh converts (some of them only temporary) as Tate, Lowell, Caroline Gordon, and Frederick Morgan, who

10

founded the *Hudson Review* (est. 1948) in their wake; but this literary minority remained a minor force.

The Agrarian apex arrived in the middle forties, roughly coincident with Tate's famous essay on "The New Provincialism" (1945). This essay followed in turn the general anthology he coedited with John Peale Bishop, *American Harvest* (1942), which united, through equal emphasis, both Southerners and New England WASPs, and appeared between such crucial compilations as Warren's *A Southern Harvest* (1937) and Tate's own *A Southern Vanguard* (1947). As cultural Agrarianism became a dead issue by the forties, esthetic formalism became their principal standard of literary self-publicity. In the early fifties emerged even younger Southern epigones, all born between 1914 and 1930, who were eager to do various kinds of academic-historical sweeping—Louis D. Rubin, Jr., Robert Daniel, Robert D. Jacobs, Walter Sullivan, John Edward Hardy, James B. Meriwether, most of whom, unlike their cultural daddies, remained in Southern universities, some of whom devoted whole books to themes and subjects their precursors treated only in essays. They were the grandchildren, so to speak, in a literary family whose father-figure, Ransom, was privately called "Pappy."

Afterwards came book-length retrospectives about the Southern writers, uncritically reiterating such honorific terms as "Renaissance" (hardly appropriate for a movement that produced, as far as the outside world was concerned, one and only one truly great writer), recording memorable anecdotes about the masters and their off-hand comments about trivial things, and still inflating the reputations of minor writers who embodied values, attitudes, and birthplaces similar to the stars of the firmament. By 1960, Rubin could note, "On one page of almost all announcement sheets from every publishing house there is announced a new Southern writer, and most are never announced more than once." With a decline in their influence, however, came cultural claims that could not convince anyone not already predisposed, in addition to irrational and unsupported derogatory generalizations about emerging younger writers with other affiliations, coupled with a defensive interest in holding professional ground already won. Of course, what in retrospect resembles a neatly systematic invasion may have actually been full of internal conflict and the result of either semi-conscious common sympathies or the fortuitous accident of similar talents befriending each other; for intrinsic in analytic history is a penchant for finding past developments far neater than they may actually have been. Only an ingénue, however, could still think that the ascendancy of the Southern literati was purely serendipitous.

III.

> Most of my friends and I were Jewish; we were also literary; the combination of the Jewish intellectual tradition and the sensibility needed to be a writer created in my circle the most potent and incredible intellectual-literary ambitions I have ever seen.
> —Seymour Krim, *Views of a Near-Sighted Cannoneer* (1961).

The same pattern of insurgence was duplicated a decade and a half later by another well-organized literary minority, the Jewish-American writers. Here again was a core of critics and propagandists; a common commitment to Marxian-Freudianism which politically branched off into the two streams of democratic socialism and neo-liberalism; the inclination to test earlier authors against these intellectual touchstones or dominant beliefs; a set of literary values which discounted both formal invention and fantasy, instead of emphasizing both intelligible (and intelligent) themes and the accurate rendering of urban social experience; a phalanx of magazines, ranging from a quarterly through a monthly through the literary pages of a weekly; a force of ambitious sometime students and protégés willing to do minor tasks for which the elders no longer had the time, guts, or energy; allies in the major reviewing media; cooperative conduits in New York publishing; anthologies that would place their names beside the acknowledged champs; and the attempt to make one of their number into the foremost novelist of his time (the Saul Bellow-shall-be-our-Greatest-Writer-or-bust-movement), which has so far conquered one international prize and has at least another to go. They emphasized not poetry and extended critical essays, like their predecessors, but fiction and book reviews, which are inherently more popular forms.

Only on the textbook front did the Jewish-American literary propagandists at first seemingly fail to complete their literary-political revolution; instead they capitalized upon a successful surrogate—the quality paperback that has progressively replaced many textbooks in the university classrooms. Jason Epstein became the crucial entrepreneur of this phase of the operation; his pioneering paperback line, Anchor Books, not only revived many of the Jewish-Americans' earlier, often neglected works, but he also commissioned some of them to write introductions to revived classics. The lucrative textbooks, needless to say, followed later. By the sixties, this Jewish-American group became the dominant literary-political force, the Southerners having politely stepped aside during the previous decade. Among the conclusive signs of the former's ascendancy were not only prestigious best-sellers by Bellow, Bernard Malamud, and Philip Roth, but anthologies and critical books recapitulating Jewish-American cultural achievements. As Robert Alter concluded in 1965, "Everyone is by now aware of the fact that literary Jewishness has become a distinct commercial asset."

What seemed at first surprising was how strongly this group disclaimed any allegiance to religious Judaism or even any interest in Jewish theology. Rather than following the rabbis, they regarded themselves as extending a tradition of secular Jewish writers—more concerned, by definition, with the people than the faith—which they interpreted as leading directly to themselves. In this respect, they resembled nineteenth-century German-Jewish intellectuals, who, as Hannah Arendt notes, "had to differentiate themselves clearly from the 'Jew in general,' and just as clearly to indicate that they were Jews." Though neither Zionist, religious, nor members of B'nai B'rith, they were still self-consciously Jewish enough to wail "anti-Semitism" when collectively criticized. However, their assertion, like that of other groups, created the preconditions for collective dismissal; a claim that is false in form invites equally fallacious denigrations.

Indeed, just as the literary Agrarians hardly typified the Old South, these Jewish-American writers were scarcely representative of American Jews, as nearly all of them were descendants of recent immigrants, New York City-born and -educated, and non-Zionist. Very few had pre-1880 American ancestors, and

13

none was Sephardic in background. Buber-boosting notwith-standing, their rationalist cultural sympathies rarely stretched as far as the intellectualized neo-Hasidism of Allen Ginsberg or certain commune hippies. These limitations and distortions partially explain why cradle Jews have often been confused with adopted Jews or converted Jews, as well as ersatz Jews and symbolic Jews (in addition to gentile writers whose names and faces happen to look Jewish); but Jewishness of some sort, at times more asserted than actual, informs all of their enthusi-asms.

The Jewish-American writers also sought to reroute the West-ern intellectual tradition, generally favoring continental (and often Jewish) precedents over Anglo-American. Leslie A. Fied-ler describes this attempted shift as fully realized:

> Through their Jewish writers, Americans, after the Second
> World War, were able to establish a new kind of link with
> Europe in place of the old pale-face connection—a link not
> with the Europe of decaying castles and the Archbishop of
> Canterbury, nor with that of the French *symbolistes* and
> the deadly polite *Action Française*—for these are all Chris-
> tian Europes; but with the post-Christian Europes of Marx
> and Freud, which is to say, of secularized Judaism, as well
> as the Europe of surrealism and existentialism, Kafka,
> neo-Chassidism...

And Fiedler himself has specialized in outlining "the Jewish-American tradition in fiction." Here, as with the Southerners, the radical revaluation of the past, along with the elevation of certain neglected figures, ultimately served to lend intellectual foundation to the current enterprise. (Indeed, as a general rule, the reinterpretation of past literature, as well as the reselection of its canon, usually reflects emerging literary-political pres-sures.)

However, the Jewish-American inclusions were, in the end, less significant than their most conspicuous neglects, some of which revealed, or caused, limitations in sensibility. The most prominent omission, in retrospect, was Gertrude Stein who, though Jewish and first-rate, was too intelligent in ways they could not understand and then too alien to their own prosaic literary tastes, as well as too wealthy, rather than upwardly mobile; too old Jewish-American, rather than new; too psychological and esthetic, rather than ethnic and sociological; as well as personally too female, and then too lesbian and too cussedly experimental. (Though she had graduated from Radcliffe with honors, a favorite student of William James, the Harvard machine neglected her, too.)

The movement's ambitions in reviving precedents were scarcely parochial, however, for just as the Southerners claimed universal, or at least national, relevance for their literary program, so did the Jewish-American writers. A few of them, especially Irving Howe, even sought to incorporate Yiddish writing into the stream of relevant ancestors, not only compiling anthologies with laudatory introductions, but dropping praise well in excess of the literature's evident merits. In an instance of critical feedback, Alfred Kazin praised Bernard Malamud's best fictions for evoking "the same deep satisfaction that I [get] from the great realistic masters of Yiddish literature." This jerry-built "tradition" served the further practical function of contributing its bit to current enterprise and of being "unavailable" to T. S. Eliot and Allen Tate. The literary Jews also sprinkled their prose with Yiddish bon mots in lieu of the Latin that the Southerners favored.

Once the core canons of current writing had been established, they could be popularized, not only in "critical essays" but in anthologies that often featured previously established eminences; and a second-generation of collections, devoted solely to "American Jewish writing," would be compiled not by themselves but others (e.g., Irving Malin and Irwin Stark, Charles Angoff and Meyer Levin). By the late sixties, what the sociologist Charles Kadushin defined as "the American intellectual elite" of literary journalists, editors, and other opinion-makers was about one-half Jewish.

Both literary Southerners and literary Jews, then, capitalized upon the absence of a single permanent establishment to invade the scene from a minority position. Though scarcely as efficient as an army, both groups realized effective organizations based upon more than polite reciprocity, and their common success demonstrates that, differences between them notwithstanding,

15

no collective literary enterprises ever *operated* so well in modern America. In that intellectual free market which is American literature's scene, both groups developed the capitalist techniques of efficient production, division of rank and labor, trading in kind, informal association for mutual advance, employee incentive, promotion, advertising, publicity, collusion, interlocking directorates, merchandizing, and dividends. Each, in the interest of its few, also capitalized upon the progressively larger American curiosity about intellectual people and produce.

Professional competition notwithstanding, the most talented members of each establishment have contributed to the other's magazines since the early forties, and during the summers they were frequently in residence together at Yaddo and McDowell writers' colonies, or at the Christian Gauss Seminars at Princeton, or as "fellows" at the Rockefeller-sponsored "School of Letters" at Indiana University. Critics from one group certified the claims of the other in neutral publications (e.g., Irving Howe's lead essay in the *New York Times Book Review,* August 5, 1965)—ecumenical gestures that usually accompanied more concrete collaborations. Primarily because both literary groups had a common interest in deposing conservative academicians, it was Robert Penn Warren who initially proposed Robert Brustein to replace the previous dean of the Yale Drama School.

It is indicative that nearly all of the prominent critics and novelists of the fifties and sixties were either Southerners or Jews or regular contributors to *The New Yorker* (which has been, since the thirties, the most powerful literature-publishing magazine to strive, crucially unlike *Esquire,* for contributor-continuity); and in Richard Howard's encompassing critical survey of forty-one post-World War II poets, *Alone with America* (1969), fifteen were Jewish and nearly as many contributed to *The New Yorker.* Not individual but collective dominance is perhaps the surest measure of literary-political success.

The Dynamics of
Literary Politicking

2

I.

> Nobody can be more meanly intolerant, more insistent on his right to be heard whatever the quality of what he says, more confident of receiving the humbly sympathetic attention that derives from his listener's sense of collective guilt than the member of a persecuted minority at a time when social attitudes are undergoing geological alteration. —Marvin Mudrick, "Podhoretz and Mrs. Trilling: The Holy Family" (1964).

> I refer to that extra dimension given to Jewish personality and life by the fact that each Jew moves, consciously or not, in the context of a long and special history and a religious-ethical tradition that lays upon him, whether as a burden or a badge of pride, the sense of being "chosen," and so creates in him the tendency, even the obligation, to carry himself "with a difference." —Elliot E. Cohen, *Commentary on the American Scene* (1953).

It is significant that both Southerners and Jews, not unlike other militant minorities, strove to overcome earlier influential stereotypes of their collective cultural sterility. The literary historian Jay B. Hubbell has documented that pre-1920 anthologies and textbooks of "American Literature" rarely included any Southern authors, while Southerners coming of cultural age in the twenties also felt obliged to dispel H. L. Mencken's much-quoted characterization of the South as "The Sahara of the Bozart": "Almost as sterile, artistically, intellectually, culturally, as the Sahara Desert. . . . [where] you will not find a single Southern poet above the rank of a neighborhood rhymster." In a 1959 Fugitive symposium, Tate affirmed that he "used to carry Mencken around under his arm." They also wanted to counter the idea of the KKK, say, as typical of white Southern culture, for the general Northern acceptance of such negative stereotypes perhaps explains how even Robert Penn Warren could have, to quote John D. Stewart, "submitted [his first two] novels to nearly every publisher in New York without success."

Similarly, the Jewish writer fought to dispel the anti-Semitic stereotypes so fashionable in the literature of 1920-40 in which, as Fiedler remembers, "The Jew [either] stands for the pseudo-artist . . . [or], as merchant-tourist and usurious millionaire, he desires now to appropriate what he never made, to buy and squat in the monuments of high Christian culture, fouling them by his mere presence." This two-sided derogatory image obviously obsessed the Jewish writer coming of age during that period; and just as he denied his traditional religion (and often his immediate ancestors as well), so did he feel obliged to measure a distance from these stereotypes by creating a new contrary image of a collective ethnic self. "The son of a bookish tradition," Theodore Solotaroff wrote in 1959, "he [the American Jewish writer] is now also economically secure enough to convert business energy more purely into creative and scholarly energy."

Literary Jews suffered genuine discrimination between the wars, if not into the fifties. Columbia University's English department had no Jewish professors between Joel Elias Spingarn's resignation in 1911 and Lionel Trilling's ascendancy in the forties. At Harvard, the poet Stanley Kunitz, who graduated *summa cum laude* in 1926, was discouraged from pursuing a doctorate because, as he was told, "Anglo Saxons would resent being taught English by a Jew." Indeed, no one of Jewish background ever gained a tenured position in English at Harvard, Yale, or Princeton until the late forties, and "Jewish quotas" upon entering students persisted at those schools until the late fifties. The National Institute of Arts and Letters still has remarkably few Jewish writers, most of whom were recently inducted, and the fifty-member American Academy, which selects itself from the larger organization, has proportionately fewer Jews.

Several old American publishing houses had no Jews on their

editorial staffs until quite recently, and certain cultural journals with national circulations had remarkably few Jewish contributors. It is not surprising, therefore, that in the Tate and Bishop retrospective of 1920-40, the only Jewish writers included were Karl Shapiro, Jerome Weidman, and Delmore Schwartz; that in an anthology collected from *Harper's* magazine, *Gentlemen, Scholars and Scoundrels* (1959), only three of the ninety contributors are assuredly Jewish—Oscar Levant, Betty Friedan, and Sigmund Freud; that in *Best Short Stories from the Paris Review* (1959), only one of fourteen contributors are Jewish; and that in Van Wyck Brooks' *A New England Reader* (1962), subtitled "From William Bradford to Robert Lowell," there are no Jewish contributors at all!

Given this record of absence, the success of individual Jewish writers made Jewishness a more opportune base, or front, for winning professional allegiance—not necessarily based, as noted before, upon a sympathy for philosophical Judaism or even an ethnic reality (as a few close allies were gentile by birth)—in much the same way that anti-Semitism had once served a similarly symbolic function for Brahmin WASPs (who might have found real Jews tolerable). As Fiedler shrewdly observed, "Philo-Semitism is required—or perhaps, by now, only assumed—in the reigning literary and intellectual circles of America, just as anti-Semitism used to be required." The analogue to *I'll Take My Stand* was *The Partisan Reader* (1946), which likewise presented the major figures and articulated dimensions of the ideology. (This last book probably contained a greater proportion of Jewish writers, as well as more New York writers, than any previous anthology of American writing.) The Black Mountain poets were similarly excluded—from the prominent magazines, from the university jobs, and from respectable anthologies. Donald Hall, who joined his coeditors in omitting them entirely from both editions of *The Poets of England and America* (1957, 1962), confessed in a 1972 interview, "It's ridiculous, but we did not acknowledge that they existed, and we weren't reading them....Obviously, I wanted to keep my mind closed." Rarely, in my observation, have literary chiefs made such admissions in print.

The literary Southerners and the literary Jews resembled each other in numerous other ways, such as an insatiable interest in parochial themes—e.g., the Southerner's feeling for the earth

19

and the recent Jewish immigrant's relationship to the city—especially if such concerns were embedded in a colleague's work. Both tried to discover, or define, "an organic relation to [their] past," to quote David Daiches' phrase. Both developed "ideologies" which served not only to unite the disparate sensibilities of writers, but also to give the admirers of each group a "handle" by which its art and thought could be most easily understood. Such ideology—basically literary Southernness and literary Jewishness—was cast as having a redemptive power that would enhance a work of art and thus rescue second-rate talents from oblivion. Nonetheless, the ideology functioned most effectively not when it was explicitly promoted, but when it was implicitly understood, or mentioned in passing, or vociferously denied (and thus implicitly evoked), becoming thereby a subconscious inducement to the sentimental loyalty of both writers and readers. One reason why the ideology best remained implicit was its intellectual limitations—just as little in life is exclusively Jewish, so even less is solely Southern, and in neither case would these strictly parochial qualities contribute much to literary virtue. These terms, to repeat, served as "fronts" to induce allegiance, rather than as encompassing or determining characteristics.

Each group developed a particular style of literary criticism that opposed, on crucial points, approaches favored by other critics; so that just as no literary Jew was a "New Critic," so did the Jewish writers develop a kind of criticism that no Southerner would practice (and neither would emulate the plot-summarizing favored by Ivy League WASPs or the breathlessly "poetic" Poundian notationalism of "Black Mountain" essayists). Spokesmen for each insisted at times that critics from other backgrounds could not interpret *their* writers as well (and that, indeed, was usually true). In the writings of both groups were broached some fairly patent contradictions between political slogans and esthetic values, but these discrepancies somehow evaporated beneath literary-political ambitions. Though John Crowe Ransom critically celebrated the Poet's love of nature, he rarely published poems about natural beauties; and few of the Jewish writers treated urban life affectionately. Similarly, just as the Southerners never realized Agrarianism, so the Jews were failed socialists, their political formulations contributing, nonetheless, to their success as American men of letters. Each group wanted to champion, if not produce by themselves, a literature for people of similarly limited experience, only to win in their success a limited percentage of their own kind, along with a more diversified public of chronic readers.

Both Southerners and Jews relished pseudo-explanations, usually based upon some kind of mythical cultural determinism, of why they, rather than another minority, should have current literary dominance—intellectualized prophecies which are fulfilled, to be sure, largely by literary politicking. At times this penchant for foisted historicism produced such far-fetched parallels, respectively geographic and ethnic, as nineteenth-century Southern writers or Hebrew poets of the Spanish middle ages! Historicism also accounts for a related tendency to see predecessors of one's kind as a hidden factor in literary history. As Robert Alter notes:

> According to such a theory, which seems to be tacitly assumed by many critics, the main currents at least of modern culture all derive from subterranean Jewish sources: a tenuous connection through three Christian generations with Jewish forebears is supposedly enough to infect the writer with a uniquely Jewish imagination, and this in turn he passes on to the Gentile world around him.

The excellences of the best writers were attributed to their parochial origins (e.g., numerous essays on Bellow, Malamud, and Roth). As late as 1963, Cleanth Brooks produced a large book suggesting that Faulkner's genius stemmed from (and thus, by implication, could only exist in) the particular kind of society in which he matured. The ideology also explains the Jewish critics' comparative lack of interest in novels populated only with gentile characters—Malamud's *The Natural* (1952) and Bellow's *Henderson the Rain King* (1959); the analogues in Agrarian literature are William Faulkner's *Sanctuary* (1931) and John Peale Bishop's *Act of Darkness* (1935), both of which regard the South not as suspended between Good-Bad but as irredeemably horrible. Certain figures in each group took the literary-political ideology more seriously than others—Tate and Donald Davidson for the Southerners, Irving Howe and Leslie

21

A. Fiedler ("Master of Dreams") for the Jews. Precisely because they truly believed, whereas the others were more inclined merely to exploit and forget, they became the most explicit sources for the movements' subsequent literary and intellectual historians.

Both Jews and Southerners tended to favor, as noted before, certain political views, as well as particular conceptions of "human nature"; and just as the Agrarians frequently refought the Civil War and Reconstruction, so did literary Jews persistently redo the Russian Revolution and the subsequent history of Marxian Socialism. As the Southerners made T. S. Eliot their principal European modernist, so Franz Kafka played a similar, fortunately deceased, role for the literary Jews. Within both establishments literary modernism was a major issue of intellectual disagreement, each having its experimental and its conservative factions; but by the seventies, even the sometime experimentalists seemed fairly traditional.

Both groups also felt strongly impelled to transcend, by means of quality, certain sociologically comparable predecessors of minor talent and achievement—respectively, those writers appearing in several polite Southern journals, and the undistinguished Jews contributing to Henry Hurwitz's *Menorah Journal* in the twenties and thirties, and *The Contemporary Jewish Record* (1938-44), both published in New York. As Ransom noted in the initial manifesto of *The Fugitive,* "The fugitive poet flies from nothing faster than from the high-class Brahmins of the Old South." (Elliot E. Cohen, *Commentary*'s founding editor, knew his precursors well because he had worked on the first journal, and his sponsor, the American Jewish Committee, had previously funded the second.) Both felt obliged to separate themselves publicly from literary trash produced by their own kind—Margaret Mitchell and Erskine Caldwell, Herman Wouk and Harry Golden—even though the popularity of these writers predisposed a larger public to accept the smaller movement's terms of self-publicity.

Both Southerners and Jews also had to distinguish themselves from more immediate competitors who were sociologically similar, though artistically inferior. The Agrarians surpassed a Charleston group known as "The South Carolina Poets" led by DuBose Hayward and Hervey Allen, as well as a New Orleans set gathered around a periodical called *The Double Dealer* (1921-6), that, curiously, included William Faulkner for a while. The literary Jews vanquished not only the Jewish patricians, epitomized perhaps by Dorothy Norman's *Twice-a-Year* (1938-48), but also the Jewish Communist writers (Michael Gold, Morris U. Schappes, Howard Fast, Albert Maltz, Joseph Freeman, John Howard Lawson), while the new San Franciscans had to transcend Yvor Winters' *Twelve Poets of the Pacific* (1937), whose members subsequently gravitated down the peninsula toward Stanford University. The literary Jews, unlike the Southerners, also felt obliged to defend their hard-won turf against subsequent writers of similar background—not only the partly Jewish "beats," whom they found epitomized by Allen Ginsberg, but later Jewish-born spokesmen for the "New Left" and the "counter culture."

Each literary machine also had its elder sages who served as helpful critics of their colleagues' unpublished manuscripts (e.g., Tate and Trilling); both groups exhibit to this day a tendency for reviving interest in neglected early works of their colleagues—as Robert Penn Warren devoted a laudatory essay as recently as 1971 to Andrew Lytle's early novel, *The Long Night* (1936), so were literary Jews forever honoring Delmore Schwartz's early poetry and fiction or Lionel Trilling's *The Middle of the Journey* (1947). Each also had mavericks whose larger talents eventually emancipated them from the chain and who then forged independent reputations large enough to warrant public excommunication. As Warren, for instance, exiled Thomas Wolfe, who had previously been included in *A Southern Harvest,* so did Philip Rahv and Irving Howe refuse communion to Leslie A. Fiedler. Each group also had its eccentric who pursued idiosyncratic, often contrary extremes, and yet remained loyal because no one else would publish him. The eccentric's waywardness and intellectual indulgences were often cited by group spokesmen as evidence of their "openness." As the historian Frank Lawrence Owsley served the Southerners, so has Lionel Abel been used by his literary-political colleagues.

Both establishments had magazines that published outsiders, so to speak, in small and irregular measure, though it was the insiders, and only they, who established each journal's identity and finally profited from its success. *Commentary,* founded in

23

1944, resembled *Kenyon Review,* started six years before, as a belated, ultimately more popular, and prestigious extension of the initial energy. Each group also had its devoted continental travelers who spread word of the emerging Americans to those Europeans most likely to become sympathetic, as well as loyal protégés who functioned as the founders' literary life insurance, perpetuating their elders' professional reputations far beyond their otherwise active lives. As most young Southern novelists revealed Faulkner's influence, so a generation of aspiring Jewish fiction writers revealed, usually at their beginnings, stylistic debts to Bellow. In each group were writers whose eminence was indebted, at least in part, to a fortunate marriage—Caroline Gordon (Tate) and Eleanor Ross Taylor, Diana Trilling and Midge Decter (Podhoretz)—or filial relationship such as John Faulkner, Martin Greenberg, and Pearl Kazin (who was also married to Daniel Bell).

Each also had its transitional figures who originally emerged from older molds and thus had certain credentials and connections otherwise unavailable to aspiring writers. While Princeton-educated John Peale Bishop and Yale-educated William K. Wimsatt served the Southerners, the Jewish movement was later indebted in various ways to such Harvard-educated writers as Daniel Aaron and Oscar Handlin. Similarly, just as the latter had its collaborating gentiles such as Dwight Macdonald and F. W. Dupee, so did the literary Southerners need their Northern-born associates—Robert B. Heilman and William Van O'Connor being two of the most prominent. In my own judgment, the most interesting individuals have generally been those marginal members eccentric and productive enough to transcend their cronies' limitations and thus make an individual contribution, often telling some (though never all) of the truth about their professional colleagues—Fiedler and Paul Goodman among the literary Jews, and Randall Jarrell among the Southerners.

In each group were individuals who refused to speak to each other at various times and for various reasons, while others were simply more comfortable with each other at a distance. (The Southerners actually saw far less of each other, the three kings—Ransom, Tate, and Warren—never spending more than a summer together since 1934.) In both domains were certain decidedly unpopular ideas which were later muffled, if not repudiated: Tate, for example, once defended social inequality on the grounds that "every class and race should get what it earns by contributing to civilized life," and suggested that the "Southerner take hold of his Tradition...by violence"; while several literary Jews rationalized the McCarthyism of the middle fifties.

From their complementary influence comes the common American critical custom of interpreting other literature in similar categories. Thus, James Joyce is regarded primarily as an Irishman rather than as an exemplary literary modernist. Their example also inspired discussions of other hyphenate American literatures, if not legitimizing the subsequent effort to make ethnic studies of all kinds into a respectable scholarly industry. Although Jewish writers have been more inclined than Southerners to criticize each other in print, each group observes a policy of regarding fellow members as the only peers or antagonists worth mentioning. In criticizing an earlier, periodical version of this essay, the novelist George P. Elliott correctly observed, "What strikes me, as a visitor [to New York], even more strongly than the intensity with which these Jews attack and praise each other is the attention they pay to one another." The "position-taking" to which the Jewish writers are inclined usually refers to the views of others within the movement rather than general intellectual discourse, reflecting not only a power-play but, more surely, the kind of product-differentiation that keeps an individual producer in literary business. Morever, underneath the intellectual disagreements of the moment is always the hint that current antagonists will be professional collaborators again. Especially in contrast to the Southerners, the Jewish-American writers seem more cohesive, if not more truly conspiratorial, not only in defending their operation but in carving out new terrain. After all, the Southerners were scarcely enterprising enough to establish a front as popular as *The New York Review of Books,* and no American literary establishment has remained as dominant for so long.

II

If one were to compile an anthology of all the unabashed nonsense written by literary critics over the past fifty years, a good many pages would have to be devoted to what has been advanced about Jewish values, vision and world view by a wide variety of

apostates, supposed descendants of Jews, offspring of
mixed marriages, or merely assimilated Jews.
—Robert Alter, "Jewish Dreams and Nightmares"
(1968).

Nowadays, the Southern movement is an anachronism; the
literary Jews, no longer bothering to quarrel with it, tend to
regard Agrarian achievements as "historical" (in an ecumenical
put down). The latter effort has continued unabated, encountering surprisingly little resistance or competition. It is clear
that its comprehensive success within the literary world specifically reflects (and capitalizes upon) general changes in American
society: the public disappearance of polite anti-Semitism; continuing guilt about earlier prejudice; the cultural, social, and
academic influence of American Jews (proportionately far in
excess of their numbers); their particular ascendancy in the U.S.
communications industries; the preponderant Jewishness of
both the theater-going audience and the book-buying public
(Bellow's readership overlapping with that of Harry Golden and
Chaim Potok); the widespread interest in Jewish manners; and
finally those new alliances between established WASPs and
upwardly mobile individuals from backgrounds previously
thought sub-respectable. Thus could the publisher Cass Canfield, long the patrician chief of Harper's, write in his memoirs,
"I have found the most alert group in recognizing good writing
to be the Jewish audience." By the late fifties, even the last
bastions of academic anti-Semitism—those English departments
at Harvard, Yale, or Princeton—had rightly succumbed to the
new pressures. There is no doubt that the social successes of
people previously discredited is a good thing, as is the disappearance of both the negative stereotype and strictly religious
discrimination; however, within the literary world twofold
assertions of group importance and group innocence frequently
distort standards of artistic judgment and fair argument.

Nowhere else do such excesses show more strongly than in
the inflation, invariably by allied critics, of minor talents. This
explains why one frequently comes across embarrassing, almost
desperate puffs, invariably by Jewish critics, of writers as various in interest, though less-than-first-rank in achievement, as
Norman Podhoretz, Philip Rahv, Isaac Rosenfeld, Diana Trilling, Harvey Swados, Lionel Abel, Isaac Bashevis Singer, Leonard

Michaels, Dan Jacobson, Theodore Solotaroff, and Irving Howe. Film critic William S. Pechter reported that the publication of the late Robert Warshow's collected essays, *The Immediate Experience* (1962), was delayed so that Lionel Trilling, one of the kingfish, could certify that, yes, Warshow, the author of only a handful of significant essays, belonged among the best minds of his generation. It is as though the Jewish critic assumed that the ultimate success of his movement lay not in the world-wide recognition of its best men but in what Irving Howe, speaking ostensibly of Yiddish literature, once called "the only subject truly worthy of a serious writer . . . the problem of collective destiny, the fate of a people."

Some reviewers and reviewing media still lie in wait to hail the arrival of another novel from a chosen Jewish writer; certain elder statesmen seem almost indiscriminate in distributing blurbs. The unbounded praise and attention that greeted Philip Roth from the beginning of his career stemmed from how closely this young man fulfilled a prior stance—critical of the Jewish middle class and yet still secularly Jewish. Other typical absurdities include extended discussions of whether or not the protagonist of a novel is Jewish (and what that fact might mean), sporadic attempts to investigate whether a distinctly "Jewish art" exists, and a cultivated, though contextually ignorant, interest in similarly secular Jewish writers around the world. Just as some young Southerners have written "criticism" only about geographically fraternal writers, so certain Jewish critics, such as Theodore Solotaroff, have built fairly respectable reputations primarily upon critical essays about the Jewish experience and Jewish authors, their remarks about gentiles being platitudinous or obtuse. In a critical book devoted to *The New Novel in America* (1970), and subtitled "The Kafkan Mode in Contemporary Fiction," all of the featured novelists are Jewish; no gentile is discussed until the book's final chapter which is devoted to "Minor American Novelists." It is not surprising, therefore, that novelists who wrote well only about Jews (Bellow, Malamud, and Roth) should have national reputations comparable to that of an earlier novelist whose memorable works dealt almost exclusively with white Southerners. Only by ethnic criteria could three writers so different in style and concerns as Bellow, Roth, and Malamud be so often discussed as though they were partners in a single enterprise. (Indeed, only if

27

he is the beneficiary of literary-political puffery can a serious novelist survive a best-seller, because one function of critical allies is to protect a respectable reputation against the likely charge of "selling out." Only the effort of literary politicians can keep a passé style or an old-fashioned novelist prominent.) As Philip Rahv once defined "proletarian literature [as] the literature of a party disguised as the literature of a class," so might Jewish-American writing be called the corpus of a clique masquerading as the literature of an ethnic group.

Further signs of distortion included several confessions of partial Jewish ancestry by patently gentile writers allied with the Jewish-American movement (e.g., Robert Lowell and Mary McCarthy), as though the one or two drops of Kosher blood, or whatever, really mattered. Alfred Kazin's assertion, while reviewing *Portnoy's Complaint,* that Jews were "the most vocal [i.e. talkative] group in human history" reveals a kind of thoughtless superlative based not upon systematic research but prejudiced sentiment. Yet another symptom was the installation, during the late fifties, of Mordecai Richler as the most-lauded Canadian writer, Dan Jacobson and A. Alvarez as the most-touted Englishmen, and Harold Rosenberg as the chief expert on "the New." Similarly untenable was the temporary appointment of James Baldwin as the chief Negro spokesman in the late fifties, even though it could be questioned whether he had the personal experience or knowledge necessary for that position. Extensively published and featured in the group's magazines since the late forties, Baldwin's essays cast his own "alienation" in distinctly Jewish terms, largely because, one suspects, he both discounts the blues tradition and has lived more of his early adult life among intellectual Jews than Negroes. (As Albert Murray noted in the mid-sixties, Baldwin "certainly knows infinitely more about the guerilla warfare of New York intellectuals than he has ever actually known about uptown street gangs.") However, Baldwin's subsequent expatriation and popular success led to his excommunication in the form of suspiciously patronizing reviews of his later books.

It is also appropriate that Podhoretz's frequent praise of a certain kind of literary-critical essay (which he once regarded as superseding both poetry and the novel) serves to aggrandize a form favored by him and his literary-political colleagues, as well as a kind of intelligence he seems to consider especially Jewish (even if also displayed by more than a few gentiles). The myth of Jewish-American superiority makes some unlikely and uncritical converts, such as gentile critics who reveal embarrassing ignorance of Jewish culture. A long review of *Herzog* in *Encounter* by a Cambridge (and, one assumes, gentile) don, Tony Tanner, suggests that Bellow's philosophically rich style had its origins in Yiddish. In fact, Yiddish is decidedly anti-philosophic, being full of witty words for the dirt (*dreck*) of human existence, while the erudite weight of Bellow's prose probably comes from his evident interest in philosophy. (This 1965 essay reveals, incidentally, the kind of international literary acceptance of Bellow that would have been unlikely a decade before.)

Philip Rahv, scarcely a gentile, finds in Bellow's work "a deep sense of humor derived from his Jewish background," rather than from more strictly personal Bellowian qualities and tastes. Even Maxwell Geismar, generally an independent curmudgeon, once published an essay on "The Jewish Heritage in Contemporary American Fiction" which reiterates the myth in the course of circumcising a few gentile writers as well. In short, as WASP inheritance or even an Ivy League education was once inflated far beyond its true import, so is Jewish ancestry often given more intellectual prestige than it merits, betraying "that fantastic delusion," to quote Hannah Arendt, "shared by unbelieving Jews and non-Jews alike, that Jews are by nature more intelligent, better, healthier, more fit for survival."

Perhaps the most ludicrous display of Semitic promotion in the guise of objective criticism is Norman Podhoretz's first collection of essays and reviews, *Doings and Undoings* (1964). A scorecard reading of this work reveals the following major critical decisions: pointed praise for Saul Bellow (as our greatest contemporary, of course), Joseph Heller, Paul Goodman, Nathaniel West, Bernard Malamud, Isaac Rosenfeld, Herman Kahn, Norman Mailer, James Baldwin, and Edmund Wilson (who writes about his philo-Semitism)—all of whom are also male; and equally sharp dismissals of Mary McCarthy, John Updike, Dwight Macdonald, William Faulkner, F. Scott Fitzgerald, John O'Hara, Jack Kerouac, Allen Ginsberg (an exception, who is, as noted before, counter-stereotypical), William S. Burroughs, and Hannah Arendt (whose fault in this case is being too critical of European Jewish establishments). Rarely before in reputedly serious critical discussion have "literary" evaluations been so facilely derived. The only subsequent book I know of equally parochial "criticism" is Robert Creeley's collection, *A Quick Graph* (1970), which infrequently sees beyond (or around) his beloved Black Mountain group. A comparably partisan Southern effort was Katherine Anne Porter's itemized objection to *Book Week*'s 1965 nominations to the pantheon of major post-World War II novelists:

> It is rather a strange list of writers supposed to represent American literature that omits the names of Peter Taylor, William Humphrey, George Garrett, Walter Clemons, Andrew Lytle, James Agee, Truman Capote, Glenway Wescott, Caroline Gordon, Allen Tate, each a first-rate artist in exactly his own style and character, living in his own mysterious gift, on his own ancestral grounds, speaking his mother tongue: if you ignore these writers, it is somewhat like leaving out the spinal column when making a man.

"It is obvious," Q. D. Leavis noted in another context, "that these are not judgments of literary criticism but gestures of social solidarity—the only kind of criticism that isn't Bad Form." Furthermore, the politicization of literature, whether by Communists or by a clique, falsely makes the author more important than what he writes; so that supposedly "literary" judgments become, in practice, assessments of a man, his professional history, or his current friends.

One cannot help suppose that Podhoretz, in issuing his collection, felt that his pretensions to "taste" would withstand close examination, if only because the Jewish-American movement and ideology had indeed succeeded so completely. After all, the clique's promotions were all but unanimously accepted, its essayists had won professorships in major universities (even though some of them lacked doctorates), its books were favorably reviewed and frequently incorporated into university courses, they gave lectures everywhere (an increasingly lucrative enterprise in the sixties), its stars amassed annual incomes well over $50,000 (and all the accoutrements of their economic class), its allies abroad profited from their relationship, its protégés and former students were becoming increasingly powerful in publishing and reviewing media, and a new periodical of the sixties, *The New York Review of Books,* its name signaling a new fronting epithet, became the movement's most popular organ.

Talents languished, to be sure; very few of the important writers produced in the sixties work that equalled their earlier achievements. As the second and third generations were successively less substantial, Robert Alter could notice, in 1965, that the movement "may be falling into a declining phase of unwitting self-parody." This sense of swelling flaccidity made the Jewish writers especially prone to more aggressive extrinsic literary-politicking, not only to protect terrain already won and to compensate for a diminishing expectation of excellence, but also to extend by capitalistic means certain ambitions that could not be realized solely by literary handiwork. As the most efficient literary machine ever created in America, it had unprecedented power to determine what writing might be taken seriously and what would be neglected or wiped out. Every serious writer who came of age during the past decade, be he or she Jewish or gentile, eventually became aware of that almightiness.

Perhaps this extravagant success, along with critical scrutinies, will end the reign of false equations—false both to critical judgment and Jewishness. Whereas collective self-inflation could once be rationalized as a necessary minority strategy, it now seems superfluous and obviously self-serving. This is perhaps the primary reason why, as we shall see, Jewishness as such did not survive the sixties as an effective literary-political slogan. Another hypothesis is that Israel's efficient victory in 1967 inadvertently eliminated whatever remained of guilty deference to mythically defenseless Jews. Moreover, it is my observation that younger intellectuals of Jewish or whatever descent are too repelled by such chauvinistic enterprise to emulate or accept it; so that the notion of calling any writer born after 1935 "a Jewish intellectual" or even "a Southern Agrarian" seems ludicrous.

One general reason for this last development is that young Americans of nearly all Caucasian backgrounds spurn ethnic and other minority-based allegiances. A more specific one is that just as young Southerners are no longer haunted by Mencken's criticism, so young Jewish-Americans have rarely encountered serious antagonistic anti-Semitism. Neither, thus, has ever felt obliged to overcome any ethnic or geographic negative stereotype or fear that public criticism of pious parochialism, such as this chapter, would fan any anti-Southern or anti-Semitic flames; and both are "American" before they are anything parochial, exemplifying precisely that generational difference in "assimilation" that is a key theme of much American-Jewish and some Southern writing. (Indeed, an earlier version of these opening chapters was dubbed "anti-Semitic" for supposedly suggesting that Jews currently "control" literary publishing; however, not only was such a charge consciously avoided from the opening paragraph, but it is impossible for any clique, no matter how unprecedently powerful, to control everything in America. Also, whereas classic anti-Semitism generalizes about "Jews" as a total group or deals in imaginary Jews who are portrayed as hidden gremlins screwing up the works, these chapters talk about real individual Jews—or, to be more precise, real writers who wanted to be publicly known as Jewish.)

If so many of the older generation came from lower-class, immigrant backgrounds and were, therefore, very much concerned with "making it" in the U. S., often confusing literary values with personal and group advance, the younger Jewish writers invariably descend from parents who have already secured a social and economic foothold in America (as did Gertrude Stein, Paul Rosenfeld, Matthew Josephson, Waldo Frank, Lincoln Kirstein, Bennett Cerf, and others before them). These younger intellectuals realize that following their literary inclinations inevitably lowers their station in life—they will earn less than their parents did, spend most of their lives in shabbier neighborhoods and houses, and probably wind up less respected by their communities—and that these expectations must be acknowledged at one's professional beginnings. They became writers or teachers largely because they would rather write or teach than anything else, and they have few illusions about such upper-middle-class aspirations as "good schools" for their children (their own "best" were, as schools, scarcely better than "average") and even less inclination to look upon the literary life as a stepping-stone to assimilation or bourgeois success. They are scarcely able to regard book reviewing and the like as Fiedler's generation did: "A method of social climbing, especially viable for young Jews." Their class-determined faults tend

32

to be, by contrast, false snobbery about literary ambitiousness and a counter-productive self-confidence that precludes both inspired anger and excess determination.

In these respects, younger Jewish writers are, needless to say, little different from downwardly mobile gentile writers. Their experience leads them to believe, again in sharp contrast to their elders, that ethnic origin is not especially determining, for what an artist or writer achieves is nine-tenths the result of his own imaginative efforts. "Writers no longer have to feel constrained," as Robert Alter rightly observes, "to betray some part of themselves by masquerading as members of the 'dominant' cultural group in the forms of literary expression they adopt." They assume, perhaps naively, that a truly serious writer does not need a literary-political organization (and the accompanying corruptions) to get American readers interested in their work, for the fact of an increasingly literate population means there need no longer be, as before, such fierce competition for the attention of so few. As American writers before they are anything else or less, the young measure themselves against all American literature rather than just a parochial segment, largely refusing to create (or join) segregated categories of self-promoted and ultimately self-deceptive importance. On the other hand, it is my observation that the young react more militantly to evidence of real prejudice than did their elders, who tended to regard inequitous discrimination and blocked opportunities as acknowledged facts of life.

Realizing how terribly politicized literary reputation-making has become, they are likely to initiate the evaluative reinterpretations of writing in recent decades, not only separating what is genuinely good and important from what was just vociferously championed in its time, but also to resurrect important authors who were unaffiliated and thus neglected. Among my choices for revived novelists, for instance, would be Vance Bourjaily, James B. Hall, Kenneth Patchen, William Gaddis, William Demby, Paule Marshall, J. F. Powers, John Howard Griffin, Alan Harrington, Wright Morris, Alfred Grossman, and Mark Harris— all of whom are well over forty. The critic Allen Guttmann has attributed the critical neglect of the last, who *is* Jewish, not to his literary-political independence, as I would suggest, but to his un-Semitic surname. "Now that Harris has published a novel blatantly entitled *The Goy* [1970], we can expect critics to be

33

more attentive." It seems likely that if Henry James, a classic goy, had written in the fifties and sixties, his novels would have gone hopelessly unknown.

The young also recognize that the living writers most worth admiring and emulating have either remained aloof from minority movements or have straddled them, and that the historical American past masters scarcely knew each other. The only valid collective prefix for such emerging authors would, thus, be "young," signifying that they came of age under certain historical, political, and intellectual influences; and, as we shall see, the negative stereotypes they found themselves obliged to repudiate characterize not Southerners or Jews but "the young." In this respect, young Jewish writers join young Southern writers, alienated as well because of their physical distance from New York publishing, in desiring a more open and truly pluralistic literary society that is respectful of individual integrity and unaffiliated, personal achievement.

III

> Meanwhile, little politburos of the insulted and injured spring up; intellectual ascendancies are established on the evidence of the loudest breast-beatings about the messiest scars on the most delicate psyches;...what was once an embattled and exacerbated ghetto culture contracts into a coterie with its own obtuse instruments of self-advertisement and self-aggrandizement, its household gods and dogmas, its doctrinaire substitutes for thought, its defense-mechanisms against outsiders and traitors. . . . —Marvin Mudrick, "Podhoretz and Mrs. Trilling: The Holy Family" (1964)

Now that the Jewish literary movement has "made it," some suspect that blacks will be the next minority group to dominate the cultural scene. I think not, for various reasons, one being that Jewish-American writers historically tied the aspirations of certain blacks to their own; so that the acceptance of Jews brought with it, certain hypocrisies notwithstanding, the acceptance of the literary blacks, at least in respectable circles. Not even a black writer as personally prickly as LeRoi Jones could claim that prejudice hindered his literary career. Although the new cultural-political segregation, abetted by evidence (and rumors) of black anti-Semitism, has severed much of this earlier

34

collaboration, there still exist certain "radical" Jewish critics who publicize, as well as rationalize, new developments in "militancy." A further reason is that, in spite of Ralph Ellison's pre-eminence and example, the most currently emergent black writers in America have not yet produced sufficient literary works that are superlative enough to win sustained critical respect. Also, the attempt to revive the "Harlem Renaissance" of the twenties is handicapped by the fact that remarkably few writers were involved and no acknowledged classics were produced. It is also unfortunate that Langston Hughes, who possessed the personal qualities of a master literary politician, died too soon, and no one so adept has since taken his place. Not only has the black intellectual scene always been terribly factionalized or subservient to self-defeating ideologies, as Harold Cruse notes in *The Crisis of the Negro Intellectual* (1967), but black writers have been further handicapped by influential racialist ideas that, by making the author and his "politics" more important than his work, serve to discourage both aspirations to unalloyed literary excellence and the sympathy of non-black readers. In short, in terms of the morphology described earlier, black literary-political efforts have so far been more skilled at capitalizing on guilty beneficence than generating literary success. (Indeed, the curious underlying theme of Irving Howe's condescending critique of Ralph Ellison, collected first in his book *A World More Attractive* [1963] and then reprinted in *Decline of the New* [1970], is that Negro writers have not been, metaphorically, Jewish enough in their devotion to group advance!)

Women writers could well be the next minority to ascend: like literary blacks, they have suffered both blatant discrimination and negative stereotypes, along with the accompanying self-deceiving rationalizations, codifying their supposed intellectual ineptitude and cultural inferiority. It is indicative that few literary women in America have had much power apart from the literary men they married. For these reasons, they are also able to exploit an accumulating reservoir of establishment guilt over past prejudice; they have another advantage in the potentially largest literate audience of their own kind. Such distaff institutions as Martha Foley's annual short story anthologies or Alice Morris' *Harper's Bazaar* during the forties and fifties displayed a sexual bias, the vogue of "gothic fiction" in part reflecting their influence; and book reviewing in the new magazine *Ms.* has been systematically biased. However, this pressure has so far been even less cohesive than that of blacks, failing so far to single out its own eminences. For another thing, the literary achievement of women, like that of blacks, has not proportionately equalled their numbers in America. The young constitute yet another literary minority, also suffering from both negative stereotyping and genuine discrimination, but whose aspirations are perhaps ecumenical enough to overcome more parochial categories.

Evidence of all kinds suggests that the next powerful supermilitant minority might be homosexual, the star writers presenting themselves as unashamedly gay in a literary extension of "Gay Activism." Nearly all literary homosexuals in the past, including a group especially powerful in the late forties, submerged their sexual bias behind another kind of literary-political program. Many new books by homosexuals were blurbed (or even reviewed!) exclusively by literary gays, though sexual persuasion itself was rarely mentioned. In the future, however, homosexuality will be presented as a respectable minority affiliation and then articulated as a sensibility of "universal" relevance. Very much like both the Southerner and the Jew before him, the cultured homosexual has been characterized in severely unflattering terms, as well as excluded from some of the literary spoils; so that a persuasive case, or a series of them, must be made for his cultural acceptability. The critical advocacy of "camp" was in part an attempt to establish a respectable, relevant tradition for a certain strain of homosexual writing. An earlier, comparable attempt was Gore Vidal's advocacy in "Ladders to Heaven" (1953), originally published pseudonymously on behalf of an altogether different, tougher style of writing (which Vidal found exemplified in John Horne Burns, Tennessee Williams, and Carson McCullers). Like other previously submerged minorities, literary homosexuals can make culturally-based claims for the special, "new" quality of the unfettered communication of their parochial content or sensibility.

Since homosexual writers have, in general, so far produced far better books than blacks or women—an achievement indeed proportionately in excess of their numbers—they are also far more likely to support their literary pretensions with works that, in crucial literary-political advance, can command the respect of the general literate audience. As public attitudes and libel laws change, what was once a source of shame will become, in literary discourse at least, a mark of pride; and what was once implicit can become more explicit (and critics will feel more free to cite specific examples).

More crucial for the theme of this book, however, is the expectation that, unless there is fundamental change in U. S. literary politics or certain incredible credibilities simply expire, writers will continue to organize along minority-based lines. Small groups will continue to succeed each other, one at a time, the transient victor lording over the others, parochially favoring certain writers and kinds of writers, all to the detriment of our indigenous cultural pluralism.

The New York
Literary Mob

I

New York is now the business center of American
culture, the amusement or frivolity center, the excite-
ment center, perhaps even the anxiety center. —Saul
Bellow, "World-Famous Impossibility" (1970).

The goal of radicalism is to improve the human condition, not to prove one's moral superiority. —Jack
Newfield, *A Prophetic Minority* (1966).

What I liked about [*The Godfather*] —and what they
dropped from the movie—was that it showed how
Don Corleone came over to this country intending to
work and make an honest buck, but there were prejudices against Italians, so he was forced into doing
things the way they were done in Sicily. . . . The one
great thing Puzo did in his book was show the Sicilian
genius for organization. —Vincent Teresa, *My Life in
the Mafia* (1973).

What began in the thirties as a collection of ambitious young
writers became, by the sixties, the most powerful establishment
ever seen in literary America; and they dominated the scene as
it had never been dominated before. Even though all of its
chiefs were "Jewish writers," they must have sensed that Semi-
tism per se was becoming, as noted before, a less effective
marquee in literary politics, so they took another minority-
defining epithet for their collective identity. "The New York
intellectuals" they began to call themselves, as most of them
lived in and around the City; and this new geographical term
capitalized as well upon the mythic cultural authority accorded
everything emanating from "New York" (and especially with its

imprimatur). Just as the prime new organ of the forties, *Commentary,* was an avowedly Jewish magazine, so the new periodical of the sixties was christened *The New York Review of Books.* This shift in collective nomenclature probably came around 1962, for as late as 1961 a *Commentary* headnote to an essay by Benjamin DeMott spoke glowingly of "the increasingly prominent Jewish writers in America," while Alfred Kazin, in a radio symposium that year about Negro writing, dismissed pre-World War II Jewish-American writers before shifting his tone to his contemporaries: "And then suddenly in the last fifteen years, we've had a group of writers, like Saul Bellow and Norman Mailer and Bernard Malamud and others, who, with enormous surprise to themselves, I think, have suddenly created five or six really good books, which are as fresh as anything can be." By the following year, sentiments expressed in such terms became increasingly rare among themselves, though not among their popularizers.

Indeed, New York had always been the Jewish-American literary establishment's home, though far, far fewer than all Jewish writers living in New York also resided inside this particular literary onion. Most of the "New York intellectuals" were born and raised there; a good many attended City College in the thirties or Columbia College in the late forties; their magazines were all published in and around New York; and by the sixties most of these people either taught in local universities or worked in publishing or allied trades and lived on Manhattan's Upper West Side. (Even when teaching in the provinces, they regarded themselves as "New York intellectuals.") As literary New Yorkers they felt obliged, however, to repudiate an influential negative stereotype of the city's cultural sterility; Allen Tate and John Peale Bishop wrote in their 1942 anthology, *American Harvest,* that New York was *not* one of the "regions" contributing to contemporary literature. These Southerners portrayed it instead as the place "where books and magazines are published, and writers go to make a living." Not unlike a previous group of New York writers—those gathered around *The New Yorker* and the Hotel Algonquin in the twenties and thirties (and from whom the new New Yorkers would continually differentiate themselves)—this younger set liked to think that their intellectual style had qualities particularly indigenous to their City. (Indeed, this difference in literary

New Yorks, along with the more authentic nativity of the newcomers, are among the principal themes of Alfred Kazin's partisan memoir, *Starting Out in the Thirties* [1965] .) None of these literary sets overlap with the "New York Poets," who are yet another, younger group, which emerged in the sixties; their marquee echoes (and exploits) the "New York School" of American painting.

Norman Podhoretz, in his autobiographical *Making It* (1968), compares his colleagues to a large Jewish family—ultimately cohesive, in spite of constant bickering and dissension; but, as shall become clear, the group's purposes and methods, abetted by their vulnerability, make the "mob" metaphor far more appropriate even when informed by irony. In his book *Crime in America* (1952), Senator Estes Kefauver summarizes the testimony of a government investigative agent named Follmer who explained:

> There is an "inner circle" and an "outer circle" of the Mafia. The inner circle is composed of men who are rewarded for "special duty they have performed in the past" or "through their standing prior to their coming into the organization." They get the cream of the rackets. The outer circle is just the run-of-the-mill type, the ones who do the heavy work and the rough things.

In a more recent book, *The Valachi Papers* (1968), Peter Maas notes:

> The Cosa Nostra [meaning literally this thing of ours] has no Mr. Big. . . . Instead, it has been governed in recent years by a *commissione* of from nine to twelve bosses across the country. The *commissione* has one main function: to keep the Cosa Nostra a going concern.

Similar hierarchies and distinctions exist in the literary mob where not everyone is as Jewish or New Yorkish as the *commissione,* nor do lesser-rank associates or even their allies and employers need to be. "But by no means does the Cosa Nostra ethnically limit its operations," Maas continues. "It is a closed society within a large framework, constantly involved with a whole spectrum of 'outsiders'—Jewish, Negro, Irish, French,

Puerto Rican, English and so on down the line." Unlike an athletic team or even a corporation whose members-executives experience a degree of autonomy and neglect, a literary mob is small and tight enough for associates to keep in fairly constant touch with each other, an individual's current work suffering from close surveillance and constant comment from his professional partisans. Not unlike its model, a literary mob or "outfit" (as the original customarily calls itself) tries to control the merchandising of pleasure.

This particular group initially came together in New York in the 1930's when several young men on the fringes of both the Communist movement and literary journalism founded a cultural journal. *Partisan Review*, as it was called, began early in 1934 as an organ of the John Reed Clubs which were themselves a Communist organization; but the magazine separated from organized Communism soon afterwards, ceasing publication late in 1936, only to be revived as an independent (and anti-Stalinist) magazine a year later. An "Editorial Statement" in December, 1937, declared an opposition to "academicians from the university, yesterday's celebrities, and today's philistines, [for] *Partisan Review* aspires to represent a new and dissident generation in American letters." Its editors then were two young Jewish radicals, Philip Rahv and William Phillips, and three Yale classmates previously associated with the very short-lived bimonthly, *The Miscellany* (1931-1931)—the critics Dwight Macdonald and F.W. Dupee, along with the abstract painter George L.K. Morris, who became *Partisan Review*'s first principal patron (three of the other editors marrying women of private means); all of them were then about thirty in age.

Once the magazine established itself, many "promising" writers approximately their age gravitated to it, including Meyer Schapiro, Sidney Hook, Lionel Trilling, James T. Farrell, Harold Rosenberg, and William Troy, most of whom had already contributed to an earlier intelligent quarterly, *The Symposium* (1930-33). Several other writers still under thirty and just starting to publish would soon also contribute to its pages—John Berryman, Karl Shapiro, Alfred Kazin, Mary McCarthy, and Delmore Schwartz; and many of these people also wrote reviews for Margaret Marshall, who was editing the back pages of *The Nation* (where opinions seemed to diverge from the pro-Soviet attitudes prevalent in the front of the magazine), while the more militant anti-Stalinists contributed to *The New Leader.*

All of these people were intellectually united by what they regarded as shared interests in the highest levels of both contemporary literature and radical political philosophy. Mostly Trotskyist in their sympathies, they had such a decided bias against Stalinism that they also opposed, as "fellow travelers," those intellectuals who were judged to be insufficiently anti-Communist. Though *Partisan Review,* to quote Fiedler again, "was born of such a marriage of Greenwich Village and [anti-Communist] Marxism," its esthetic predilections were nonetheless considerably less radical than those found in such periodicals as *transition* (1927-38) or *View* (1940-47). *Partisan's* young contributors also shared aspirations to "brilliance" based upon polemical wit and/or strictly post-1800 literary-political-historical literacy. By the late forties, they successfully developed a characteristic style of literary criticism that neglected technical-formalist concerns, strictly stylistic perceptions, or consistent analytic methodology. Instead, they emphasized both general humanistic-political meanings and professional evaluation (with criteria that were, by necessity, vaguely articulated). Not "insight" but *importance* was their rationale for these approaches, but the rewards were less intellectual than commercial. "They just took over all the techniques of Stalinism," remembers the anarchist Kenneth Rexroth, "hatchet reviews and logrolling and wire-pulling and control of foundations and academic jobs and so forth."

Partisan followed the earlier example of *The Dial* (1920-29) in cultivating a steady interest in intellectual life abroad, eventually regarding itself as the American outpost of an international community of "intellectuals," while its writers styled their self-image upon the European model (previously scarce here) of a free-floating critical "intelligentsia." By the middle forties, *Partisan* would garner contributions from such European ex- or anti-Communists as Arthur Koestler, André Gide, George Orwell, Ignazio Silone (all of whom thus became implicit allies in their strictly parochial literary-political battle with the Jewish Communist writers). When such European eminences passed through New York, *Partisan's* writers and editors became their local hosts. The magazine also scored literary-political coups by printing several English translations of Franz Kafka and, religious-political differences notwithstanding, the poetry of T.S. Eliot. After the war, *Partisan* also published the first American translations and expositions of Parisian existential philosophy, even though none of its contributors ever became professed existentialists. The magazine remained, until the sixties, more hospitable to European avantgardes than to comparable American experimentalists.

However, its initial commitment to literary modernism was generally compromised through its neglect of the more radical post-World War II innovations, which were routinely criticized only after the authors' reputations had been established elsewhere. (This could be partially attributed to their belated discovery that their modernist heroes, including Kafka, had symbolist, rather than realistic imaginations, plus conservative political outlooks; and the resulting crisis contributed to a decreasing interest in all imaginative writing not produced by their literary-political associates.) By the late forties, circumstances became prosperous and exciting enough for the magazine to appear monthly for a spell. Its major patron during the post-war decade was Allan D. Dowling, a sometime poet and novelist, whose role was assumed in the late fifties primarily by Louis G. Cowan, the originator of radio's "The Quiz Kids" and the producer of television's "The $64,000 Question." By the late fifties *Partisan Review* had completed one milestone in its evolutionary cycle by becoming the American magazine most read by the European intelligentsia.

Though internal squabbles occurred all along, the first severe break in *Partisan*'s editorial operation came in the summer of 1943 when Dwight Macdonald resigned, protesting its growing political conservatism, its increasing literary emphasis, and finally most of his colleagues' support of U.S. involvement in World War II. Out of his attempt to revive a new, radical political position came a magazine, *Politics* (1944-49), which was edited by Macdonald with Paul Goodman (another *Partisan* castoff) as its featured American contributor. This editorial dalliance with home-brewed anarcho-pacifism lasted five years. After the demise of *Politics,* not only was Macdonald (though not Goodman) quickly brought back into the fold, but, as an Exeter- and Yale-educated WASP, a former employee at *Fortune* magazine, and perhaps the slickest of the mob's penmen (all in diametrical contrast to Goodman), he also became a staff

44

writer for *The New Yorker.* A witty and tough-minded critic, except when flattering his professional friends and supporters, Macdonald made a specialty of demolishing highly favored WASPs—not only Henry Wallace, the last gentile apostle of fellow-traveling Jews, but Van Wyck Brooks and Archibald MacLeish before the war, then James Gould Cozzens, Ernest Hemingway, Tom Wolfe, and the authors of the Revised Standard Version in the years thereafter.

In 1945 came another new organ, more parochial in its aims and origins, yet ultimately more popular in its purposes. Like the other mob magazines, *Commentary* had well-defined editorial biases and authoritarian leadership. In the splintered history of the Jewish-American magazines, it came to represent a faction less Zionist than *Jewish Frontier* or *Midstream,* less religious than orthodox journals, less theological than *The Reconstructionist,* more patriotic than politically radical Jewish magazines, and more assimilationist (or less parochially Jewish) than them all. Then as now, *Commentary* more closely resembled *Harper's,* say, or *The New Republic* than other Jewish magazines; the difference was a peripheral, almost haughty interest in the general state and problems of American Jewry. The American Jewish Committee, which sponsored the founding of *Commentary,* also represented old Jewish America, mostly German in ancestry, pre-twentieth century in immigration, and largely American in culture (Podhoretz: "Perhaps the classiest tone of any Jewish organization"), rather than the new Jewish America of recently arrived Eastern Europeans. It is indicative that *Commentary*'s offices have always been (unlike those of *Partisan Review* for most of its New York life or *The Nation* or *Politics*) north of 23rd Street and New York's downtown ghettos and bohemias (just as those of *The New York Review of Books* would be yet further uptown).

The contributors to *Commentary*'s first issue (November, 1945) included George Orwell, Mary McCarthy, Louis Kronenberger, Harold Rosenberg, and Paul Goodman, all of whom had previously written for *Partisan.* Apparently, it was *Commentary*'s subsequent success that persuaded the emerging writers to adopt Jewishness as their initial common badge. As its founding editor, Elliot E. Cohen (1899-1959), told Podhoretz, then a junior editor, "The main difference between *Partisan Review* and *Commentary* is that we admit to being a Jewish magazine and they don't." The new magazine subsequently became distinguished for some of the earliest and most penetrating analyses of that new social phenomenon called totalitarianism, as well as displaying a rabid anti-Communism that was especially merciless with Jewish Communists. As Podhoretz remembers *Commentary* during the fifties: "All articles were [then] carefully inspected for traces of softness on Communism." The magazine also published some first-rate impressionistic sociology of both contemporary America and popular culture; yet in nearly every issue would be something about the social and intellectual fortunes of Jews. Implicit by this time in this "herd of independent minds" (Harold Rosenberg's phrase) was not only a certain talent for creating public interest in themselves and their talmudic arguments, but also a strong sense of their own cultural elitism which Podhoretz characterized as:

> The conviction that *others* were not worth taking into consideration except to attack, and need not be addressed in one's writing; out of that feeling as well [came] a sense of hopelessness as to the fate of American culture at large and the correlative conviction that integrity and standards were only possible among "us."

Since the most familiar device for restricting conversation is snobbery, intellectual disputes were customarily conducted wholly within the herd—between *its* political conservatives (Irving Kristol and Daniel Bell) and *its* radicals (Howe and Macdonald), *its* esthetic modernists (Harold Rosenberg and Clement Greenberg) and *its* artistic reactionaries (Kazin and Rahv)—with all of them generally neglecting or dismissing similar arguments and examples forged outside their immediate corral. The only "American intellectuals" described in their self-conscious polemics were, predictably, themselves. Furthermore, they collectively developed the tone of privileged conversation into which the reader, especially of numerous self-symposia, supposedly felt gratified to be admitted. Nonetheless, such symposia, along with their resulting debates, constitute not intellectual history, which has higher standards, but the social history of "intellectuals," in addition to an awful lot of journalistic make-work.

The strongest "critical" energies were devoted to the elitist task of separating intellectual culture, especially their own, from lowbrow and middlebrow. They emphasized artistic standards while denigrating their moral superiors and ethics while criticizing their esthetic betters, thus underscoring their own artistic incomprehensions. From this exclusionary impulse came the custom of dismissing as "cultish" all those cultural reputations prevalent *outside* their immediate circle. (Only by such double standards could William S. Burroughs' eminence be "cultish" and Saul Bellow's not.) For that reason, too, they consistently disparaged the professional integrity of other writers and magazines, especially those belonging to competitive establishments. "The fact that writers cooperate and collaborate with its editorial standards," wrote Delmore Schwartz in 1950, "does not lessen but rather illustrates the extent of *The New Yorker*'s power." The same charge could be leveled at the mob magazines and their lesser writers. Isaac Rosenfeld and Robert Warshow repeated this attack on *The New Yorker* (and its favorite contributors, especially Salinger), which was echoed in turn by such loyal second-generation epigones as Hilton Kramer (in a 1959 polemic in *Commentary*). The post-1963 attacks on Hannah Arendt, who had by then become identified with *The New Yorker,* fall into this tradition, as does Irving Howe's criticism of the magazine's refusal to print letters-to-the-editor, plus the more recent and predictably negative critiques of those associated with Clay Felker's *New York* (e.g., Dwight Macdonald, among others, on Tom Wolfe). From this elitism also stems the characteristic mob posture (which has long outlived its reality) of dramatizing itself as an embattled minority, along with the tendency to fabricate inappropriate dichotomies (then taking "a position" behind one of them), as well as for portraying themselves as the last independents, even while screaming in chorus.

These New York writers opportunely filled a fortuitous vacuum in literary power caused by a major war (in which, unlike the Vietnam conflict, literary people actually served)—much as the young writers of the twenties had capitalized upon a comparable vacuum. (As Malcolm Cowley noted of his own contemporaries: "We started to publish in the postwar years, when our youth was a moral asset. People seemed to feel that an older generation had let the world go to ruin, and they hoped a new one might redeem it.") Into the onion's orbit and their magazines' pages came several rising young intellectuals who, though never fully-accredited members of the mob, acknowledged nonetheless a degree of mutually dependent destiny—the sociologists C. Wright Mills and David Riesman, the historians Arthur M. Schlesinger, Jr. and Richard Hofstadter, the literary critics Randall Jarrell and Eric Bentley, the philosopher Hannah Arendt, in addition to the eminent older critic, Edmund Wilson, who had briefly been married to Mary McCarthy (herself a sometime paramour and assistant editor of Philip Rahv). Within the history of significant American thought, which only occasionally overlaps with the mob's career, these magazines made their most significant cultural contributions in the late forties. (Indeed, their prime intellectual deficiency after 1960 was a sensibility honed on the literacy and thought-patterns of those earlier decades.) By the early fifties they came to recognize themselves as a powerful establishment; as early as 1956, the critic John W. Aldridge, then still more of an advocate than an enemy of literary youth, judged that, "The formerly liberal journal, *Partisan Review,* has lately become the chief organ of a new intellectual orthodoxy."

Post-World War II politics of both magazines tended to be neo-liberal and anti-Communist with *Partisan* showing a greater cultural latitude than *Commentary.* The drift away from European socialism reached its height in 1952 with a *Partisan* self-symposium entitled "Our Country and Its Culture" in which most of the contributors voiced surprisingly affirmative evaluations of the American experience, compromising the earlier ideal of bohemian recalcitrance. This kind of positive cultural thinking infiltrated a new Anglo-American magazine, *Encounter,* hatched in London in 1953 with a mob-allied American coeditor and financed (as it was later revealed) partly by CIA money supporting this and other leftwing, but anti-Communist cultural ventures. Since many New York regulars contributed to *Encounter,* it became their first European popular front. Regarding the reasons behind such surreptitious support, Podhoretz shrewdly judged, "The fact that the CIA knew about *them* was itself a measure of how far, for better or worse, they had already traveled from their monastic confines of the thirties." Many of them also contributed to *Perspectives U.S.A.* (1952-56), a lavishly thick, culturally patriotic periodical sponsored largely by the Ford Foundation and destined primarily for distribution abroad. Its solicitation of mob writers was likewise indicative. They capitalized, in short, upon the plush opportunities, both literary and economic, available to non-Communist intellectuals during the Cold War.

This new affirmativeness, along with their predominantly ambivalent responses to Senator Joseph McCarthy's anti-Communism, produced yet another schism in the New York literary mob. The dissenting faction, led by Irving Howe, gathered around a new periodical called *Dissent* which claimed to be "democratic socialist" or more "radical" in its political outlook (supposedly in contrast to the neo-liberalism of the others). Over the years, however, *Dissent* has shared contributors with its former antagonists and, like them, concentrated more upon negative critiques of America and modern society than upon articulating any positive ideology or comprehensive visions for change. It has also been the most orthodoxically Jewish of mob periodicals, not only in consistently having the highest proportion of Jewish contributors, but also in excluding women completely from both its "editorial board" and "contributing editors," as well as from the various anthologies culled from its pages such as *Voices of Dissent* (1959), *The Radical Papers* (1966), *The Radical Imagination* (1967), and *Beyond the New Left* (1970). *Dissent* has also opposed, with utter harmony, nearly all strains of independent youth, whether literary or political, Jewish or gentile.

By this point it should become clear that even "ideological" disputes within the mob often mask literary power plays where ideas and issues represent not insights or intelligence, but either imprisonment in one's own intellectual history or an investment in one's writing career. (A decade later, such anti-radicals among the mob as Daniel Bell and Irving Kristol, finding the old magazines unsympathetic to their most serious work, founded *The Public Interest*.) Though politics usually provided the divisive issues in the mob's history, most of its polemicists were more interested in attitudinizing, reputation-deflating, position-taking, or literary-politicking than in political philosophy or extended sociological analysis. As a result, none of these "intellectuals," though mostly Marxist, made any definitive contributions to Marxist theory or criticism. Even a mob-apologist like

49

Irving Howe judged in 1968 that, except for Hannah Arendt's *The Origins of Totalitarianism* (1951), "The contributions of the New York intellectuals were not to political thought."

In the fifties, too, a constellation of younger, mostly Jewish, New York writers formed on the fringes of the mob—Chandler Brossard, Anatole Broyard, Seymour Krim, William Poster, Alan Harrington, David T. Bazelon, Manny Farber, Milton Klonsky (all born between 1916 and 1924)—most of whom emphasized feeling over intellect, experience over erudition, pop culture over "Art," Bohemia over academia, though most were, by familiar standards, quite intellectual, erudite, and artistic, if not eventually academic too. They were, in other words, too close to the mob to be regarded as non-competitive. These biases engaged them in a love-hate affair with the *Partisan-Commentary* crowd—an ambivalence epitomized in Brossard's anthology, *The Scene Before You* (1955)—which left their professional careers peripherally entwined with the mob. Except for brief flings with *Neurotica* (1949-51) and *The American Mercury* toward the end of William Bradford Huie's editorship (1945-52), this group lacked an editorial power base in book or magazine publishing, though some of its attitudes and flair for self-promotion eventually flowed into early "beat" writing (John Clellon Holmes [b. 1926] chronicled this connection in both his *roman à clef* entitled *Go* [1952] and his memoir, *Nothing More to Declare* [1967].) It is no surprise that deflating this group, in concert with the beats, became a favorite exercise of young men strictly on the mob-make such as Norman Podhoretz (b. 1930), in his much-reprinted "The Know-Nothing Bohemians" (1958) and Theodore Solotaroff (b. 1928) in his "All That Cellar-Deep Jazz" (1961).

II

> For this Claremont daguerreotype, Trilling sits in his proper suit as the Heavenly Father, Mrs. Trilling makes a quick change from Archangel to Madonna, and Podhoretz—still muttering at the prospect of a mocha-colored grandchild—irritably straightens his crown of thorns. —Marvin Mudrick, "Podhoretz and Mrs. Trilling: The Holy Family" (1964).

Intellectual differences notwithstanding, by the middle fifties members of the New York literary mob learned how their individual reputations were intermingled with its collective destiny and vice versa. Not only did individuals recognize common causes and attend crowded parties at which, though quarrels were common, collective solidarity was reaffirmed, but they also endeavored to mention each other's names and works whenever possible—mob-rolling, so to speak. As each other's best press agents, they developed one flair for sponsoring well-promoted public symposia with themselves as the starring panelists and another for getting an increasingly larger public interested in their personal histories and conflicts, which were both intramural and interpersonal. As New Yorkers, rather than San Franciscans, they were, like professional athletes on New York teams, more likely to be noticed and publicized by the New York-based national media.

Even though bickering among them was as common and passionate as that within the real Mafia, there was a similarly overriding sense of collective interest in their dealings with the larger world; and that double perspective accounts for those peculiar reversals—love-hate feelings—that inform their comments about each other. Those who won great success with cultural publics or authorities outside the mob were subject to envious criticism from within; but since they and only they, as elitists, were "qualified" to review each other in public print, the same people subject to criticism from within would nonetheless be vehemently defended from and against outside attack. The spoils of bourgeois success overcame the Bohemian penchants for artistic impracticality, intellectual integrity, and social disengagement; and though they still liked to think of themselves' as an "intelligentsia," their life-style and incomes already made them squarely middle-class. They accepted, if not echoed, the modern writers' critique of contemporary civilization as easily as they surrounded themselves with its encumbrances, such "paradoxes" being both the root and the symptom of further hypocrisies.

By this time, too, it became clear that Lionel Trilling had become the closest semblance of a chief this disparate tribe had—or, as Podhoretz testifies, "in fact, the family's single most influential member in the 1950's." As the first Jewish professor of English at Columbia since Spingarn early in the century, Trilling had a position respected by all, even if begrudgingly. His fine academic monographs on *Matthew Arnold* (1939) and *E.M.*

51

Forster (1943), along with his novel, *The Middle of the Journey* (1947), and the long essays he collected in *The Liberal Imagination* (1950) made an influential, if ultimately minor, contribution to the post-war decade's neo-liberalism. His wife, Diana Trilling, had been a regular contributor to Margaret Marshall's columns in *The Nation* throughout the forties; and although Mrs. Trilling became a prominent target of sneers from within, she nonetheless had the implicit power of critical opinions that invariably echoed and forecast her husband's.

As an elder statesman before his years, Trilling was chosen to write the extended preface to *The Partisan Review Reader* (1946), and he would specialize for many years thereafter in long, solemn introductions which displayed his mastery of two typically Trillingesque techniques—qualified statements and praise by innuendo: "And I do not mean to assert that *Partisan Review* in itself contains the best of our literature but only that it is representative of some of the tendencies that are producing the best." Even in his 1965 collection of essays, *Beyond Culture,* most of the American contemporaries respectfully cited by name are long-term professional friends. His essays and blurbs were always featured in their magazines, and some young writers then on the make would emulate both his convoluted prose and his characteristic critical strategy of relating the book at hand to the assertedly current (though sometimes fictitious) *Zeitgeist*—using literature to review "reality" (or an asserted definition of it), rather than the author's literary craftsmanship. Some of his former graduate students like Stephen Marcus (b. 1929) would ritually cite Trilling as a fount of expertise, an exemplar of literary intelligence, and a touchstone for comparative critical judgments. It was only appropriate that Podhoretz's critical debut should have been an essay in praise of Trilling's *The Liberal Imagination* published in 1951 in F.R. Leavis' *Scrutiny,* thereby helping establish both his mentor's eminence in England and his own currency at home.

Commanding considerable influence within both literary and academic milieus, Trilling advised not only the young editors like Epstein and Podhoretz, but chairmen who were hiring staff at other universities. Indeed, Trilling's ascendancy legitimized the pursuit of an academic career in the minds of those who previously had doubts. He also joined John Crowe Ransom and F.O. Matthiessen, kingpins in their own establishments, in organizing the Rockefeller-financed Kenyon School of Letters, which subsequently moved to Indiana University and employed Trilling's literary associates as summertime teachers. "He manages to preserve," Fiedler noted in 1956, "a remarkable aura of respectability not granted any of his colleagues." He also acquired sufficient public eminence to front, in succession, two book clubs in the fifties, Reader's Subscription and the Mid-Century. However, so over-inflated had Trilling's reputation become by this time, especially in comparison to his rather modest achievements, that pricking it became a general sentiment, particularly outside the mob. While his sometime admirers either defended their former chief or stepped aside, Trilling himself wrote fewer essays and devoted his energies instead to compiling textbook anthologies.

What was most conspicuously absent so far in this clique's development were allies in the large publishing houses—the essential intermediary channels between a group of ambitious writers and their possible public. No established editors had yet served them as successfully as Albert Erskine, Jr. and, to a lesser extent, David McDowell, had sponsored some of the literary Agrarians. Although the New Yorkers' own magazines prospered with increasing circulation while their names were becoming more widely known (with Marjorie Farber and then Harvey Breit becoming their principal editors on *The New York Times Book Review*), only a few of them had actually published books, mostly with James Laughlin at New Directions; and these trial balloons had not then been particularly well-received outside their immediate camp. This misfortune partially explains why the best writers, such as Trilling and Kazin, Macdonald and Rosenberg, became so accomplished as literary essayists, as well as why, perhaps, they honored so vociferously the preceding generation's most accomplished and persistent reviewer, Edmund Wilson. When publishers finally offered book contracts, most of them customarily followed Wilson's example of delivering not an integral work but a collection of previously published pieces. (The rationalization was that some of the essays were rich enough to equal a book; but one suspects that these writers simply lacked the wherewithal that finishing a book demands—not only the stamina and determination, but also a major idea or subject meriting sustained elaboration.) Some of them, like Irving Howe and Philip Rahv, would collect their own best essays many times over, as well as reprinting them in those textbooks and anthologies they later came to edit (many of which served the literary-political function of including both their colleagues and themselves with the past masters).

The first crack in the book-publishing barrier came in the early fifties when a fresh Columbia College alumnus named Jason Epstein became an editor at Doubleday. After a bout of typical editorial drudgery, he saw that just as "mass-market" books could be reprinted in paperback, so could titles of more specialized interest, which could then be marketed not just in drugstores and the like, as were earlier paperpacks, but on college campuses and in legitimate metropolitan bookstores (such as, fortuitously, the Doubleday chain). His line, christened Anchor Books, used finer paper and binding than the cheap reprinters, as well as charging higher prices; and the list capitalized upon a growing post-war audience for high-cultural writing. More important to this history was the fact that his early titles included Trilling's *The Liberal Imagination,* Edmund Wilson's *To the Finland Station,* Kazin's *On Native Grounds,* and F.W. Dupee's *Henry James.* Epstein, born in 1928, epitomized those of his generation who, in Barbara Probst Solomon's analysis, "set out to be the grand entrepreneurs of the intellectual; young men of the future, they sensed that the safest way to proceed in those uncertain years was by packaging the past." In this respect, he set a deleterious example for subsequent aggressive young Jewish editors—Arthur A. Cohen (b. 1929), Aaron Asher (b. 1931), and John J. Simon (b. 1935), all of whom were chiefs of Meridian Books, an early Anchor imitation, in addition to a later Columbia College alumnus, Peter Mayer (b. 1936), the precocious editor-in-chief of Avon Books, who likewise followed Epstein's precedent by issuing yet another paperback edition of Trilling's single, slow-selling novel, *The Middle of the Journey* (1947). Epstein also founded his own short-lived periodical, *The Anchor Review,* edited by Melvin Lasky, who later coedited *Encounter;* the contributors to its two issues predictably included Dupee, Macdonald, Koestler, and Kazin. The commercial success of his Anchor line not only repudiated the trashy image the paperback book had acquired, but it brought increasing power to Epstein, who became a mob *capo* in his own right. Whereas this young man of commerce once needed to win the respect of older writers, now it was they who vied for his favor.

Another omen of possible popularity came in the wake of Saul Bellow's third novel, *The Adventures of Augie March* (1953). A Chicago boy, born in Quebec, Bellow published his first story, "Two Morning Monologues" (1941), in *Partisan* when he was twenty-six; and especially after he moved to New York, the mob took a more solicitous interest in his career. That Bellow was chosen to be their premier novelist, rather than Harvey Swados, say, reflects a modicum of literary taste, no doubt; but the process of inflating his reputation, as we shall see, reflected not rare critical judgment but the more common techniques of American advertising and publicity. Bellow's first novel, *Dangling Man* (1944), was favorably reviewed by Diana Trilling in *The Nation,* by Irving Kristol in *Politics,* and by Edmund Wilson in *The New Yorker.* His second, *The Victim* (1947), received another warm reception from Diana Trilling again, from Leslie A. Fiedler in *Kenyon Review,* and from Elizabeth Hardwick who prophesied in *Partisan* that "it would be hard to think of any young writer who has a better chance than Bellow to become the redeeming novelist of his period."

All this snowballing sentiment created the expectation that Bellow's third novel, parts of which had been appearing in *Partisan* since 1949, would be a large and truly major work. When the book arrived, twice as long and far more pretentious than its predecessors, Trilling hailed *The Adventures of Augie March* as "nearly as remarkable an achievement as I had hoped for," his language betraying his biased expectation. His recommendation made the novel the monthly selection of the Readers' Subscription. Kazin called it "plainly one of the richest of the twentiety-century novels," while Robert Gorham Davis, another Columbia professor, praised it on the front page of *The New York Times Book Review;* and although lesser, unaffiliated reviewers had not generally favored Bellow's novels before, this time they swam along with the drift. *Augie March* escalated soon after publication, not only to become a best-seller but also to win for Bellow the first of his three National Book Awards. For many years thereafter, Bellow's books would be partially prepublished then ritually praised in mob print, often in such unpersuasively extravagant terms as these blurbs from Philip

Rahv and Norman Podhoretz, respectively: "The finest stylist at present writing fiction in America" (a testimonial that earnestly trips over itself); "A stylist of the first order, perhaps the greatest virtuoso of the language the novel has seen since Joyce."

Bellow's great triumph inflated the entire mob (the fortunes of each American establishment, as noted before, depending in part upon the professional success of its most touted member). Whereas the literary Southerners acquired a great interest in making William Faulkner a world-famous novelist (after it became clear that James Branch Cabell, in the twenties, and then Robert Penn Warren simply would not be the best bets), so the enterprising New Yorkers made a similarly great investment in Bellow. Indeed, it seems in retrospect that his fictions, as if to give a good return on their capital, conveniently embodied his admirers' main preoccupations (the much-touted writer writing about the themes his touters toot)—ambivalences toward military conscription in World War II in *Dangling Man*; American anti-Semitism in *The Victim*; the naiveties of liberalism in such stories as "Looking for Mr. Green" (1951); the acceptance of both America and an urban childhood in *Augie March;* the fear of American "failure" in *Seize the Day* (1956); the neuroses of both the creative mind in *Henderson the Rain King* (1959) and the intellectual in *Herzog* (1964); an aging Jew's contempts in *Mr. Sammler's Planet* (1970).

Enterprising on his own, Bellow managed to flirt with all the respectable dowagers, publishing his fiction not only in *Partisan* and *Commentary* but also in *Hudson Review, The New Yorker,* and *Esquire,* as well as reviewing for *The New York Times Book Review* and elsewhere. With the support of Arthur A. Cohen and then Aaron Asher at Meridian Books, he founded *Noble Savage* (1960-62), a semi-annual whose eclectic inclusions nonetheless reflected his own literary politicking. In an essay originally drafted in 1959 but not published until his *Doings and Undoings* (1964), Podhoretz snitched, "There is, indeed, a sense in which the validity of a whole new phase of American culture has been felt to hang on whether or not Saul Bellow would turn out to be a great novelist." Fiedler, a few years before, praised Bellow as "perhaps of all our novelists the one we need most to understand, if we are to understand what the novel is doing at the present moment." Although Bellow, a notoriously contentious personality, would continually deny the mob's contribution to his public reputation, even forsaking New York City for upstate Hudson County and then Chicago, the literary mob nonetheless supported *Herzog* and *Mr. Sammler's Planet,* both of which brought him literary prizes and great commercial success. Even as late as early 1973, Pearl K. Bell, the wife of Daniel Bell and sister of Alfred Kazin, published in *Dissent* a comprehensive denunciation of all recent novelists as inferior to her touchstone, Saul.

The role that Bellow played in fiction and Trilling in criticism was originally assigned to Delmore Schwartz in poetry (just as the Southerners had nominated John Crowe Ransom and Allen Tate respectively for the last two positions). Born in New York in 1913 and educated at N.Y.U., Schwartz had an extremely precocious success, not only contributing to the first issue of the revived *Partisan* in 1937 (along with Trilling, Edmund Wilson, and Mary McCarthy), but also publishing many important things before he turned thirty. Unlike his colleagues who tended to specialize in only one genre, Schwartz excelled at poetry, short fiction, and criticism. In the early forties, he was chosen not only to be an associate editor of *Partisan Review* (taking Macdonald's vacated place) and a literary advisor at New Directions, but also the coveted Briggs-Copeland instructor in writing at Harvard (signifying, unlike the first honor, success well outside the immediate circle). He also won the support of Allen Tate, king of the Agrarian prince-makers and a master literary politician, who had shrewdly picked him, along with Randall Jarrell, Robert Lowell, and John Berryman, to become the major poets of their generation. (Tate also preceded Warren in publicly identifying Faulkner as "the most powerful and original novelist in the United States.") Schwartz willingly assumed his role, producing a great quantity of prose that, like his poetry, steadily declined in quality over the years, in addition to loyally executing mob tasks such as praising *Augie March* as superior to its prime literary model, *Huckleberry Finn,* "by virtue of the complexity of its subject matter"! However, Schwartz's life turned tragic, his first marriage broke up, his good looks dissipated, and he suffered frequent bouts of alcoholism. From the middle fifties to his death alone in a Times Square hotel in 1966, his former literary associates regarded him as "too crazy" to see socially or even to publish. Prior to the sixties, as Norman Mailer once noted, "The verdict of history might have found them [the mob] destructive of more talent than they liberated."

Schwartz's position as the outfit's poet laureate was subsequently assumed not by a Jewish poet such as Karl Shapiro, who was too provincial and intransigent, or Allen Ginsberg, who led his own minority interest, but by Robert Lowell—a move reflecting the "popular-front" strategy dominant in the late fifties. Soon after graduating from Kenyon College in 1940, Lowell accepted Allen Tate's invitation to encamp on his Tennessee lawn; and though speedily established as the youngest Agrarian (b. 1917), Lowell also began to publish his poetry in *Partisan* as well. By the late fifties, he had moved permanently to New York with his second wife, Elizabeth Hardwick (b. 1916), a Kentucky-born novelist and critic on the mob's fringes since the late forties. Blessed with enough private means to support a reputation for personal hospitality, as well as a knack for public utterances that were both portentous and platitudinous, Lowell became an incomparable literary politician, not as an initiating organizer like Tate and Trilling, but as the much-hyped protégé of established powerhouses. He won top nomination from not just one but two and then three of the most auspicious American literary cliques. (Jarrell, when he lived in the north, began to forge a similarly ecumenical role, contributing like Schwartz and Lowell to both establishments' magazines; but once he moved south permanently, the New Yorkers lost interest in him.) The supreme accolades that were once Schwartz's now went to Lowell, who also acquired a Harvard professorship (thereby completing the triangle), along with a cover story from *Time* (making a square). Quite conveniently could he claim a personal ancestry that included both Jewish and Harvard, as well as Southern, strains! By the late sixties, Lowell became a factor behind other powerhouses, not only scoring a publicity coup by befriending Senator Eugene McCarthy during the latter's Presidential campaign, but also giving "frequent consultation" to Carolyn Kizer during her administration of the poetry programs of the National Council on the Arts. Since Lowell had been so publicly opposed to the U.S. government's involvement in Vietnam, this role struck some skeptics as hypocritical; but only a true master could be so guileful in separating literary politics from other politics.

Now and then an effort was made to put him up for the Nobel Prize, but just as a professional backlash was beginning to jell, Lowell left New York (and his wife) for an extended sojourn in England.

It should be noted here that the New York mob customarily regarded theater as a less serious art, *Partisan* usually assigning women to "chronicle" it (Mary McCarthy, Elizabeth Hardwick, Susan Sontag); had not Arthur Miller been so insufficiently anti-Communist, he could well have become "our dramatist." Instead, like the Southerners before them, the New Yorkers had no playwright laureate.

Cultural Prosperity and Its Perils

4

I

> The people of these higher circles are involved in a set
> of overlapping "crowds" and intricately connected
> "cliques," ... although this often becomes clear to
> them, as well as others, only at the point at which
> they feel the need to draw the line; only when, in
> their common defense, they come to understand
> what they have in common, and so close their ranks
> against outsiders. —C. Wright Mills, *The Power Elite*
> (1956).

> There is no such thing as a New York intellectual
> establishment. It just looks that way from the out-
> side. —Jason Epstein, to a reporter (1965).

In the sixties, fortunes took several new, increasingly prosperous turns. Jason Epstein, frustrated at Doubleday, initiated a
power struggle that led to his resignation (while Podhoretz,
curiously, was offered the same Doubleday job at a higher
salary). Not the sort to suffer unemployment for long, Epstein
soon became vice-president at Bennett Cerf's Random House
where the Agrarians' Albert Erskine had gone some years
before. It would soon become the most powerful firm in
American literary publishing, acquiring, about this time, two
of the most prestigious Jewish-owned publishing houses, Alfred
A. Knopf and Pantheon Books. This new position put Epstein
in charge first of the Modern Library (of hardbound reprinted
classics) and then of Vintage Books, a quality paperback line
which was founded some years before in imitation of his own
Anchor at Doubleday; he also served as senior editor in Random House's trade division. With an unfettered editorial hand,
he became the mob's chief spoilsman, swiftly reprinting earlier
editions of Robert Lowell's poems and Edmund Wilson's essays

as well as offering Modern Library introductions to his favored critics. He also did books by regulars who had previously lacked loyal publishers, for example, Paul Goodman, David Bazelon, and Dwight Macdonald. Epstein's success with their books persuaded other publishers that, as Podhoretz put it, "There was not only prestige to be gained from publishing family-type writers, but perhaps even money, and not in the very long run at that."

Thanks to his success, Epstein became an increasingly greater powerhouse in mob networks. Although he previously regarded himself as primarily serving a literary generation older than himself, he later tried to overcome his earlier prejudices by contracting books from his contemporaries and juniors—even his college acquaintance, the poet Allen Ginsberg. "A fantastically generous young man with a real flair for the extravagant gesture and a carelessness about money," is how his friend Podhoretz describes Epstein in his very quotable and mutually incriminating memoir, *Making It* (1968):

> Leaving a cocktail party, he would invite ten people to dinner, and take them to some appallingly expensive restaurant, priced far beyond the resources of either his expense account or his salary as a junior executive, and never turn a hair at the sight of a bill that would have given me a heart attack on the spot. If he traveled, it had to be first-class; if he bought a pair of shoes, it had to be from an English bootmaker who came once a year to the Plaza to fit his customers; and then he would spend thirty dollars sending them over to London by airmail to get them resoled.

At the same time that Epstein became more radical (or, to be more exact, a prominent publisher of "radical" books) in the late sixties, he would typically indict out of the left side of his mouth the inequitable structure of income in the U.S. and out of the right judge that "you can't live well" in New York on less than fifty grand annual income and two servants. A secretive person, inclined to assertions of patently false modesty, he capitalized on modern capitalism as eagerly as he criticized it, coolly profiting in both mind and body.

As his contract with Random House permitted Epstein to found and pursue other business, his ambitions took yet other forms, such as his own firm for reprinting classic juveniles—the Looking Glass Library—with Podhoretz as transient editor-in-chief and both Edmund Wilson and W.H. Auden as advisory editors. This series was later sold to Random's juvenile division. His greatest extracurricular coup lay in founding *The New York Review of Books,* early in 1963, in his own duplex apartment at 33 West 67th Street, as the first masthead dutifully declared. His wife, Barbara Epstein (b. 1929), who had been an editorial colleague at Doubleday, was duly installed as coeditor with Robert B. Silvers (b. 1929), a conscientious manuscript man who had previously been a junior editor at *Harper's,* a coeditor of the *Paris Review,* and Alfred Kazin's acknowledged helper at collecting his fifties essays into *Contemporaries* (1962). Elizabeth Hardwick, a neighbor on 67th Street, became an advisory editor. (According to Philip Nobile's informative "A Review of the *New York Review,*" the original choice for Silvers' job was Erik Wensberg, a younger Columbia College alumnus who had founded *Columbia University Forum,* yet another popular front, a few years before, and later became a junior editor on *The New York Times Book Review.* In 1972, Podhoretz told Merle Miller that he had also been asked but declined for practical reasons. "I had been involved with Jason on two previous enterprises, and I had no reason to believe this one would be more successful.") The initial undated issue, published early in 1963, capitalized not only upon the intellectual decline of *The New York Times Book Review,* but also upon an extended New York newspaper strike which, by knocking out that prime competitor, left an accumulation of publishers' advertising money otherwise uncommitted.

There is no doubt, however, as Podhoretz testifies in his book, that "Jason Epstein had had the idea for a paper like *The New York Review* for a long time," and he became a frequent contributor to his own magazine, not only of reviews but also of letters-to-the-editor. According to Nobile, Epstein would also hang around the office in the earliest days, opening the morning mail, writing headlines, and even soliciting reviewers. The first "Statement of Ownership," published in the issue dated October 22, 1964, lists him among "the stockholders owning or holding one percent or more of total amount of stock"—the others were his wife Barbara, Silvers, Elizabeth Lowell (née Hardwick), Robert Lowell, the *Review*'s publisher A. Whitney Ellsworth, the poet James Merrill, and Blair Clark, who subsequently managed Eugene McCarthy's Presidential campaign. Nobile reports that the Lowells and the Epsteins, along with Silvers and Ellsworth, risked none of their own money, instead getting a rather remarkable collection of high-class WASP backers to fund the enterprise. Those six chose themselves the "board of directors" and controlled fifty-one percent of the corporation's stock. By the following year, these six names were superseded by "New York Review, a Limited Partnership." By 1971, the other names disappeared into "NYREV, Inc." which, like the other title, shows no obligation to account for *its* ownership in public print.

All kinds of evidence suggests that, much legitimate reviewing notwithstanding, *The New York Review* was from its origins destined to publicize Random House's (and especially Epstein's) books and writers. Only a year before, Epstein had established a precedent for himself by contributing to *Partisan Review* (to whose "Publications and Advisory Board" he then belonged) a favorable review of W.H. Auden's *The Dyer's Hand* (1962) which happened to be one of his own publishing projects at Random House. The following year, he published in *Commentary* a generalized case for children's classics not unlike, to be specific, those of his own Looking Glass Library! Also in 1963, the *Bulletin* of the American Library Association published Epstein's promotional talk on how he cofounded "a book review of our own" which he portrayed as a redemptive force in a dreary landscape, nonetheless plugging with one hand a product he was peddling with the other. In the first undated issue of the *Review,* ten of the fifty-seven books reviewed were published by Random House—either the imprint itself (five) or one of its three subsidiaries, Alfred A. Knopf (three), Pantheon (one), and Vintage (one); its competitor nearest in number was Harper & Row with three books reviewed. Nearly all the reviewers, who contributed their pieces gratis, were members in loyal standing of the New York literary mob (Kazin, Howe, Mailer, Dupee, Glazer, Vidal, Marcus, Mary McCarthy, Phillips, and Rahv). An editorial rule evident in the first issue holds: Do unto others as, or if, is done unto you. Thus, as Goodman submits a piece, so is there a review of his latest book—ditto,

W.H. Auden and Dwight Macdonald; as Jules Feiffer and Edward Sorel contribute illustrations, so are their "non-books" reviewed, all suggesting the periodical might be called *The New York Review of Each Other's Books.*

One curiosity then noted by the publishing executive Allen Ullman was that "at least four reviews are written by Random House authors [Auden, Styron, Warren & Macdonald], and there is a special article by Paul Goodman, who is principally published by Random House." Five more reviewers would soon have books published by Random House—Bazelon, Edgar Z. Friedenberg, Robert Jay Lifton, Howe, and Epstein himself; and books by *all* of these writers would be reprinted as Vintage paperbacks, which was Epstein's particular editorial domain. His own first review the following fall honored Edmund Wilson's *The Cold War and the Income Tax,* for, though that book was published by Farrar, Straus, Epstein had published some of Wilson's other titles at both Doubleday-Anchor and Random House-Vintage. The back page of Vol. II, No. 1 of *The New York Review* (Feb. 20, 1964) includes a list of seventy-five of the magazine's prior reviewers, eighteen of whom were, or soon would be, Random House authors. In a sample issue dated December 14, 1964, one-half of the fourteen reviewers were, or would be, similarly associated with Random House. Thus, it is not surprising that most of the non-reviewing materials such as essays or the occasional poems would come from Random House authors, if not from forthcoming Random House books.

Macdonald also helped launch the business by contributing to *Esquire,* whose regular film critic he then was, a polemical essay attacking *The New York Times Book Review,* sneering at *Saturday Review* (a lesser competitor), then hailing the arrival of a new book review (thus echoing not only a demand made a few years before, at Silvers' editorial invitation, by Elizabeth Hardwick in *Harper's,* but also the hearty welcome Macdonald himself had given Epstein's Looking Glass Library in *The Griffin*). Podhoretz wrote a review that announced that "everyone I know" wrote for the magazine. And so on and so on. ("Where, one might wonder," Ullman asked in a letter to *Esquire,* "was Mr. Macdonald when all these independent and completely objective editorial decisions [regarding books and reviewers] were being made?") Although writers customarily denigrate the quality of reviews and reviewers, every publisher knows how incomparably powerful they are for selling *literary* books and establishing "serious" reputations. By printing much longer and far fewer reviews than *The Times Book Review, The New York Review of Books* could also give a more concentrated push both to certain issues and reviewers as well as to selected books.

In short, then, *The New York Review* became, first, the most popular front of the ever-enterprising New York literary mob; and second, an extension of Epstein's own publishing designs. The evolution from the first emphasis to the second is the central theme of the magazine's own history to 1967 or so. Even though his own name did not appear on the magazine's masthead, its success ushered Epstein and then Silvers, who became progressively more assertive, to the core of the onion, succeeding Trilling (who, symbolically, has never contributed to *The New York Review*) and signaled thereby a concomitant general decline of the mob's intellectual, moral, stylistic, and entrepreneurial tone. (The paper's opening issues had back-page advertisements announcing a new publishing firm named Stein & Day, whose president, Sol Stein, had served the mob in ways similar to Epstein—e.g., founding the Mid-Century Book Club; but aside from loyally publishing Leslie A. Fiedler's many books, Stein has since gone his own way.) "Neither time nor space," announced an editorial in the second issue, "have been spent on books which are trivial in their intentions or venal in their effects, except occasionally to reduce a temporarily inflated reputation or to call attention to a fraud." However, these homilies would, as we shall see, be repeatedly violated.

Such collusive enterprise continued into the seventies as Random House's growing enthusiasm for leftish critiques, for instance, coincided with that of *The New York Review*, each publishing the other's almost exclusively male-Caucasian "radical" authors, both exploiting the growing sentiment of protest —Paul Goodman, Noam Chomsky, George Lichtheim, Tom Hayden, Stokely Carmichael, Bernard Fall, Oscar Lewis, H. Stuart Hughes, Edgar Z. Friedenberg, I.F. Stone, Christopher Lasch, Jules Henry, Jean Lacouture, Jane Jacobs, Dwight Macdonald, Robert Jay Lifton, Robert Heilbroner, Paul Jacobs, Gar Alperovitz, Seymour Hersh, Ronald Steel, Franz Schurmann, William Appleman Williams, Francine du Plessix Gray, Eugene Genovese, Eric Hobsbawm, Ralph Stavins, Michael Rossman, Marcus Raskin, Tom Bottomore, Gore Vidal, Peter Dale Scott,

Frances Fitzgerald, Kirkpatrick Sale, "Health-PAC," *all* of whom eventually appeared in Vintage paperbacks as well. The magazine's radicalism burgeoned with the issue dated August 24, 1967, whose cover had a sketch and recipe of a Molotov cocktail; for although Random House-Vintage was neither selling bombs nor reviewing them, it did publish several books about urban disorders and commissioned a few more.

The featured essays in *The New York Review* were invariably by Americans, some of them contributing more to enterprise than "criticism," while scores of eager Englishmen, mostly recruited from *The New Statesman* and appreciative of dollar rates-of-pay, filled "the back of the book" with semblances of legitimate, albeit puffy, reviewing. (Mob moguls born after 1925, perhaps reflecting Trilling's influence, are more Anglophile than their continentally-inclined predecessors, while the British writers were more adept at accommodating themselves to the tone and prejudices of yet another new medium.) Most of the American contributors were Easterners by residence, and most of the Easterners were New Yorkers or Bostonians; so that the *Review*'s reports on protests at Berkeley were, as one critic observed, "often done by visiting profs from Harvard and Brandeis." Moreover, though aimed at a fairly young audience, if not squarely at the graduate student-young instructor, approximately three-quarters of its contributors were, like its editors, born between 1915 and 1936; and not until very recently has the magazine published more than a dozen writers born after 1937, none of them, by my count, contributing more than thrice. (It has published even fewer blacks, Italian-Americans, and Spanish-Americans, as well as absolutely no Chicanos, Puerto Ricans, Indians, or Chinese-Americans.) Those few young writers asked to contribute have generally been treated so high-handedly that most of them have come to despise the magazine. One was short-changed, another was asked to enlarge his essay to twice its original length before the editors cut it down to its initial size, while a third was asked to abridge his polemic into a letter-to-the-editor. As an exporting (and exploiting) medium, it sells far more to blacks and young people than it buys from them.

The magazine's success at its publicizing endeavors made it, in Tom Wolfe's phrase, "the chief organ of the radical chic," its critics noting nonetheless that its pages were more committed to the New Politics than New Art or to any other examples of "the new sensibility"; but precedent suggests that were its owners capable of investing in avant-garde activity, *The New York Review* would undoubtedly publish critics predisposed to it too. The magazine became noticeably thicker by the fall of 1965 as the essays became much longer; and before the decade's end *The New York Review*'s circulation steadily approached a plateau of 90,000. As its fattening issues were riddled with full-page advertisements purchased at nearly a thousand dollars apiece, its managers would claim it "money-making"—not only for all its implicit subsidiaries and beneficiaries, but also, unlike the earlier mob magazines, in its own right. (Success had the further benefit of making even *The Times Book Review* more responsive to mob writers.) By 1971, *The New York Review*'s political radicalism began to subside, perhaps in response to intra-mob criticism or the general mood, one friend of Epstein's telling Nobile, "He's not radical but quite fashionable, and when things change, he'll change." Back in 1963, Epstein wrote: "There is finally a point beyond which a publisher cannot go against the tide. Eventually he risks drowning."

Although Epstein's radical titles sold comparatively well, continuing to justify his earlier Random House editorial decisions in their favor, Bennett Cerf, hardly a fire-eating radical, and his colleagues sometimes spurned this policy. They had previously resisted Epstein's ambition to publish Barbara Garson's *Macbird* (1966), a heavy-handed script that probably attracted the mob (and antagonized others) because it vulgarized their own increasing antipathy toward President Johnson. Even though Macdonald produced an extravagantly laudatory notice for *The New York Review*, and both Lowell and Robert Brustein provided blurbs, Cerf kept his top-dog authority. Nonetheless, all this advance publicity helped sell over 100,000 copies of a privately published edition, as well as make the play an off-Broadway hit—the mob unable, alas, to reap the rewards of its own endeavors—while the playwright Garson subsequently disappeared.

Nonetheless, by the late sixties, *The New York Review*-Random House machine had become so effective at publicizing (and then exploiting with appropriate titles) the anti-Vietnam sentiments of book-buying America that Cerf's own biases, for what they were, deferred to publishing success. By then, too, Epstein

68

had become the most powerful of Random House's senior editors, all of whom operate fairly autonomous fiefs (and thus implicitly compete against each other); so that Philip Roth, for instance, found, upon completing *Portnoy's Complaint,* that Epstein could obtain a far larger advance than his prior Random House editor could offer. As Roth switched editors, Epstein, in turn, got credit within the firm for sponsoring the pre-puffed best-seller.

All this prosperity notwithstanding, Epstein must have recognized, one suspects, that adversities might force him to create his own firm, for his power, after all, was based upon his experience and success in book publishing. Partially to prepare for that possibility, *The New York Review* hit upon an especially opportune scheme for quickly raising its own funds—by founding, early in 1968, a lecture agency that would capitalize, first, upon the spectacularly rising fees paid to eminent lecturers; second, upon the rather low operating expenses required by such an enterprise; and third, upon the *Review*'s capacity to publicize its clients in spacious advertisements in its own pages. Furthermore, of the original seventeen political-literary lecturers, seven were already Vintage authors; nearly all of them were also embedded in the New York literary onion.

The final factor in the agency's operation and subsequent success was the magazine's increasing circulation to university addresses outside New York. A 1966 survey reported that 45 percent of its subscribers were academics by residence while 70 percent lived beyond the Middle Atlantic states. A more sophisticated survey by Charles Kadushin and his associates found *The New York Review* to be the "most influential" magazine among America's 275,000 academics. However, since only a fifth or so of its subscribers actually *lived* around New York City, it became clear that, like *The New Yorker* before it, *The New York Review* has been largely directed at people residing outside the city, the magazine catering to their cosmopolitan aspirations and exploiting the cultural authority of "New York." (Nor are "Florida oranges," after all, destined largely for customers in Miami!) This thrust explains why cultural activities within New York City are neglected in its pages, except for occasional theater reviews—not of off-Broadway or off-off, to be sure, but of the uptown mainstream that outlanders are likely to sample on a visit.

Since the primary business of Vintage Books–*New York Review* could be defined, by this time, as peddling certain reputations and ideas (in the form of accompanying books) to provincial academics, this lecture agency seemed the most lucrative means of extending the operation's best developed competence. It is revealing, in this respect, that the agency's prime mover, A. Whitney Ellsworth, told a *New York Times* reporter, "We think the same kind of quality that has appealed to university audiences in *The Review* will appeal in the selection of intellectual entertainment"; and he quoted with apparently naive glee a professor in Alaska (!) who sent this reply to the opening announcement: "We will be glad to have anyone you send us." Epstein, whose stockholdership in *The New York Review* had publicly disappeared behind a new corporation, nonetheless joined the board of directors of Review Presentations, Inc.; and this "service of *The New York Review*," as it is subtitled, charged comparatively hefty prices, "with special discounts for series bookings." Customarily taking a third of the gross, it quickly became more profitable than its parent organization. Many of its "acts" also contributed their talents to the Eugene McCarthy 1968 Presidential campaign, whose New York City machine (plus its cabaret named "Eugene") was, in some ways, also a "popular front" of the New York literary mob. This interest in rather conventional theater prompted Nobile to characterize the *Review*'s politics as "to the left of Carnegie Hall [its neighbor on New York's 57th St.] and to the right of most of what is commonly associated with New Left politics."

Even though Epstein stayed with Random House, *The New York Review* started to issue books under its own imprint, most of them by regular contributors (Herbert Kohl, I.F. Stone, John Schaar, Sheldon Wolin) or drawn from itself (*Trials of Resistance*); and these were distributed by Vintage Books, naturally. In 1971, NYREV, Inc. purchased for "an undisclosed amount of cash" *Kirkus Reviews* which remains, after *Publishers Weekly*, America's most powerful prepublication reviewing medium, thereby adding yet another speaker to its publicity-amplification system. Eighty percent of *Kirkus*'s 4,500 subscribers are libraries across the country, one percent are booksellers, nineteen percent are publishers, reprinters, book clubs, review editors, and even other reviewers.) Although Ellsworth piously declared that the *Kirkus Reviews* would remain "absolutely editorially independent" and its management unchanged, not only did *The New York Review*'s earlier editorial hanky-panky render his assertion dubious, but this change in ownership at first went suspiciously unreported in the *Kirkus* publication itself. Although there was no precedent for one reviewing medium purchasing another (or any apparent strictly-business reason for the accession), the obvious objections to this monopolistic takeover were, once again, publicly silenced. *The New York Review* publicized *Kirkus* by printing occasional excerpts of its reviews, and in 1972 it assimilated *I.F. Stone's Bi-Weekly.*

II

> This bent toward careerism of modern Left intellectuals as a social caste is worldwide....The new elite was less concerned with social criticism than with the imminent rewards of banding together. The fact that a new togetherness, not new ideas, was its aim accounts for the murderous style of its factional fights and its vile treatment of dissident individuals—Harold Rosenberg, "Death in the Wilderness" (1959).

Meanwhile, Norman Podhoretz, the mob's most lauded "young critic" in the fifties and a generally faithful publicist, joined Epstein at the onion's core, becoming, at the age of 30 in 1960, the editor-in-chief of *Commentary*, following the death of Elliot E. Cohen the year before. In its pages was Podhoretz's own precociously successful American career launched; for along with other cultural entrepreneurs such as Irving Kristol, Clement Greenberg, and Nathan Glazer, he had been an associate editor during Cohen's reign. *Making It* reveals that Podhoretz thought of himself as rescuing the declining magazine for "the family" from which it had drifted away during Martin Greenberg's interim regime, since Podhoretz, like Epstein, regarded himself as serving not his peers but his predecessors. "Rarely do young men," notes Barbara Probst Solomon, roughly their contemporary, "get together for the express purpose of bringing fame and fortune to a generation already established." Podhoretz's opening issue featured Trilling, Dupee, Kazin, Goodman, Marcus, and Kristol, as well as the first of three installments from Paul Goodman's much-rejected manuscript, "Growing Up Absurd," which Podhoretz delivered to his friend Epstein to publish as a book. It became one of the latter's first radical good-sellers. Not only would much else excerpted from forthcoming books similarly appear under Random House imprint, but Epstein's titles (and authors) were featured in the back pages of *Commentary.*

The magazine thrived under Podhoretz's editorship, updating its design and increasing in both circulation and physical size (even becoming a more lucrative advertising medium). As ever-enterprising as *The New York Review*, it established its own conglomerate of cottage industries—a nationwide network of discussion groups, reprints of earlier articles (sometimes with specially prepared "study guides" destined for the classroom), its own book club (whose offerings included the Old Testament on subscription), such religious ornaments as Chanukah candelabras, "Commentary cards" (for use as notepaper or greetings), and "A Treasury of Chassidic Songs." Despite all this enterprise, *Commentary* still preserved its traditionally critical relationship with a predominantly bourgeois audience—such as the *Commentary* custom of automatically criticizing the latest cultural enthusiasms of its readers. The usual target was a best-selling author (or book) with "serious" pretensions, whether Herman Wouk, J. D. Salinger, Harry Golden, Katherine Ann Porter, Edward Albee, or John Barth. (Mob authors and operations were, of course, excepted.) In 1966 appeared *The Commentary Reader,* introduced not by Trilling, who was passé by then, but by Alfred Kazin, whose characteristic sentimentalities and ambiguities in many ways epitomized the magazine in that period.

Podhoretz also acquired his own popular front by becoming, for two years, a regular and well-paid book reviewer for *Show*, a slick, mass-circulation magazine published by Huntington Hartford. Podhoretz's essay about the newly founded *New York Review of Books* admitted not only that "everyone I know" wrote for it, but that, "All these reviewers inhabit much the same intellectual milieu." Only in the sixties did members begin to acknowledge the mob's existence in public, though always insisting that it had less cohesiveness and power than the evidence suggested. The truth-telling memoir entitled *Making It* (1968) that Podhoretz published with Random House (after it was rejected by Roger Straus who had commissioned it for a fairly extravagant advance) revealed explicitly what others had earlier come to suspect—that he had exchanged the decent ambition of critical concern with intellectual truth and literary excellence for the bourgeois pottage of fame, power, and money; so that even in writing a "critical essay," he confessed he found the second set of concerns more motivating than the first.

By the late sixties, he and Epstein had a personal falling out, initially over *Making It,* which Epstein disliked, and then over the political issues of both the politics of the Vietnamese war and the 1968 New York school teachers strike in which militant blacks antagonized the predominantly Jewish teachers' union. As the conflict exacerbated, the two long-term collaborators found themselves stuck holding antipathetic bags. As each refused to mention the other in print, so other sores of disagreement, such as anti-Communism and student protest, were opened. Nonetheless, even though henchmen of each went along with their boss, this quarrel, unlike the wars with the literary Communists, was not violent enough to make anyone lose or quit his job, for this schism within the larger church was relatively amicable. No one this time, unlike the fifties, suffered the middle-class misfortune that really hurts—a sharp decline in one's standard of living; and Podhoretz and Epstein continued to move in overlapping social circles and to keep a lot of mutual friends.

After this split, *Commentary* began to take positions closer to those of the socio-political conservatives of *The Public Interest*, often publishing the same writers and becoming as self-consciously middle-aged; and *Commentary* developed a flair, shared by its editor, for debating spurious issues. One could assume that articles were once again "carefully inspected for traces of softness"—now toward the New Left or the "counter culture"—while its occasionally hysterical anti-radicalism, abetted by an anti-anti-Semitism that wailed about largely imaginary devils, seemed reminiscent of the fifties. Its accumulating attack upon *The New York Review* climaxed with an expensively-commissioned long polemic by the sociologist Dennis H. Wrong, who criticized, with occasional brilliance, just the political evolution of the other magazine. Given the depth of *Commentary*'s animus, it is odd that this essay failed to mention its practical corruptions (i.e., its Random House biases)—the most reasonable explanation of its continued silence on this score being that such revelations (already made in publications of smaller circulation) would necessarily raise questions about why Podhoretz's magazine (and *its* herd of independent minds) had not looked into such dishonesty before. Indeed, the fact that certain secrets are kept suggests that more skeletons can be found in the closet and that each knows they, like two disputing families within a single Mafia, will once again be doing business together. The name of their game is not war—not even literary war—but monopoly.

Partisan Review likewise became more popular during the sixties, though considerably less purposeful and consequential. In 1963, *Partisan* sold itself to Rutgers University, its offices and files moving to New Brunswick (even though most of its senior staff continued to live in New York); and its proudly anti-academic heritage suffered mortal sabotage. Moreover, just as Richard Poirier, then chairman of English at Rutgers, became a coeditor of *Partisan,* so William Phillips, the magazine's primary editor at the time, became an English professor at Rutgers. Since Philip Rahv, Phillips' partner all those years and already a professor at Brandeis, found his wishes continually overruled, he established his own review, *Modern Occasions*, initially publishing it with Farrar, Straus & Giroux (1965). After officially resigning from *Partisan* in 1969, he revived *Modern Occasions* in 1970 as an independent journal that resembled *Partisan* in size, design, and middle-aged contributors. (In the first issue, the youngest was Philip Roth!) Terribly narcissistic in its endeavors, this magazine tried to seem more "radical" than its progenitor while remaining opposed to the young and the new; and that contradiction perhaps accounts for the hiatus after a few issues. On yet another hand, Louis G. Cowan, *Partisan*'s principal patron, remained chairman of its "Publications and Advisory Board," having already founded Chilmark Press with Phillips as his primary literary advisor and Random House as his distributor; and perhaps the only Chilmark title not reissued from British plates was Phillips' first-ever collection of essays and stories, *A Sense of the Present* (1967).

Superficially more open to young writers, especially if they studied with any of the editors, *Partisan Review* made, until around 1970, an apparent practice of publishing new people once and only once, escorting them on stage for a brief bow before leading them away, perhaps in the hope that all those one-shot contributors would, in their own subsequent biographical notes, prominently list *"Partisan Review"* among the magazines in which they had previously appeared. Its prime literary contribution had been made years before, however; in Irving Howe's 1963 estimate, "PR not only helped establish a new school in American literature—the writers of urban, 'alienated' and (in not merely the literal sense) Jewish fiction—and a distinctive tendency in American literary criticism—what might be called the New York social critics." By the 1970's, though its issues were often much fatter, *Partisan* seemed disspirited and undirected, having lost its initiating role in the mob's intellectual life, surviving mostly, it seemed, to sustain the literary reputations of those still associated with it.

Nonetheless, the New York literary mob's power and wealth generally increased, along with its avarice and corruption, from the beginning of the decade. Nearly everyone became a university professor, a few assuming endowed chairs, all of them inevitably desiring to increase the prerogatives and privileges of that profession, as well as addressing young audiences from whom they expected agreement. Other previously recalcitrant highbrows became publishing executives, like Kristol for a spell, or plushly salaried middlebrow newspaper critics, like Hilton Kramer, who were at the same time still responsive to demands from within the onion. (Kramer, for instance, while frequently protesting the corruption of the art scene, remains oddly silent about similar dishonesty in literature.) When Richard Kluger resigned his editorship of *Book Week*, the second most powerful newspaper book supplement, Theodore Solotaroff took his place; the latter soon moved on to establish in 1967 *New American Review* as yet another popular front in the widening circle of accomplices. When Willie Morris became editor-in-chief of *Harper's* early in 1967, certain mob writers became regular contributors; and Podhoretz's wife, Midge Decter, became executive editor in a top-level troika (and reportedly its most persuasive decision-maker)—in sum, temporarily transforming *Harper's* into yet another popular front. (Thus, for a spell, were two of America's most powerful cultural organs governed from a single dining table.) When Decter became managing editor of Norman Cousins' *World* (est. 1972), taking particular charge of the literary pages, the same familiar names now joined alumni from the *Saturday Review*.

By the sixties, some of the outfit had become extremely prominent not only on the lecture circuits, but in Washington during the intellectually-attuned Kennedy administration (Podhoretz, inevitably a follower, had *his* audience with Johnson!); and nearly all of them capitalized upon the prosperities of the decade. Incomes above fifty grand annually—from position, royalties, lectures, consulting, magazine commissions, publishers' advising, and expense accounts—were not uncommon. Whereas the self-proclaimed intellectual might once have been ashamed of living too well off his trade, guilts and apologies of that sort disappeared by the middle sixties. These intellectuals rented large New York apartments, hired full-time servants, bought houses in the country (and even such amenities as yachts), and provided well for their retirements. "It was disconcerting to discover," writes Willie Morris, "that political liberals and radicals, whose warmth of spirit [sic] I admired, all had summer homes, as I myself would one day." The life style they favored was no longer bohemian but upper-middle class, their children going to the best private schools. Some, like Trilling, Epstein, and Silvers, joined New York's most culturally prestigious private club, the Century; while scarcely bohemian or radical, this alliance provided a social link to older literary New Yorks. None of America's beneficence seemed beyond their pocketbooks. Indeed, the pride that some of them took in reciting America's prosperity (while opposing the bohemian radicalism of the young) seemed, in context, to rationalize their personal success.

The most successful by his own handiwork was Norman Mailer, a genuinely popular writer of Jewish background (South African, rather than Eastern European) but independent career-origins. He had supported Henry Wallace in 1948 (and was thus thought to be a Stalinist) and then was peripherally allied with the love-hate anti-Partisaners until Macdonald, Howe, and Podhoretz conscripted him into the mob in the late fifties. By 1962 he received Diana Trilling's public imprimatur and came to be more generally touted, always with reservations, as a possible prince to King Saul in the royal family of Jewish-American novelists. Other reputation-makers called him, to introduce a professional category ignored by the Agrarians, "our best journalist," with an ambiguously possessive pronoun—a phrase that had sometimes been used before to honor

Dwight Macdonald. Their support, along with *Esquire*'s and Mailer's own talents for publicity, helped establish him as, in Marvin Mudrick's phrase, "the great American writer for the people who don't read." Mailer's new fame, like Bellow's, complemented the "outfit's" own increasing eminence, and thus created a growing audience for such collective self-studies as *Making It*. As a writer of opportunistic spirit and idiosyncratic passions, Mailer exploited his admirers' publicity without succumbing to their authority, instead going his own way— subsequently making films, exercising his talent for public hyperbole, running for Mayor of New York, and forging a small-scale literary machine of his own. As Seymour Krim, one of his earliest champions, observed in 1969, "I can't move in Manhattan life today without having him imposed on me."

By the sixties, most of New York's literary mob were so busy with secondary activity—whether lecturing, reviewing, slick-journalizing, jockeying for position, enjoying spoils, getting attention from a yet larger audience, or simply tending to their growing families—that most of their announced primary projects went chronically unfinished: Kazin's book about nineteenth-century American literature, Kristol's on twentieth-century ideas, Trilling's about literary modernism, Podhoretz's on the thirties, Rahv's on Dostoevsky, Solotaroff's on recent fiction, Kramer's on modern sculpture, Rosenberg's on action painting, Mailer's multi-volumed opus starring Sergius O'Shaughnessy. One likely reason why these works remained incomplete is that, given such over-inflated reputations, the finished products would inevitably disappoint readers and reviewers, and this fear, in turn, rationalized subsequent "holding actions." Of nearly everyone it could be said: Yes, he did his best work years ago. Or: He writes much less nowadays than before. Not unlike John Updike's prototypical "Jewish novelist," Henry Bech, "His reputation had grown while his powers declined."

Although the novelist George P. Elliott noted in *The Nation* in the late 1950's that a coterie of New York writers had a presumptuous way of using the pronoun "we," no one except such old war-horses as Kenneth Rexroth seemed courageous enough to decry the mob in print until Renata Adler's essay on "Polemic and the New Reviewers" in *The New Yorker* (July 4, 1964). A sometime graduate student at Harvard who had, at the

77

age of 24 in 1962, become a staff writer on *The New Yorker,* she produced a witty and devastating analysis of the mobsters' characteristic intellectual fallacies, as well as their predilection for quoting each other. Although she never pursued the sociological analysis suggested by her literary insights, she ranks among the first to identify a suspicious cohesiveness among supposedly autonomous minds. Nevertheless, simply by appearing in *The New Yorker,* her piece inadvertently contributed to the old battle between the two literary New Yorks.

In the summer of 1965, *Social Research,* an academic journal, published a superficial survey by the economist Robert Lekachman on "The Literary Intellectuals of New York." He named names, 149 of them, one-third of whom were English. "What these individuals have in common is contributions during 1963, 1964 and the first five months of 1965 to *The New York Review of Books, Commentary,* or *Partisan Review."* Though failing to examine beneath the surface of his evidence (e.g., his acceptance of Englishmen, most of whom contributed back-page filler to *The New York Review,* as equal members), Lekachman did make two perceptive points: "Most of the hundred and forty-nine have appeared in at least two of three journals. Many have been the subjects as well as the authors of reviews and articles." Secondly, "These periodicals meet what might be called the self-consciousness requirement in the definition of a cohesive intellectual class." However, Lekachman accepted too uncritically those pretensions to intellectual excellence that are unfounded, especially since so few of the remaining American hundred can claim any cultural achievement greater than reviews and articles. Since these "intellectuals" are not, by and large, the creators of "intellectual history," it would be more appropriate to characterize them as a literary clique or mob. In 1965 also appeared, in *Hudson Review,* my own essay on "Militant Minorities," which was expanded to become the opening two chapters of this book.

The following spring, Victor S. Navasky's "Notes on Cult: or, How To Join the Intellectual Establishment" appeared in *The New York Times Magazine.* Navasky, a former lawyer just beginning his writing career, opened by quoting Adler and me on the existence of a literary establishment and then proceeded to examine whether our charges were true. He concluded that we were wrong, but rather than make the analysis his judgment demanded, he resorted to the journalistic device of gathering extended quotations from various people involved, most of whom made it implicitly clear that something very powerful and fairly tight did indeed exist.

One predictable response to such scattershot was an increasing public self-consciousness within the mob itself. In 1968, editorial chieftains Howe and Podhoretz each published an extended apologia. While the former typically expressed pious nostalgia for a more radical past, the latter transcended his cynical pose to make risky revelations not only about the existence of a cohesive "family," but also about a few (though less than all) of the loathsome practices of its auspicious members. (It was not for nothing that Epstein refused to publish the book which was sponsored with success by another autonomous senior editor at Random House; and *Making It* has, significantly perhaps, never been Vintaged.) Podhoretz's memoir also suggests that economic and social-climbing motives have generally superseded the drive for purely literary achievement. Reworking T.S. Eliot's (unacknowledged) metaphor of literary reputations as a stock-market, Podhoretz acknowledges the bullish value of various non-literary criteria:

> Did so-and-so have dinner at Jacqueline Kennedy's apartment last night? Up five points. Was so-and-so not invited by the Lowells to meet the latest visiting Russian poet? Down one-eighth. Did so-and-so's book get nominated for the National Book Award? Up two-and-five-eighths. Did *Partisan Review* neglect to ask so-and-so to participate in a symposium? Down two.

However, in a patently disingenuous attempt to bluff away inevitable criticisms, Podhoretz concluded that, "By the mid-1960's, however, it had all but completely disintegrated," thus reiterating Epstein's arrogant deceit, quoted before in an epigraph, of denying in one phrase what is acknowledged in the next, confirming, if not illustrating, a criticism in the course of denying it—a fault less typical of intellectuals than politicians. "It is fashionable," notes Navasky, "for the N.Y. intellectual establishment not only to deny its existence but as a corollary to deny its influence." In fact, since the mob most clearly

reveals itself in defense, members can be (or used to be) identified as those who most vehemently deny its existence, just as
mysteriously prosperous Sicilian-born "businessmen" ritually
declare, "Mafia. What Mafia?"

The truth is that, schisms and criticism notwithstanding, the
New York literary mob remains ultimately as powerful, self-
protective, and avaricious as it has been throughout the sixties.
Portnoy's Complaint became a best-seller in 1969, not only
redeeming their earlier investment in Roth's reputation, but also
emulating similarly successful novels by McCarthy, Bellow, and
Malamud. Mailer's projects continue to command spectacular
prices and prestigious publishing prizes, while Robert Lowell's
books, no matter how poetically thin and verbose they become,
are still habitually given prominent laudatory reviews in nearly
every major medium. The epithet "New York intellectuals" still
gets enough respectable publicity to perpetuate the deceit implicit in the phrase itself. Were that phrase to be publicly
discredited as the lie it is, the mob would need to adopt another
collective front (or perhaps publicly disappear!). As very politicized people, these "social men of letters," to use Q.D. Leavis'
phrase, display an impulsive pettiness of both favor and disfavor
more typical of politicians than writers.

When the sociologist Charles Kadushin surveyed American
cultural periodicals in an effort to identify, by systematic quan-
tification, an "intellectual elite," he produced a list of seventy
people which he divided into four ranks. Of the eleven in the
top group, only John Kenneth Galbraith is not included in my
chart of the "New York Literary Mob." Of the next group of
ten, the two exceptions are Herbert Marcuse and Daniel Patrick
Moynihan. Though representation on the lower levels is more
heterogeneous, members of the mob still predominate. The
mob's own magazines have been especially successful in reaching the cultural powerhouses of their own generation; by 1970,
according to Kadushin's survey, "the three journals read most
regularly by the chairmen of the major American colleges and
universities are *The New York Review of Books, Commentary,*
and *Partisan Review.*" The paid circulation of its most popular
front approached 100,000, and a survey prepared in 1966 for
The New York Review's prospective advertisers characterizes its
regular readership as "highly educated, active and sophisticated

consumers" with a median income of over $15,000 and an average age of forty.

One further indication of the outfit's persistence is the continuity of contributorship within the onion's inner skins, although individual writers have favored different magazines and alliances at various points in their careers. Another is the absence of stark disagreements over which living writers are (and are not) important and which intellectual issues are more major than minor. (This may also explain why every non-Communist participant in the cultural Cold War is still functioning prominently, no matter what his past position or, even, his possible collaboration with the CIA.) Individuals still speak possessively of "our intellectual community," symposia at the egregiously misnamed "Theater for Ideas" still draw full houses, parties are still crowded, and high-class hostesses are still willing to give them. Polemics preaching unity within diversity still appear, while positions and proximities within the onion have changed only slightly. Their memoirs serve the incidental functions of supplying subsequent intellectual historians with raw materials for laudatory scholarship. Although Schwartz died in the sixties and Goodman in the seventies, Kazin and Howe, Bellow and Lowell persist; though Martin Greenberg all but disappeared and his brother Clement joined Trilling in premature near-silence, Rosenberg has become a *New Yorker* columnist. And so on and so on.

The mob's inner leaves closed shut in the sixties, for just as no one born after 1917 (Robert Lowell) ever became a full-fledged Agrarian, so no one younger than Sontag and Roth, both born in 1933 and the last nearly unanimous promotions, has become a fully accredited New York intellectual—not even Jeremy Larner, who has been conspicuously on the mob-make since the early sixties. His first novel, *Drive He Said* (1964), not only acknowledged their intellectual preoccupations, but also won a prize juried by Leslie Fiedler and Mary McCarthy. In addition to coediting a book with Irving Howe, Larner followed the mob's nearly unanimous support of Eugene McCarthy by becoming one of the Senator's speech writers; he then accompanied their rejection of him with a critical attack on the man and his ineffectual campaign, published not in a core periodical, of course, but a popular front, *Harper's,* and then as a book,

The Man Nobody Knows (1970). Early in 1973, another ambitious young writer, Alan Lelchuk (b. 1938), who had been Rahv's assistant editor on *Modern Occasions,* echoed Larner in publishing a terribly modish novel, *American Mischief,* in which many of the mob appear as stars on the cultural landscape. Late the previous fall, Philip Roth, writing in *Esquire,* selected *American Mischief* as his favorite book by a young American and also praised it as "a brilliant and original comedy."

Most of the young people published in mob periodicals were not only conservative in taste and cautious in professional demeanor, but also, as noted before, invariably former students (like Larner himself) of mob chieftains. Indeed, conservative magazines like *Dissent* and *Commentary* offered short careers to precocious writers echoing their elders' criticisms of the New Left. Young critics such as Steven Kelman and David Bromwich survived only as long as their judgments coincided with the drifts of their sponsors. (The easiest way to distinguish young servants from independent critics is to check where else they have been published—the former appear only within the safe circle of allied magazines, while the latter have diversified support.) Symptoms on all fronts showed that, in both their esthetics and literary politics, all mob magazines were reactionary posing as liberal or even "radical."

It seems that those mob elders born before 1910 (e.g., Rahv, Trilling, Phillips, Rosenberg, and Greenberg) had just one child or none, making them distant from the young in general (while he who was most reborn, Leslie Fiedler, has six children!). Trilling became notoriously inaccessible in the sixties even to his Columbia pupils, his published remarks about "students" suggesting he *knows* them as a Southern planter "knows" his darkies. ("That to some of us who teach and who think of our students as the creators of the intellectual life of the future, there comes a kind of despair.") Since they wanted to believe that younger writers would succumb to the coercive pressures of bourgeois America (and the literary establishments) as easily as they did, they were especially critical of the talented ones who remained recalcitrant (starting with Allen Ginsberg). Diana Trilling, for example, revealed her sentiments on the matter by saying about Ginsberg: "Then why should I not also defend the expectation that a student at Columbia, even a poet, would do his work, submit it to his teachers through the normal channels of classroom communication, stay out of jail, and, then, if things went right, graduate, start publishing, be reviewed, and see what developed, whether he was a success or failure?" It is again indicative that no one listed on the illustrative chart was born after 1942. (The average age of Kadushin's elite was fifty-five in 1970; none of his seventy were born after 1934. Four of the eight women mentioned are married to other listees.) What Philip Rahv noted of an earlier literary generation—"While the writer thought he was allying himself with the working class, in reality he was surrendering his independence to the Communist Party"—was true again, except that as "Literature" succeeded "the working class" in this equation, so did the "New York literary mob" in its dealings with young writers come to resemble the Communist Party, rewarding with one hand while supervising with the other.

The mob's unity and unanimity became particularly visible when challenged en masse, for disagreements are forgotten when mutual self-preservation becomes the primary need. It has become customary within the mob to charge that literary experiment is "finally exhausted" and that "the young don't seem nearly as interested in writing fiction and criticism as their counterparts of my generation" (Irving Howe)—both charges functioning to protect their own professional investment. Recognizing that too many people were already partaking of a limited amount of cake, they wanted to close off the inflow and create a professional situation that would discourage increasing numbers of talented young. (For similar reasons, as Peter Maas observed, the Cosa Nostra offered no new ranking memberships from the early thirties to the middle fifties when it vainly attempted to rejuvenate its operation.)

These sometime socialists practiced a literary politics that was, needless to say, detrimental to the welfare of the majority. Not even the newest of the mob magazines, *The New York Review,* has ever launched a young writer of acknowledged promise—the closest semblance would be Robert Mazzocco, a poetry critic scarcely published elsewhere—while new names in other journals seem undistinguished and undistinguishable. Those young writers mature enough to do adult literary tasks automatically became devils in the mob's demonology—competitors to be feared and put down, underlings against whom all discriminations are theologically just. In truth, the

83

mob *needed* the young, much as Israel has needed the Arabs—as a threat to unite factions that would otherwise be disputatious.

It was not as imaginative writers or even as critics that the New York literary mob most obviously succeeded for they produced no more than a few distinguished books, along with many essays and cartloads of reviews. As literary politicians and publicists, by contrast, the mob can be credited, in retrospect, with the genuine cultural achievement of replacing lower-middlebrow opinion with upper-middlebrow in America's semi-official literary circles. Thus, Edmund Wilson, rather than J. Donald Adams; Robert Lowell, rather than John Ciardi; Saul Bellow, rather than John Steinbeck or John O'Hara, have become the most honored American writers. The mob's most salient collective quality has been its persistent dominance—for more than two decades—while it still has enough internal energy to last another decade, perhaps two. However, the absence of younger people finally will circumscribe the potential duration of its hegemony, for without fresh blood every aristocracy depletes and disintegrates. In spite of the inevitable fear of exposure, in spite of intramural quarrels, in spite of the economic recession at the beginning of the seventies, business was still prospering as usual.

The New York Literary Mob During the Past Decade

THE CENTER

Jason Epstein	Norman Podhoretz
Irving Howe	Robert B. Silvers

THE INNER LEAVES

Daniel Bell	Melvin J. Lasky
Saul Bellow	Robert Lowell
Midge Decter	Dwight Macdonald
F. W. Dupee	Norman Mailer
Barbara Epstein	Steven Marcus
Leslie A. Fiedler	Willie Morris
Elizabeth Hardwick	William Phillips
Alfred Kazin	Richard Poirier
Hilton Kramer	Philip Rahv
Irving Kristol	Harold Rosenberg

Philip Roth
Meyer Schapiro
John J. Simon
Theodore Solotaroff

Susan Sontag
Roger Straus, Jr.
Lionel Trilling

THE MIDDLE LEAVES

Lionel Abel
Sherry Abel
A. Alvarcz
Aaron Asher
Pearl Bell
Robert Brustein
Lewis A. Coser
Louis G. Cowan
Stephen Donadio
A. Whitney Ellsworth
Edgar Z. Friedenberg
Nathan Glazer
Paul Goodman
Clement Greenberg
Caroline Rand Herron
John Hollander
Murray Kempton

Frank Kermode
Richard Kluger
Myron Kolatch
Neal Kozodoy
Jeremy Larner
Christopher Lehmann-Haupt
George Lichtheim
Marion Magid
Bernard Malamud
Mary McCarthy
Conor Cruise O'Brien
George Plimpton
Arthur M. Schlesinger, Jr.
Peter Schrag
Mark Strand
William Styron
Diana Trilling
Erik Wensberg

THE OUTER LEAVES

Daniel Aaron
Henry David Aiken
Robert Alter
Hannah Arendt
Eve Auchincloss
W.H. Auden
James Baldwin
David T. Bazelon
Eric Bentley
Marshall Berman
Shirley Broughton
Francis Brown
Catherine Carver

Bennett Cerf
Christopher Cerf
Alfred Chester
Noam Chomsky
Arthur A. Cohen
Neil Compton
Paul Cowan
Frederick Crews
Robert Craft
David Daiches
Robert Gorham Davis
Candida Donadio
Theodore Draper

Martin Duberman
George P. Elliott
Joseph Epstein
Leslie Epstein
Irving Feldman
Moses I. Finley
R.W. Flint
Eugene Genovese
Albert Goldman
Richard Goodwin
John Gross
Oscar Handlin
Michael Harrington
Tom Hayden
Robert Heilbroner
Gertrude Himmelfarb
Berenice Hoffman
Richard Hofstadter
Sidney Hook
Richard Howard
Dan Jacobson
Roger H. Klein
William Kolodny
Louis Kronenberger
Alan Lelchuk
Herbert Liebowitz

Robert Jay Lifton
Seymour Martin Lipset
Wallace Markfield
Saul Maloff
Peter Mayer
Jonathan Miller
Hans J. Morgenthau
Martin Peretz
V.S. Pritchett
Dorothy Rabinowitz
Jack Richardson
David Riesman
Bayard Rustin
Peter Shaw
Isaac Bashevis Singer
Barbara P. Solomon
George Steiner
I.F. Stone
Harvey Swados
Wylie Sypher
Virgil Thomson
Gore Vidal
Michael Walzer
Edmund Wilson
C. Vann Woodward
Dennis H. Wrong

The Forms and Functions of Literary Power

5

I

By the powerful we mean, of course, those who are able to realize their will, even if others resist it. No one, accordingly, can be truly powerful unless he has access to the command of major institutions, for it is over those institutional means of power that the truly powerful are, in the first instance, powerful. —C. Wright Mills, *The Power Elite* (1956).

Literary intellectuals are no different from other mortals when it comes to many of the things to which they themselves are often in the habit of pretending superiority. The occupational hazard of the literary intellectual is to believe that he is redeemed by consciousness. He knows, for example, what mean-spiritedness is, and he is, of course, against it; therefore, he need have no further worries about falling into it himself. He is opposed to all the vices and in favor of all the virtues; and this, of course, makes him a righteous man without further ado. —Norman Podhoretz, *Making It* (1968).

Since literary power is a slippery concept, whose existence is continually denied or discounted, it seems wise to begin with several fairly verifiable observations made from disparate perspectives. These notes, in turn, will suggest some themes worth developing.

Literary power resides in the intermediary channels that funnel writing (and literary opinion) to the public, simply because they select to expose the reading public to certain issues and ideas rather than others. Secondly, the power of an individual periodical depends upon both the numerical size and the cultural leadership of its audience—both the quantity and the quality of its circulation. Those two factors circumscribe the potential influence of its contributions, for quantity without quality is as literarily impotent as quality without quantity. *The New York Times* is thus more powerful than *The Daily News; The New York Review of Books* is culturally more powerful than *Commentary* perhaps, *Esquire* probably, and *Partisan Review* for sure.

Since no one in advanced society can communicate to strangers without institutional means, book publishers have power over the future of literature simply because they select, from an abundance of possibilities, what to print, promote, and distribute to possible readers. Decisions about these processes function to make one book, or one writer, or one subject, or one viewpoint more available than another. Reviewing media have a similarly selective power, simply because they review much less than everything that is published. As both book publishers and review editors have the authority to accept or reject what passes through their channel, both function as gate-keepers to readership.

A book publisher is especially powerful when he can dominate a domain, either because no other firm cares about the subject or because its possible competitors lack certain commercial advantages. In England, for instance, Pelican Books, which is the cultural paperback line of Penguin Books, has the best-displayed and best-distributed primers on a spectrum of academic subjects. Thus, its choice of authors or manuscripts can determine not only which academic specialist will become well-known, but which of several possible positions or methodologies in an academic field will be most popularly purveyed. A change in Pelican's literary editors, for instance, can cause a shift in favor from Bloomsbury-style criticism to Leavisite, while all others suffer neglect.

Control of the channels by which certain intellectual materials primarily reach their most receptive public means a capacity to determine what ideas or individuals are broadcast over that channel. That control in turn grants the possibility of power, not only over what reaches a particularly receptive

88

audience, but also over the expression of writers previously (or possibly) contributing to that medium.

Power is not synonymous with influence, which can exist apart from power. Influence is based upon respect for an individual, while the sources of power are institutional. James Baldwin, Allen Ginsberg, and Norman Mailer are influential writers with no institutional connections, because their opinions can sway large audiences; and the capacity for great influence makes them ideal choices for literary tasks that exploit their strictly personal authority such as blurbing or introducing a new book.

Personal power, by contrast, extends initially from institutional power; so that just as a free-lance art critic will become more powerful as curator of a museum, so would an unaffiliated literary critic advance in power by becoming editor of a cultural review. Individual power stems from control over institutional avenues to an especially attractive audience.

Literary agents gain power from the numbers they represent which gives them leverage at contracting their client's manuscripts or soliciting higher fees, as well as collecting debts; but this is a power strictly of and for the marketplace. Agents do not constitute a channel of communication and cannot, by themselves alone, control one. They can, however, impose pressure upon those empowered to make editorial choices, as well as favoring one medium (or editor) rather than another.

Since the power of an intermediary channel depends, to repeat, upon the composition of its audience, the principal drama critic of *The New York Times* can reportedly "make or break" a new Broadway production. This power stems not from professional respect or even from personal influence, but from the fact that, since the *Times* is the most literate surviving daily newspaper in the urban center of live American theater, its readership includes roughly ninety-five percent of those people likely to see a play during its opening weeks. "You must remember that it is not I who have this power, it is the drama critic of *The New York Times*," its current incumbent, Clive Barnes, noted. "It is the power of the position, not the person." A favorable review from Barnes does not necessarily generate a success, but a negative notice will probably discourage the initial audience. (The plays most likely to overcome this negative power are those with either superstars or sufficient advance sales to survive the opening weeks.) And a new play that does not succeed in New York is not likely to be performed elsewhere in the U.S. or turned into a movie.

The *Times'* film critic has a comparably determining power—not over all films, to be sure, but over those European and art films aimed at more sophisticated film-goers, most of whom regularly read the *Times;* for quality cinema, unlike opulently-budgeted trash, needs favorable notices to survive. The film critic of *The Daily News,* with his one-to-four-star ratings, might, by contrast, have more effect upon the immediate fortunes of a Hollywood blockbuster; but given the amount of money invested in the film, its distributor will probably disregard all reviews for the popular verdict. The producer of a network television program follows similar signals in the form of audience "ratings"; for at this level of cultural merchandizing, the only critic with any clout is the massive public.

The dance critic of the *Times,* to continue the comparison, has less effect upon a dance company's or choreographer's immediate audience, most of which consists of loyal fans, than upon its subsequent fortunes (with booking agents, foundations, etc.). Since no other notice is so prominent, the judgment of the *Times* dance critic will also affect the company's international reputation, in part because only in New York, among the world's cities, are all of the world's major companies seen (and thus comparatively evaluated). The art and music critics of the *Times,* by contrast again, are uninfluential, partly because the paying audiences in these arts are much smaller and geographically more diffuse. Pop art, for instance, prospered for an entire year before the *Times* critics even bothered to notice it. Critical power in these arts resides in periodicals of smaller, more specialized, and yet national circulation whose readers can thus dismiss the *Times'* critics (and their typical recommendations) for many of the same reasons that drama producers can dismiss John Chapman of *The Daily News.* At this cultural level, the size of the audience notwithstanding, opinions make neither reputations nor sales.

In *The Art Crowd* (1973), Sophy Burnham notes that art critics frequently praise artists whose works they possess, and that artists sometimes give their works gratis to supportive critics (or even worse, allow the friendly critic to select a piece from the works currently in the artist's studio). Her book also

90

reveals that art museum trustees and curators have been known to support the scheduling of an exhibition of an artist whose works they personally possess; and since museum retrospectives are extremely prestigious, especially if the living artist has not been honored before, one likely result will be an increase in the value of the artist's work (and thus the trustee's paintings). At *Fortune* magazine, by contrast, reporters are forbidden to buy or sell stock in a company they investigate until a month after the article has appeared in print; and the Investment Advisors' Act of 1940 prohibits a securities analyst from recommending a stock without fully disclosing his own (and his firm's) interest in the company. Both policies are designed to insure that adjudication is not compromised by proprietorship. Burnham also notes that one of the reasons why Doré Ashton was pressured into resigning her position as a *New York Times* art critic (1955-60) was her marriage to a noted painter, Adja Yunkers. Not only had Ashton mentioned his paintings in her columns, but she generally supported the painterly style, Abstract Expressionism, that was associated with his name.

In part because the Sunday edition of *The New York Times* has a greater national circulation than the daily, as well as a readership more sophisticated than, say, *Time*'s or *Newsweek*'s, the front page of the *Times Book Review* has unparalleled positional power. Nothing else can claim a comparable audience. Its editors, like those at other "book reviews," choose not only what titles will be reviewed, but whether these selected books will be treated alone or in tandem with others, how long the commissioned review will be, who will write it, whether the submitted text is "acceptable," and where it will be positioned in a forthcoming issue. Because nearly all of the *Times Book Review* is written by outside contributors, the medium's available power is apportioned to individual writers who are thus granted a temporary license for wielding it. However, since the journal's publisher and editors retain control over the processes of appointment and apportionment, a reviewer can assimilate a medium's possible power only by constant prominent appearance within its pages (if he does not first get depressed from contemplating the power of these decisions-makers). Furthermore, the strength of a securely established institution like the *Times Book Review* customarily survives changes in management.

A survey by Julie Hover and Charles Kadushin noted that *The New York Review of Books,* though its circulation is smaller than the *Times,* commands more influence upon intellectual powerhouses, such as the editors of other magazines and university department chairmen. It thus has more "power to make or break reputations" in those circles. They continue: "Only two persons who were mentioned more than twice as having the power to make or break reputations were not connected with journals. However, one of the persons, the critic Edmund Wilson, was said not to use this power." As Leslie Woolf Hedley noted in another context, "The people still reading books have little or no control—barring fortuitous accidents—in establishing a writer's fame."

Barbara Bannon, the review-editor and principal fiction reviewer of *Publishers Weekly,* is said to be the single most powerful book touter in America; but the power of her prepublication notices depends not only upon her reputation for commercial perspicacity, but upon their regular appearance in a medium that is especially popular with bookstore managers. "My theory about publishing a book," Truman Capote once remarked, "is that everything—the reviews, the interviews, and everything else—has to happen within two weeks of publication. If it's scattered, it's not going to work. But if it all comes together simultaneously, you'll spin right up the list." Book reviewing in other media, whether little magazines or provincial newspapers, tends to have little influence beyond (or even within) their immediate readerships. Indeed, provincial book editors customarily take their cues from the New York media; so that only a few days after the *Times Book Review,* especially, features a certain title, free-lance reviewers across the nation often receive invitations to review it.

A further factor which can add to, or subtract from, the power available to a position, is the persuasiveness of the individual writer. Only by this criterion of personal strength was Kenneth Tynan more powerful than his successors at *The New Yorker* or was Walter Kerr probably a more powerful *Times* daily critic (1966-67) than his predecessor, Stanley Kauffmann (Jan.-Aug., 1966), and perhaps his successor as well. However, Kerr's retrospective reviews, currently printed every Sunday in the *Times,* lack positional clout, in part because that column is unprecedented and thus lacks, unlike the daily space, the power accruing to an established outlet. Absence of tradition also undermines the possible power of the sensible drama critics for New York's television stations. Critics writing for magazines of smaller circulation are often more persuasive in advocacy, which is to say that if they recommend a new play, a higher percentage of their readers will actually go see it. Needless to say, no necessary correlation exists between critical persuasiveness and institutional power.

The editor of a newspaper has the power to decide what events shall be regarded as "news." Unless an event is reported, it is not "news" and has no public existence beyond earshot of those initially present; and what is not news cannot possibly become "history." Nonetheless, the criteria of newsworthiness are so limiting and capricious that the medium excludes many happenings that could become historically important, simply by denying them any initial exposure. Similarly, a new book that is not reviewed at all is not likely to become available to literary history or literary criticism.

As public notice of any kind makes a new book news, bad reviews are generally more helpful than no reviews at all. Bad reviews can rarely "unmake" a best-seller whose immense audience already lies beyond the influence of reviewers, though negative notices have been known to dampen whatever aspirations a book or its author may have had for literary prestige or a professional prize. A severely unfavorable review may also damage a writer's professional reputation (and, thus, his chances for promotion or future jobs), and it may dissuade publishers from contracting the writer's work again. (Indeed, it is almost impossible for a "serious" reputation to survive unfavorable reviews in prominent places.) Perhaps reviewing is most decisively powerful in its neglects, as any title that is ignored completely makes a splash no greater than a Library of Congress card; it has practically no chance at all of establishing any sort of communications beachhead.

The primary power of selective book reviewing is bringing a new title to the attention of an audience; a secondary power is influence over sales. Among its tertiary effects are the status of the "reputation" by which an author's future books will be contracted and sold. Attention at the beginning creates the possibility of more attention at the outer circles, while neglect at the beginning makes the other benefits unlikely. Similarly, by printing selections from a new book prior to its publication, a periodical can boost its fortunes enormously, because a choice morsel might persuade review editors, as well as customers, to digest the whole.

Positional reputation, along with the quality of its large readership, gives *The New Yorker*'s columns immense power over the fortunes of a book prepublished in its pages; yet the typically weaker quality of its book-reviewing makes most notices there inconsequential. No critic can "make" a creative writer's reputation, nor can any reviewing media. However, a periodical that offers regular publication can help considerably. J. D. Salinger and John Updike, as well as John Cheever and Donald Barthelme, among others, owe their initial fame to the continuing support of *The New Yorker.* At minimum, such support contributes to the realization of possible eminence. No other slick magazine "makes" literary popularity, though appearance in the pages of *Esquire,* say, will add much to a writer's growing fame. *New York Times* staffers are attractive to publishers because their names appear constantly in prominent print; but it is debatable whether anyone ever wrote an excellent book while working at the *Times.*

Just as the loyalty of a respected book publisher or periodical can make a cultural reputation, so the absence of sustained support can cause unjust neglect. This is one reason why Ernest Hemingway, F. Scott Fitzgerald, and Thomas Wolfe were immediately prominent while William Faulkner's novels were so long neglected, or why Richard Hofstadter acquired more fame than C. Vann Woodward, or why the critics Lionel Trilling and Edmund Wilson seem overrated while Kenneth Burke and Northrop Frye are comparatively unheralded. Here, too, not advocacies but omissions provide the clearest index of literary power.

Ideas and their spokesmen not recognized by the intermediary channels are likely to remain unknown even to literate people, no matter how important the ideas are (e.g., information theory, analytic philosophy, formalist esthetics, systems thinking). Most of Marshall McLuhan's *Understanding Media* was written in 1959, but not until it was published in 1964 could it be reviewed. Since it was scarcely noticed upon publication, not until large-circulation magazines ran articles about the man and the book did his ideas become popular.

The fortunes of individuals depend upon publicity which usually comes in the form of critical notice. "Promotion," writes Francis V. O'Connor, "is the essential prerequisite today for all other forms of patronage," because it justifies expenditures all along the cultural line—by publishers, by foundations, by universities, by government agencies, by individual customers. Reviewers and "critics" certify value with the art-buying public that is skeptical by nature, but nonetheless eager to invest in whatever seems "promising." Book editors will compete to get a literary writer reported to be "liked by people at the *Times Book Review,*" while the rumor of opposite sympathy will jeopardize possible contracts. Favorable notice will generate not just further contracts and perhaps sales, but offers of academic positions.

Truly major critics have an influence that transcends the power of any periodical in which their writing appears. For that reason can their best work often be successfully collected into a book, or could Stanley Kauffmann, unlike Howard Taubman, remain influential after relinquishing his position as *Times* drama critic. Power can come to the artist whose advice is solicited by powerful institutions such as universities and foundations—as Aaron Copland served American music, so have Robert Lowell and James Dickey functioned in American poetry.

Professors close to particular publishing houses can influence their editorial decisions over scholarly and semi-scholarly manuscripts, and "literary advisors" can affect a publisher's choice of new poetry and fiction, all of the selections in a genre sometimes reflecting the enthusiasms of a single sage. If an influential critic champions an unpublished or neglected text in prominent print, it will probably become commercially available. Thanks to Dorothy Parker's plug in *Esquire,* Alan Marcus' novel, *Of Streets and Stars* (1960), which was privately printed after seven years of fruitless traveling, found both a hardback publisher and then a paperbacker. An influential writer can also shape the decision-making of impressionable young men coming into their own editorial power; it was precisely this kind of power-behind-power that Lionel Trilling, say, had over the policies of several young editors in the fifties or Eric Bentley once had over literate theatrical directors-critics-producers.

II

> Power itself is but one means, though perhaps the supreme one, for manipulating people. —Harold Rosenberg, "The Heroes of Marxist Science" (1959).

A purer form of individual power in literary politics depends not at all upon fame, professional achievement, intellectual influence, or even one's writing; this power depends instead upon institutional position, pure and simple, whose possible leverage depends in turn upon access to a flow of money and/or a large audience. As money bestows cultural power only to the extent that it can be institutionally leveraged, dollars are culturally ineffective without a commanding position. The extent of that personal power depends, in turn, not only upon the particular institution's capacity to grant a lucrative or professionally enhancing favor or to amplify a message or reputation, but also upon an individual's rank in that communications hierarchy. The most recent example I know of a single writer "making" an artist's reputation would be Thomas Hess, who, as both principal critic *and* the editor-in-chief of *Art News,* championed Willem de Kooning in the early fifties. (Hess also owned some of the painter's work.)

A further rule is that one has more positional power if he can expect to get some sort of patronage in return. In an elementary example, Professor X, invited to lecture at Professor Y's university, will probably try to induce his own institution to extend a comparably lucrative invitation in recompense, almost as a matter of etiquette. Indeed, whether such a commission is forthcoming may become an implicit test of X's power. Power of this sort is applicable if the position to be filled has few stipulations, requiring merely a writer, say, rather than a Henry James expert or a Hindu poet. Once a prolific host in New York, the novelist Vance Bourjaily became more powerful on the University of Iowa's creative writing faculty where, as Merle Miller noted, "A great many people who used to be guests at Vance's parties have gone to Iowa City for an academic year, a semester, or overnight." And they in turn help keep alive Bourjaily's reputation in New York.

Editors have been known to play comparable games of reciprocity. Just as Willie Morris, assuming the chief editorship of *Harper's,* prepublished sections of Norman Podhoretz' *Making It,* so did Podhoretz feature sections of Morris' *North Toward Home* in *Commentary,* moderate sums of money and a good deal of favorable advance book publicity changing hands in the process. (And *Commentary*'s favorable review of Morris' autobiography appeared adjacent to a large ad for *Making It*!) This institutional power further explains why writers who also edit so often seem unduly flattered in critical print, or why these writers make particularly attractive clients for literary agents who can then ideally exploit the client's editorial medium as a channel for the agent's other properties; and more than one magazine or anthology edited by a client of agent X is chock full of agent X's other writers. However, without control of a communications channel, the "powerful" suddenly become powerless.

As both poetry editor of *Paris Review* and a prolific poetry anthologizer during the fifties, Donald Hall got invited to read and publish his own poems in far more places/periodicals/anthologies than he otherwise would, or his work otherwise merited; but once Hall relinquished his editorial position, his poetry almost disappeared from public view. As director of poetry programming for the BBC for the past decade, George MacBeth in England has unparalleled professional power and even poetic eminence, though his many works are, by contrast, unknown in America. The closest semblances in America would be Howard Moss, who has been *The New Yorker*'s principal poetry editor for over twenty years, and Richard Howard, who has been advising both publishers of poetry programs and awards-committees on their beneficences, as well as selecting poetry for the *New American Review* since 1971. Successful, though undistinguished, careers can be based entirely upon "connections," while fortune of any kind would be impossible without them.

Editorial patronage can include other forms of lucrative commission, such as writing a well-paid introduction to a new book or anthologizing some classic texts in the public domain (to which no reprint-permission fees need be paid). "If you play the game," Paul Goodman told a *New York Times* reporter, "you get $2,000 for editing the short novels of Henry James and pasting together an introduction from stuff somebody else has written." It is a yet more lucrative assignment to edit one's own series of books, commissioning one's professional associates and protégés to produce each one and then splitting the royalties on each title—as, for instance, Irving Howe as "General Editor" has done with his "Literature and Ideas Series" for Fawcett paperback, thus solidifying professional ties through an interlocking network of spoils.

One New York editor has been known to encourage his academic contributors (who earn professional credits, on top of small money, by publishing in his pages) to invite him to give the most lucrative lectures at their own universities. It follows that were this man to lose his position, the power at his command, as well as his lecturing business, would disintegrate considerably. The capacity to grant favor assumes the threat of withholding it, as well as the grantor's possible removal from his sources of leverage. Upon observation, I have noticed that literary powerhouses will generate talk on almost anything except "literary power." All artists, like magicians, are secretive about the tricks of their trade. Nonetheless, as a general rule, the location of real power must precede any explanation of equally real powerlessness.

Once separated from control over channels of communication, those whose existence depends upon power, unlike respected artists, become vulnerable to cultural extinction. It is thus possible that Norman Podhoretz could be the Charles Angoff of his generation—powerful and respected while entrenched in an editorial position (Angoff, born in 1902 and still alive, was H. L. Mencken's assistant on *The American Mercury* in the early thirties), forgotten once separated from it. Similarly, were Hilton Kramer or John Canaday to quit their positions at *The New York Times,* their power base would disintegrate and their names disappear from artistic discussion. Once Saul Maloff resigned as *Newsweek*'s regular book reviewer, he was lost, his subsequent novels scarcely surfacing; once Granville Hicks retired from the *Saturday Review,* he went too. A popular medium "makes" a critic, simply by publishing him regularly. "It is fairly humbling to remember," Clive Barnes once judged, "that if I close the case of my typewriter, I would be forgotten in two weeks flat." (Does anyone still remember the movie critic Bosley Crowther? The art critic Stuart Preston? The music critic Olin Downes?) The composer Virgil Thomson reports that, when he resigned from his position as music critic of *The New York Herald-Tribune,* a friend asked, "But how will he get his music played?" And in truth Thomson's pieces are no longer heard so often.

Collective power in literary politics means, first, the capacity to make a work of writing, or group of writers, far more popular and respected than it, or they, would otherwise be. In addition, it means the capacity to thwart, rather than merely criticize, the claims and careers of professional antagonists. Collective literary power is thus based not just upon friendship and comradely backslapping, but also upon interpersonal organization, institutional leverage, and effective action. To protest that the New York literary mob is "not a conspiracy" does not prevent units of it from behaving like one. Since the loudest voice so often wins in American culture, the power of any cabal depends upon how effectively it can not only marshal a public chorus, but also exploit the existing amplification systems and construct its own intermediary channels. Since power generates professional success, which usually generates money in turn, mere publication or the esteem of one's colleagues are not the only stakes in literary politics. Should an influential position or an acknowledged reputation begin to decline because of its own insufficiencies or changes in cultural attitudes, its public survival depends upon the strength of the clique and/or the publicity media predisposed to it.

The power of a particular literary establishment can be gauged not only by the average annual income of its individual members—always a good criterion for measuring any kind of success in America—but also by the effectiveness of both its collective promotions and its unanimous demolitions, as well as, perhaps, the prevalence of its most obvious intellectual deceits. Although no cartel in pluralistic America can gain control of everything—even within Manhattan itself literary life is too diffuse—no operation in earlier literary politics was one-half as powerful or as successful as the New York literary mob, and none, as noted before, ever sustained its dominance for so long.

The mob's composition can be compared, as noted before, to an onion; within its leaves are constellations of associates with varying degrees of proximity to the core. By the sixties, Epstein and Podhoretz, both late-comers and popularizers, assumed cushions at the center. Each had an important publishing position, affording him not only a comfortable income and a corporate expense account for lunches and travel, but also the power to bestow spoils and readership upon favored writers. All this meant, in practice, that the patronage of both moguls had to be courted and that no one within their circle of favor would dare criticize them, especially in print. Close to the core were their working associates, at Random House and *Commentary* respectively, and regular contributors to the key magazines, plus elder literary statesmen; but even within this last category, an individual's relationship to the center was continually subject to change, depending upon whether he received any beneficence, or helped his colleagues in their designs, or simply lived in New York.

Further leaves consist, on one hand, of more occasional contributors, such as those academics invited once a year to posit a predictable point of view on a key issue (e.g., interpretations of the Cold War or the New Left) and, on another, of young men on the rise, usually in non-mob institutions, such as the sub-editor at *The New York Times Book Review* who wants to make his professional mark by "getting more intellectuals into the paper," or the fresh-faced editor at the paperback house eager to have such eminences write forewords to his reprints of classic texts. Further out, but still within the onion, is the little magazine editor or provincial reviewer who treats mob merchandise with special favor, generally in return for nothing more than an invitation to a literary party and/or occasional publication in one of the mob magazines. Writers and editors on the outer skeins are also less beholden to the center than those within, while literary people entirely unresponsive to signals, threats, or favors from within are, by definition, completely outside the onion.

One sign of collective power is the capacity to co-opt either a possible antagonist or the chief of a neighboring institution. Soon after Willie Morris became, at 32 in 1967, the editor-in-chief at *Harper's,* he announced a laudable desire to bring "young writers" into the magazine. Even though the outgoing chief editor, John Fischer, reportedly favored Mississippi-born Morris as non-New York and non-Jewish (and had, thus, selected him to replace Robert Silvers after the latter's departure four years before), the mob quickly incorporated the new man into its designs. Midge Decter became executive editor, Norman Mailer a featured contributor, Irving Howe a regular reviewer, while Podhoretz himself swapped preprints with Morris. The promised "young writers" were, to be sure, older than Morris himself. (Deceived by this promise, Morris' own chiefs reportedly wondered why, according to their own surveys, his magazine was not attracting genuinely younger readers.)

One conspicuous sign in the sixties of the New York literary mob's collective muscle was the marshaling of sufficient advance publicity and prominently favorable reviews to make new novels by Mary McCarthy, Bernard Malamud, Saul Bellow, and Philip Roth into best-sellers. This process depends upon accretion which functions most effectively when pushed with optimal persistence. As Truman Capote testified of *Portnoy's Complaint* while chatting on the Johnny Carson Show (of all people, of all places): "They promote each other continuously—this little clique of writers, of which Philip Roth is the youngest and, in many ways, the most brilliant. They started the drum going for this book a good year and a half ago, so it was inevitable that it would turn into what it was, because they were really pushing for it." Since such literary power is largely tied to position and, implicitly, to purse strings, the ultimate power of any group (or individual) depends upon how many positions can be won or influenced, how powerful these positions are, and how much patronage can be effectively apportioned. Of course, not everything so enthusiastically puffed actually becomes popular—not even commissars can make people read, fortunately; but there is no doubt that, thanks to mob support, certain books and authors have won audiences far, far larger than would otherwise be theirs.

III

> For the fact is that the cultivated in general do *not* realize how completely reviewing has ceased to have anything to do with criticism; honest and intelligent reviews still occur, but the function of reviewing (the legitimate function) has lapsed. —F. R. Leavis, "The Literary Racket" (1932).

The truth—never to be forgotten—is that the primary business of literature is selling books, and the most effective kind of advertising toward this end is favorable publicity. Therefore, such superficially prestigious processes as earning favorable reviews or well-publicized awards provide public attention that, in turn, incidentally contributes to this commercial goal. Reputations are forged by middlemen stationed between the published book and its likely audience, and their function is creating an image of the writer and his work—the terms or "handle" by which a larger public can grasp a more complex entity. In the old days, prior to the hyper-commercialization of literature, favorable attention in the literary journals changed nothing more than the prices of a writer's first editions; but nowadays, a growing audience increasingly responsive to upper-middlebrow opinion is liable to purchase en masse the latest work of a highly-touted author.

Literary "prestige" can be converted into money, however, only if that reputation is widely publicized and the prestigious have something to sell. For this reason does a publisher oblige his famous author to "produce." "Under capitalism," notes David T. Bazelon, "the reputation of individuals has been commercialized—literally turned into money." Since high-level reputations produce far higher sales than before, there is, to put it baldly, more money nowadays in cultural repute.

The essence of "building a reputation" is mobilizing the expectation of wide publicity for a writer's, or even a publisher's, latest ventures; so that the publisher and his writer, as well as their professional allies, became symbiotically entwined in establishing, or sustaining, each other's claims to importance. Therefore, too, every time a touted author produces a new title, both his own reputation and, by extension, his publisher's— their ability to mobilize support—are tested in the weeks following its publication. Merely issuing a book today requires no great effort—anyone with enough money to pay the printer and the copyright office can do it. The real predicament is that a book, unlike a periodical, begins its public life with few assured readers. The word "publish" comes from the Latin *publicare,* meaning to announce publicly; however, what separates the powerful publisher from the amateur is his capacity to make the book's existence known in the media perused by book-buyers. As Mrs. Leavis noted of a contrary example, "The more cultured a country, the less its publishers would have to spend in forcing books on the public attention." In the U. S., by contrast, the more sales the publisher expects, the more resources must it expend, the harder must its employees push.

Quality alone, needless to say, has never insured the media's notice or even the attention of regular book reviewers, for the enterprise of reviewing extends not from literary criticism but book publicity. (That accounts for why book publicists and publishing editors frequently become reviewers, and vice versa.) In practice, reviewers and review editors must be persuaded that in the piles of books inundating their offices are certain authors and titles which deserve their professional attention. Since they cannot possibly examine everything in this flood, publicity and advertising and prior fame all function as complementary factors, guiding their preliminary selections. Therefore, reviews, especially in the more popular presses, largely reflect prior interest in the author, the efforts of the publishers' publicity departments (who favor certain titles over others), as well as the effectiveness of advertising (which also implicitly subsidizes most book-reviewing media). "Publishers," F. R. Leavis once noted, "are clients of the Advertising Manager, as the most conscientious editor can never be allowed to forget." Prominent reviews may also reflect prior notice in such prepublication services as *Publishers Weekly* (with its influential "forecasts") or *Kirkus,* which are themselves responsive to the pressures of publicity managers. They may also reflect the propaganda of literary cabals such as the New York mob. Publishers and literary powerhouses, unlike prepublication services, aim to promote public interest in the man or his work for the sake of selling his produce.

Since so many books are published, the few that are chosen for prominent or widespread review have a genuine advantage in the marketplace. "Responsible booksellers will volunteer," Q. D. Leavis noted long ago, "that Arnold Bennett, for instance, had only to mention a novel in his weekly article to sell an edition." Books with pretensions to cultural quality *need* favorable reviews, if only to sell to libraries, especially if the title's fortunes are too modest to warrant any corporate advertising. Not only will the editor at a paperback publisher cite favorable reviews to justify its reprinting of a new hardbound title, but the reviews accorded a "serious" first novel or collection of poems will usually determine whether a writer's second can be commercially published. In this case, editors assume that hardback sales, no matter how negligible, are not the best index of "promise." A severe denunciation, though, may persuade the publishers not to advertise a new title or, even worse, not to send it to the stores at all, thereby killing the book at birth.

The merchandizing of books depends, in general, not only upon advertising and prominent reviews, but also upon *publicity* in the newspapers and over the electronic media. That last fact explains why publishers are so responsive to communications channels with massive audiences or why, ever since radio's "Invitation to Learning," the electronic media can make certain literary "personalities" far more famous than their works. Thus, when contracting a proposed "big" book, some publishers consider whether the author's personality can be "sold" to the media moguls and then to the media-watching public, the assumption being that both groups are more interested in "personalities" than books. (The only hitch is that the personality might succeed, while his books remain unsold or unread.) "Editors of the competing revolution books are in complete agreement on one thing," notes the reporter Gail Sheehy. "Publicity, such as the Chicago conspiracy trial, is the best thing for sales." With authors not so famous, the publisher may initiate, for the sake of publicity, such special promotions as prominent advertising, blurbs from several famous writers, personal letters to possible reviewers, plus a lecture-media tour by the author. For an effort so grand, the author's own capacities for friendship and self-promotion become merely supplementary.

Publishing's subservience to the mass media also explains why established (i.e., prepublicized) celebrities can often fetch ridiculously lucrative contracts for books that they may not write or which invariably disappoint and lose money when and if they appear. The principle also accounts for why no one would publish Marshall McLuhan's *Counterblast* (1969) until he became a celebrity; then and only then did he sell an eccentric manuscript written over a dozen years before. His growing notoriety simply made McLuhan's work a more valuable publishing property. (A writer made famous by publicity becomes dependent upon it, especially if his writings do not support his reputation, and so needs more publicity, rather than new books, to keep his name before his public.)

A final factor fomenting sales—word-of-mouth recommendation—can become the most powerful force in making a best-seller, but this ultimate advertiser, unlike the others, cannot be effectively initiated or even accurately predicted. Since this last realm is ultimately beyond the range of an individual medium's voice, the aim of any literary merchandizer is effective mastery of the preliminary factors, partially to generate word-of-mouth enthusiasm—a chorus by extension, so to speak. High sales customarily breed more sales, the "best-seller list" itself also providing the powerful publicity that prompts more advertising and keeps such titles best-selling. A new book in public hands also functions as an implicit advertisement until the largest possible market for a particular title is saturated. Conspicuously rare, however, is the serious book that sells more than 10,000 hardback copies without any of these complementary publishing initiatives; and although one or two alone may not sell that many books, all of them usually will. Publishing promotions have less direct effect upon what intellectuals think than upon the sources they cite for insight and example (which incidentally serve as advertising). In that latter respect, publishing publicity can ultimately affect the range and possibilities of serious thought.

By the middle sixties, to return to the history sketched before, the New York literary mob in its various strains, but especially at its nexus in Epstein's domain at Random House-Vintage, dominated *The New York Review of Books,* still regarded by innocent readers as an "independent" reviewing medium, as well as *Commentary* and *Partisan Review.* Certain editors in other intermediary publications, notably *The New York Times,* its *Book Review* (though *not* its Sunday *Magazine*), *Harper's,* and the syndicated *Book Week* (successively edited by Richard Kluger and Theodore Solotaroff), were predisposed to collaborate. As these included nearly all of the most powerful amplifying literary institutions in America, fashions and reputations initiated in their pages quickly spread to other media. Early in 1971, NYREV, Inc. took over the *Kirkus Reviews,* as noted before, which provides advance notices mostly to libraries, major bookstores, and provincial reviewers—even John Leonard, then working as a *New York Times* daily reviewer, confessed to inspecting it regularly. In the late sixties, outfit authors became quite conspicuous on the daily morning NBC network *Today* show. Identifying his most effective ally,

John J. Simon, Epstein's closest colleague at Random House-Vintage, told reporter Gail Sheehy that "virtually every articulate author on the *Today* show sells books"; and in Douglas Mount's judgment, "There is perhaps nothing that can sell more books faster than the *Today* show." When I.F. Stone, Charles Reich, and other Random radicals appear on *Today*, let there be no doubt that "politics" need not interfere with business.

The management of "reviews" has always been a particular mob forte, not only because pretentious reviewing media function as classy doormen, admitting only a few titles into the party of the cultural public's notice, but also because, as already noticed, reviews are especially necessary to establish "reputations" that in turn can fetch publishers' contracts and impress America's booksellers. This explains why most mob "critics" have generally written more reviews than extended explications (which the earlier Agrarians favored), or why they should have been so eager to co-opt existing media and found a new one with more concentrated focus, in addition to why they were, especially in the fifties, so persistently critical of established American book reviewing. As late as 1963, Epstein could publicly dismiss *The Times Book Review* as "the work of tired hacks, lame professors, breezy illiterates"; however, vituperation of this last sort disappeared from mob writing by the mid-sixties. Precisely this drive to control intermediary media reveals they found literary power more motivating than the primary task of, say, writing a good book.

6 The Leverages of Collaboration

Mass cultural communications is a basic industry, as basic as oil, steel and transportation in its way. Developing along with it, supporting it, and subservient to it, is an organized network of functions that are creative, administrative, propagandistic, educational, recreative, political, artistic, economic and cultural. Taken as a whole this enterprise involves what [C. Wright] Mills called the cultural apparatus. Only the blind cannot see that whoever controls the cultural apparatus . . . also controls the destiny of the United States and everything in it. —Harold Cruse, *The Crisis of the Negro Intellectual* (1967).

That was my first lesson in gambling. If you see somebody winning all the time, he isn't gambling; he's cheating. —Malcolm X, *The Autobiography* (1965).

Literary reviewing media have the power, noted before, to decide what will (and will not) come to their audience's attention, and the possible power of a particular medium depends upon the quantity and quality of its readership. Although *The New York Review* had become the most powerful American cultural organ in the sixties, the publicizing purposes apparent from its beginnings have persistently favored Random House-Vintage produce in several ways. Since its editorship has neither changed nor been diffused among assistants, only two people have ever officially chosen books or reviewers, or apportioned space: Robert Silvers and Barbara Epstein; and they alone must be judged initially responsible for the striking, if not shocking, disparities. For instance, in all of the 1968 issues, as surveyed in 1969 in Harry Smith's *The Newsletter*, "17 of 73 books singled out for individual review (more than 23%)" were published by the Random House conglomerate—far more than any other publisher received, and more in sum than those from such quality-minded houses as Viking (one), Grove (one), Holt (two), Harper (five), Houghton (one), Oxford (one), Doubleday (one), Macmillan (two), Harvard (one), and Princeton (one) *combined.* Furthermore, it is these few featured titles—an average of three in each issue—rather than titles reviewed in tandem with others that receive especially extensive attention. While it is true that Random House's multiple imprints make it larger than most of the other firms listed in the above comparison, the latter ten published more than six times as many titles in the previous year (3618 to Random House's 586). Were this comparison to add the sums of houses publishing good books and yet completely shut out of individual reviews in this period—for example, McGraw-Hill, Horizon, Norton, and Dutton—the ratio would be even more ludicrously lopsided. In this period, Random House also "led in total number of books reviewed—41 (no other publisher having as many as the 19 for the Knopf imprint alone, firms such as Scribner's, Simon & Schuster, Bobbs-Merrill, Morrow and Putnam's getting less than five)."

The Newsletter's survey also revealed that twenty-five percent of *The New York Review*'s reviewers that year already had Random House books in print, "37% of them reviewing books by other RH authors," and that, though the periodical claimed to be tougher than other scrutinizing media, Random House books "received favorable notice in 3 out of every 4 cases." Of the essays other than reviews published in *The New York Review* in that period, well over half came from writers already published by Random House. In the self-featured "Fifth Anniversary" issue, dated September 26, 1968, and emphasizing essays over reviews, four of the fifteen contributors were Random House authors, three Knopf, and one Pantheon, some of them contributing material soon to appear in Random House books or even a *New York Review* pamphlet; four of the seven English-language books reviewed in that issue also had Random House imprints.

Even the occasional poems published in its pages reveal a similar bias. In Volume IX, dated between July 13, 1967 and January 4, 1968, two of the four poets published in the *Review* were regular Random House authors, Paul Goodman and W. H. Auden. The third was co-owner Robert Lowell, whose *Life*

Studies (1959) had once been a Vintage book; the poet Philip
Levine was the ringer. In reading through these issues, I sensed
that the letters-to-the editor around that time displayed similarly disproportionate favoritism toward Random House produce,
not only since previous contributors to the *Review* are more
likely to write the editor (and have their letters published), but
also because many of the controversies aired in these columns
implicitly publicize the Random House books and writers reviewed and published before.

Predictably, the Random House combine also purchased
twice as many advertising pages as its nearest competitor in the
year surveyed, taking the center spread of the Fifth Anniversary number. In a *buffo* understatement, *The Newsletter*
found "the Random House team with top billing in NYR,
[its merchandise] in the spotlight issue after issue." In the
following years, the next largest advertiser would be the ever-
enterprising New York Review Corporation itself, its ads peddling both calendars and lapel buttons with David Levine caricatures, jig-saw puzzles, a "Vietnam Curriculum," the increasingly
miscellaneous wares of its booking agency, Review Presentations, Inc., and then back issues at an escalating rate of $.75,
$1.50, and $3.00, as well as such cottage industries as its own
books and pamphlets, its own efficacy as an advertising medium
and, finally, the Arno Press offset reprint of its first five years
of issues.

My own analysis of the cumulative index to this five-year
retrospective reveals the following corroborative information:
Of the five poets to appear four or more times in the first five
years—Auden, Goodman, Lowell, Mark Strand, and Robert
Penn Warren—four had previously appeared in Vintage Books,
which, as noted before, has largely been Jason Epstein's domain. Of those twenty-three essayists contributing at least three
articles (other than reviews) in the first five years, sixteen were
Random House authors, fifteen of them also appearing in Vintage editions—Auden, Chomsky, Epstein, Friedenberg, Goodman, Hofstadter, Howe, Lowell, Macdonald, Morgenthau,
Pritchett, Ronald Steel, I. F. Stone, Stravinsky, Edmund Wilson. (The exception, when last I checked, was Robert Brustein.)
Of those fifteen essayists appearing at least four times, to survey
a rarer atmosphere, eleven had been published by Random
House and ten by Vintage (with the same exception).

Reviewing is the major business, however, of *The New York Review,* and here the implicit biases are reflected not only, as noted before, in the selection of books, but in the choice of both featured reviews and regular contributors. The selection of reviewers is more crucial in this publication than elsewhere, since *The New York Review* differs from its competitors in throwing more spotlight on its writers—perhaps more than is shined on the books they review. Not only are the reviewers' names often put on the front cover, but beneath the table of contents are fairly generous bio-bibliographical notes, while David Levine caricatures the authors reviewed (by customarily blowing up their heads and shriveling their bodies).

The five-year index divulges some significant information about the principles of editorial policy. Of the forty-five writers reviewing ten or more times, twenty-three have been Random House authors. If the Englishmen are removed from this survey (including such part-time Americans and Vintage authors as the late George Lichtheim, Frank Kermode, and Conor Cruise O'Brien) a more devastating statistic emerges: Fifteen of the remaining twenty-three have been Random House authors, most of whom are also represented in Vintage Books; and none of these fourteen was born after 1933. Since most of these percentages exceed one-half, it is not unfair to conclude that, on the whole, what is often featured in the magazine is *more likely than not* to reflect a Random House-Vintage investment.

The Newsletter quoted the *Review*'s editor, Robert B. Silvers, as contending it "unfair to consider [Random House] as one publisher." Not only are its several divisions not entirely autonomous, in fact, but even as separate imprints, the study notes, both Random House and Knopf "each still have more books individually reviewed than any other single publisher." (These statistics could have been more personally specific, if not damaging, had the surveyor access to those charts, circulated exclusively within the firm, showing which Random House books were sponsored by Epstein himself, either as "Random House" titles or through a "Vintage" collaborative commitment, rather than one of the other senior editors in the firm.) Silvers also contended that "we have never chosen books for review on the basis of who published them—or reviewers"; yet given his own position and the identity of his colleague, his evident bias can scarcely be unconscious. Moreover, a *New York Review* reviewer would have to be incredibly unsophisticated (or perhaps British) to be unaware of its especially close association with a certain American book publisher.

In another survey, which I took of volumes XVII and XVIII, running from July, 1971, to June, 1972, I counted thirty-seven publishers having books singled out for review; yet only six of these firms had at least three titles individually honored: Harper & Row, three; Holt, three; Viking, three; Pantheon, three; Random, four; Knopf, nine. Of the forty-five or so writers contributing essays (apart from reviews), fifteen were Random House authors; and another essayist (Adrienne Rich) was pre-publishing her preface to a Vintage book. Of the ten writers publishing at least two essays, all except Mary McCarthy have been Random House authors: Chomsky, Craft, Friedenberg, Goodman, F. Du P. Gray, Hobsbawm, Paul Jacobs, Pritchett, I. F. Stone. Twelve of the twenty reviewers publishing two or more notices have been Random House authors. Of the seven poets published in this year-long period, three belonged to Random House (Spender, Warren, and Kenneth Koch); but two of the others were dead foreigners (Cavafy, Mandelstam), another was John Berryman, while the last ("Richard Murphy") was curiously not identified. Nor is his name otherwise familiar.

What this operation also illustrates is that no book review need "buy" or pressure writers whose outlook can be safely ascertained in advance. Instead, by matching books with shrewdly chosen reviewers, editors can exploit predictable inclinations and gauge with fair success how key books will be treated. *The New York Review* once selected W. D. Snodgrass, a poet who rarely writes reviews, and yet a former protégé of Robert Lowell, to cover *The Old Glory* (1964), a trilogy of plays by the magazine's co-owner. Imported from the midwest for this purpose, Snodgrass produced a laudatory notice and flew home. This exemplifies an "honest" kind of review management—picking a reviewer who need not be "bought out" or need not compromise his opinions because the gist of his notice can probably be predicted in advance. With so many Random House-Vintage authors reviewing RH-V books, one could also expect a measure of intellectual likemindedness. These facts suggest that the *Review*'s interest in "quality" has largely been confined to a commercially circumscribed world. All this partially explains why other publishers have discovered that favorable notice in *The New York Review* does not sell too many of *their* books; yet most of *The New York Review*-Vintage promotions seem to succeed quite well (especially to "radicalized" teachers and students in provincial universities).

In practicing the management of reviews, the editors at *The New York Review* have at times suggested how a supposedly independent critic might approach an assigned title; and should the editor disagree with the reviewer's evaluation, it has not been uncommon for him to ask his commissioned writer to revise his piece accordingly. The mechanics of this process were revealed by Norman Mailer in a letter addressed to Robert B. Silvers and dated February 22, 1965, in which Mailer remembers that *The New York Review* had commissioned Midge Decter to review Mailer's collection of essays, *The Presidential Papers:*

> Her submitted piece was, in your opinion—I quote your label—"over-inflated." That is to say, it was unfavorable. Changes were requested. The reviewer refused to make them. The review was not printed. No review of *The Presidential Papers* appeared in *The New York Review of Books.* Only a parody. By a mystery guest. Now, we have my new book, *An American Dream.* I hear you have picked Philip Rahv to review it, Philip Rahv whose detestation of my work has been thundering these last two years into the gravy stains of every literary table in the Eastern Seaboard.

Silvers refused to publish this correspondence, quoted above only in part, which appeared instead in *Partisan Review* and then in Mailer's next collection of essays, *Cannibals and Christians* (1966); Decter's balloon subsequently appeared in her husband's *Commentary* (October, 1964).

II

> But we do not believe that the greater number of clients of the "higher journalism" realize how preponderately the reviewing they read is what it is—oil for the cogs of the publishing machine. —F. R. Leavis, "The Literary Racket" (1932).

How else, it is asked, can control of a "review of books" be exploited to aid other commercial operations? For one thing, it can introduce literary material that might otherwise get lost in book publication. *The New York Review* once devoted many pages to the complete text of Robert Lowell's new play, *Prometheus Bound* (1967), in type so untypically small and tight that it could not be read by anyone except theater people interested in producing it. Many of the magazine's excerpts from forthcoming books, especially those preprinted at great length, come from titles soon to appear under a Random House-Vintage imprint—Noam Chomsky's polemics, Tom Hayden's report from Newark, V. S. Pritchett's dreary memoirs (in no fewer than three installments from the first volume and one from the second), Epstein's own book on the Chicago conspiracy trial. Some of these preserialized Random House titles were favorably reviewed as well (Pritchett's two books were given, respectively, in a shrewd example of review-management, to John Gross and Karl Miller, two fellow regular contributors to *The New Statesman*'s literary pages).

Stephen Spender's *Review* essays in 1968 on the student revolts, to cite another instance, soon appeared as a Random House-Vintage book whose preface untypically (and suspiciously) neglected to acknowledge its periodical origins; and the frequent publication of Igor Stravinsky interviews, beginning in 1965, followed the composer's shift in publishers from Doubleday (1959-63) to Knopf in books of 1966 and 1969. Indeed, since it was commonly known that not Stravinsky but his American associate, Robert Craft, wrote most of the composer's witty English lines—even, as Lillian Libman's memoir reveals, after the octogenarian composer was too ill to speak intelligibly—*The New York Review*, along with *Commentary* and *Harper's*, were guilty of publishing material they knew was mostly ghosted. A further peculiarity of these late "Stravinsky conversations" is that the leading questions are attributed not to Craft, as in the earlier volumes, but to these magazines' own editors, who reveal not only a musical literacy otherwise unknown in their editorial activities but also identical inquisitive styles. The obvious conclusion is that their own sophisticated lines were ghosted, too!

A special issue devoted to "The Education Nightmare" (October 9, 1969) featured contributions by John Holt, Ivan

Illich, Christopher Lasch, Eugene Genovese, Sheldon Wolin, John Schaar, and Herbert Kohl, all of whom, except Holt and Illich (surprisingly), were, or soon became, Vintage or *New York Review* (book) authors. Holt, who never wrote for the magazine again (unlike the others), was hired to review a Random House book—George Dennison's *The Lives of Children.* Kohl, who authored both a pamphlet and a book published by the New York Review, Inc., was also the featured figure in a full-page advertisement by Review Presentations, Inc., for speakers and seminars on "New Forms of Education," a field in which, to be sure, Random House-Epstein had already made yet other kinds of investment. Epstein's own featured essays advocating school decentralization, beginning in June, 1968, echoed not only a book he had contracted, David Rogers' *110 Livingston St.* (1968), but also his Random House editorial proposals to produce books designed for more *local* adoption, in addition to his multi-graded elementary school newspaper entitled *New York, New York* (1966-68) which was designed to compete with *My Weekly Reader* for purchase by the Board of Education. (Since his own children went to private schools, the vested interest behind his passionate prose was probably less familial than commercial.) Epstein planned to publish comparable papers in other cities; but since the prolonged 1968 New York school strike caused the demise of this enterprise, his interest in schools dwindled. Whereas the biographical notes accompanying his earlier essays identified Epstein as a "vice-president of Random House," the contents-page columns now coyly referred to him as "an occasional contributor to *The New York Review.*"

Similarly, what the *Review* is featuring Random House is also publishing. A lengthy preprint from Kenneth Koch's book on the teaching of creative writing, *Wishes, Lies and Dreams* (1971), coincided with Random House's assumption of its distribution (after the original publisher's bankruptcy) and preceded both the title's appearance in Vintage format and Koch's becoming a Random House author. The *Review*'s specialist in Russian literature, a Smith professor named Helen Muchnic, was a veteran Random House author; approximately one-third of Professor Muchnic's recent collection of fugitive pieces, *Russian Writers: Notes and Essays* (1971), originally appeared in *The New York Review.* After Gore Vidal became a more frequent contributor, Random House published *Homage to Daniel Shays*

(1972) in which seven of the concluding ten essays (or 94 of the last 108 pages) initially appeared in *The New York Review*. This book was favorably reviewed in the magazine by Stephen Spender, another Random regular. The *Review*'s favored experts on literary modernism, Frank Kermode and Roger Shattuck, were both Vintaged, as was its prime music critic, Virgil Thomson, whose autobiography (1966) was published by Knopf. The *Review* found a reviewer of cookbooks, the sometime-pianist Michael Field, just after he became a Knopf author, and since Field's premature death, cookbooks have been ignored. In a contrary twist, a book plugging a *Review* product (rather than the reverse), the only outright advertisement reprinted unrevised (or unretouched) within Mitchell Goodman's radical compendium, *The Movement Toward a New America,* (Vintage-Knopf, 1970), is a display-with-a-coupon on page 302 for *The New York Review*'s "Vietnam Curriculum"! As Conor Cruise O'Brien noted of the CIA-*Encounter* collaboration, "The beauty of the operation . . . was that writers of the first rank, who had no interest at all in serving the power structure, were induced to do so unwittingly."

Periodicals can also foster interests and enthusiasms that, if successfully popular, can be complemented by appropriate books (their contents, for the moment, being another issue). For only if there is something to sell can the propagation of even "radical" attitudes be turned to commercial ends. The magazine's relentless criticism of Lyndon B. Johnson (also reflected in David Levine's increasingly malicious caricatures) coincided with Random House-Epstein's enthusiasm for books of a similar nature (e.g., *Macbird*), neither institution, when last checked, caring so adamantly about Richard Nixon. *The Review*'s persistent interest in the Chicago conspiracy trial—not only Jason Epstein's own critique, but large chunks of the transcript—undoubtedly helped the sales of Bobby Seale's Random House-Vintage book, Abbie Hoffman's *Woodstock Nation* (Vintage, 1969), Tom Hayden's *Rebellion in Newark* (Vintage, 1969), plus a Random House book by Anthony Lukas that featured an extended profile of Jerry Rubin, in addition to both an anthology published by the *Review* itself and culled from its own pages, *Trials of This World* (1970), and Epstein's own Random House-Vintage book on *The Great Conspiracy Trial* (1970). Not only did Epstein personally shepherd other reporters around the Chicago affair, but his proposal for Random House to publish the complete trial transcript was assumed, instead, at his suggestion, by Chelsea House. According to Philip Nobile, it was Epstein himself who initially asked Roger Wilkins, a former Assistant Attorney General, to review the Bobby Seale book for *The New York Review* (though the resulting essay never appeared in print).

The New York Review's constant coverage of the Chicago Seven and other political show trials represents a circuitous type of radicalism which appears to be based not upon criticism of social inequity or the advocacy of revolution, but rather a sentimental sympathy with the "civil disobedience" of personally estimable revolutionaries, coupled with a distaste for their prosecutors. Though the conflict between them is scarcely the central injustice, the dramatization of it facilely elicits melodramatic emotions. In this circumstance, poor defendants like Bobby Seale become noble gladiators inspiring lots of journalistic copy, while the reader joins a radical reporter in listening to an incarcerated activist defending his exploits—a double distancing that seems both voyeuristic and paternalistic, as well as raising ironic questions about for whose benefit these show trials were staged.

> By the summer, as the attorneys for the defense prepared their appellate briefs, Rubin was back in Cook County Jail. Of the eight defendants, he was the only one to have been charged under state as well as federal law for his part in the convention disturbances. To these state charges he pleaded guilty. His sentence was sixty days in jail.

With that perspective-defining paragraph, which portrays poor Rubin fading away into the incarcerated distance, Epstein closes his book.

Whatever was hyped in one medium would at times be peddled through another. *The New York Review*'s interest in the Black Panthers complemented Random House-Vintage books by Eldridge Cleaver, Bobby Seale, the New York Panther 21, and their attorney, Gerry Lefcourt, as well as a contract to Murray Kempton for a book on the subject (that was later cancelled, the author taking it to E. P. Dutton), plus a Review Presentations' package on "The Black Experience"; while Tom

Wolfe joked that none other than Robert B. Silvers himself was one of the N. Y. literary cocktail circuit's most prominent "Parlour Panthers"! All of the articles by and about the Berrigan brothers accompanied the purchase, by Review Presentations, Inc., of exclusive distribution rights to Lee Lockwood's film about Brother Dan, *Holy Outlaw* (1970), which was, needless to say, also prominently advertised in the *Review*'s own pages. The *Review*'s sustained interest in both student dissent and Communist China, rather than other popular issues, similarly complemented the large number of titles on these subjects that Random House was publishing. In the issue of February 10, 1972, I. F. Stone discussed the exemplary Medvedev brothers in a long essay which was interrupted by a full-page ad for their latest Knopf books. "Thus writers of high achievement and complete integrity," O'Brien continues, "were led unconsciously to validate, through their collaboration, the more purposeful activities of lesser writers [and editors]."

The magazine's comparative neglect of the Middle East probably reflects, by contrast, not only, as Dennis H. Wrong perceived, a likely unwillingness to risk splitting its loyal audience (largely Jewish, though "radicalized"), but also the parallel scarcity of Random House-Vintage titles on the subject. This last factor might also account for the lack of reviewing interest in theology, esthetics, nearly all domains of science, futurology, architecture, art criticism, avant-garde art in any form, dance of any kind, and even Chomsky's linguistics, which are published by Mouton in Holland, in addition to much else of intellectual importance. Common lack of interest also accounts for the neglect, on both ends, of Marxist philosophy—the kinds of titles published by Beacon or Herder & Herder—and guerilla theater, along with other forms of radical art.

III

In the name of free enterprise, up to two-thirds of American manufacturing has been metamorphosed into a closed enterprise system. While businessmen spoke the language of competitive capitalism, each sought refuge for himself. Price-fixing, parallel pricing, mergers, excessive and deceptive advertising, tariffs, quotas, subsidies, loan guarantees, political favoritism, and preferential tax treatment—all have

created a system of what Senator Estes Kefauver
aptly labeled "corporate socialism—a collective run
by business, not government." —Mark J. Green, *et al.*,
The Closed Enterprise System (1972).

It should be apparent by now that *The New York Review of
Books* represents something more duplicitous than mere "aggressive publishing"—to quote an American-style rationalization; for at the root of its operation is a huge deception. Book
publishers have been known to establish magazines to publicize
their own activities—those are called "house organs"—while
others have founded a journal that is especially predisposed to
publishing their writers (e.g., Grove Press's *Evergreen Review*);
but never before had an American book publisher founded a
periodical that served both of these functions *but* eschewed
these identities. Whether or not *The New York Review* is
"better" or "more radical" than *The Times Book Review* or *The
Saturday Review,* as its apologists would have it, is really not
the issue here; what is appalling is the unprecedented degree and
extent of what normally would be called *corruption.* Indeed, in
most other quality-conscious industries, this kind of apparent
collaboration between manufacturer and a putative reviewing
medium would be publicly exposed; but since the produce in
question is not a dentifrice or toilet paper, whose poor quality
might inflict universal physical misery, but a culture's books,
only intellectuals have sufficient reason or knowledge to complain.

However, one of the more remarkable attributes of this mob
(like the real one) is getting those who are especially
exploited—customers, competitors, and duped collaborators—to
go along with the deception, if not defend the entire operation.
Those who could have protested seemed either implicated or
afraid, and those who might have (or had) noted in print what
writers might say among themselves were unknown or unpublished. It is depressing to record that I have met "critics" who
insisted that such collusion did not exist, all the data notwithstanding, or that it could be expected (and was thus morally
unobjectionable), as well as capitalists who insisted "That's the
only way such books can be *sold* in America"; plus "radicals"
who sometimes rationalize that since the *Review*'s ends were
"mostly correct," its means were not to be questioned. Not
only are all of these cynical responses morally inadequate, but

they are also decidedly unintelligent. *It was, after all, indubitably improper for a manufacturing executive to found in his personal residence a public medium supposedly scrutinizing both his own and his competitors' produce and then installing his wife to comanage it.*

The fact of close personal relations between husband and wife—specifically between a Random House vice-president and the coeditor of an adjudicating medium—immediately raises the question of possible conflict-of-interest; so that what might otherwise be regarded as similar editorial enthusiasm becomes, given this conjugal circumstance, a symptom of intentional collusion. "That I could, even if I chose to, advise these people [*The New York Review*'s editors] how to run their magazine is untrue," Epstein once replied, in a letter to the editor of *The New York Times Magazine.* "Nor is there truth in [the] theory that since I am married to one of the editors, our thoughts are alike." However, "thoughts" are not the crucial issue here, as Epstein must know, his assertions evading the initial charge of one publisher's egregiously excessive influence. That this operation was anything but covert, and yet so scarcely exposed, remains a devastating comment upon American intellectual life. *Quod erat demonstrandum.*

What is more shocking is that so-called "serious writers," with an occasion to reveal truth, neglected to do so. Willie Morris recalls in *North Toward Home* (1967) that on his first job-hunting visit to New York, in the spring of 1963, he called upon an editor at an unamed publishing house clearly resembling Random House—"'an editor who published *the important things,* and who in that very year had helped start, by raising the necessary funds, an ambitious book review." When asked what kind of publishing job he might like, Morris mentioned the new review, and the book-publishing editor felt sufficient, first-person proprietary authority to reply, as Morris quotes him, "Not a chance, I'm afraid. We scarcely have enough money for the next number." However, Morris, portraying himself as an innocent Southern boy, fails to note what must strike the skeptical reader—that by 1966, when he finished his memoir (after two years as an editor at *Harper's*), he might have reported that it was ethically peculiar for a book publisher to found a book review and then act as its personnel department as well, assuming functions of management along with ownership.

Magazines seemed no more courageous. Indeed, had another public adjudicatory institution compiled such a compromised record, it would have been ripe for exposure in *The New York Review*.

Indeed, it was *The New York Review*'s (and Epstein's) commitment to "radical" literature that deceived so many of the mob's potential critics who failed to see that, no matter how important the books, the success of this interest was riddled with capitalism's vices. It should never be forgotten that nonsectarian commercial publishers sell books, not ideologies, and this means they aim to publicize not viewpoints but authors. The theme of a publishing promotion is not that Paul Goodman is right—that conglomerate bureaucracies should be dismantled, for instance—but that Goodman is an important mind whose books should be purchased. (Reading them is, of course, another matter.) The basis of *The New York Review*'s much-vaunted "radicalism" resides less in presenting anti-establishment viewpoints than, as noted before, in publishing (and publicizing) the Random House radicals and/or reviewing their books. Remarkably few of Vintage's many "radicals" have contributed to the *Review*—less than ten, by my count: David Halberstam, Staughton Lynd, H. William Domhoff, Donald Michael, Gabriel Kolko, R. D. Laing, Jonathan Schell, Edwin Reischauer, James Weinstein, Howard Zinn, and Justice William O. Douglas—nearly all of whom, incidentally, were originally sponsored not by Epstein, but by other Random House senior editors. The appearance of, say, David T. Bazelon or George Lichtheim or Tom Hayden or Gar Alperovitz in the magazine's pages roughly coincided with the publication of their Random House-Vintage books; their disappearance likewise accompanied their departure to other publishers. Such pillars of radical integrity as I. F. Stone, Edgar Z. Friedenberg, and Noam Chomsky have, in contrast, remained ensconced within both boats. Rare has been the "radical" contributor to *The New York Review* who has not been, or is not now, or never will be, a Random House author. (Confront one of them with evidence of collusion, I once discovered, and he will plead personal ignorance of such chicanery, along with gratitude that his own writings appear there.)

Random House's success with books of this kind inspired young radical writers to knock upon its door with manuscripts to be considered for publication; and since they were nearly all refused, these books could, in theory, be submitted elsewhere. Pantheon and Knopf, the Random House subsidiaries, also published radical titles; and although editors at those firms were forever claiming autonomy from the parent company, they knew that their argument for publishing a certain highbrow manuscript could be strengthened if they got an advance commitment from Vintage to reprint the work as a high-priced paperback. If Vintage refused, however, the case for publication would be jeopardized, in effect giving Epstein a pocket veto over some of his colleagues' operations—particularly the radical or intellectual titles they wanted to publish.

A radical writer rejected by Random House (or refusing to deal with them) was "free," of course, to take his work elsewhere; but all too often a sympathetic editor from another house would reply, "You know that I'd like to do your manuscript, but we don't know how to publish this kind of book. Why don't you try Random House—they know how so much better." There was a growing market for such writing, to be sure; but only Random House seemed to have the promotional assistance necessary to reach the "intelligent" and academic segments of it successfully. By subsuming within himself the complementary roles of producer and collaborating-publicist, Epstein became the implicit czar of radical criticism in America, choosing not only whom Random House would publish but also, so the evidence suggests, who would be invited to contribute to *The New York Review* and perhaps to join the lecture agency as well, in this conglomerated celebrity-making machine.

It is worth repeating that this multiple operation has been based, like book-publishing itself, upon serving (or exploiting) an individual author, rather than articulating a perspective or ideology. Indeed, one likely reason why Random House-Vintage's anthology of *The High School Revolutionaries* (1970) did poorly was that its very young contributors, unlike more experienced adults, were not susceptible to this personality-publicizing process. Praeger's title on the same subject, John Birmingham's *Our Time Is Now* (1969), sold far better.

In general, other publishers belatedly floating radical books fared poorly unless their authors were already national celebrities. The most famous left critic never to appear in *The New York Review* has been Herbert Marcuse, whose books come not from Random House but from Beacon Press. (That absence may account for why his books have been consistently criticized in the periodical's pages and may partially explain why his eminence was established in Europe before it spread to the U.S.) Indeed, unless the radical book-writer already had a national reputation approaching Huey P. Newton's or Michael Harrington's, those who would not deal with Random House were, no matter how brilliant their work, left largely unpublished (or diffused through magazines). In contrast, both fame and fortune came to nearly all *New York Review*-Random House radicals, and that success represents an episode not in intellectual history, but the history of intellectual promotion. One incidental effect was an insidious control over what was thought (and, thus, not thought) by thousands of radical readers.

One measure of true literary power is a capacity to suppress the instinctive recalcitrance of serious writers. Epstein once concluded an editorial conference over a certain veteran author's first book with, "Oh, I could have written this . . . and it would have been better." The writer, though known to the world as a proud and argumentative man, took his lumps like any lesser mobster who knows his place, for there really was nowhere else for him to go. (Farrar, Straus rarely publishes politically leftward books, though the firm shares with Random House a similar commissarship over collections of literary criticism.) Contrary to what "radical" critics usually imply, "American" culture remains more free and plural than the literary world; censorship and nothing but is the ultimate threat of any editorial monopoly. "The fault of the CIA was not that it corrupted the innocent but that it tried, in collusion with a growing number of insiders, to corner a free market," Jason Epstein once wrote in a remarkable essay (that probably could not have been published outside *The New York Review*'s pages). Though that was not, in my judgment, the central fault of the CIA (whose aims were different), Epstein's indictment, and precisely that indictment—trying to corner a free market in collusion with a growing number of "insiders"—can also be leveled at *The New York Review*-Random House operation.

7

Literary Rule
and Professional
Violence

I

No matter how lowly the birth of the leader, any man automatically becomes upper class when he becomes a member of the power elite. —Albert Murray, *The Omni-Americans* (1970).

Self-righteous bullying fanatics are self-righteous bullying fanatics regardless of the cause they support; and they are as much a threat to the central values we defend when they bully on our side as when they bully on our enemy's. —Wayne Booth, *Now Don't Try to Reason with Me* (1970).

Still, the willingness and ability of insiders to blow the whistle is the last line of defense ordinary citizens have against the denial of their rights and the destruction of their interests by secretive and powerful institutions. —Ralph Nader, *Whistle Blowing* (1972).

It is difficult to define exactly the extent and degree of the New York literary mob's actual power, in part because it fluctuates over time and place while much of it remains hidden, but mostly because we simply have no terms for comprehensively measuring such phenomena. A further hazard in the analysis of literary power is the chronic difficulty in separating the mechanisms of power from the influence of autonomously persuasive ideas. In his sociological study of the reading preferences of American intellectuals in 1970, Charles Kadushin identifies "an oligarchy of influence [structured around] eight journals—*New York Review of Books, New Republic, Commentary, New York Times Book Review, New Yorker, Saturday Review, Partisan Review* and *Harper's*"—three of which are securely within the mob, three more of which are very susceptible to the mob's promotions, and all but one of which were then published in New York. (*Saturday Review* subsequently moved to San Francisco and died.) Kadushin attributes especial influence to "those who write most often for the leading intellectual journals" and identifies the editors as "chief gate-keepers of the intellectual elite."

It is also clear that a group or institution can "control" a literary domain only insofar as it can monopolize the channels disseminating it widely, such as radical critiques and literary reviewing. For a spell in the fifties, the New York literary mob probably had a similar authority over writing by non-sectarian Jewish-Americans. In practice, a young literary writer of Jewish descent submitted to the mob's magazines first, perhaps expecting editorial favor based upon ethnic sympathy. A few were admitted in small measure, usually in the back pages, until it could be seen whether or not they fell into line with the current editorial ideologies. If not, the young Jewish writer generally found other opportunities closed, in part because of actual anti-Semitism (still alive at the time), but also because his opening publications typed him as a "Jewish writer," and, thus, a product of an establishment which other cliques avoided. This power over social destiny, analogous to that of a ghetto elder, might explain why so many older non-mob, first-rate, Jewish writers did not become prominent until the sixties (e.g., Stanley Kunitz, Louis Zukofsky, David Ignatow, Irvin Faust, George Oppen, Kenneth Koch, Charles Reznikoff, Harvey Shapiro, Armand Schwerner, Stanley Edgar Hyman). By analogy, if only one collection of black writers or literary feminists became exclusively ascendant today, the writers most likely to suffer neglect would be those blacks or women *not* associated with the dominant group.

The general indices of the current power of the mob's three inner leaves are these: At least one member gets inducted every year into the National Institute of Arts and Letters (though few have yet to enter the more exclusive National Academy); mob writers usually sit on the selection juries of the National Book Award (but not the Pulitzer Prize) and win these awards regularly (Bellow getting an unparalleled three); their enthusiastically-sponsored novels become best-sellers and non-fiction titles good-sellers (*The Fixer, Advertisements For Myself,* etc.); and associates teach at Columbia and the City University

124

(though not at Fordham or N. Y. U.), as well as at S. U. N. Y. and Rutgers (though rarely at Yale and Princeton). They are especially adept at fetching fellowships from the Guggenheim (Kazin has had four), Ford and Rockefeller foundations (though not from the National Endowment for the Humanities); they were conspicuous throughout the sixties at the YMHA Poetry Center (at that time the most auspicious of New York's cultural showcases); nearly all of the writers now have regular publishers and the expectation of respectful reviews when and if their books appear, as well as easy access to several periodicals; they have allies in all but a few of those publishing houses interested in literary work and most of the quality paperback houses, in addition to a few of the mass reprinters and most of the major reviewing organs. Nearly all of their critic-publicists have published at least one collection of their "pieces"; they can recite certain common sympathies like a well-drilled chorus; most earn more than $35,000 annually and have positions that include some patronage that can be exchanged for personal spoils; almost everyone who wanted an academic job is by now a full (if not chaired) professor at a major university—even the most eccentric or obnoxious individuals; and writers publicly questioning their power and procedures have duly suffered for their courage. Though having no direct control over channels of mass communication (those with audiences larger than 500,000), the mob's media manage nonetheless to have an enormous influence upon those who run the slick sheets; and this power of opinion-making partially explains the remarkable nation-wide dissemination of particular ideas and attitudes, as well as reputations once exclusively confined to a sophisticated minority.

Though no mob, literary or otherwise, can control everything in America (or even within New York), this one still has particularly comprehensive authority in upper-middlebrow political and literary criticism. Since its dominance in certain styles of political criticism—notably extended "radical" critiques—is nearly pervasive, first-rank radical critics completely outside the mob's onion are all underrated (e.g., Buckminster Fuller until recently, Robert Theobald, Murray Bookchin, Harold Cruse, Carl Oglesby, David Horowitz) and intelligent conservatives are generally unknown (e.g., Jeffrey Hart, Ernest Van den Haag, Murray Rothbard, George Grant). Since most of

North America's well-known literary critics operate from within the onion, very few well-known American literary reviewers under sixty have survived totally independent of mob support: Hugh Kenner, John Simon, Stanley Edgar Hyman, and Vivian Mercier are four; a fifth is hard to find. The dominance of the mob, along with its characteristic critical strategies, partly explains why such older first-rate literary theorists as Northrop Frye and Kenneth Burke have been neglected, and why fiction criticism in this country is generally less sophisticated than poetry criticism, especially in dealing with the modern classics.

Never before in America has any literary machine been half as powerful as the New York literary mob; perhaps the only equally powerful literary clique in modern times would be "Bloomsbury," which has by now been somewhat discredited for ignoring the major talents and developments of its own time and place (D. H. Lawrence, James Joyce, Gertrude Stein, among others), and for having an ill effect upon subsequent British literature. (As Stephen Spender noted recently, "Ultimately the values whereby Bloomsbury excluded [various eminences and issues] from serious discussion were snobbish.") That example reminds us that, then as now, such a concentration of literary power is ultimately inimical not only to the free dissemination of intellectual goods, but also to the future of intelligent writing.

The mob also functions as a well-oiled publicity machine, largely at the service of informing the public about itself. The fact that such a parochial definition of "the New York intellectuals" has become so widely accepted or that they are so often recognized, as well, as "the American intellectuals" is evidence of powerful promotional machinery. This kind of "achievement" belongs, to repeat, not to intellectual history but to the history of intellectual advertising. (The principle of appropriating a general term for one's particular wares is scarcely American. Nearly all of the French "new novelists" of the early sixties were published by a single Parisian house!) Irving Howe, for one, customarily uses the once-honorific epithet "intellectual" to refer not to all people possessed of intelligence and erudition and capable of abstraction and empirical verification; his "intellectuals" are only those urban-born, ex-bohemian academics over forty now teaching in universities—like the New York literary mob or just himself rhetorically extended. When

Podhoretz says of his colleagues, as he often has, "on the whole I would say these are the most intelligent people in America," he makes not a genuine critical judgment, but a collectively self-promotional blurb suitable for quotation. (And advertisements for *The New York Review* draw freely upon this kind self-generated illusion.)

What is equally distressing is how easily these deceptions have spread to Europe. When the BBC commissioned the British poet-critic A. Alvarez (b. 1929) to do several radio programs on "American artists and intellectuals" after the John F. Kennedy assassination, no one there objected to his severely limited reportorial survey. His interviews, reprinted in a Penguin paperback *Under Pressure* (1965), covered twenty-one people, all of them born between 1904 and 1930, most of them residents of New York or its environs (e.g., Auden, Arendt, Baldwin, Bellow, R.P. Blackmur, Hardwick, Hofstadter, Howe, Lowell, Mailer, Podhoretz, Rahv, Trilling). All but a few were regular contributors to literary journals where, relentlessly pushing their names into print, the greatest "pressure" they suffered was deadlines. Nearly all of these twenty-one belong, of course, to the New York literary onion. In a review of this scandalously unrepresentative book I noted at the time:

> Some can be said to have absolutely no appreciable achievement, either as critics or creative writers; rather, they are intellectual celebrities who are indefatigable participants in self-conscious, self-glorifying symposia, respondents to questionnaires, signers of petitions—the sort who raise both hands, rather than their books (if any), whenever "writers" are counted. Some are classic literary examples of what the historian Daniel Boorstin calls pseudo-celebrities—"people known for being known."

The American sections of *Under Pressure* thus realize a double deception—one by Alvarez upon his readers and listeners, the other by the mob upon Alvarez, whose own writing had appeared in mob U. S. magazines and whose next book, an inconsequential collection of reviews entitled *Beyond All That Fiddle* (1969), was issued here by Random House. The fear I expressed at the time was that Alvarez's parochial picture of

American literature, especially in the format of a cheap paper-back, would influence subsequent European critics and survey-ors; and, as we shall see, indeed it has.

It is not only erroneous but dangerous to equate "American artists and intellectuals" with contributors to a few New York-based journals; yet the fact that so few should be regarded as representing so many deserves, of course, a sociological explana-tion. New York is not by any means "the heart of American culture," as Robert Lowell told Alvarez's listeners, but the center of native cultural business. What cultural "heart" Ameri-ca has is, paradoxically, its network of fertile universities and research institutes. Nonetheless, most new ideas and cultural reputations must be established in New York before their dis-semination elsewhere in the nation; and as noted before, this explains why every literary machine tries so hard to influence, if not infiltrate, those media. That false sense of America also rationalizes the northeast bias of *The New York Review,* as well as its comparative neglect of writers residing in the South and Midwest. "New York," notes Saul Bellow, "is the principal producer and distributor of the mental goods consumed by the large new public. The present leaders of culture in New York are its publicity intellectuals."

New York has also functioned, throughout American history, as the primary channel for commerce with Europe, and what has always been true for dry goods remains true, longhaul jets notwithstanding, for cultural produce. Because visiting jour-nalists and publishers have always come first to New York, ideas and reputations prevalent there, rather than in Chicago or San Francisco, are those most likely to be exported abroad. (And New York-based writers are, in turn, also more likely to be influenced by fashions current in Europe.) As a result, whoever dominates literary opinion in New York can successfully shape Europe's impression of contemporary American culture. The drummers in this selling process are those New Yorkers who offer hospitality, if only sumptuous lunches and dinners (ideally on a corporate expense account), to visiting dignitaries whose favor is then won; and the mob entrepreneurs have always been extremely adept at unloading their over-inflated wares on im-pressionable Europeans. Salesmanship of this order accounts for a highly striking anomaly noted by the London critic Edward Lucie-Smith in his recent anthology of post-World War II British poetry—that Robert Lowell should be the contemporary American poet most praised by powerful (i.e., America-visiting) London critics and yet least imitated by the current poets. This discrepancy also indicates a considerable distance, especially in their sense of American writing, between the professional British appraisers (and the messages they receive) and British writers.

An ironic virtue of *Under Pressure* is the rich lode of oral statements that reveal, better than their writings, the literary-political style of the mob. For instance, any clique which manufactures its own eminence usually resorts to exclusionary procedures. Just as the WASP debutante director controls the list of acceptable guests, so can Norman Podhoretz shamelessly inform Alvarez, "The only intellectual I take seriously who could be said to be involved with anything like a cult of violence is Norman Mailer." As "we" hold a monopoly of serious opinion, all others are, it is assumed, consigned to another realm (with the "frivolous"?), non-recognition becoming snobbery's most convenient scalpel. (Kadushin has described the editors of "reputable" journals as salon hostesses deciding who will become recognized as "an intellectual.") The only non-writer that Alvarez interviews is, curiously, the actor Zero Mostel, and the Englishman's selections confirm the mob's snobbish presupposition that professionals in other cultural trades, no matter how personally brilliant or intellectually eminent, cannot deal intelligently with platitudinous questions.

The same Upper West Side myopia enables Podhoretz to assert, quite erroneously, that, "There is no tradition of decent poverty in New York," though his generalization might be true only for "everybody I know." In this and other statements, the semblance of critical judgment or even mere description masks underlying literary-political purposes; so that every opinion uttered by a mob "critic" should be closely examined for its ulterior motive. It follows that social gatherings among the mob serve multiple functions—among them, solidifying the membership, spreading important messages, and perhaps initiating a business deal or two; and literary outsiders are invited only to be impressed or inspected for their possible usefulness. Soon after *Ramparts* made its first big splash in 1965-66, the editors were "honored" with a party at Robert Lowell's, to which the boys from California were innocent enough to arrive late and leave early. Other compromises notwithstanding, they never did fall within the onion.

II

> Thus a New York hoodlum of good standing in the national crime syndicate has no difficulty in arranging for a colleague in Kansas City, Chicago, or on the West Coast to do him a little favor, such as collecting a gambling debt or rubbing out a competitor, and so forth. The favor, of course, is returned as the occasion arises.—Estes Kefauver, *Crime in America* (1952).

In dealing with attacks themselves, literary mobsters try to disqualify their critics by the vulgar device of personalizing, often fictitiously, the "causes" of the attack. Thus their critics are portrayed as suffering from "rejection" or "sour grapes" or similarly low motives, an *ad hominem* argument designed to rationalize wholesale dismissal of the charges. To "explain" away Edgar Z. Friedenberg's negative review of *Making It*, Podhoretz told not one but two reporters, "I had just rejected two of Friedenberg's pieces. Hell hath no fury like an author scorned." Victor Navasky quotes Susan Sontag attributing criticism of mob journals to someone who "probably has trouble getting published in these magazines." When Jason Epstein heard about this book, he told a reporter that "Kostelanetz is an ambitious little hustler who has no talent and has been rejected everywhere. He's a bad writer who used to hang around *The New York Review,* and I used to throw him out—and you can quote me on that." In fact, we met just once, several years ago, when I interviewed him in his Random House office for a *New York Times Magazine* essay about the "culture boom"; and since he had nothing worth quoting, I departed swiftly, entirely under my own steam. Not only have I never set foot in *The New York Review*'s office, but it is also odd, if not symptomatic, that Epstein should fancy himself the oversized bouncer of an office in which, so he has elsewhere assured us, he has no policy-making role.

On second thought, only an editor desiring police powers would take particular pride not in initiative or advocacy but *rejection.* Since editors deserve recognition only for what they publish—*not* for what they don't—the editor who says that a much-published writer "has been rejected everywhere" is exceeding his professional role. This epithet, in the mouth of an editor, reveals an ambition to function as a reviewer or, more fearsomely, a desire to control the writer's destiny by imposing a new definition upon his career. Indeed, if one hears any editor take public pride in rejecting a controversial manuscript or an individual writer, be sure that he wants to receive social credit for contributing to its non-existence; but if he is rejecting writing already in print, he must, on deeper levels, be calling for its eradication. If, therefore, an editorial powerhouse says that something already well-known "should not have been published" (rather than saying "it is unpublishable"), the implication is that the manuscript ought to be censored. By boasting of his exclusions, a publisher is really asking us to honor his capacities for censorship.

Every successful mobster knows that his fortune depends not only upon the non-recognition of his potential competitors, but, more important, upon his power to intimidate, if not professionally destroy them. Since literature is an occupation for "gentlemen," professional attacks usually take distinctly white-collar forms. Writers on the fringes of the mob are always vulnerable to excommunication for reasons both literary-political and strictly qualitative; because those in editorial authority always have the power not to publish writers who have previously been favored. After Benjamin DeMott contributed a thoroughly condemnatory review of Podhoretz's *Doings and Undoings* to *The New York Review,* its columns ran some exorcising letters to the editor, and DeMott never again appeared in any of the key mob periodicals. Podhoretz's own memoir reports that soon after he published at the age of 24 a youthfully negative review of Bellow's *Augie March,* a novel that mobsters were supposed to praise, a drunken poet warned him at a party, "We'll get you for that review if it takes ten years." Also intrinsic in literary power is a capacity to get aspiring lackeys to attack antagonists or possible successors, and most of the establishment-sponsored essays (and anthologies) critical of the New Left were filled with younger writers and second-raters practicing literary-political hatchery. However, rare is the co-opted lackey who survives beyond his original coup.

Critical judgments in mob magazines often carry literary-political designs, for one aim of neglecting or condemning an antagonist or his books in amplified media is to persuade publishers not to risk their fortunes and reputations on the offending writer again. Fire-bombing jobs customarily go to new writers trying to make the mob—as tests of their sensitivity to ulterior purposes. In 1963, Richard Gilman, then in his late thirties and just emerging into prominent print after years of neglect, published several short pieces in *Commentary.* He was then assigned a review of Wallace Markfield's *To An Early Grave* (1963), a *roman à clef* containing satirical portraits of several mob writers. The major figure, Leslie Braverman, is clearly the late Isaac Rosenfeld; the novel also includes a satirical sketch of a bumptious young man ("Bruce Siskind") closely resembling *Commentary*'s editor-in-chief. Gilman's rather laudatory review was rejected outright; something more astringent by a *Commentary* junior editor, Marion Magid, appeared instead. Not only did Gilman never write for that magazine again, but *Commentary* subsequently greeted the appearance of his first book, *The Confusion of Realms* (1969), with a ritualistic massacre by Gore Vidal. In the course of researching a double profile of Epstein and Podhoretz, Merle Miller discovered, "Of the more than 50 people I talked to, only a handful would talk on the record. Why? One writer who was more honest than most said, 'Because my next book is going to be reviewed in *The New York Review* and, hopefully, in *Commentary* too.'" One effect of intermediary power is intellectual, or reportorial, intimidation.

Another episode in review-management followed the appearance of Ralph Ellison's collection of essays, *Shadow and Act*, a year after his awesomely sage critique of Irving Howe's intellectual intimidation of Negro writers. Not only was this clearly a book that reviewers could not ignore, but its publisher was also Random House (through Albert Erskine, Jr., whose editorial domain was established before Epstein's ascendancy). Mob responses included Norman Podhoretz's condescending review in *Book World, Partisan*'s terminal postponing of the favorable review that the distinguished critic Joseph Frank had written and then rewritten on commission, plus a general vendetta against Ellison. When R. W. B. Lewis submitted his commissioned notice to *The New York Review of Books,* "I was asked to revise," he wrote me, "partly for clarity and partly because it was felt I had praised the book too warmly." This revision, he continues, was "well buried among the ads at the very back of the magazine."

Not even the best American writers, or the most prominent of their own kind, remain immune to intimidating pressures. Leslie A. Fiedler reports that a critical essay on *Partisan Review* he wrote in the middle fifties in another magazine "brought down on my head actual excommunication, in the form of an indignant letter from the editors of that journal barring me forever from its pages." (Politically ill-advised at that time, this excommunication was rescinded a few years later.) When Saul Bellow attended a White House festival of the arts in June, 1965—an invitation that Robert Lowell refused in an announcement to the press—the mob's response was virulent. Eric F. Goldman, in *The Tragedy of Lyndon Johnson* (1969), notes that Bellow received

> what he called "pressure from the New York crowd," letters, phone calls and telegrams from intellectuals and artists demanding that he withdraw from the festival. As Bellow described it, this was . . . vitriolic denunciation, charges of turncoating for publicity and preferment, even hints of literary blackmail. Bellow's report was not the first I [Goldman] had heard. The novelist Ralph Ellison, who was coming to the festival as a member of the National Council on the Arts, had spoken of the same treatment.

During the festival Bellow encountered Saul Maloff, then a book reviewer at *Newsweek* and a second-rank fellow-traveler who, as Goldman remembers, not only accused "our greatest novelist" of hypocrisy but "did not stop [there]. He spoke of 'turncoats' and said, 'We made you and we can break you.' " (Maloff has publicly denied making such a statement but since he also asserts, in a letter to *Harper's*, where Goldman's memoir first appeared, such untruths as "only Bellow, none other, 'made' his reputation, and he did that solely by means of his great gifts," there is reason to doubt Maloff's intelligence on this subject. Maloff never sued, while Goldman did not rescind his report, which he still regards as accurate.) For all their talk of challenging the political establishment, writers, as a rule,

133

largely intimidate not politicians but other writers. In the end, the actual range of their activity—ideological disputes, position-taking, attitude-striking, and so forth—rarely extends beyond the realm of literary politics.

Literally "rubbing someone out" is, of course, illegal and despicable, and literary people are, by and large, law-abiding, even when avaricious and dishonest. Instead, their "contract," to use the underworld term for commissioning a gunman, takes the form of trying to snuff out a victim's professional life—not in public by means of argument or review but by machinations, below the belt of print, that are designed to keep the challengers unknown and, if possible, unpublished. White-collar mugging, as we shall call it, takes such sub-print forms as persuading editors not to publish (or review) the offending writer again, erasing names from manuscripts, or organizing a campaign of whispered intimidation. One minor move is an informal covenant which rules against ever mentioning these critics' names in mob periodicals. Contributors acknowledging such covenanted writers in their own manuscripts will find either these blackballed names or the entire piece excluded from print. Those who criticize the outfit *in toto* or imply such a comprehensive condemnation (e.g., DeMott) are usually treated with more severity. In part because "the New York intellectuals" have had a fairly cordial press in America, the kind of printed criticism that would scarcely fluff a veteran politician will move literary mobsters to spiteful reactions. Young critics of Jewish descent have been particularly susceptible to such proscription, perhaps because they, unlike comparable gentiles, can be regarded as wayward sons deserving punishment.

When Renata Adler's critique of "The New Reviewers" appeared in *The New Yorker*, she not only received hate mail, one letter threatening to bust her typewriter, but mobsters close to *The New Yorker* put pressure upon the magazine's editor, William Shawn, to fire her, one of them even threatening not to write for the magazine again. Richard Kluger, then editing the weekly *Book Week*, took to his own pages to attack her essay in the course of defending her targets ("No one now writing regularly about new books in America does so more lucidly, more thoughtfully, or more interestingly, than Norman Podhoretz"). Furthermore, a personal vendetta, often conveyed in her presence or through friends, was so effective that she wrote nothing for several months afterwards; and although the New York literary mob prosperously survived her critique, she never again returned to the subject.

When Adler was appointed principal film critic of *The New York Times* early in 1968, the mob again marshaled its weaponry, repeatedly circulating the rumor that she would soon be fired. When close friends of hers were asked if this were true, they sometimes asked from whom the rumor came, and the "source" was often some stinker within the onion. Since the *Times*'s chiefs have, to their credit, remained as unaware of the mob's ways as its literary reporters, white-collar mugging here took a form of circulating a self-fulfilling prophecy—if enough people think and say something will occur, it is likely to come about. This rumor-mongering persisted long after Adler acquired tenure at the *Times*—long after, too, it became clear that no movie reviewer in recent memory ever wrote as well for a daily newspaper. (For good reason was her collection of film reviews, *A Year in the Dark* [1969], dedicated to her *Times* editors, just as her other collection, published that year, *Toward a Radical Middle*, was dedicated to William Shawn.) Nonetheless, among the pressures that finally drove her into premature retirement early in 1969 was precisely the snowballing prophecy that fulfilled itself.

When my own piece on the mob appeared in *Hudson Review* in the autumn of 1965, a similar attempt to mug me was launched. However, I was a more elusive figure than Adler, in part because few of them had actually met me, a sometime graduate student in history then living in a low-rent Harlem housing project, but also because I had spent the previous year in South London. Although I had contributed six reviews and one longer essay to *The New York Times Book Review* between 1963 and the summer of 1965, not until 1970 was I invited to write for them—and then only once again. Although a book I coauthored was reviewed in the summer of 1965, none of my later books was noticed until November 7, 1971, and not in a commissioned individual review but among several others in an anonymously authored "Et Al." I was reliably informed that an assistant editor on the mob-make was fulfilling the contract.

But as Adler's essay (published the year before my *Hudson Review* piece) had gained importance from all of the public objections to it, it was decided that my own essay needed only one "official" reply; and the events following this decision provide another instructive illustration of literary power-politics. Podhoretz invited to lunch a gentile novelist, George P. Elliott, who was then courting the mob's favor while yet remaining a contributor to *Hudson Review,* whose editorial board included his wife Mary Emma Elliott. Having agreed to draft a polemical reply to me, he first wrote me a note "directly to ask whether you are a gentile or a Jew?" It took no great insight to suppose him wondering which of two vulgar "sociological" explanations to use; but since I had already written that my own generation did not take ethnic-religious categories too seriously, I had no qualms about telephoning him directly and declaring, in a gross imitation of my Harlem neighbors, "I'se cullid, but I'se white enuff to pass." He filed his polemic nonetheless, and I answered it. *Hudson Review* never published me again either; nor has my name ever since been mentioned in its pages. A young critic on the mob-make submitted a personally nasty letter-to-the-editor of another periodical that had published an essay of mine. When he heard that my reply would charge that his *ad hominem* remarks were patently designed not to argue any genuine issues, but to please the mob with his low opinion of me, he cancelled its publication (and thus my response) and instead sent copies of his note (though *not* my response) to everyone in the mob he knew. Most of the time, the mob refuses to acknowledge my existence; even as late as 1969, Irving Howe, replying to a letter-to-the-editor in which my name was mentioned, closed haughtily with, "But, who is Richard Kostelanetz?"

White-collar mugging occurs for various reasons and in various ways, but the form is always the same—the powerful exploiting their leverage against the situational weakness of the powerless and/or the innocence of the good-hearted. Its function is analogous to that of a grass bust, which is nowadays a demonstration arrest designed not only to deflate a key antagonist and prevent repetition of the offense, but also to scare the hell out of his sympathizers. A young writer I know once drafted a memorial essay about an older writer who was on the fringes of the mob. As soon as his literary associates heard that the essay would be printed by a vulnerable periodical, they coerced the young writer, the deceased's widow, and the magazine's editor to drop the piece on the ostensible grounds that "only someone of XYZ's own generation had the right to memorialize him in print." Just as, to quote Victor Navasky, "It is better to be attacked by an establishment comrade than to be praised by an outsider," so it is an unwritten law of the outfit that only a member is truly "qualified" to review another's work—even after his death.

A young writer I know courageous enough to criticize Irving Howe in print has never been able to contribute to any of the magazines with which Howe has been associated, although this writer's essays have appeared in many other periodicals. Not only does Howe's name frequently pop up in stories of literary mugging, but it is Howe, as we shall see, who credits the mob (and himself) with helping "destroy" the Stalinist writers and who implores everyone to deal as effectively with the young. When Jonah Raskin (b. 1942), the author of *The Mythology of Imperialism* (1971), was denied tenure at S.U.N.Y.—Stony Brook, one reason cited by his senior colleagues, according to Raskin, was a critical and perceptive review of Howe that had appeared in the year before in *Scanlan's Monthly.* "The Irvings of this world call me Stalinist," Raskin later recollected, "but I'm the one who is being purged." Indeed, Howe once compiled a symposium on the radical young, entitled *Beyond the New Left* (1970), in which the subject is manifoldly condemned by contributors all well over thirty-five, writing not for the young, to be sure, but for their fellow elders of Zion. Frequently caught in hypocritical stances, he once denounced mass culture and its debasements while regularly writing unsigned book reviews for *Time;* he also criticized "intellectuals" who became professors soon after he took a professorial job at Brandeis, as well as continually demanding that "intellectuals" resist the blandishments of capitalism while he himself royally succumbed.

It is unfortunate that, when an intellectual articulates a "position," the fate of his ideas becomes entwined with aspirations for personal success so that he comes to develop a "vested interest" upon which his fortune depends and which must be defended against all comers. This means not only that "an intellectual" can be a socialist in print and a capitalist in life—a discrepancy exemplified by Howe—but also that he can change his political advocacies without appreciably changing his life style. By such processes, however, does a prosperous intellectual, no matter how "radical," become not only proud of his eminence but professionally conservative (e.g., Howe again), especially when confronting the young.

When a widely published independent writer finds his work suddenly excluded from outlets in which it had previously appeared, there is, as a rule, good reason to suspect a professional mugging. If the writer is excluded from *all and only* those outlets under the influence of a certain literary powerhouse, the pattern will usually reveal the identity of the mugger (and perhaps the reasons for it as well). To criticize one's antagonists in print is legitimate, even if masking ulterior motives; but it cannot be reiterated enough that mugging, whether physical or professional, should be relentlessly condemned and eliminated. "Competition" in a free society means surpassing one's foes, not rubbing them out.

In truth, the New York literary mob has not become magnanimous or high-minded with its collective success. Just as no literary clique ever pushed itself harder into eminence on such slender cultural achievements, so none has been as ruthless and smug in its operation, or so eager to capitalize upon provisional prosperity, or as glib with self-serving rationalizations, or quite as tenacious in retaining transitory power for longer than its normal life. A serious "intellectual" only two decades before would have apologized to his peers for taking a lucrative position, or for earning over $30,000 a year, or for having more than three children, and he might have tried to retain visible ties with his bohemian past. By the sixties, however, these limits disintegrated, as mob capo Jason Epstein complained, "In New York there are few respectable or comfortable ways of being poor or even middle class. To be without money in New York is usually to be without honor." Not Epstein, however, but Irving Howe became the prime apologist for this bohemian sell-out, blaming the morally absolving demands of American bourgeois existence: "I mean the whole business—debts, overwork, varicose veins, alimony, drinking, quarrels, hemorrhoids, depletion, the recognition that one might prove not to be another T. S. Eliot." (At least poor Charles Van Doren was high-minded enough to claim a desire "to increase public respect for the intellectual life and the teaching profession"!)

Once a writer-professor-editor decides to support his family at levels above his salary, he works primarily not to protect his job, which is customarily tenurial (and, contrary to the bohemian myth, he cannot quit), but for his surpluses, which largely represent rewards for "reputation" or past achievements. This development means not only that commercial interests supersede unsullied literary ones, but that he must also cultivate both his self-image and his benefactors with more attentive care, as well as necessarily adopt a conservative professional outlook. For one thing, he must also oblige his associates to erase all possible challengers, much as a bourgeois home-owner fights to prevent the influx of blacks who might jeopardize his property values; and the Nixon recession, with its cutbacks in academic expenditures, tended to make him even more aggressive at protecting income levels that simply could not be sustained. (The hard, tragic truth is that protecting such surpluses is practically impossible in a culture as fundamentally volatile as America's.) All these developments, though perceived, have encountered few professional objections, and that is a most depressing and damning fact.

III

> As a group, our sample had little awareness of persons who were up and coming in the intellectual world. Many were unable to think of any up-and-coming persons at all, while others named such 'newcomers' as Norman Mailer [b. 1923] and John Updike [b. 1932]. —Julie Hover and Charles Kadushin, "Influential Intellectual Journals" (1972).

The most serious threats to the mob's dominance were first those previously in power, such as the WASP establishments and then the weakened literary Agrarians, and now those younger people and writers outside New York who could do many of the same tasks better (and other ones besides). The greediest literary powermen nowadays oblige themselves to create a situation in which the more intelligent young (other than their own students and sycophants) remain powerless and vulnerable, thus discouraging not only the presently emerging generation but subsequent ones as well. This development explains why no one younger than Philip Roth and Susan Sontag has become an inner-circle member of the New York literary mob—and those two entered a decade ago. It also explains why mobsters continually assert that "the young," to quote Howe again, "don't seem nearly as interested in writing fiction or criticism."

Back in the forties, the anti-Stalinists in the mob helped drive into obscurity and silence not only outright Communists, but those leftists who refused to be so anti-Communist (called "fellow travelers"). Committees of "Cultural Freedom" were formed, often with financial help from the CIA, partially to exclude both groups from the over-crowded literary profession (a genuine disagreement in political philosophy functioning as a front for a disingenuous literary-political power play). Once the Communists were so mugged, other groups served a similar victim's role in the literary mob's typically thirties' demonology—apologists for mass culture in the early fifties, the "beats" around the decade's turn, and then the young in the late sixties (all of whom met a professional violence initially honed on the Communists and the anti-anti-Communists). When such intellectuals talk "activism," the context of their remarks—the scene to which such talk relates—is really the professional world of writers or literary politics. The people most likely to be hit by their fire are invariably not politicians but other writers.

This most powerful of American literary mobs has used its steadily accumulated power to repudiate certain kinds of unjustified discrimination and make literate Americans aware of certain otherwise neglected writers. As Norman Mailer judged in 1968: "But they did not grow over the years, no schools of criticism developed from them, no seminal ideas, no ferments—just an endless series of brilliant but tactical papers. They were guardians, rather than catalysts." They had the power to exclude from common discourse all kinds of writing and ideas they could not understand; so that not only were they largely responsible for certain currently widespread limitations in, say, literary taste, political criticism, and sociological perception, but even their own brighter protégés would inevitably succumb to an imaginative and intellectual bind. Whatever internal intellectual energy that once was there is no longer communicable, even to those apprenticing themselves to the established style and prejudices; and most of the fresh names in their magazines nowadays are interchangeable and easily forgotten. In the seventies, some of the neo-conservatives in the outfit criticized the pathetically decimated Black Panthers as culturally inimical; but the truth remains that the New York literary mob represents a far more serious threat because it is wealthier and more powerful within its intermediary domains, as well as more successful at resisting outside challenge.

In addition to making "criticism" a servant of collective self-publicity and fostering a prejudice against the young, the New York literary mob undermined much of the respect we have for "the intellectual life," as well as eliminating the possibility of freely formed intra-professional criticism. Since professional opportunity and morality have necessarily become major issues within the community of serious writing, among the primary literary-political tasks confronting the young is the repudiation of the mob's negative prophecies and then the restoration of an atmosphere of personal possibility, general self-scrutiny, and moral leverage in dealing with the larger world.

The Rule of
Corruption
and Repression

8

I

As a matter of fact, the whole word "corruption"
doesn't come up any more. I think a few years ago
Clyfford Still could call Robert Motherwell an "old
whore," or somebody could call somebody else
one, . . . but, you know, you can't do that any more.
There is no one artist who could call any other artist
an old whore. That is the kind of time it is. —Ad
Reinhardt, in an interview (1966).

No matter how much venality and deception is uncovered, the rules of journalism require that each
instance be treated as an aberration rather than part
of a larger problem. Those who attempt to report in a
broader context are accused of forfeiting their objec-
tivity. They have the choice of becoming pariahs and
losing their access to sources of information or [be-
coming] commentators and losing their credibility as
reporters. . . . It's all right occasionally to point out
that a bit of paint has been chipped off the social
machine but not to ask where the machine is taking
us. —Robert Stein, *Media Power* (1972).

Dishonesty and greed have always poisoned cultural
communication—advertisers, to cite a widespread example, frequently influencing or censoring copy in magazines; but never
before have such poisons infected literary society to such a
pervasive degree. Within this circumscribed domain, the New
York outfit is scarcely the only force currently inimical to the
possible future of intelligent writing. Although no other cabal is
more pernicious, it must be understood that other powerful
factors also block the emergence and circulation of literature.
The unprotested dominance of the New Yorkers creates, to be
sure, an atmosphere of avarice and corruption in which shady

operations and even muggings are tolerated too easily, if not disingenuously rationalized as "shrewd business." (By this same kind of capitalistic rationalization, needless to say, most any kind of gangsterism or even the Vietnam War can be made acceptable.) The pervasiveness of such behavior sometimes causes writers who are scrupulous by nature to act in less-than-honorable ways—current "art" imitating previous inventions in art, so to speak. When even *their* activity goes uncriticized, other high-minded writers begin to wonder if their gut integrity, intrinsic to the art and ambition of writing, might not be their greatest professional liability; yet as long as everyone remains quiet, there can be no leverage for change. It is also hypocritical, though characteristic of the times, for a cultural celebrity to moralize about something he knows substantially little about—foreign policy, say, or the quality of Afro-American life—while refusing to notice similar inequities and repressions on the literary scene about which he surely knows and probably feels much, much more.

All histories of the American underworld explain how the success of one gangland operation usually breeds a rash of imitators which are rarely as successful as the original model. If only to avoid needless bloodshed, each new operation carefully respects the autonomy and turf of its predecessors. As in the underworld, so on today's literary scene—the New York mob's model of marital collusion, for instance, breeds its successors, none of which are as elaborately powerful. One of these gathered around the literary agent Lynn Nesbit, born in the late thirties, but more sympathetic toward a literary generation several years older than herself. She began with the Sterling Lord Agency but soon branched out on her own, setting up a literary department within an increasingly prosperous, multipurpose enterprise called Marvin Josephson Associates which later assumed Ashley Famous Agency and became "The International Famous Agency." Her writers were particularly favored by certain publishing editors—for instance, the late David I. Segal and Hal Scharlatt, both of whom moved through a succession of houses. Christopher Lehmann-Haupt, successively an assistant editor in *The New York Times Book Review* and then a regular reviewer in the daily *Times,* was a loyal collaborator, as well as Nesbit's neighbor on Greenwich Village's Charlton Street. (Apparently a responsive sort of "critic," he had once puffed a book sponsored particularly by his wife, Natalie S. Robins, as an editorial employee at Random House [Lucille Clifton's *Good Times* (1969)]; and in his pre-Christmas survey of December 1, 1969, six of the twenty books he recommended were published by Random House itself.)

It was Lynn Nesbit's good fortune, in 1966, to marry the critic Richard Gilman (b. 1926), then a drama reviewer at *Newsweek*. He soon became the literary editor at *The New Republic* which had, during the sixties, become the most successful of the liberal weeklies. As editor, Gilman published several of his wife's clients and commissioned reviews of their books, one partner plugging what the other was peddling. As a sometime book reviewer, Gilman himself was generally a tough critic; however, two of his wife's accounts, Donald Barthelme and William H. Gass (published by Segal at three different houses), received in *The New Republic* the laudatory and extended notices that Gilman also reprinted in his first collection of criticism, *The Confusion of Realms* (1969). Even though his enthusiasms may have been genuine, it is always wise to avoid the appearance of conflict-of-interest.

For several reasons, it should be noted, agentry makes a more propitious base for literary operations than publishing; for while both publisher and agent have a vested interest in selling clients' books (and enhancing their commercial reputations), an agent allied with reviewers can quickly turn all signs of "reviewers' interest" into persuasive demands for higher advances which the agent then shares with his writer. Publishing spoils, in contrast, are diffused throughout a corporation which can, however, compensate especially successful editorial effort with salaries and increased bonuses. Furthermore, since an agent places his writer's books with different publishers, the agent remains invisible—it is hard to tell from the outside whether reviewer Y is commercially tied to writer X. Nonetheless, precisely by this publicizing process do allied writers, publishers, and agents develop a burgeoning stake both in boosting all of their claque's assertions and in increasing the greeny fluff of divisible pie.

Developing its own competence at Review Management, this Nesbit-Gilman mini-mob made a concerted push not on behalf of a literary or political critic (still the New York mob's all-but-exclusive domain) but, rather, with a new novelist (thereby respecting, as well as capitalizing upon, the other mob's decreasing interest in new fiction). Rudolph Wurlitzer's first novel, *Nog* (1969), published by Scharlatt, then at Random House, came armed with blurbs by other Nesbit clients; and Harry Smith's *Newsletter* reported that when the novel arrived at the *Times Book Review,* Christopher Lehmann-Haupt successfully advocated that it be singled out for a level of attention rarely accorded a first novel—a thousand-word review printed within the magazine's front seven pages. Unable to get approval for any surely sympathetic reviewers, Lehmann-Haupt was obliged, according to *The Newsletter,* to ask a less predictable young novelist and critic, Richard Elman, to take the assignment. The negative notice that Elman submitted opened with the innocently made suggestion that *Nog* was a novel Richard Gilman would write if the critic could write fiction. Obviously disappointed with Elman's performance, Lehmann-Haupt adamantly insisted that unless the reference to Gilman were cut as irrelevant, the review would not be published. Since Elman based his allusion solely upon Gilman's critical essays, rather than any close personal connection to Gilman-Nesbit-Wurlitzer, he succumbed to Lehmann-Haupt's editorial pressure. When the abridged version finally did appear, David I. Segal, then chief editor at Harper & Row, promptly wrote a dutiful letter-to-the-editor vulgarly attempting to discredit Elman, for Segal's own wife, the novelist Lore Segal, had already praised *Nog* in Gilman's section of *The New Republic.*

Suffering, however, from an incomplete education at their literary business, this imitative mob failed to develop an appealing minority-based "front"; and interconnections subsequently disintegrated. Just as neither Wurlitzer nor Gass, poor pawns in other men's games, ever quite equalled Philip Roth either artistically or commercially, so Gilman departed from *The New Republic* to teach at Yale Drama School and Nesbit subsequently became more interested in movie rights and other sub-literary game. Moreover, the fact that the mugging of Elman was so mild, compared to what the New York mob might have done, indicates that this particular literary machine would never displace its model.

Improbity has become so acceptable in U. S. cultural life that no one seems to mind that many books excerpted for prepublication in *The American Scholar* often appear under the Harcourt, Brace imprint, the magazine's chief editor also serving as a senior associate of the book-publishing firm, or that the critical articles in *Artforum* have disproportionately featured artists represented by the Leo Castelli Gallery. Even superficially innocuous proceedings, such as the selection of poets for the first *American Literary Anthology* (1968), become riddled by decisions relating less to critical values than literary-political ambitions. Sponsored and founded by George Plimpton, *Paris Review*'s founding editor, the *American Literary Anthology* was established to select works (supposedly the best) that had appeared in little magazines the year before. Thanks to a grant from the National Endowment for the Arts, each writer selected would receive $1,000 for a long piece or $500 for a short one, while the magazine publishing him would get one-half those amounts respectively. The winning pieces would also be reprinted in an annual volume published in rotation by commercial houses, the government guaranteeing against possible losses. "It is difficult to understand," quipped Curt Johnson, the editor of *December*, "why our culture agency should have to underwrite commercial publishers. That's the CIA's job, isn't it?" And elsewhere he noted, "The *Anthology*'s first budget allocated $17,000 just to prepare the first volume's manuscript for the typesetter, a feat equivalent to spending $500 to get a shave."

The poetry judges for the first issue were John Ashbery, Robert Creeley, and James Dickey, all noted poets in their forties. A close inspection of the twenty-nine poems included in the book reveals that nearly all of the poets selected were professional allies of one of these three men. Ashbery, as doyen of the "New York School" of American poetry, is probably responsible for the appearance of the other members of that mini-mob—Joseph Ceravolo, Kenward Elmslie, Kenneth Koch, Harry Mathews, John Perreault, Clark Coolidge, Peter Schjeldahl, Aram Saroyan, and Ed Sanders. All of them except Mathews and Coolidge lived primarily in New York City where they saw each other regularly at poetry readings at St. Marks-in-the-Bowery Church and New York University; and all have been published, along with Ashbery himself, in both *Paris Review* and an anthology called *The New York Poets* (1970), edited by Ron Padgett and David Shapiro. Most of them also wrote for *Art News* when Ashbery served as its executive editor. Creeley, as a prince of the Black Mountain poetic association, probably chose that group's king, Charles Olson, and his own former teacher Louis Zukofsky, as well as his fellow Black Mountaineers Robert Duncan, Edward Dorn, and John Wieners, in addition to closely allied "beats"—Allen Ginsberg, Michael McClure, Denise Levertov, and LeRoi Jones, all of whom (except Duncan, then "disenchanted with anthologies") also appeared in the parochial collection that Creeley coedited with Donald M. Allen, *The New Writing in the U.S.A.* (1967) and, except for Zukofsky, also in Allen's earlier *The New American Poetry* (1960).

Ashbery or Creeley, or both, probably chose Ezra Pound, who was then hardly either young or unknown. One could wager that James Dickey selected Lawrence Lieberman, who had published a monograph on Dickey's work, as well as Richard Howard who wrote the next longest critical essay on Dickey; and five fellow non-New York enthusiasts for nature poetry— Louis McCarty, William Stafford, Thomas Whitbread, Gibbons Ruark, and James Wright. These last selections represent, at least, an intellectual-critical commitment rather than literary political allegiance. Since the reviews he collected in *From Babel to Byzantium* (1968) reveal more eclectic sympathies than Creeley's *A Quick Graph* (1970), one suspects that the remaining three selections were his as well. Since the other judges were all at least forty years old and mostly academic, such priming of protégé-pumps is perhaps predictable.

The obvious suspicion is that the judges did not vote by majority rule, as might be expected of a multi-man panel, but made individual selections; however, nothing within the book's preface explains the procedures that Plimpton later revealed to Smith's *Newsletter*—that the judges never met together since each was "asked to make a specified number of choices to go directly into the volume." As chairman of the enterprise, Plimpton apparently found no reason to invalidate the balloting. Indeed, with everyone less interested in articulating standards or discovering unknowns than in rewarding friends and compatriots (if not finally themselves), it was not surprising that the first *Anthology* included six items, all poems, from Plimpton's own magazine, two more than its nearest competitor (in *all* genres). Two more items, both poems, came from *Nice,* which was personally published by the *Paris Review*'s enterprising poetry editor who had also previously published two of the three poetry judges in the latter's pages; two more items came from

The New York Review of Books which, though scarcely a little magazine, has been chiefly edited by Robert B. Silvers who had long served as one of *Paris Review*'s senior editors.

Not only is it illegitimate to establish a tax-exempt foundation whose principal beneficiary becomes oneself or one's enterprise, but these sweepstakes with government (taxpayers'!) money in public purview patently represents backslapping and reciprocal payoff where membership on a giveaway committee constitutes a license to extend the designs of those who established the program and those who were selected to judge. In another government pork barrel for "gifted but unrecognized writers," six well-recognized old pros in a "Literary Study Group" received, according to Curt Johnson's exposé, three grand apiece (or $18,000) for nominating twenty-nine deserving youngsters for a total of only $37,500, in sum raising the old question of who is doing whom a favor and why? Johnson also reports that at the Coordinating Council of Literary Magazines, whose aim it is to aid small literary journals in practical ways, "Administrative expenses run upward of 20 percent of its budget, though by my calculation, they run closer to 30 percent." Its largest grants have gone to *Partisan Review*, whose chief editor, William Phillips, is chairman of the CCLM board and whose managing editor, Caroline Rand Herron, was salaried manager of CCLM's New York office. Most government support, Johnson concludes, goes to established institutions and "writers who had already spent half their lives riding gravy trains."

Therefore, no contributor to little magazines may expect to be selected to the *Anthology* unless he has a colleague on the appropriate selection committee; and since the judges, as established literary politicians, are liable to belong to thriving cabals, no writer would possibly expect selection unless one of his particular cabal were represented. Since Duncan and Levertov were among the poetry judges for volumes two and three respectively, Black Mountain had its forces permanently represented; and Ashbery, who served as a poetry judge for volume one, was chosen to appear in numbers two and three. All this interrelation explains why, as several of the first *Anthology*'s reviewers noted, the sweepstakes "discovered" so many writers who scarcely need further notice, and so few of the many kinds of recent American poetry were finally incorporated into any and all of the *American Literary Anthologies*. In addition to

149

misrepresenting the pluralistic reality of American literary achievement today, this selection procedure discriminates against writers who are young, unestablished, and independent—precisely the people who are most likely to forge a future for intelligent writing.

It is by comparison a minor sin that a publishers' organization should sponsor prizes such as the National Book Awards, which are chosen by highly unrepresentative sets of judges, during "National Library Week," and whose primary purpose seems to be publicizing year-old titles that might otherwise go unknown or unsold. If nothing else, almost every American library will purchase the champion along with a few of the finalists—this game selling losers as well as winners; for *all* the titles are publicized in both the book-award association's prominent advertisements and its news releases, where the winners are billed as "The Most Distinguished Books of 19--." A further problem is not just that the wrong books are chosen, as some critics say, but that the same few literary publishers are ritually honored along with a university press or two to preserve the semblance of integrity, while first-rank titles from other publishers, including some of the best, never reach the finals.

One reason why books from certain publishers are favored is that their authors also dominate the selection panels. In 1972, Farrar, Straus, whose books were victorious in the categories of fiction and children's literature, had two of its regular authors on the former panel and one on the latter; and the finalists in each of those categories included yet another Farrar, Straus book. (Donald Barthelme, a judge for fiction, won the prize for children's literature.) The chronic omissions, by contrast, can be partly blamed upon the procedures of the National Book Committee which customarily presents the judges with a list of likely books and asks publishers to send selected titles to the judges' homes. However, since the NBC's small staff cannot possibly read all the new titles, even their preliminary selection reflects the loudest promotions of "prominent" publishers and cultural politicians.

Since the judges themselves are asked to nominate the finalists, the books chosen to compete invariably reflect the particular enthusiasms, if not the cultural alliances, of individual panelists. Particularly in poetry where reputation-making is so politicized, the NBA selections reflect distinctly private passions.

150

In 1972, the poetry finalists included books by Frank O'Hara and David Shapiro, both of whom had worked closely with one of the poetry judges, Kenneth Koch; and the year before, Allen Ginsberg, then a judge, staged a vociferous protest when his old friend and colleague, Gregory Corso, did not win the grand prize. Judges have also been known to nominate books by writers with whom they are editorially involved. In 1972, the finalists in the "Arts and Letters" category included collections of criticism by B. H. Haggin and John Simon, both of whom contribute regularly to *Hudson Review* whose chief editor, Frederick Morgan, was one of the arbiters in that category. An early galley of Norman Fruman's *Coleridge, the Damaged Archangel* acknowledged the help of Stanley Burnshaw, a veteran poet and editor whose interest in the book dated back to his days as a Holt vice-president. After his name was duly removed from the book's preface, he made this work *his* first choice for the Arts and Letters prize; not surprisingly, Burnshaw's current publisher is also Fruman's. Here, as in the *American Literary Anthology*, the choice of prize winners depends less upon "standards" than upon the selection of judges. What is more symptomatic, of course, is that the literary world should regard as prestigious a contest that is just as self-invented and ultimately bogus as Hollywood's Academy Awards. "The rules of journalism," as Robert Stein, editor of *McCall's,* notes, "require that each instance be treated as an aberration, rather than part of a larger problem."

II

The result is that much good literature is never published, and much that is published never receives its due. And it is barely possible that if more good literature from a variety of points of view from a variety of schools had been published in this country over the past 25 years, ... [there] would [not] today be good writers staring out windows in Florida, Indiana, Rhode Island, California, pondering the realization that the meaning of their whole lives has been squandered by rather easily describable conspiratorial maneuvers they are forbidden to describe—because conspiracies don't exist in this country. —Curt Johnson, "My Culture Agency Problem—and Yours" (1970)

151

Most everyone who writes with seriousness wants eventually to publish—short works in magazines and longer writings as books—and thus communicate beyond his immediate audience. However, what opportunity these publishing media once offered has by now become increasingly constricted. New writers innocently putting their manuscripts into the mail assume opportunities which, for various identifiable reasons, no longer exist. For one thing, although magazine writers and magazine readers are probably as numerous as ever, there are fewer general magazines. *Look, Life,* and *The Saturday Evening Post* all died soon after their editorial policies turned more youthful, the last two clearly suffering from mismanagement that killed editorial touch; and no new mass journal except *Rolling Stone,* perhaps, has taken their place. The death of *Collier's, Story,* and *The Saturday Evening Post* left fewer well-paying magazines open to fiction; and since new journals do not fill this gap, it is absolutely impossible for a writer (except those connected with *The New Yorker*) to earn a living from short stories, no matter how fine. There are fewer outlets for extended critical essays as distinct from book reviews, while stuffy cultural periodicals like *Daedalus, American Scholar, Southern Review,* or *The Public Interest* rarely have any contributors under the age of thirty-five.

It was more disheartening to discover that certain new publications and editors who announced themselves as open to the young really were not, such as *Harper's* during Willie Morris' reign and Theodore Solotaroff's *New American Review,* both of which began in that highly deceptive summer of 1967. The former eventually set a policy against considering unsolicited manuscripts, thereby making explicit an attitude that would remain implicit in other establishments—they simply were not looking. The latter exemplified the common editorial principle of exploiting the prestige of the avant-garde while favoring fogeys over fresh goods. A salaried reader-poet at *Paris Review* once told me that he never found a publishable poem among the unsolicited manuscripts sent to the magazine, suggesting not that none exist, as he would have liked me to believe, but that he was not looking too hard. More than one of the *Paris Review*'s non-salaried "scouts" have reported that their own recommendations are never published, largely because, as they learn, the circle of acceptable contributors is circumscribed in advance. In a genuinely revealing aside, Norman Podhoretz noted that his own first editor at *Commentary,* the late Robert Warshow (1917-1955), "genuinely loved the young (no easy thing to do, as I was subsequently to find)." Sympathy of this sort was more rare in Podhoretz's own editorial generation than it was in Warshow's.

The fortunes of new and young writers are made even more hazardous by the fact that the seats of literary power—on that *Anthology* and elsewhere—are now occupied by men in their forties and fifties who established themselves in the post-World War II boom. No entrenched generation in our cultural history has ever been so aggressive and tenacious, so affluent and yet avaricious. As one kindly veteran, the novelist Glenway Wescott (b. 1901), noted in passing in the early sixties, "I have the impression that the mutual promotion and the competitiveness [in these generations] are both more specific and energetic than they were in my generation." American literary institutions have come to resemble the Israeli parliament where, as Amos Elon noted, the members' average age was 43 in 1949 and 63 in 1969. The hegemony of these literary powers is further threatened by the sense that the recent work of its major figures fails to equal earlier achievements. Indeed, one theme of sixties criticism was disappointment with previously established creative talents, their financial prosperity notwithstanding. Commitments exclusively to their contemporaries, and only to their kinds of work, explain why most of this literary generation strikes younger people as dead from the neck up.

Furthermore, new writers are naive if they fail to understand that every long-established magazine has, to differing degrees, a vested interest in its reigning style and positions along with its literary-political allegiances, whatever they may be. Neither a magazine based upon profit-motives nor one desiring influence can allow its stylistic-intellectual-political "formula" to be violated. The pretense of editorial openness and liberalism is merely a typical American deceit because the rhetoric of opportunity, like that of equality, is culturally *de rigueur.* Since an editor's power and income depend upon continuing success of his institution's vested interests, all established periodicals are editorially less innovative than conservative, less open than closed. Magazines, like radio stations, are run not to win the audience's attention but to keep it—to prevent the buyer from turning away once he has exposed himself to the medium. That explains why everything within a periodical's format seems tailored to certain preconceptions which are themselves based upon a characterization of the lowest common denominators of its particular audience.

Most emerging writers want to contribute to the periodicals their peers are reading—they desire access to the young audiences that certain institutions have won; yet such reasonable aspirations are often compromised, if not stymied. If a young writer invited to contribute to *The Village Voice* writes that the West Village is too bourgeois, or that the East Village or SoHo are both more authentic bohemias and more attractive places to live, that Norman Mailer is a windbag with an overblown literary reputation, that so-called "good" schools are scarcely better than "bad" ones, or that mixed-means theater is usually more interesting to watch than off-Broadway, he will not last long on *The Village Voice* if he slips into print at all. An aspiring writer would not last much longer on *Commentary* if he judged that "black anti-Semitism" was negligible or often imaginary, or that Irving Howe was "a cultural policeman." He would survive no longer on *The New York Review* (were he invited at all) if he said that Allen Ginsberg or Kenneth Rexroth are more admirable poets than Robert Lowell, that certain avant-garde writing is consequential enough to merit serious critical attention, that provincial academics are easily conned by New York sharpies, that collusion between publishers and reviewers is unethical, or that a literary mob exists and is powerful.

Authoritarian editing of this kind is less a matter of censorship than the means by which the magazine cultivates both its "image" and vested interests, as well as protecting its readers from the real world to which they all belong. As Joseph Bensman and Israel Gerver perceived, "The merits of any particular *art product* are viewed by its owners as less important than the maintenance of the institution." Since every established magazine has a limited idea of what kind of writing and what subjects might currently be appropriate in its pages, nearly all U.S. periodicals would be forced to refuse, for one ludicrous editorial reason or another, most great contemporary literature, even in the particular genres they favored. Editorial policies usually function, in Mrs. Leavis' words, "to close the [magazine] to genius, talent and distinction, and to force instead a kind of anemic ability to satisfy the reading habit." Because such policies both cause and reflect the narrow range of the magazine's contents, most periodicals of opinion can be read rather quickly, each new issue largely repeating its predecessors.

Furthermore, any thriving magazine reasonably loyal to its writers has more than enough willing and sympathetic people to do its necessary tasks, and is thus interested in aspiring newcomers only for their capacities to extend the reigning style and prejudices without intruding into domains already apportioned to regulars. A new writer applying for admission is not likely to get past the magazine's door unless his evident prejudices accord with the magazine's traditions and he can fill a clear gap in its current coverage and/or handle an assignment that the regulars cannot, or would not, fill themselves.

In their dealings with young writers, such magazines invariably establish a kiddie principle whose first rule is that bright, aspiring young writers are as expendable and interchangeable as slaves on a plantation—and increasingly abundant in supply. As the amenable new writer gets more back-page work to do, those who fail to fall into the assembly line—say, by violating the company's established stylistic and ideological biases—are shipped "down river" and easily replaced. The ever-increasing influx of new talent is one reason why rates of literary pay have not advanced with inflation.

Another tenet of the kiddie principle holds that the most opportune subject matter for a young writer is the enthusiasms of his own generation. Although the newcomer might feel obliged to reaffirm his editor's "ideas" and stereotypes about the young, anyone with any sense of his own integrity and taste might well avoid "adult" fields where a magazine's hierarchy of reputations is already fixed and to accept youth-cult subjects which allow him more latitude of opinion. The same editor who does not care about this younger critic's taste in rock would, by contrast, generally take an overweening interest in whether or not his commissioned writer likes a certain playwright or novelist. The working assumption is that only established writers can adjudicate other notables in old-boy pages, even if precisely the same criticisms are made. It's not what you say, but who you are.

"One of the most depressing things," a New York editor in his twenties told the reporter Douglas Mount, "is the idea that young editors are expected to produce 'young' books. Publishers pander so to fads." Many well-known young writers are haunted by the anomaly that their more facile "youth" work gets easily into print, while their more considered, more "adult" efforts—the writing they regard as more consequential—remains unpublished or less known. If a publisher asks a good writer or editor to focus on only one of his ten interests, they capitalize on only one of his ten available talents, which is their privilege. However, not only is the writer or editor who is rewarded for his immaturity likely to feel professionally frustrated, but his readers are receiving only one-tenth—or losing nine-tenths—of his possible communication. Furthermore, just as editorial moguls have distinct, albeit changing, conceptions of what an "authentic" black writer should look and sound like, so in the late sixties they expected their youth expert to have long hair, a hirsute face, hip clothing, beads around his neck, a joint in his mouth, and "groovy" speech. The truth, never to be forgotten, is that the older Caucasian generation controls the media that articulates not only white America's current stereotype of black people, but also the older generation's pet picture of dumb, dissolute youth. Just as most black-oriented radio stations have white owners, controlling imagery with one hand while the other rips off profits, so most youth-oriented publications are owned by people well over forty.

The pervasiveness of these limitations partly explains why it has been all but impossible for young intellectuals to write for readers both young and old; why young political columnists are so few even though everyone knows that American youth have much political intelligence and voting power; or why so few *literary* critics emerged in the past decade; or why young critics with academic credentials find it difficult to publish interpretations of the classics; or why those independents who want to report their discoveries in avant-garde writing have been equally frustrated. The repressive situation, rather than the absence of talent or desire, also explains why no young critic today could possibly emulate Edmund Wilson's honorable example of exposing and explicating the best of his contemporaries. It explains how Ihab Hassan's pseudo-hip symposium about "The Humanities in Revolution," published as *Liberations* (1970), has no contributors born after 1928; and why so many lists of "intellectuals" or "writers" signing a public protest, giving a

156

series of lectures, or participating in a conference rarely include anyone under thirty-five; and why Jonathan Cott, whose essay on "Poetry" for *The New American Arts* (1965) remains a definitive treatment of the early sixties, was never asked to write again on poetry or even review young poets (he has since turned largely to rock criticism and interviewing). "It is prejudice when you can't get an apartment," Langston Hughes once noted. "It's probably prejudice when a skillful writer cannot publish because of some arbitrarily decided notion of what is or is not, as they tell me all the time, parochial material, of narrow interest, and so forth."

Attitudes of this sort also account for why some "rock critics" on established magazines are rather unlikely young writers, some of whom are musically incompetent. The best of them have been honest enough to be disturbed not only by the negative stereotype they help propagate, but also by the growing sense that their audience probably has a more intimate and discriminating sense of the music. Even after these young writers were accepted into an established magazine's family of regular contributors, they usually found their ambitions to write on non-kiddie subjects thwarted ("Remember, David, that you are our 'rock critic' "); as a result, most of them have grabbed every opportunity to do other kinds of writing elsewhere. The three issues of the periodical *US* (1969-70), published by Bantam Books and edited by Richard Goldstein (b. 1944), suggest that it was founded largely to allow rock critics to write on adult subjects, ranging from radical feminism to Charles Dickens. Similarly, large-circulation magazines will consider innovative writing only after its author has become a literary celebrity—William S. Burroughs, Allen Ginsberg, and John Barth being among the favored few.

In dealing with the young within their trade, established writers and editors continually reveal the temper of the time. In the epitome of generational tokenism, *World,* the magazine that Norman Cousins established in 1972, had a regular "youth columnist," plus a youngish part-time drama critic, Stephen Koch, though rarely publishing anyone else under thirty-five. A compendious, superficially open-minded anthology of recent fiction, *How We Live* (1968), coedited by L. Rust Hills (b. 1929), a sometime *Esquire* fiction editor-reviewer, and his wife, contains nothing by anyone younger than Philip Roth (b.

1933), while the list of 287 "names to watch" includes no one born later than 1939. Nonetheless, whenever young writers *are* included in old-boy anthologies of poetry, say, those who are chosen are invariably unrepresentative of their generation, rather derivative in style and ambitions, and often destined to be forgotten. When an old magazine tries to open its pages to independent young writers, its editors encounter abusive ridicule from the magazine's former supporters. Thus, Saul Bellow (in my judgment no friend of the young or new writing) tried to devastate *Partisan Review*'s William Phillips, at best a nodding acquaintance, by saying, "What frightens him is that he may not make it with the young and that people in New York will think him a silly dry old stick who is *out* of it."

Similarly, personal distance did not prevent older political writers from interpreting the protest activism of the radical young (usually to coincide with notions that these writers had about earlier protest movements); and until 1967 or so, unlike the thirties, all the books about "radical youth" (except for David Horowitz's pioneering *Student* [1962]) were written by older people who provided activist young readers with preliminary definitions of themselves and their behavior. The problem was not that young writers could not, or would not, or did not, produce such manuscripts, but that publishers placed their contracts with "more reliable" political authors (which is to say, older and more established). Because many literate young people have tended to regard everything appearing in reputable print far too literally, some of them echoed these old-fashioned interpretations before forging their own. By 1967 when the underground press began to make its impact, some of its liveliest writers were gingerly asked to contribute to more established publications—not, to be sure, on general-interest subjects such radicals treated in their own papers, but, given the kiddie-principle, the strictly circumscribed area of "youth culture."

III

I see hundreds of people coming round with children's books. I don't know what the rejection rate is on children's books, but it seems that the books that get published do so by accident. —Milton Glaser, "Most Are Bad" (1973).

Though books are theoretically a freer form of expression which evade the intimidation of advertisers and the formulas of periodicals, American book publishing has been no more open to the serious young writer than the world of magazines. By the early seventies, I began to regard the publication of literary books by young unknowns as reflecting miraculous breaks in a steadily constricting system. One truth that scarcely bears repeating is that most American publishers and editors simply do not care about the future of intelligent writing (at least not on company time). Their devotion to either the dollar or purely practical information places them outside, or beneath, the concern of my scrutiny which deals with those who care (or think they care). It has been reliably estimated that less than two dozen firms prominently publish literary books in America and that less than 50 people, all of whom work in New York or Boston, make the crucial decisions about what (or what not) to publish. Around this decision-making core work hundreds of assistants with varying degrees of access to their chiefs. It follows that what an individual editor in a possibly literate publishing house does "to make money" for his firm means less to this critique than what he regards as "serious" publishing. (Cookbooks, diet books, and travel guides clearly do not count. Nor do textbooks, which customarily popularize knowledge, rather than advance it.) The abundance of bad stuff drives out the good, in publishing's version of Gresham's Law, only by the editorial default of those who know what is better. Given the demands of both mass society and capitalist enterprise, it is not surprising that so many bad books are published; but what is terrifying are certain identifiable, industry-wide developments which keep so many better books, and talented writers, so much intelligent thought and experimental writing, unpublished. And even if good manuscripts get into print, they are often unadvertised, unreviewed, unavailable in bookstores, and unpurchased by libraries. Writers who are justifiably disgusted are inclined to dismiss publishers as "stupid idiots," but the reasons for their failures are more subtle, multiple, and scrutible.

To start with the first step, it should be understood that since publication requires the investment of money, publishers must be conned into doing good books. Unless the proposed project is a sure-fire best-seller (e.g., an ex-President's memoir), the burden of proving its publishability rests with the author and then with the firm's editor who, by extension, sponsors the author's project before the money sources. It should also be acknowledged that literate editors have dual vanities, wanting not only to make money for their firms but also to publish what they (and their colleagues and editorial competitors) will regard as estimable. They may also seek the friendship of authors they respect since the motives that got them into publishing rather than real estate persist, even if continually tempered by commercial considerations. On laudable projects they are prepared to lose money—senior editors having a larger license for losses than their juniors—for not everything published has been done primarily for a profit. That explains why a publishing editor, if asked what he "does," will probably recite not his money-makers but his most noted authors and titles; for no matter what a serious editor does to make money, he must do good books or else be considered (and perhaps consider himself) inferior. The assumption is that on the side, so to speak, he runs a lucrative business that supports his more memorable endeavors. It is these familiar signposts, customarily, that will be mentioned in his obituary, and most histories of publishing in general, or individual firms, speak not of profits but consequential titles issued. Needless to say, the existence of two kinds of publishing, with two kinds of books, forces editorial rhetoric to jump from one track to another, and this dichotomy has also been known to split apart a single editorial head.

Editors' loyalties are divided in other ways as well. They function as intermediaries between the author and their employing publisher and, thus, ideally represent the demands of each against the other, for among their purposes is preserving an amenable author-publisher relationship. In practice, however, an individual editor's stance on this spectrum of sympathy can vary enormously in the course of a publishing relationship. As an intermediary, the editor can support the author in asking the publisher for a larger cash advance; on the other hand, he can also represent the publisher in asking the writer for revisions in a completed manuscript. Some writers, particularly inexperienced ones, are especially sensitive to such suggestions; yet if the editorial demands become too imposing, a book comes to be written not for an audience but for a single man who nonetheless claims access to a larger public. In the Frenchman Robert Escarpit's formulation, the publisher "attempts to influence his authors in the interests of the public and the public in the interest of the author; in a word, he tries to induce a compatible writer-public relationship." Ultimately, an editor proves his value to his employer by delivering manuscripts that are profitable.

One fact distinguishing the present from the past is that dangerously few young editors have been especially interested in the best writing of their own generation; and these few incipient Maxwell Perkinses have found their immediate designs foiled and their sense of long-term obligation frustrated. Some learned that their superiors really hired them for assistance with their own projects rather than considering the new editor's own interests and recommendations, while others discovered, with disturbing frequency, that their superiors simply did not like, if they understood at all, the cultural enthusiasms of the young. Thus, well-intentioned young editors spent some of their most enjoyable office hours reading manuscripts that, frustratingly, their superiors would decline largely for inept or inadequate reasons. In addition, not only were these editors subject to the kiddie principle, but they also suffered what Douglas Mount defined as "an unarticulated prejudice that says you have to be around for quite a while before most of the people you need to know to publish books will give you the time of day." One reason for the delay is that a young editor is tutored "to think like a publisher" until he learns why he cannot publish the manuscripts that, several years before, would have excited him most; for the process of "editorial training" is designed to make his taste and decision-making as demonstrably conservative as that of his colleagues. Furthermore, when a young person joins an aging commercial establishment, his elders often fear that he might discover or initiate kinds of successful business that they had not considered before; so that those young editors who try to innovate, especially if indelicately, do not last very long in book publishing. These circumstances partially explain why large firms so rarely publish unsolicited manuscripts—no more than a few each year of the hundreds that are submitted and channeled into what is fondly called "the slush pile."

Instead, several young editors gained notoriety among their writing contemporaries by approaching the most conspicuous of them with the attractive claim to be "our generation's editor" (partially because book publishers are promiscuous flirts, always eager to "make friends" with those who might someday, in some way, be professionally useful); but these editors invariably returned a negative decision on whatever was submitted. In my observation, editors of this stripe also tend to take pride in what they "reject," which suggests that they receive such an abundance of good manuscripts that they can be very, very selective; however, he who rejects everything is, by definition, unselective. As noted before, editors are not reviewers saying "yes" or "no" to works presented to them, but potential sponsors who can change things only by saying "yes." A negative decision, unlike an unfavorable review, has no meaning because it indicates that nothing will happen, no book will appear in print, no communication will take place. Any fool can reject a manuscript, but acceptance, in contrast, requires intelligence and initiative (which accounts for why letters offering editorial acceptance are invariably more intelligent than those announcing rejection). In publishing, as in writing, you get points only for what you put into print—not for what you don't.

While other industries hired young managers attuned to the tastes of both young customers and young suppliers, publishing remained a generally conservative business, scarcely susceptible to innovative initiatives. Nonetheless, the breach in the market grew, beckoning to be filled and probably at a profit, too, if only an established publisher dared to open his operation to the literate young who constitute a larger book-buying public than ever before. The first to mount a significant project with young editors and young writers was Doubleday, establishing in the late sixties an imprint called "Projections" and giving its advocates, two editors named Matt Harris (b. 1942) and Ken Robbins (b. 1945), a vague mandate to publish several books annually. Doubleday also sponsored a large party to which many of New York's young writers and agents were invited, creating an impression of genuine intentions. Given such an unprecedented license, Harris and Robbins made several important and successful choices, including books by Earl M. Rausch, Frederick Barthelme, and Duane Michals. As well, they behaved within

162

the firm as honest and outspoken editors would and should. In less than a year, however, the Doubleday brass was so offended that, although the books did reasonably well, Harris quit and Robbins was peremptorily fired, the series subsequently disintegrating through neglect. All the commercial possibilities aside, the practice of young people writing and editing for each other was, and probably still is, too radical a precedent for big-time book publishing. The cutting paradox is this: Although most bookstores are in or near universities, and most books are destined for young readers who read and purchase books more abundantly than their elders and predecessors, publishers are slow to acknowledge the reality that movie producers discovered after much misfortune—that audiences today have radically different tastes from those of a decade ago. "The only losers," as A.J. Liebling once remarked in another context, "are the readers."

The Rationales
of Suppression

9

Yet the unpublished book, even the unpublishable one, often does cry out for attention. And today there is a whole literature of such works, what we might call *la bibliotheque imaginaire,* or more accurately, *la bibliotheque invisible,* circulating from hand to hand in the manner of the underground literature of contemporary Russia, to be thumbed over by literary agents, duly checked in and out again by publishers' readers, as far away from the printing presses a year after composition as they were before the authors had completed their first drafts. No one seems to have taken a census of all-but-professional writers lacking only the sanction of a single voice (or editorial committee) to become more published and professional.—Herbert R. Lottman, "The Invisible Writer" (1970).

The curious system of trade and traders which has grown up with the purpose or result of interposing itself between literature and the public...—Ezra Pound, "Summary" (1917).

The earliest publishers were primarily booksellers who closely observed the responses of their book-buying public; however, the growth of the business brought an increasing distance between editor and reader, forcing the publisher, in turn, to seek other signs of public response. The commercial problem, as noted before, is that a book, unlike a periodical, begins its life with no assured readers; and whereas a periodical addresses a single public with some degree of homogeneity, the produce of most trade publishers is aimed at a variety of publics ranging from intellectuals to hobbyists. For lack of any better criterion,

165

American publishers have come to base their crucial decisions upon precedents, so that an editor proposing a publishable manuscript on subject X argues that it should sell as well as previous books on subject X. By similar logic, it is thought that a new novel by XYZ should sell as successfully as its predecessors which the new one sufficiently resembles, and probably receive equally favorable reviews as well. Even in juvenile publishing, as the designer Milton Glaser observed, "The criteria are the usual: How similar is a new title to other successes, how significant is the author's name already, how closely does it cling to established formulas." The operative assumption, admittedly questionable, is that the people who liked the earlier work will also purchase the new one. (For a spell in the fifties, the fad-conscious pundits suggested that the super best-seller would deal with Lincoln's doctor's dog.)

Since precedents supposedly reveal not only the existence of a definable audience but its dimensions, the success of John Rechy's *City of Night* (1963), for instance, indicated a large interest in explicitly homosexual fiction. Rule-by-precedent also prompts publishers to demand revisions that will bring a potentially popular manuscript closer to commercially-proven stereotypes. As an anonymous author noted in *Encounter:* "They seem almost to demand that each new book should sell at least *as* widely as the book that made the breakthrough into success. Obviously, this is impossible, but the attitude is taken for granted; it is their right to get a best-seller every time." In truth, a literary product tailored for a particular audience is, like a textbook, usually born lifeless.

Commercial decisions regarding an accepted manuscript—printing, pricing, and advertising—are generally based upon a precedent-supported estimate of its expected sale. The editors at Harper & Row did not expect much response to a first novel by Erich Segal, since first novels usually have a small sale, the author was unknown, and a few other publishers had previously rejected the manuscript. As a result, the initial printing was quite modest—no more than that accorded other first novels; but subsequent fictions resembling *Love Story* (1970) would be more extravagantly published. Although Dr. David Reuben's *Everything You Always Wanted to Know About Sex* (1970) had also been widely rejected and contracted at a modest advance, the imitative pro-sex manuals would, thanks to the Reuben precedent, be contracted for larger advances and published with more commercial fanfare. Nonetheless, example after example suggests that intrinsic to all publishing decisions is a self-fulfilling prophecy: Publishers generally sell best the titles that they think will sell best. Efforts at advertising and publicity, for instance, more often than not produce commensurate results, while neglect at the home office usually produces a lack of interest in the book stores.

A publishing house also tends to construct a set of precedents based entirely upon its own particular experience, and these identify the kinds of books it "knows how [and thus, by contrast, doesn't know how] to publish." Though the categories of such home-grown policies differ enormously from house to house, they rule with nearly absolute authority within their immediate domain and in part define the character of the firm. Some publishers proudly boast that they do not issue literary books at all, no matter how fine. Even in those houses potentially sympathetic to intelligent writing, the rule of precedence makes editorial decisions a fundamentally conservative process, discriminating against both the new author who has not established his "track record" and manuscripts that are drastically different from anything seen before. That partially accounts for why, as Glaser observed, even though juvenile publishing has traditionally been more responsive to creativity, "most juveniles remind you of something you've seen a couple of hundred times." In practice, too, publishing precedents are often selectively cited, if not misinterpreted, as gambits in editorial debate, since they are at base so arbitrary and variable. It also seems indubitably amateur to base a pretense to "knowing what will sell" to a fickle public primarily upon an approximate measure of what did awhile back. Indeed, the strict rationalization of precedent can completely prevent the chance-taking that not only makes publishing more interesting than real estate, but might also produce a surprising success. There was no precedent for the sales, say, of *Jonathan Livingston Seagull* (1970).

Since publishing houses tend to be understaffed, considering how much work there is to be done, and since editors working in the office are subject to constant interruptions, decisions are often made in excessive haste, editors preferring the conservative, methodical routine to the exploration of alternatives. As they tend to want the books they think they want, or precedents rule they should want, most editors are rarely capable of responding to proposals they had not thought of before. Even if an individual good-seller successfully overcomes an editorial piety of what "cannot sell," such as the one proscribing West Indian novels or another stigmatizing radically-designed books, publishers will remain skeptical until several winners establish a new precedent. In spite of the critical and commercial success of Thomas Pynchon's *V.* (1963), nearly everyone in big-time publishing has long believed "there is no market" for mature and/or experimental first novels by young writers, thereby also killing much of the opportunity for issuing the books that might repudiate this policy. The bias against experimental fiction is so pervasive that had not *Lolita* succeeded so royally in 1958, it seems doubtful that Nabokov's true masterpiece, *Pale Fire* (1962), would have appeared in print at all.

Even the so-called literary publishers do remarkably few first novels, no matter the author's age. When *Panache* magazine asked American firms how many first novels they published in 1967-70 (four whole years), the survey revealed the following statistics: Farrar, eight; Viking, eight; Scribner's, seven; Holt, six; Grove, five; Grossman, five; Atheneum, five; Dutton, four; Atlantic, two; New Directions, one; Braziller, none—no more than two per year apiece out of the hundreds of completed "literary" manuscripts that were available. It is typical that book editors were continually declaring their "strong desire for a Vietnam novel"; however, only a few appeared while more than 42 publishers rejected an anthology of poetry by Vietnam veterans, *Winning Hearts & Minds* (1972), that was collectively self-published to favorable reviews. Kenneth Rexroth, after surveying American publishers of poetry, reported that half do just one or two books a year while "the largest commercial publishers and the small avant-garde specialists [ten percent of those queried] average the same number yearly—five." Such tokenism is, needless to say, conducive to cutthroat competition among the sellers and exploitation by the buyers, but hardly conducive to courageous writing by those who were chosen.

As first novels usually fail to turn a profit (or even get reviewed), a contract for a second is, in general, no easier to come by. Furthermore, since most novels are customarily issued in hardback, in deference to the refusal of the reviewing media to consider original paperbacks, and since the retail price of hardbacks is so high, the primary buyers of hardbound fiction are suburban ladies whose tastes thus determine the fortunes of novelists whose books are not paperbacked. Several firms reportedly have introduced the editorial category of "literary fiction," as distinct from mere "fiction," to classify novels destined not for suburban ladies but a smaller university audience, putting "literature" (and its sponsoring editors) yet further on the defensive. Here as elsewhere, so many *wrong* reasons and indices inform those decision-making processes that, in turn, determine the life of art, ideas, and people.

Subservience to precedence also explains why publishers totally avoid experimental poetry even though, as Kenneth Rexroth accurately observes, "only avant-garde poetry sells, or ever has" (aside from trash like Rod McKuen's); and the audience for serious poetry is increasing faster than that for fiction. Examples like this illustrate that American publishers know considerably less about "what won't sell" than their declarations suggest; for gamblers though they be, they favor conservative principles of wagering. Indeed, all this accounts for why, in spite of a growing public for poetry, the fortunes of poetic communication today are no better now than they were in the mid-twenties when Edmund Wilson reported that even the best of his contemporaries "are having difficulty getting their poems published." As non-publication is not only a cultural reality but a personal predicament, everyone involved in literature today knows at least one good much-published writer—not just poets—broken in spirit by the misfortune of an "unacceptable" manuscript.

Enlightened editors often contend, in reply, that the business is now more open to experimental literature than before, one of them telling me about recent titles "that could not have been done a decade ago"; but as the forms and frontiers of advanced writing have changed drastically in the interim, the kinds of radical works that *could not have been written* a decade ago (such as those discussed in the latter chapters of this book) remain, as we shall see, almost totally unpublished and thus invisible to both publishers and critics (and the literate public). Moreover, precisely on this issue of precedence does publishing diametrically differ from serious writing, for the great books or the great ideas, the ones really worth doing, are drastically unlike anything done before. It has also been my observation that the same editors who boast that "everything good gets published" are those who are least likely to publish a previously unsolicited manuscript.

The rule of precedence also explains publishing fads, one great success breeding its numerous imitators; so that not only did *The Sensuous Woman* (1970) beget *The Sensuous Man* (1971), but a dozen different editions of *Pride and Prejudice* are currently in print, each new one trying to succeed on the reputation of its predecessors. Similarly, once Claude Brown's *Manchild in the Promised Land* (1965) sold so well, publishers developed a new and eager interest in Negro and Puerto Rican authors who told similar stories of their ghetto youth (and reiterated the same sociological clichés). The precedent established was not for "black books" in general, but only for a particular kind (and plot and theme) until it appeared that the market for this cliché was satiated. If several publishers have successful volumes on a "hot" subject, such as rock or women's liberation, yet others will turn ripe for something similar. However, once the sales for such books show symptoms of dwindling, publishers will rule the fad has "been killed" even though the movement generating the fad, such as women's liberation or rock music, will continue to prosper. All this partially explains why current editorial procedures are hardly conducive to intelligent publishing or why the book industry is so self-involved— more subservient to its own current myths than any larger reality; but since such myths invariably change, a short personal memory seems more typical in the trade than a long one.

The principle of success's imitations is one reason why so many indisputably bad books (or redundant paperbacks) are published. Another reason is gang-selling which is the insistence that less desirable titles be purchased along with the most desirable. This is practiced not only by agents peddling books to publishers, but more often by hardback houses leasing rights to paperbackers. A third reason is that the few publishers owning their own printing plants are obliged to produce far in excess of what might otherwise be prudent. "A big publishing house like

Doubleday," notes Dwight Macdonald, "must have hundreds of titles a year to keep its presses busy; the overhead goes on, the more books produced the cheaper [it is] to produce each one." A chief book reviewer at *Time*, Timothy Foote, among others, once proposed the "United States publishers . . . should publish fewer books," which seems attractive in theory; but *publishing precedent suggests that more good manuscripts than junk would disappear from public view.*

By the sixties, decisions in publishing houses were made either by a committee in which sales executives sometimes participated (the most conservative method), or by an experienced senior editor acting autonomously as his own sub-publisher, so to speak. The former arrangement usually smothered the "inexperienced" young editor (and also the woman editor); but in the latter arrangement, the young editor's opportunities depended not upon his appeals to the firm's editor-in-chief, as was customary, but upon his rapport with his immediate superior. Since a senior editor's aims were usually more particular, purposeful, and parochial than those of an editor-in-chief, the young man fell into line rather than forging new paths. It was also more common, as noted before, for the literate young editor to follow the example of such earlier editorial whiz kids as Jason Epstein and Arthur A. Cohen, the original quality paperbackers, who made themselves the servants of an older generation of established writers, rather than publishing their own contemporaries. The trouble has been that quality paperbacking as an editorial process represents not the discovering and nurturing of new talent, but the purchasing and refurbishing of established reputations; "leech publishing" was Alan Swallow's epithet for it. In truth, the established system itself eventually compromised the radical and generational impulses of those young editors who survived within big-time publishing. (The classic example of finkiness—admittedly extreme in content, though not untypical in form—was the under-25 president of a pop record company who reportedly cancelled contracts with fourteen groups for "promoting and glorifying hard drugs" and then, in an interview, echoed all the ignoramuses over forty by including marijuana among "the hard drugs.")

Never before, in brief, had an emerging literary generation

171

found the book publishing situation so bleak; for in sharp contrast to earlier times no young editor had established himself as serving the best writers of his generation—nor did any literary agent. In an anthology of *Young American Authors* (1967), to cite one selective example, I noted that no single publisher had more than two of the thirty-eight authors under contract; the fact that no house had more than that indicated that nobody then was particularly looking. Though the fact of that book's publication would seem to refute some contentions made in this chapter, most everything else about the collection confirms it. The book also went unreviewed, as did the several other "young" anthologies published about that time (even though, one would think, their collective appearance was itself newsworthy); and the few notices typically concentrated more upon the book's purposes or my polemical introduction—the *existence* of young writers being the crucial issue—instead of considering the individual selections or their general quality. Moreover, most writers included in the book were unknown to reviewers even though some of them had been published frequently (and I, for one, had appreciated their work); and a few contributors wrote to tell me that, indicatively, they had not known before of most of the others.

Soon after *The Young American Writers* appeared, several contributors on their own initiative sent me book-length manuscripts with the hope that I could place them with publishers. Some of the works were extraordinary, which made me suffer the pain of not knowing who to show them to. My anthology's publisher, the trade division of Funk & Wagnalls, was squashed by its conglomerate owner, and other New York houses, for all the reasons noted already, were not receptive.

The writers I favored in 1967 have not, by and large, fared particularly well since then with commercial publishing. Though Joyce Carol Oates and Renata Adler have become more famous, Frank Chin's novel, part of which I included, still remains unpublished, as are novels by Eric Felderman, Arno Karlen, Kenneth King, in addition to R.H.W. Dillard's collection of stories, *Dance, Wolf, Dance.* Kenneth Gangemi's *Olt* was published in England before its acceptance here to surprisingly cordial reviews; however, three of his later experimental novels have, at last count, never appeared in print. Tom Veitch's *The Luis Armed Story* has appeared only in Germany, the original

172

English-language text still awaiting a native publisher, while Ronald Tavel's remarkable novel, *Street of Stairs,* appeared only in a severely abridged form, its publisher defaulting on his promise to do the entire book. In the twenties, Scribner's and Liveright earned their high reputations (and subsequent fortune) by publishing many of the best of the emerging young writers. No firm since then has even tried. "Prejudice," Langston Hughes continues, "doesn't keep a writer from writing. If you're colored, you can write all you want to, but just you try to sell it, that's all."

II

> The great mystery in the publishing of poetry is not the unprofitability of good poetry, once it gets published, but the difficulty it has of getting published in the first place, and the astonishing bulk of mediocre, utterly characterless verse that does get published, year after year. —Kenneth Rexroth, *The Alternative Society* (1970).

Indeed, if the manuscript submitted to me were not only good but stylistically unusual (as many of my selections were), I felt even less optimistic. Only three years before, nearly two dozen American publishers rejected the manuscript that became John Barth's *Giles Goat-Boy;* and since that novel eventually was a best-seller as well as a critical success, and its sparsely-touted author became an acknowledged great innovator, the indisputable fact is that a lot of Eastern literary editors did not recognize the inventive, popular masterpiece that passed before their eyes.

Nearly as many missed an invitation to do Richard Brautigan's fiction a few years later and Kerouac's *On the Road* (1957) a decade before. Typically, publishers regard the successes accorded these writers, as well as Borges and Beckett, to indicate not a potential audience for serious writing, but "mysterious exceptions" to sanctified precedent.

It is not surprising, therefore, that many of England's best experimental novelists have never been published here, even though reprinting books already published in English would not be expensive: the fictional works of Wilson Harris (eleven), B. S. Johnson (seven), Andrew Salkey (five), Derek Ingry (two), as well as Tom Phillips and Sidney Goodsir Smith (one master-piece apiece). Of the seventeen American writers included in Eugene Wildman's path-breaking international anthology, *Experiments in Prose* (1969), only three have ever had commercial publishers for their creative work. Of the seventy or so American contributors to my own recent anthology of innovative fiction, *Breakthrough Fictioneers* (1973), less than twenty have ever had their creative books commercially published; and although most of the thirty or so Europeans in this anthology have had works commercially published in their native countries, books by only three have appeared here, these statistics, like the others, suggesting a serious loss of other kinds of possible communication. It should also be noted that, here and elsewhere, I am citing *published* texts and authors because these works cannot be dismissed, as is the custom, as "unpublishable in its present form."

Even by the seventies, it was practically impossible to place a book that was innovative in appearance unless its author (or coauthor) was a youth-cult celebrity such as Marshall McLuhan or Buckminster Fuller, Abbie Hoffman or Jerry Rubin, the precedent predisposed to celebrities negating the rule opposed to radical design. (Over thirty of them, however, declined Abbie Hoffman's *Steal This Book* [1970], which, unlike *Woodstock Nation* [1969], was more radical in content than design.) Although visual poetry was an international movement, all the American anthologies of "concrete," as it was initially called, were issued by small presses; and a commercial publisher has yet to issue a single one-man collection of such work. Visual poetry rarely, if ever, appears in *Poetry* or other old literary journals, and it could be said that the complete absence of it, along with other avant-garde forms, in the poetry magazines and anthologies is one symptom of literary opportunism in its current form, impressing academics by the neglect of what they consider "not poetry." (Indeed, resistances to this hybrid art remain so strong that a recent Farrar, Straus anthology of Filippo Marinetti's *Selected Writings* [1972] omits *entirely* his pioneering contributions to the genre!) Nor has a book-length visual fiction ever been commercially produced in the U.S. except as a juvenile; it is appalling that some of Edward Gorey's more radical tales sneaked out through publishing's side door.

For certain classes of writing, U.S. publishing has repealed "freedom of the press" by default, totally without Congressional intervention, as specified in the Constitution; and spurned writers have discovered that viable alternatives, in contrast to theoretical ones, are not immediately available. Since there is no real discrimination in either commercial acceptance or rejection, "Yes" is as culturally meaningless as "No"; and since more bad books than good flow out of the publishing houses, any claims for the literary authority of the industry are hard to respect. Indeed, a radical manuscript that presently remains persistently unpublished gains a certain cachet in discriminating circles, not only for the work's intrinsic integrity, but also for its implicit criticism of currently established systems. In truth, the same large firms that published the "modern classics" we read in college are failing to publish the literature our children will study with respect. "The only losers," to quote Liebling again, "are the readers."

The problem in its largest terms in both America and most of Europe is this: The same boom in child-bearing, education, and leisure that produced an increase in both the populace of literate readers and the number of serious writers has not been accompanied by comparable expansions of the channels of communication. The recent decrease in both marriage and child-bearing among the intellectual classes, coupled with the increases in socio-cultural welfare, means that many more people have more free time to pursue serious literary work. The creative writing programs sponsored by American academies not only have increased the supply of competent young writers, but also have given their older teachers more time to write, as well as more incentive to be published.

All these developments increased the competition for available printed space. In the most drastic discrepancy, more people produced more short stories than ever before for fewer and fewer outlets. Albert Drake testified that a "university-subsidized quarterly" he once coedited received about "four stories a day"—or 360 per quarter—of which, given the magazine's editorial allocations, only two were published. As more and more talented writers emerged and the quantity of quality doubled or maybe tripled in less than two decades, the existing channels, while prospering, became less and less responsive to new blood.

Since commercial publishing has failed its responsibility to the future of literature and will probably continue to do so, serious writers who are young, who live outside New York, and/or whose work is unusual or counter-stereotypical, can no longer approach the possibility of publication with much hope. Half, maybe more, of the consequential literature written today does not get commercially published, and too much valuable energy is continually wasted in the futile search for channels hopefully open to intelligent communication—too much is wasted upon finding the means, rather than creating the ends. By the seventies, it became clear that there were only two reasons why even the best of the unestablished writers' books might ever appear in money-making public print—someone in sufficient editorial power strongly wanted to see his manuscript done or publishers simply needed books, new books of any kind, to sell.

III

The old regime will seek to isolate the new by performing upon it the easy surgery of political falsification. . . . Every effort, in short, will be made to *ex-communicate* the new generation, so that their writing and their politics may be regarded as making up a kind of diabolic totality, which would render unnecessary any sort of rational discussion of the merits of either. —*Partisan Review,* "Editorial Statement" (Dec., 1937).

An author's writings represent an investment of time and energy that, if successful, produces dividends without further labor; so that every successful writer has property to protect against a possible decline in value. Whereas successful elders in earlier times were sure of their perspective and the wisdom of their patiently accumulated experience, the acceleration of historical changes has brought doubt and anxiety to this expectation of authority. It is also true that every established generation predictably defends *its* youth, with varying degrees of chauvinism, as superior to subsequent cultural adventures and adventurers. That is natural and, as such, perhaps acceptable; but what is unprecedented today, as well as unacceptable, is the vehemence of the establishment's attack upon the literate young. It was Malcolm Cowley who noted in *The Literary Situation* (1954) that the writers emerging at that time seemed "silent" because they had published fewer books and magazine articles "than their predecessors had published at the same age. That was largely the fault of publishers and editors." The emerging generation today has been yet more drastically silenced.

Derogatory images of intellectual youth have flooded the literary press; and though young people have found these characterizations of themselves incredible beyond belief, they have failed to perceive how such negative portraiture has served to rationalize the emerging McCarthyism of "the intellectuals." A typical sort of denigration eagerly identifies sub-literate (or ex-literate) young publicists as epitomizing the supposedly lesser intelligence of an entire cultural generation. Thus does the drama dean Robert Brustein, no friend of any young other than his favorite students, offer the following example of "historical" contrast: "The strong, intelligent politics of Marx and Trotsky are drowned out by the mindless yippie yells of Abbie Hoffman and Jerry Rubin." What seems at first a criticism of political style is actually a professorial judgment which, by contrasting two sets of personalities and their intellects, functions contextually as a literary-political attack upon the radical young, flunking them as "mindless." It is also unfortunate that many young people, so humbled by intellectual reputation and so credulous about everything appearing in accredited print, believe such nonsense about themselves, even though their own experience suggests contrary self-interpretations. When they accept such slanderous nonsense, young people succumb to imaginary symptoms rather than ·confront real problems. In truth, because the older generation controls the media in which such generalizations about the young are made, the contrary view about their intelligence and maturity does not often appear in public print.

The key manifesto in the decimation of the literate young (making explicit those repressive sentiments that might otherwise have remained implicit) is the concluding part of Irving Howe's awesomely self-serving essay on "The New York Intellectuals," originally published in *Commentary* (October, 1968) and subsequently reprinted in his book, *Decline of the New* (Harcourt, Brace, 1970), and elsewhere. Occasionally revelatory in spite of its apologetic purposes, this essay (quoted before) charts the intellectual and social success of the New York mob, celebrating their supposed achievement and rationalizing their desire for ever-increasing incomes. It also acknowledges intellectual limitations and laments the loss of both coherence and missionary spirit, especially in the face of a new challenge. The earlier literary-political "achievement," in Howe's view, came in helping "destroy—once and for all, I could have said until recently—Stalinism as a force in our intellectual life, and with Stalinism those varieties of Populist sentimentality which the Communist movement of the late thirties exploited with notable skill." The real success, however, lay not in devastating Stalinism, which died largely of its own insufficiencies, but in wiping out Communist writers; for, as noted before, when the New York literary mob talks political activism, the context of their remarks—the scene of their real action—is literary politics.

The latest challenge to the mob is, predictably, the "new sensibility" of "a rising young generation," which is portrayed as a threat to western culture. Into an ashcan marked "new" and "young" Howe dumps everything he dislikes in contemporary culture (including some junk that none of the young or new would claim), often without the academic courtesy of first-hand acquaintance and by the use of such discreditable techniques as guilt-by-rhetorical-association. Fomenting an ideology of literary-political repression, Howe speaks of a "rising younger generation of intellectuals [which] matters, thus far, not so much for its leading figures and their meagre accomplishments, but for the political-cultural style—what I shall call the new sensibility—it thrusts into absolute opposition both to the New York writers and to other groups." His Marxian rhetoric continues: "Though linked to New Left politics, it goes beyond any politics, making itself felt, like a spreading blot of anti-intellectualism, in every area of intellectual life." Howe's dramaturgy portrays "the younger generation of intellectuals" as cultural heirs to the Communists, in spite of their anarchist sympathies and professional disorganization. Nonetheless, their arrival should inspire "enough energy and coherence to make possible a sustained confrontation" with the "new sensibility"; and his call for a professional pogrom goes out not only to all the old cold-warriors, but also to an increasing number of fellow-travelers in academia and publishing.

Philip Rahv likewise connects the new and the young as Culture's primary antagonists by charging in his latest book that the criticism of contemporary writing, once the domain of first-level critics, "has been preempted by younger men, swinging reviewers rather than critics in any proper sense of the term, who . . . welcome every whim of fad and fashion as a creative 'breakthrough' and a 'new' conquest of imaginative experience." He continues, "In a situation of this kind, the appearance of another Leavis, or Eliot, or critics of like caliber, is no longer to be expected"—his Higher Authority denying in advance the possibility of merit. Indeed, the fact that Howe and Rahv edit two of America's more powerful quarterlies should indicate how established their literary-political viewpoint is, as well as how "open" their pages are to independent young writers, new literature, or contrary views about either subject.

So accustomed has Irving Howe become to portraying his end of the mob as a beleaguered minority that he suggests the young are more powerful (which is news to everyone I know). The tipoff to the contrary truth is that they seem, like the devil in Catholic theology, invisible enough to be indescribable. "Not yet fully cohered," Howe writes in this same essay, "this new cultural group cannot yet be fully defined, nor is it possible fully to describe its projected sensibility, since it declares itself through a refusal of both coherence and definition." Lines like these illustrate the familiar maxim about power corrupting, not only an intellectual's career but his perception of the world. Howe's essay talks, in the end, not of real people but of a cause to unite the mob (along with its allies) and extend its collective life; for Howe's real interest is not high criticism or intellectual values but low literary politics.

The real "threat" of young writers lies, of course, in the possibility that the best of them might be more honest, more literate, and perhaps more talented, as well as more victimized (and perhaps more humane) than their immediate predecessors. The supposed "adoration of the young" is clearly a myth propagated not by young writers but by their elders, justifying all sorts of exploitation and repression, as well as inviting, merely by the phrase itself, resentment and *ressentiment.*

Howe's judgments and invocation also constitute a self-fulfilling prophecy whereby the powerful class holds that the powerless, such as blacks, are generally inferior because their "accomplishments are so meagre." The deceit is that many genuine accomplishments go unrecognized, in part because the powerful cannot afford to recognize them, but mostly because the channels of communication have prevented their public dissemination. In this case, the high odds already discriminating against young writers are further stacked by the mobilized prejudice of the cultural handicappers, thus all but insuring that no fresh horse gets beyond the gate (at least in those races duly fixed). Never before has an entrenched generation been so aware, and yet neglectful, of the intelligence of the young. By decimating professional opportunities, literary old-boys have successfully prevented the emergence of both "leading figures" (who would then be identified by name) and "accomplishments" which could then be publicly acknowledged, these discouraging circumstances thus "proving" the prophecy about the absence of literary talent. (Needless to say, should no one emerge at all, what is *actually proved* is not the absence of talent or ambition, but the real efficacy of such a focused professional beating. Thus do muggers mug in more ways than one.)

If, as I suspect, the tradition of literary professionalism is dying, a primary reason is simply all the resistances to the evolution of writing. As the New York literary mob at its worst had, in Howe's testimony, previously "allowed their anti-Communism to become something cheap and illiberal," so had Howe indulged the mob's generational antagonism; and he differs from other no-less-than-forty-grand-a-year ex-radicals in being not untypical but more explicit. All this rationalized aggression seems, it should be noted, more typical of a military-industrial executive whose company produces a technology of declining usefulness; perhaps the next step will be a demand for a government subsidy!

When an individual writer loses access to the channels of communication because of circumstances beyond his control or for reasons other than intrinsic quality, the result is a personal tragedy that may, like illness or injury, take its deleterious toll; but when a whole class of writers encounters such disadvantage, the resulting losses are collective, affecting readers as well as writers. (Among the more obvious symptoms is a lack of generational intelligence at a time when the conflicts of our culture are more generational than anything else, and pervasive confusion in the articulation of those dimensions of collective consciousness customarily shaped by reading.) For the blockage in communication is, indeed, an instrument of repression. These developments have effectively destroyed what Lewis S. Feuer shrewdly calls "the generational equilibrium," which he identifies as the primary reason why America has so far largely avoided generational conflict—"when no generation feels that its energies and intelligence are being frustrated by others, when no generation feels that solely because of its years it is being deprived of its proper place in society." That the world is conservative is inevitable, but that it should be murderously so, as well as corrupt, is not acceptable. A further, equally ferocious misfortune is that the avarice of culture's powerful class has successfully eliminated or alienated those emerging writers who are, in spite of intellectual differences, most likely to honor and remember in print whatever legitimate achievements their predecessors have made; so that the price of the established generation's greed, which never comes cheap, is finally their *own* ignominy and cultural death.

All this self-interest, hypocrisy, corruption, and repression remain, of course, minuscule, compared to what happens throughout American society today. Not only are the sums exchanged in the editorial-industrial complex quite negligible compared to those involved in a defense contract, but no literary mafia is one-tenth as mean-spirited and destructive as the original one. The more essential charge here is that just as the corruption of policemen debases their collective reputation, so has the literary world failed its self-image, precisely because it reflects rather than transcends the larger society; and the guardians of culture seem to be no better than the guardians of the peace at exposing and eradicating internal corruption. Not only its literary powerhouses but the system itself exhibits moral fibre no tougher than that of a military-industrial corporation nibbling at the public pie, plus a resistance to the idealistic young equal to that of the American Medical Association.

It has been commonly understood that art and literature forge a different, special realm, representing and sustaining what is best in man and his works; and precisely in the preservation of ideals and possibilities, as well as the endless exposure of hypocrisy and constraint, does writing have its social role. "It is one of the great themes of the sixties that intellectuals as a group felt they should themselves supply to a democracy those public virtues not accounted for by mere electoral representation," notes the critic Ronald Berman. "All kinds of demands have been made, not the least of which is that intellectuals should embody our moral impulses." However, in comparison to the exemplary behavior of certain heroic artists and intellectuals in Russia, who have risked their lives to preserve certain conceptions of opportunity and human decency, Americans of the same generation and profession seem to exploit public faith in literature's reputation for their personal profit. The depressing truth is that the intellectual world has sacrificed its integrity and openness, along with its capacities for courage and reform, especially of itself. As these facts alone forbode the likely end of intelligent writing, so the restoration of that moral leverage along with opening the channels of cultural communication must be counted among the most necessary and difficult tasks confronting my own generation.

The Literary-
10   Industrial Complex

In New York, the editorial center of the country, the writer is much less important to the complicated heavy industry of literature in the 60s than the three "practical" figures mentioned above [the Agent, Editor and Publisher]. He can be operated on, bought, sold and dismissed, because he is not as significant (and can always be replaced!) as the men and women who use him for their own purposes. . . . Words are deadly cheap to the people who puff your writer up, because they are playing for higher stakes and in a game where the writer is a mere idiot child whimpering about verities that every "adult" knows are nuseryschool jazz compared to the mammoth merchandising network. —Seymour Krim, "The Unimportant Writer" (1962).

But, in a sense, shrewd gambling—finding, promoting and exploiting winners—is what hardcover publishing is all about these days. —Robert Stein, "What Am I Bid for Lyndon Johnson?" (1971).

As publishing has grown more competitive, the fortunes of a book have come to depend a great deal on timing, presentation, price, jacket design, the number printed, the method of advertising, the possibilities of serialization, television and a dozen other forms of publicity. —Michael S. Howard, *Jonathan Cape, Publisher* (1971).

Developments within the industry itself made young and unknown writers less essential than before. For one thing, book-publishing became a far more profitable business in the sixties, expanding steadily from 1955 to 1967, thanks first to the affluence of a larger reading public which also had more leisure time, and then to the post-Sputnik boom in higher education. As increasing numbers of students needed texts and related books, there were more governmental expenditures, especially during the Johnson Presidency, for books of all kinds. Though distractions to reading were more plentiful, more books were bought and presumably read than ever before. The U.S. book-buying public grew to over fifteen million people. The impact of television notwithstanding, between 1960 and 1970, according to Ken McCormick, Doubleday's former editor-in-chief, total annual book sales rose from $1,130,000 to a gross of nearly $3 billion. While receipts from "trade books" rose from $460 million to $1,305,000,000, "trade textbooks in 1960 accounted for almost $350 million and in 1970 almost $870 million." Acknowledging the continuing rise in retail prices, McCormick notes that, "Inflation allows for some of the increase, but not all that much." Individual firms grew along with the industry. Harper's, for instance, which annually sold about $2 million worth of books during the twenties, now grosses over $60 million a year. Employing less than a dozen full-time salesmen then, it presently has over two hundred distributed among several "divisions."

The impact of this boom has had many dimensions, only some of which are readily apparent. Not only do good books get more readers than before, but those few very successful "trade" books do spectacularly well, earning far more money, mostly from subsidiary rights (paperbacks, book clubs, movies), than ever before. Also, everyone associated with a hugely prospering title commands unprecedentedly large salaries or advances. The boom has also brought unexpected success to certain small-sized literary houses whose best books continue to sell steadily, long after they were originally published; for since a thriving "backlist" requires neither promotion nor a new typesetting, it customarily earns a higher rate of profit than a firm's new publications.

The steady increase in retail prices (nearly doubling over the past decade for books of comparable size and length) has more than sufficiently compensated for an equally steady increase in the costs of book production. High retail prices have also contributed to the precipitous increase in the number of book clubs—from fifteen to over a hundred in the past decade; for if the initial publisher kept the list price of a hardback exorbitantly high, then the book club (as well as the reprinter and the remainder shop) could offer their customers the appearance of greater savings. Another popular by-product of prosperity was described by the publisher William Jovanovich as " 'made' or 'packaged' books that are conceived and produced for people who really do not read. One recognizes them instantly and conveniently by their titles—*Sexual Satisfaction in Marriage, How to Take Ten Strokes Off Your Golf Game, Pictures of the Civil War.*"

The larger American trade publishers—the literary-industrial complex—responded to the new prosperity by developing a consuming interest in the big killing. Individual firms differ, to be sure, but certain practices and assumptions have become almost pervasive. Anything offering the promise of hugh success now commands a comparably huge advance, which is often several times larger than what was available only a decade before. Authors of previous best-sellers are particularly favored, partly because the rule of precedent suggests that their next book will continue to attract a large audience, but also because such stars radiate an "aura" that seduces publishers as well as readers.

Not only are literary agents more adept at scoring extravagant contracts for patently hyper-commercial properties, but editors make their reputations not upon the solidity and breadth of their commitments but upon a few fortuitous choices—"big books," as they are called. Indeed, if the sponsor of a recent super-seller is not rewarded within his own firm, he usually receives offers of lucrative positions elsewhere; and top-level jobs are lost, by contrast, on a run of unprofitable extravagances. Oscar Dystel, the president of Bantam Books, speaks for his colleagues in judging that, "There is no disastrous situation in publishing which cannot be saved by the publication of one really big best-seller." (Here and elsewhere, most statements made by insiders about "publishing" in general also reflect, upon close inspection, the practices and aspirations of their particular firms.) Paperbackers like Bantam have learned how to initiate their own "big books," which are mostly "specials" dependent upon "big" newspaper stories such as *The Pentagon Papers* and *Attica.* Even supposedly more prestigious houses such as Quadrangle or Atheneum concentrate not upon developing a variously excellent list, but upon publishing a small number of books, a preselected few of which demand optimal performance from the middle-sized firm's promotional and marketing personnel.

In both large firms and small, merely identifying a forth-coming title as "the big book" serves to mobilize all the editors, promotion people, and salesmen who are customarily prepared to respond to the expectations of their commander-in-chief; and, for reasons noted before, supreme effort usually pays off. As Simon Michael Bessie, president of Atheneum, rationalized to a *New York Times* reporter: "The book that is successful in the marketplace is immensely successful—either in its own sales, or in its book club or paperback sales—and earns a great deal of money, before taxes. The book that fails, fails." It follows that the publishers privately most envied (though publicly despised) are no longer those with a broad base of quality merchandise, but Bernard Geis and Lyle Stuart, small-list daredevils who specialize in venally conceived, frugally advanced, and vulgarly promoted best sellers. Back in the late fifties, Alfred A. Knopf himself rejected *The Chapman Report* (1960) by Irving Wallace, two of whose books he had published before, even though he knew this one would be a super-seller. Knopf's reason was reportedly the new book's salaciousness (by fifties standards). It is hard to imagine, by contrast, a prominent publisher today refusing a comparable commercial opportunity.

Even among the more reputable firms, the lushest book contracts go either to authors with a "track record" of best-sellers or to celebrities so famous that a publisher can assume a large book-buying public will want to read their words. Advances of this latter kind are, needless to say, especially risky, not only because the product, even if ghost-written and heavily edited, might be abominable, but also because books take so long to be written, and then produced, that the new author's celebrity or the issue on which it was based might disappear from public view.

Only by such a "principle," nonetheless, could McGraw-Hill, Dell paperback, and the Book-of-the-Month Club commit nearly a million dollars to Clifford Irving's promised *Autobiography of Howard Hughes,* a book they had never seen, whose origins were dubious, and which was eventually exposed as a hoax. "The way this book was handled illustrates the whole philosophy of the publishing industry," Irving noted, on his way to jail. "Go for the big blockbuster, the book that is going to sell hundreds of thousands of copies and make millions of dollars, and never mind about writers." Some might rationalize that the profits earned by the blockbuster could then be devoted to more estimable books. However, as Susannah Lessard perceived, "The bulk of the money which comes in from one best-seller will have to be turned into buying and promoting the next one." The best-seller is not an economic foundation for Literature, but an insatiable end in itself.

Exorbitant advances are also justified within the firm by the principle of the loss-leader—the single enticing book that is worth contracting at almost any price, even if it alone loses money, because it will induce every bookstore manager in the country to stock the firm's other new titles. These front-runners also serve to publish—to announce the existence of—the firm's entire current output within the trade, much as advertisements in *Publishers Weekly* aim at telling salesmen what they ought to feature and retailers what they ought to stock. It must be understood that publishers' salesmen compete in practice not for individual customers, but for the limited display space available in the retail outlet. Thus, they fight primarily for the interest and enthusiasm of the bookstore's manager.

As America has less than fifteen hundred retail outlets for new hardbacks, the competition at this local level can be fierce; and one unfortunate effect of the quality paperback revolution has been a tougher battle for bookstore show space, bad books again driving out good ones. Once on display, however, books compete with each other for customers—thus the emphasis upon attractive dustjackets. Since unsold hardbacks are customarily returned to their publishers for credit usually within a few months of their arrival in the store, a salesman is reluctant to "lend" a title that will not be displayed, just as the manager is reluctant to display a title that will not sell quickly. This explains why few bookstores in America stock any unheralded titles or, indeed, any hardback books at all, apart from reference classics, that are more than a year old. The competition for paperback display space in drugstores and at newsstands is even more severe, as the paperback distributor is allowed to remove titles that do not sell, ripping off the cover, which is returned to the publisher for credit, while the rest of the book is destroyed. The average "shelf life" for a mass paperback is 11½ days— much like a fresh vegetable in a grocery store; and more than half of the paperback books in America are, in an epitome of atrocious waste, squashed, unread, back into pulp simply because they are cheaper to destroy than return.

In the final accounting, hardback publishers lose far less money on unprecedented projects (or high quality ones) than upon books like those that are currently successful, for the rule of precedence is as much of a trap as a treasure. In general, less money is lost on proposals offered to publishers than on their own "brilliant ideas" for initiating a quick killing. One reason for this is that the larger the initial investment in a book, the greater the likely cost to push it onto the marketplace—not only with advertisements (generally accorded only to best-sellers or books expected to be), but with publicity efforts and promotional expenses. This accounts for why publishers, as a rule, lose more money on *shlock* they expect to be lucrative, or large advances, or advertisements and over-printings of expected big-sellers than on anything resembling genuine literature, which can generally be contracted at a comparatively low price. Even in "risk capital" there are double standards.

Indeed, high-flying publishers lose so much money on inept investments that they partially compensate by selling books at several multiples of the physical object's actual cost; and because this manufacturing expense divides into two parts—the cost of preparing the master plates and the cost of printing the actual books—all *re*printings require only the second kind of expenditure. This progressive decline in production costs—in hardcover down almost to the per-unit levels of a paperback—is what makes a true best-seller so profitable, aside from subsidiary rights, regardless of its costs in author's advances or editors' energy. Publishers can, therefore, sometimes advance huge sums that, by normal rates of royalty, could not possibly be earned back, for the publisher is bound to make far more profit than the book's author for comparatively less work—in sum, partially preparing the manuscript, paying the printer, and peddling the produce. The rest, as they say, is "overhead."

Such probable best-sellers, helped by advertising and promotion, also fetch lucrative subsidiary contracts *before* publication, not only from paperback publishers, the mass magazines, and the book clubs, but also from movie producers; so that the money lost on the hardbound alone can be swiftly recouped—the original edition becoming a "loss leader" in other ways as well. In the evolution of the business, the dollar-volume of paperbacks has become twice that of hardcover books in spite of the lower per-unit retail price, and the book clubs have come to sell twice as many hardbacks as all American bookstores. When slick magazines excerpt from the blockbuster and the reviewing media feature it, what is reinforced is not just the fortunes of that particular title but the operation of the entire literary-industrial complex. Therefore, in contracting such milkable cows, hardback publishers find themselves thinking less of a large public of possible readers than of the recent selections of a few subsidiary-media moguls who in turn supervise channels running to a massive audience.

It would be naive to say, however, that such mass-moguls simply "give the public what it wants," for not only do popular tastes change too radically in time to be considered a fixed entity, but very large sales also reflect as self-fulling prophecies what the media moguls think the masses want and thus promote in massive ways what is available and what has already been bought. In Q.D. Leavis' classic aphorism, "What the public wants is not felt, until supplied." Furthermore, these chiefs at the book clubs and the paperbackers were themselves influenced by conservative and faddish precedents developed entirely within their own operation. In practice, if a hardback publisher wants to know if a prospective title "can sell a million" paperbacks, he gets his answer not by doing a personal survey or any comparable research, but simply by querying a paperback chief.

It is symptomatic that the fortunes of novelistic fiction have grown increasingly dependent upon film; for since a successful film can sell innumerable paperbacks, the interest of the prospective reprinter often depends upon the appearance of a movie with the same title as the book, drastic differences in plot and theme notwithstanding. These practices produced a shift in the center of editorial reasoning. If a new novel is not destined to become a movie, then it probably is not worth mass-paperbacking; if a manuscript of fiction is not likely to be mass-paperbacked (since no quality paperbacker reprints new fiction), then the novel will probably not be hardbacked either. Suitability to the mass media determines not only whether a novel will be offered to a large audience, but whether it will be published at all. The true czars behind the dissemination of

American fiction reside not in New York but in Hollywood—
not in the libraries but in the screening rooms.

For these reasons, hardback publishers who were once economically modest have become wholeheartedly attuned, if not
subservient, to the kinds of very popular fads previously restric-
ted to movies and mass-magazines. From these practices has
grown a literary star-system, not unlike that of Hollywood in its
heyday, which emphasizes those few sure-fire writers and types
of work with supposedly "proven" subsidiary-rights appeal—
Herman Wouk and Irving Wallace, for example, each fetching
million-plus contracts in the early seventies. Since these writers
are "bigger," so to speak, than any of their possible publishers,
they can switch imprints without worrying about any loss of
continuity. As publishers *need* Wouk or Wallace more than they
need a publisher, the leverages of literary bargaining are reversed. Indeed, what these superstars need is not "a publisher"
in the conventional sense, but a hardback distribution system
for their prepublicized product. (Writers are sometimes asked to
celebrate these lucrative contracts as indicating "more money
for writers"; but such token extravagances also siphon off the
available supply, keeping the rest of the scribbling tribe discon-
solately poor.) Into the book-publishing industry has come the
kind of boom-or-bust hysteria more typical of Broadway or
Hollywood, where the possibility of great profit is weighed
against the likelihood of an expensive loss.

Moreover, precisely because "subsidiary rights," as they are
called, are often more lucrative than sales of the hardback book
itself (and have the extra commercial advantage of necessitating
no further manufacture), hardback publishers are thus in the
absurd entrepreneurial position of primarily providing sub-
contractors with suitably exploitable raw material which is
originally produced not by the publishers themselves but by
their authors. However, since these formats, including the hardback book, are actually subsidiary to the work's original form
(an unpublished manuscript), publishers are no longer issuing
books but parlaying primary publication rights into secondary
profits. Authors have thus become sharecroppers who get a
percentage of the receipts earned by the plantation owner who
initially bankrolls them.

Comparable hyper-commercialization in the record business
has produced, in Eric Salzman's testimony, "a bubblegum in-

dustry [where] quick easy profit replaces independent adventurous judgment and taste. The small profit margin is a thing of the past, and the art has once more given way to business." Since records destined to have a minimal circulation have become less feasible to a large company, Columbia Records killed, in 1970, its fine contemporary music series of the late sixties. (As fewer and fewer serious recent pieces are recorded, the gaps in musical communication today are increasing.) Especially after the prosperity produced by rock, even the once-prestigious labels are devoting more attention to the potential big killing, similarly favoring a select few very popular musicians and composers to the neglect of the many. The fear in both the record business and book-publishing is that this obsession with block-busters might backfire, the bubble breaking; similar procedures, entrenched in Hollywood during 1955-65, contributed to the death of the old movie-making studios.

All this industrial emphasis upon "big books" and celebrity-hunting has sapped prior editorial interest in anything more modest. Not only are less lucrative projects and their authors treated begrudgingly, but books that do not "take off" upon publication are quickly neglected. As Richard E. Snyder, the "associate publisher" at Simon & Schuster, explained the process: "Any publisher knows that if a serious book with a favorable and major review in *The New York Times Book Review* hasn't 'made it' by *one month after publication* [italics mine], it simply isn't going to." Since Snyder's own firm practices rapid-fire boom-or-bust publishing, "It was then we made an unhappy commercial decision [about a certain new title]: we would devote our time, energy and money to promoting other books." Once shunted aside, the new book is remaindered (to chains like Marboro at prices below manufacturing cost) and classified "out of print" more rapidly than before, its death sometimes coming within a year after publication. Publishers play roulette making many bets, only a few of which will score, while the deck is cleared of losers; but unlike roulette players, they are able to pour more money and attention into their winners. Who would dare say that literary publishing was never meant to be a surrogate for gambling?

This hyper-commercialization, as well as the accompanying attitudes, explains why book publishers are so eager to influence the media of review and publicity, and why the interests of

191

junior editors are ignored, and perhaps why the business seems less attractive to literate young people (as well as why no American literary-industrial employee has written a counter-conventional or first-rate novel in a long, long time). Indeed, if editors seem personally defensive, one reason is the knowledge that their best books or even their personal favorites are not crucial to their professional fortunes; and if they seem hypocritical, as well as stuffed with excuses for not doing the books they know they should, one reason is that their culturally sophisticated rhetoric is continually undermined by the demands of commerce. If they sometimes seem secretive, one reason is the recognition that most of their daily activity is culturally (and thus conversationally) indefensible.

These developments brought massive distribution for a few titles and negligible circulation for the many which, no matter how good, quickly disappeared from public view. This neglect partly explains why all but a few American writers today earn most of their incomes from sources other than book publishing. In American PEN's recent survey of its membership, all of whom must have published at least two literary books (or an equivalent) to join, it was revealed that most had earned less than $3,000 from their writings in the previous year. Largely because the academies and the government give most writers salaries (for other work), they can afford to sell their writing for rates lower than the normal per-hour value of their labor. Some can be induced to accept financial arrangements that would otherwise be dismissed as intolerable, because they need book publication per se as a leverage toward professional promotion. Among all the individuals involved in book production, only the writer is encouraged to feel that he should *not* expect to make a decent living from his work. As a result, nearly all quality writing in the U.S. is, in the end, externally subsidized.

This boom-or-bust atmosphere only aggravates the increasingly dialectical relationship between the haves and the have-nots in the writing community, where, as in professional sports, a few are overpaid while the majority are exploited. (And, because of the influx of new writers, the populace of insulted and injured is constantly increasing.) Rare nowadays is the serious professional who does not feel a bit demoralized when he hears of yet another multi-million-dollar advance for the literary equivalent of soap opera. Just as art historically preceded its commercialization, so writing precedes publishing; but when the leverages are reversed, as now, commercial publishing nearly smothering the art of writing, then the cart is pulling the horse. While the top of the literary world boomed, various bottoms fell out.

A few once-serious writers responded to this new prosperity by providing publishers with manuscripts susceptible to promotion as salacious best-sellers: Mary McCarthy, Truman Capote, David R. Slavitt (also known as "Henry Sutton"), and Philip Roth, to name a prominent few, none of whom has ever equalled, artistically, his best previous work. (Indeed, what separates *Portnoy's Complaint,* for instance, from well-written pornography are inferences based upon its cultural context— Roth's history of appearing primarily in literary magazines, coupled with a Madison Avenue publisher, and the support of reputable critics, all of whom helped make the book, to quote Marvin Mudrick, "the first Kosher pornographic novel.") Since importance is almost exclusively equated with monetary success, most publishers assume that whatever costs a lot of money must therefore be important, while their editorial employees have come to assume, thanks in part to the efforts of certain agents, that no writer can be truly good unless his contracts are expensive. To make matters worse, more than a few writers and critics who should know better are succumbing to these heavy gusts from the marketplace.

II

> The present system tends to assist the circulation of indifferent and bad books and to retard the circulation of really good books, especially those by writers who have not yet established reputations. —Stanley Unwin, *The Truth about Publishing* (1926).

These new commercial opportunities, along with the prospect of an unending boom in education, persuaded text and trade publishers to merge with each other in order not only to "cover the field," as they put it, with "big books" at all levels of literacy and education, but also to centralize distribution and impress growth-minded stockholders. William Morrow, which assimilated both William Sloane and Reynal & Hitchcock, fell to Scott Foresman, while Intext Educational Publishers acquired three New York hardback houses, a mass paperback (Ballantine), a Texas el-hi textbook house (Steck-Vaughn), and a West Coast college textbooker (Chandler). Harcourt, Brace, whose long-time president William Jovanovich added his own name to the masthead, took over Academic Press, which specializes in scientific books and journals, and Johnson Reprint Corporation, which reissues scholarly-scientific books and periodicals. Random House was primarily a trade house until it organized the Blaisdel Publishing Company to produce science texts for colleges and technical schools; it also merged with Alfred A. Knopf early in 1960 and assumed its college textbook department, acquiring both Beginning Books with its juveniles and Pantheon with its first-rate trade list, as well as all of a Chicago-based school and library jobber named Library Publishers, Inc., plus a partial share of Accelerated Instructional Materials Corporation, in addition to L. W. Singer, which did elementary and high-school textbooks. In response to such voraciousness, the price of Random House's stock, initially issued at eleven dollars per share in 1959, soared over forty dollars by 1961. As Bennett Cerf remarked around that time, "It comes as rather a shock suddenly to find Wall Street tycoons embracing us and waving certified checks in our faces, since it really wasn't too long ago that the financial world dismissed publishers as pipe-smoking dreamers."

Prosperity also made larger corporations, especially communications conglomerates, eager to acquire book publishers; and many of the more successful traditionally independent houses were purchased at awesomely high prices. RCA assumed Random House early in 1966 in exchange for stock then worth approximately forty million dollars; and the corporate owner of the *Los Angeles Times* acquired New American Library, World, and Harry N. Abrams in separate transactions. ITT purchased Howard Sams, which had previously acquired Bobbs-Merrill; the New York Times, Inc. assumed Arno Press and Quadrangle Books, along with a few more radio stations; Dun & Bradstreet took over Thomas Y. Crowell; and Time, Inc. got both Little, Brown and the New York Graphic Society. National General conglomerated Bantam Books; and Holt, Rinehart & Winston, itself the product of recent mergers and acquisitions, fell to CBS for over $200 million in stock in 1967.

The fact that Holt's profits for the previous year were only

$6.6 million suggests that CBS, like other acquisitive behemoths, expected publishing to become far more profitable. A large house's prize assets include a thriving backlist (that accounts at best for as much as three-quarters of the annual income), experience at producing educational materials (that could ideally be adapted to the conglomerate's other communications media), literary properties (that could be used not only in television serials but in video tape recordings), and contracts with currently good-selling writers. The visionary assumption of corporate theory was that a marriage between the publisher and other media would beget an all-purpose communications and education company, whose diversification would be complementary. Not until the seventies was this dream exposed as illusory.

Takeovers made large firms into even larger literary-industrial complexes, so that book-publishing was, as *Business Week* noted in 1970, "evolving into an industry of giants and dwarfs, with middle-sized companies a vanishing species." If new conglomerate money stayed in the publishing house, one change was both higher salaries and better employee-benefit programs. Another was larger cash advances for blockbusters, thereby accelerating a development that was already in progress; and the firm's previous owner felt gratified that these inflated sums no longer came out of his own pocket. The parent super-complex could help its publisher in ways impossible before, such as publicizing Random House books over its NBC television shows. Given all this support, it seems ungenerous to note that book publishing might be emulating newspaper and television monopolies by eliminating the competition prerequisite to "free communication," or that some of the same sugar daddies are also profiting heavily from military-industrial imperialism.

In the end, however, most of the new owners were more troublesome than beneficial. Some insisted upon moving the publisher's offices into high-rent midtown Manhattan skyscrapers, which not only increased the operating overhead but usually produced a less congenial working atmosphere. Employees were shifted around in counter-productive ways, while the bureaucracies burgeoned with Parkinsonian perversity. The inevitable breakdowns in communication and coordination were customarily blamed, should the author complain, upon "organizational kinks." Although trade publishing represented a minuscule dimension of the entire conglomerate, its editors were

195

scarcely left alone. Decisions regarding the publication of new manuscripts became even more rationalized, while the new owner tried to reform accounting procedures that had traditionally been imprecise. And, too, the money men sometimes insisted upon participating in the editorial action, although subsequently absolving themselves of responsibility for bad decisions.

The conglomerate's financial department often raised the official "break-even point," which is the much-cited convenient fiction for the minimal number of copies a book must sell before becoming profitable (and thus a debating point in editorial meetings), even though this new higher sales figure had less to do with explicit production expenses than the reallocation of increased overhead. Whereas a hardcover editor once had to promise minimum sales of 3,000 copies, he now had to justify the expectation of 10,000, if not more; and if a mass paperback could once think in terms of 40,000 for a quality project, now nothing less than a projected buyership of 100,000 could convince the ultimate decision-makers. The money men also raised the minimum annual sales requirement, that is the number of books that must be sold each year to keep a published title currently in print—about a thousand in hardback, 40,000 in mass paperback; otherwise the book would be remaindered or sold for pulp. Since these decisions were made by computer, classics were cut along with trash. Victor S. Navasky writes that one Macmillan computer "declared all of Yeats out of print, because his books weren't selling enough copies per annum, until some clerk in the billing department recognized the name and brought it to somebody's attention." The demands of commerce exercise an implicit censorship independent of a book's content, not only before publication but afterwards. For instance, by overpricing a new book, the publisher jeopardizes not only its sales but its possible communication. In totalitarian societies, a book is censored at the point of production; in literary-industrial societies, censorship occurs at later points along the communication line.

For all the money the conglomerate poured into its new division, it wanted to pull out as much, if not more, quite quickly. The chiefs of the parent company expected its new publisher to attain profits commensurate with their inflated investment, thus often insisting upon "profit ratios" (upon

196

capital invested) or "surplus cash" far beyond the capabilities of any competitive publishing firm. By egregiously overestimating the money-making potential of publishing, the conglomerate jeopardized the health of its new acquisition. Publishing was never meant to be so profitable; and the fact that it was briefly lucrative scarcely indicated that the boom would go on forever. The American idea of corporate growth, as Douglas Mount notes, "is alien to the editorial process; it introduces something that doesn't belong at all."

In order to satisfy these demands in the course of protecting their own jobs, editors scrimped on present expenditures, largely by cutting down upon investments in future projects, particularly if they seemed commercially marginal (for example, in young or unconventional writers). Tight-fisted management increased current profits (and cash to be "bled") for the parent conglomerate by jeopardizing the publishing firm's future. What the new interloper sometimes failed to recognize was a financial truth indigenous to the industry—that the lack of available cash partially reflected the comparatively large amounts committed to future business in the form of yet-undelivered manuscripts. In publishing, as in the husbandry of trees, seeds must be planted and then allowed a few years to grow; without seeds, there can be no timber to harvest.

When the Nixon depression caused a severe decline in book sales, a further cutback on contracts followed, partly in order to sustain the illusion of continuing "profits," while authors were pressured into honoring outstanding contracts, often rushing into print projects that might not have fully matured. In other cases, the desired surplus could be earned only by selling away a whole series or division, much as a tree farmer might dispose of a whole forest. Policies of this kind left some experienced editors wondering whether, should their conglomerated firm survive, it would have enough books to field a substantial new list.

Sometimes the firm's former proprietor, who was customarily retained as a top manager, found himself fired by his new employers usually for failing to meet the prescribed new profit quotas. Or he quit on his own initiative before the pressure of demeaning demands. His departure generally caused his more loyal associates to leave as well, which led in turn to the hiring of an entirely new team to take comprehensive command. This change in editorial leadership usually caused the departure as well of previously faithful authors, along with their contracts for books-in-progress. Since the most eminent of them usually followed their previous editors who were shrewd at managing their divided loyalties, the editorial successors inherited not a thriving publishing house but a disintegrating ship. Thus, in order to hire experienced editors who might bring *their* loyal authors, the conglomerate promised not only higher editorial salaries but a larger budget for contracts. To "rebuild the list," these new executives often had to pour a good deal of fresh money into enticing expensive established writers, catch-as-cash-can, from elsewhere, on the operating assumption that the large firm "needed" best-sellers for management to survive. "The most publicized editors," in Cass Canfield's observation, "are those who contract for a large number of books carrying big advances."

However, since an extravagant investment in Big Names, while impressive at first, would probably not be recouped, these editors were themselves forced into a panic and, inevitably, a premature departure, thereby perpetuating the cycling disintegration. One of my own recently conglomerated trade publishers had four editors-in-chief in as many years; another lost all but one of its senior editors the autumn my book appeared, while a third has had three presidents in the few years since a conglomerate purchased it. In no example known to me did these new executives do remarkably better than their predecessors, though, it should be noted in their defense, that few were given sufficient time (at least a decade) to establish a strong publishing program. And since these hired saviors were themselves invariably fired too soon, most of their constructive work was wasted. This new money was rarely "smart," in spite of its claims to financial sophistication, precisely because its demands were editorially so dumb and thus, in the end, financially counterproductive.

All this editorial transience helped sabotage the traditional writer-editor-publisher relationship, where both writer and editor felt he had a growing stake in the long-term professional fortunes of one another and their commonly supporting firm. Editors today, on the one hand, have less personal pride in their publishing projects, many of which they inherited either from a direct predecessor or a recently departed colleague. On the other hand, when a senior editor leaves a firm, those contracted writers who do not flee with him often find that his successor has considerably less enthusiasm or responsibility for their particular work. Thus, when an editorially-abandoned new book appears, no one remaining in the firm particularly cares about its fortunes with promotion, advertising, and sales departments. Victor S. Navasky tells of a major publisher "whose computer celebrated publication day by sending out the message that the book, which was not yet in the stores, was 'Out of Print.' Because the editor who signed up the book had moved on to another job, the error was not discovered for two weeks."

Editorial transience also resulted in the shifting of authors' loyalties from editors to literary agents who, given the nature of their business, rarely had as much time for, or interest in, the quality of a writer's manuscript or his professional growth. The passion that certain agents had for "auctioneering" choice properties further threatened author-editor stability. Although some transient editors carried their few favored writers from house to house, agent-editor and agent-writer relationships began to seem more stable than those between writers and publishing houses. To make matters worse, some large firms discovered that they could get along with fewer editorial employees (and secretaries), thus increasing the book-loads of the remaining editors, as well as decreasing the time available to editor-author relationships and line-by-line manuscript editing. "Publishers" were slowly turning into mammoth sales outfits whose principal competence was not editorial but distributional.

The new avarice also seemed on the verge of swallowing the traditional trustworthiness of publishers—the principle upon which the custom of accurately accounted royalties has so far been based. One frequently hears reports of short-changing on royalties, but only a former baseball player, Jim Bouton, has documented his adverse experiences. (Sales of his best-selling *Ball Four* [1970] were transferred from one rate of royalty return to another, cheaper schedule, thus decreasing the money due him by more than one-half.) It should be no surprise, of course, that when money becomes tight, writers are invariably the first to feel the publisher's squeeze. To quote *Your Book Contract,* published by the Author's Guild: "Experience has taught [publishers] that authors are more squeezable than paper suppliers, printers and distributors." Indeed, one obvious

199

fear is that unless an appropriate investigative agency is established either by authors or publishers, the former may need to sue persistently for sums contractually due them, much as rock groups nowadays must regularly browbeat semi-scrupulous record companies. Another fear is that, given current profit-hungers, publishers may no longer be trusted to print an author's work exactly as it was written or that they may come to offer contracts that, like those familiar to movies and television, deny the author his traditional control over the final text.

What is ultimately threatened by all these developments is the industry's traditional respect for the individual writer and the integrity of his work. As Seymour Krim concludes, "The writer becomes a tool of the economy instead of its spiritual leader and conscience."

III

> It was a different problem for the still younger writers, those born after 1905, who in 1930 still had their reputations to make. They had the bad luck to come forward at a time when there was no demand for college graduates with literary ambitions. The magazines, shrunk to half their former size, had no room for new writers; the publishers had no money to risk on first novels that might never be finished, nor had they jobs to offer on their now smaller staffs. —Malcolm Cowley, "How Writers Lived" (1948).

"Financially oriented executives are taking over where traditionalist genteel editors used to hold sway," oozed *Business Week* in 1970, and it mentioned that the new president of Harper & Row had come from a career on Wall Street, via a position at the U. S. Treasury Department. Although those interlopers could usually turn enough tricks to increase short-term profits, the long-term results of their illusory business-likeness were generally disastrous for all concerned. American industry frequently makes the mistake of regarding "proven executive ability" as omnicompetent in any enterprise, but, in truth, the kind of experience gained in manufacturing lamps, say, will have limited uses and value in publishing. Books remain a specialized kind of enterprise, requiring not only skills at administration and finance but also a certain taste for, and knowledge of, books and authors, plus a high degree of individual judgment, experienced leadership, and continuity of personnel. Crucial dimensions of the business depend upon the sure appraisal of the possibly multiple potential of manuscripts and the initiation of symbiotic, though easily undermined, relationships with educated, taste-conscious, and headstrong people. "Publishing," notes William Jovanovich, "succeeds or fails finally on the judgment of which books should be published and which authors should be encouraged and supported." Thus, a publishing executive imported from another business and lacking either these special qualities or indigenous expertise often makes decisions for strictly financial reasons rather than various factors peculiar to the trade. If he does not have at least a "feel" for books, he will never understand why certain titles should be more successful than others or why certain intangible qualities give a publisher a particular identity in the minds of both readers and bookstore managers. Indeed, some of these carpetbaggers had offices so bare of books that merely visiting them would depress an author and even an editor, further demoralizing editorial incentive. "And with the departure of each individual who knows the difference," the agent John Cushman once noted, "mass sales become the only criterion." Certain firms continue to carry the names of individual publishers who, though still alive, have been managerially phased out, such as Frederick A. Praeger and Alfred A. Knopf.

More fearsomely, these financial managers' forays into editorial decisions usually function to undermine the official editor's confidence and autonomy; and when they try to persuade a writer or his editor to alter a manuscript, their manner and likely illiteracy alienate the firm's authors as well. Proposals that seemed profitable to a money man could strike even his most popular author as insidious, and should a conflict arise, the latter, rather than the former, was more likely to exercise his freedom of movement. The former was slow to learn that "good business" is often bad business in publishing. Even in some of the more literate houses, the sales manager, or even the treasurer, began to acquire more editorial power, especially in dealing directly with the firm's president, than the official editors who were dismissed as impractical. Thus, outside book packagers, usually more money-minded than writers or even agents, found such sales managers and money men more worthy of their persuasions than the official editor-in-chief. Whereas publishing could once be called, to quote Jovanovich again, "one of the most civilized of worldly pursuits," it and its people are, by now, largely indistinguishable from the rest of U. S. business.

Victor Weybright, the founder of the New American Library, reports that after the *Los Angeles Times* purchased his firm, they hired the management consultants, McKinsey and Co., who advised that editorial authority be delegated "almost entirely to marketing executives." To Weybright, an intelligent and successful paperback publisher, such a decision exemplifies "the pitfalls of over-organizing a sensitive enterprise into a device for killing the spirit and threatening the profits." One predictable result of conglomerate intrusion, as in New American Library's case, was Weybright's own resignation and then a decline in quality that also brought a decline in sales, especially to the firm's previously loyal customers; for it is a rule peculiar to today's publishing, whether of books or magazines, that not profit but loss follows a conspicuous decline in the editorial quality of a successful publisher's product.

When a mammoth specialized company, such as a newspaper or a broadcaster, ventures into another specialized kind of business for which it has neither the experience or internal competence it rarely manages this new speciality as successfully as its original forte. For example, just as Norton Simon, Inc., with its base in Hunt's Foods, failed to redeem its investment in Wheeling Steel, so its foray into founding a trade-book house under the McCall imprint quickly disintegrated. In other cases, certain top-level conglomerate decisions reveal a gratuitous insensitivity to the idiosyncracies of a publishing enterprise—one instance being a communications combine that sealed all its warehouses for an annual inventory the week before Christmas, just as the demand for books was reaching its peak.

A further trouble with outside takeover of a publisher is that the conglomerate mentality undermined much of the original owner-operator's energized commitment to his creation and his passion for his product, both of which had been essential to a small company's survival in a highly competitive and volatile culture-industry. Analogously again, the rare-book business, which prospered spectacularly in response to increased library-buying in the middle sixties, was similarly jeopardized by expansion, conglomeration, and the shift from entrepreneurial control to managerial; and once experienced bookmen left the business and the boom ceased, knowledge merely of inventory and cash flow could not prevent a long-established company's death. Another kind of specialized business is sports; CBS's ill-advised purchase of the New York Yankees contributed to that ball club's precipitous decline both in quality and income. (Having paid 13.2 million in 1964, CBS sold its stock in 1972 for only ten million—a loss of 25 percent.) By contrast, the Memphis-based Stax Record Company, which had sold out to Gulf & Western, had the wisdom to buy itself back and survive. The conservative truth is that the publisher functions best when his love of books is tempered by a desire to stay in business, in contrast to providing profits for an absentee owner. In enterprises of taste, the best policy seems to be concentrating authority and direction in the same entrepreneurial hands; so that while the public sees the published produce, only the owner-operator peruses the balance sheet.

Once a small division of a large conglomerate becomes unprofitable or the general future of an industry turns dark, it generally becomes more expedient for the parent company to sell away its new acquisition, cash-as-catch-can. Thus, Reader's Digest, Inc., disposed of Funk & Wagnalls' trade department (which still had assets in its back list); Western Publishing, its Pegasus line; and Cowles Communications, its newly-established trade-book division. Or the conglomerate can simply kill the unprofitable firm as an inept investment buried in a multi-million dollar balance sheet, no matter how prestigious the publisher's name had once been. Thus, did the Times-Mirror, Inc., scuttle the World Publishing Company, and thus, by analogy, did ABC-Paramount allow Westminster Records to disappear, although it had once been a fine classical label which they purchased at considerable expense. A paradox peculiar to advanced capitalism is that, profit-hunger notwithstanding, such giant corporations can more facilely "afford" to lose not only a whole operation but also a lot more money than a smaller, specialized organization, all without even trembling at their foundations.

When economic depression resounded through publishing, about a year after Nixon's accession, editors not only had less money to advance to authors, but, more fearsomely for the future of writing, their toughened profit-mindedness also eliminated nearly all interest in commercially marginal books. Library budgets were cut down, along with governmental expenditures for education, private cultural donations, and other prior fallouts from prosperity. Since textbook publishing had become less lucrative, publishers hoped to compensate for this slack by making their trade departments even more profitable, though that was scarcely possible at this time. Thus, the search for "big books" became even more desperate, while manuscripts once published for reasons of prestige or professional pride were now "rationalized" as uneconomical. This process of "cutting down the lists" also eliminated many young editors who had sponsored such commercially modest books, few of whom had the "track records" of their seniors, some of whom were on the verge of challenging established systems. Not since the recessions of the early fifties had so many outstanding contracts been cancelled, or so much editorial personnel been "laid off," and the first to go were typically not upper echelon executives but their less paid juniors. Those youngsters who remained were caretakers, processing their seniors' projects rather than issuing their own. A small army of literary professionals was forced into unemployment, press agentry, public relations, or ghost writing. Smaller editorial staffs meant less time for unconventional, unprecedented decision-making or line-by-line editing of a forthcoming book.

Just as several good university quarterlies disappeared around 1970 (e.g., *Kenyon Review* and *New Mexico Quarterly*), even university presses, traditionally less subservient to economic pressures, were cutting down their lists, a few houses disappearing completely in the academic depression. "The tragedy of this to me," noted the president of the Association of American University Presses, "is that many young scholars will not have that important early book published; life will be made much more difficult for young scholars." The result on all fronts was not only an undermining of confidence and continuity, but a generational decimation comparable to that occurring at the same time both in academia, where few non-tenured junior professors were promoted and many young doctorates were unemployed (while salaries for senior staff continued to rise), and on Wall Street where "go-getters" in their twenties had also been threatening to change the dominant atmosphere. Those most severely injured by depressions are not the entrenched class which keeps its position, its connections, and most of its wealth, but the rising underclass, like young writers, because economic adversity depletes available capital and opportunity. Indeed, it is my further hunch that this widespread generational devastation may soon be regarded as the prime "conservative achievement" of the Nixon years. While the top continues to boom, various bottoms fall out.

Even the senior editors showed less interest in publishing "prestige" titles which, though they lost money, would probably enhance both their own and the firm's morale as well as its image among discriminating people. The resulting trouble is that an editor unable to do the best manuscripts available to him eventually loses his enthusiasm and his professional reputation, if not his self-respect. A desperate sense of prior overextension also forced some publishers to prune their forthcoming lists of titles that were less likely to make a profit—some "marginal" books were rejected after they had been accepted or even placed into production, the publisher usually forfeiting the author's advance. Only such hysteria could make so much non-publishing more worthwhile than publishing. Even worse, some publishers gained reputations for attempting to offend contracted authors, by tricking them into breaking outstanding contracts on their own outraged initiative, thus obliging the writers to return the publisher's prior advance. All these developments account for the sense of malaise that afflicted the industry in the early seventies.

So great was the growing reluctance to do books that lacked "an immediate ascertainable buyership," as one chief editor told me, that a title like John Barth's *The Sot-Weed Factor* (1960)—the actual example we were then discussing—would no longer be worth publishing precisely because it, unlike *Giles Goat-Boy* (1966), did not become profitable until several years after its first publication! As this editor explained, "Publishers now feel obliged to make money much quicker than that." That any business should become so hard-nosed is perhaps predictable, but publishing is supposed to be different. Not all of its merchandise, which happens to include works of literary art and intelligent thought, can be entirely appraised in terms of dollars and cents. "The danger," Jovanovich explains, "is not that a few houses will come to dominate American publishing, . . . but that the large publishing house will fail to accomplish the better ends to which its great resources might be put." Since only a few of Johann Sebastian Bach's works were published in his lifetime, most were unavailable until the nineteenth century while some remain completely lost.

Editorial authority became so restrictive by the early seventies that illustrated or unusually designed books were totally unacceptable. Most of the young authors who received generous advances were either celebrities, such as star athletes or Lt. William Calley, or journalists wanting to write about subjects of general youth interest (macrobiotic cooking, hallucinogenics, rock, nudity, and other fads). Publishing had traditionally been more open and pluralistic than, say, American theater, and that was a prime reason for an earlier sense of professional possibility in writing; however, the circumstances creating such an opportune situation have since disappeared. Indeed, the charge that more good books go unpublished today than ever before implicitly questions the industry's oft-uttered claim that it serves rather than undermines the liberal ideal of free communication. If important creativity and thought remain uncommunicated, then the industry as a whole is abridging the First Amendment by default, totally without governmental intervention. Though the motives of the literary-industrial complex were fundamentally economic, the results of its operation, in response to history, are inevitably cultural and political, because it shapes the flow of communication and thus the life of art, ideas, and people.

IV

> Lawlessness is most often associated with crime and riots, but there is lawlessness and corruption in all the major institutions of our society—matched by an indifference to responsibility and consequences, and a pervasive hypocrisy that refuses to acknowledge the facts that are everywhere visible. —Charles A. Reich, *The Greening of America* (1970).

One rationale for the conservatism of publishing has been the feebleness of the reviewing media which, instead of acting as the industry's critical conscience and challenging either their closed enterprise system or their editorial irresponsibilities, usually serves to reinforce the currently established prejudices and practices of the literary-industrial complex. Indeed, American book-reviewing has been remarkably susceptible to a gamut of compromising pressures, ranging from insistent requests by established writers to the promotions of parochial powerhouses, from the wiles of editors to marital collusion, from the puffery of phony publicity machines (e.g., The National Book Award) to the shifting winds of powerful fashion. It is not surprising, given such circumstances, that absolutely none of the American book reviews, not even the more pretentious or prestigious, can present a laudable record to the scrutiny of subsequent intellectual historians. Furthermore, no established medium or prolific reviewer is particularly interested in "new" literature or young writers. *The New York Times Book Review,* for a barometric instance, has run commissioned surveys on black writing, women's lib books, Catholic fiction, American Indian work, west-coast publishers, and almost every other special interest, but it has never directed attention to young writers as a class, or to new literary publishers, or to writing done between the coasts; and rarely does it notice avant-garde literature. As noted before, the real power of this Sunday medium, in contrast to *The New York Review,* lies less in its advocacies than its omissions, for any kind of notice, whether favorable or unfavorable, inspires more interest (and sells more books) than complete neglect.

Much evidence suggests that *The New York Times Book Review,* between its ads, its charts, and its reviews, sells books with the same authority that its magazine section sells ladies' underwear (on ads alone). Most publishers pour more than half of their advertising budgets into its pages, filling two-thirds of the available page-space. Neighborhood libraries are especially susceptible to *The Times Book Review*'s emphases and recommendations (while those at universities tend to rely more upon both *The New York Review* and *Library Journal,* the latter reviewing about 6,000 of the approximately 24,000 new titles published annually, whereas *The Times* covers less than 2,500). *The Times Book Review*'s ads, reviews, and best-seller list tell retail bookstore managers what titles they ought to stock in abundance. This list, it should be noted, epitomizes self-fulfilling prophecy, because it tabulates not actual sales by gross number—real best-selling—but an evenly-weighted survey of what selected bookstore managers *think* is selling in their stores.

Such impressions are invariably swayed not only by the wiles of publicity and advertising, but also by the manager's own reading tastes. (And for various reasons, such as regional distribution or an obscure publisher, some very popular titles never make the best-seller lists.) America's most influential book-review functions primarily to serve not Literature or Criticism but Commerce, while less commercial houses and writers are, in contrast, customarily ignored. It is worth noting that America's most powerful reviewing media, as well as its largest publishing houses, are located within a mile of each other in midtown Manhattan.

Dwight Macdonald discovered some years ago that *The Times Book Review,* like other similar media, regards books as "news" and so devotes attention to what is most generally talked about. However, since it also tries to review books soon after publication (and commissions such reviews several weeks before), the only talk heard by its editors comes from the large publishers' publicity departments, the prepublication services or people within *The Times* itself. (That last custom accounts for why, as Gay Talese noted, "Books by *Times*men were rarely panned and were nearly always given generous, if not extensive, treatment in both the daily edition and the Sunday 'Book Review.'") Otherwise, a publisher's large advance promotional campaign for a reasonably respectable title all but insures a review, not only in *The Times* but in *Publishers Weekly* and other prepublication services; so that, as noted before, reviewers' attention largely reflects the efforts of publicity and advertising departments. Indeed, even if both the book and its author are destined for obscurity, proficient publicity departments endeavor to create an aura of "importance" so that the book's existence must be noted in print; yet they are obviously more predisposed to push those titles that, given current interests and attitudes, will win immediate media acceptance as "important"—a snowballing process inherently closer to journalistic and faddish values than literary ones. "Importance" is not synonymous with "excellence," though more easily identified.

With these principles in mind, it is worth considering a dated, but still relevant, close survey of *The Times Book Review*'s pages in 1968, as reported in Harry Smith's *The Newsletter,* which concludes that the medium's largest advertisers command reviewing attention disproportionately greater than their advertising space, while smaller advertisers suffer disproportionate neglect. "Most of the book companies placing more than 20 pages of ads had a review total approaching the ad page total, [and they] tended to receive more than half as many review pages as ad pages," says the survey. For instance, Random House, with 74½ pages of advertisements, had 58 pages of reviews; Harper & Row, with 29¼ pages of ads, had 22¾ review pages; Little, Brown, also with 29¼ ad pages, had 21 review pages. Less endowed advertisers received proportionately *less* attention—numerically measured either by reviews or review-pages to ad pages—except for Oxford University Press with seven reviews for 13½ pages of ads. Dutton had 4½ pages of review for 16½ ads; Lippincott had 3¾ for 16½; and Harvard University Press had "negligible" notice for 9¼ pages. In more ways than one, therefore, reviewing space has been indirectly "for sale"; he who pays the piper gets at least a tune.

In this year-long period, Random House, the biggest advertiser, had twice as many of its books selected for individual review as any other competitor or combine; and in that regular *Times Book Review* feature of "New and Recommended" adjacent to the best-seller list, the Random House imprint alone appeared 29 times, Knopf 26 times, and Pantheon just eight times (between June 2 and December 1), while Doubleday had 23 nominees in comparison and Harper & Row only 22, both of them, as noted before, publishing as many books annually as all of Random House.

It is the most damning contrast to note that even though the decade's major avant-garde publisher, the Something Else Press, ran occasional advertisements in *The Times Book Review*, only one of its many titles was ever mentioned in the *Times'* pages by 1970—Emmett Williams' *Anthology of Concrete Poetry* in a general essay on the subject. (In my one *Times* piece of 1970, on "pop publishing," I found good reasons to mention Merce Cunningham's *Changes* [1969] and R. Meltzer's *The Esthetics of Rock* [1970], both published by Something Else; but never again, by the end of 1972, was a Something Else book reviewed in its pages.) The only book from City Lights Press recently reviewed was Allen Ginsberg's *Planet News* (1968); books from university presses, even if written by truly major minds (e.g., Richard Hofstadter's *The Idea of the Party System* [1969], published by the University of California) go all but unreviewed; and never in my memory did *The Times Book Review* even mention the West Coast poetry publishers, Oyez and Unicorn, Dave Haselwood and Nova Broadcast—or Follett-Big Table in Chicago; or the House of Anansi, The New Press, and Coach House in Toronto; or New Rivers and Croton Press in New York, some of which have nonetheless advertised in the medium, and all of which have published important titles that are worthy of critical notice. (Other small publishers such as Black Sparrow, Broadside, December, and Swallow have, by my count, had their books reviewed once and only once in recent years.) It is not surprising that books emerging from counter-conventional backgrounds and professional outlooks should encounter resistances in the cultural marketplace—the history of reviewing is full of such scandals—but the more depressing truth is that the powerful *Times Book Review,* by discriminating against small and young publishers, serves to discourage the independent initiative necessary for the future of intelligent writing.

The absence of younger writers among the chosen reviewers is noticeable and appalling; and if someone young is asked to contribute, whatever faults (or discomforting virtues) he shows are blamed upon his youth (and, thus, upon youth in general). Whole groups of young writers, such as those who publish primarily in small-circulation magazines, have gone completely unnoticed, while commercially published books by young authors are rarely reviewed. Revealing its cultural conservatism, *The Times Book Review* also has neglected such path-breaking titles as Norman O. Brown's *Life Against Death* (1959), John Cage's *Silence* (1961), Joseph Frank's *The Widening Gyre* (1963), Marshall McLuhan's *Understanding Media* (1964), Edwin Denby's *Dancers, Buildings and People in the Streets* (1965), Allan Kaprow's *Assemblage, Environments & Happenings* (1966), Edward T. Hall's *The Hidden Dimension* (1966), Oliver L. Reiser's *Cosmic Humanism* (1966), Ludwig von Bertalanffy's *General Systems Theory* (1968), Vladimir Markov's *Russian Futurism* (1968), Jack Burnham's *Beyond Modern Sculpture* (1968), Mary Ellen Solt's *Concrete Poetry: A World View* (1968), Noam Chomsky and Morris Halle's *The Sound Structure of English* (1968), Michael Kirby's *The Art of Time* (1969), Don McDonagh's *The Rise and Fall and Rise of Modern Dance* (1970), F. M. Esfandiary's *Optimism One* (1970), Edmund Carpenter and Ken Heyman's *They Became What They Beheld* (1970), Murray Bookchin's *Post-Scarcity Anarchy* (1971), John Brockman's *37* (1971), and Jeff Berner's *The Innerspace Project* (1972).

Enthusiastic notice of Ralph Nader's *Unsafe At Any Speed* (1965), one of the past decade's most consequential books, was buried at the end of a survey-review of books about autoracing and sports cars! Of the humanistic philosopher Maurice Friedman's many works, none except the first (a biography of Martin Buber) has ever been reviewed, nor have any books by the most eminent advocate of an opposite position, scientific philosopher Rudolf Carnap—these examples demonstrating the principle of philosophic impartiality-by-comparable-neglect. Though the collected essays of the New York literary mob are customarily reviewed, similar books by such major literary theorists as Kenneth Burke and Northrop Frye go unnoticed. Never in recent memory has *The Times Book Review* noticed an obviously self-published book, even though, given the developing situation, many consequential titles have been and will continue to be privately financed; and it rarely reviews books that originally appear in paperback, no matter how important.

The Times' customary rationalization for neglecting a book on an avant-garde subject is, "We can't find anyone to review it." However, since the crucial critics of avant-garde art and thought rarely appeared in its pages, one can suspect that they simply never looked for such a reviewer. As always, such anti-avant-garde books as Gerald Sykes' *The Perennial Avant-Garde* (1970) or Harold Rosenberg's *The De-Definition of Art* (1972) get individually reviewed, while those favoring the new art (and explaining it) are just as predictably ignored. It is my considered estimate that all American book reviews without exception neglect as many important books as they cover. Even more depressing is the reluctance of the supposedly more high-minded reviewing media such as the liberal weeklies and monthlies to forge higher, tougher, and more relevant critical standards than those of the mass media.

The New York Times Book Review was run from 1949 to the end of 1970 by Francis Brown, a former history teacher and *Times* veteran (b. 1903), who reportedly displayed little interest in imaginative writing in general, youth and literary innovation being merely further outside of his square of concerns. It was

Brown who fostered an editorial atmosphere, also advocated by his imperious Sunday *Times* chief Lester Markel, of regarding favorable reviews as more "fit to print" than negative notices. The latter, when submitted, were customarily reduced, reassigned, rejected, or retired onto a surplus pile. Because puffs were expected, a former employee once told me they would often be arranged, either by assigning a title to a professionally predisposed reviewer or by accepting the latter's request for it. Thus, what would be said in a forthcoming favorable review was often known in advance to the author or his publisher. Not only did the medium epitomize unexceptional criticism, but new writers with styles striking enough to transcend the gray pages never appeared again. Under Brown's aegis, book-reviewing approached levels typical of travel reportage where most subjects are indiscriminately praised in columns adjacent to *paid* advertisements, both Sunday sections being all but totally dependent for their advertising revenues upon the sponsorship of what they supposedly aim to scrutinize. (That they are "trade papers," so to speak, may explain why tougher scrutinies of both far-away places and literary people usually appear in *The Times Magazine.*) In reevaluating its policies, *The Times Book Review* tended, as Dwight Macdonald observed, to be more responsive to pressures from "the big publishing houses," whom they implicitly served, than the criticism of respected literary people. It also favored Columbia University's faculty, many of whom were Brown's neighbors on Morningside Heights. Tough-minded critics rarely reviewed for *The Times,* and it has never tried to emulate the hard-headed seriousness of, say, the paper's business section.

At the beginning of 1971, Brown was duly pensioned and replaced by John Leonard (b. 1939), a prolific novelist and journalist with a knack for impressing his elders, who had previously been one of *The Times'* daily reviewers. Though his age signified the possibility of necessary change, both his fairly conservative public personality and the character of his patronage, along with initial evidence of his reign, suggested otherwise. His opening issues included extended interviews with Saul Bellow and Robert Lowell, even though neither had published a new book, and then one with Mary McCarthy, who had. In the first abundant summertime "Selection of Recent Titles" in Leonard's reign (June 5, 1971), only four books by Americans younger than himself were chosen—three conventional novels and a kiddie biography of an SDS revolutionary. *The Newsletter,* surveying the first three months of his regime, reports that the large advertisers still receive proportionately more reviewing space for their books than smaller advertisers.

The Times Book Review has since favored younger reviewers, most of whom teach at New York universities, and allowed token interest in small-press publications. The reviews are longer, more intellectual, and more critical, ending Brown's rule of puffery, while Leonard's own back-page editorials raise serious literary-political issues that, nonetheless, are never fully confronted. Though big-time publishers have criticized these changes, reportedly threatening to reduce their advertising expenditures (which declined anyway during the last few years), Leonard's medium is still their prime commercial colleague.

There is no doubt that book publishers have become increasingly dependent upon newspapers and television, not only for discovering subjects of popular interest, but also for promoting their titles and authors. This shift partially explains why both newspapers and communications combines, realizing their crucial role, have purchased publishing houses. Given *The Times Book Review*'s power and position as a satellite of a closed enterprise system, its servile conservatism is perhaps as inevitable as its susceptibility to fashion and publishers' pressure; but given *The New York Times*'s investments in book publishing—the purchase of both Quadrangle Books and the Arno Press—there are legitimate reasons for simply establishing a rule against its reviewing those imprints. What must be avoided, here as well as in the management of *The New York Review of Books,* are conditions conducive to collusion. If *The Times Book Review* were not the only large-scale weekly book review in America, its faults would not be so dangerous; but until alternatives are founded and sustained with sufficient support, it will continue to dominate, unchallenged.

Not only *The Times* but other American book reviewing media are, in the end, just another cog in the machinery of the editorial-industrial complex that is hyper-commercial, spiritually stultifying, humanly corrupting, anti-literary, anti-young, and anti-new. Instead of challenging such dangerous developments, or criticizing literary corruption, or redressing the balances of power, book reviewing merely contributes to the current decline. From the viewpoint of commerce, this "service" can be rationalized, I suppose; but unless good books are published as frequently and proudly as before, censorship has increased. Unless they are reviewed, their capacity to communicate is jeopardized and important ideas must be lost; unless literature is allowed to evolve in as many ways as possible, intelligent writing will come to an end, no matter how fine the quality or ambition of the emerging writers; and unless certain cultural endeavors are appropriately supported all along the line of communication, they will disappear from public view.

The crucial truths are as succinct as these.

The Rules
11 of Ignorance
and Philistinism

I

Here is the epitome of our cultural situation. Briefly
put, it is that there exists a great gulf between our
educated class and the best of our literature. —Lionel
Trilling, "The Function of the Little Magazine"
(1946).

But so far every attack on the "formalist" aspect of
modernistic painting and sculpture has worked out as
an attack at the same time on superior artistic standards. —Clement Greenberg, "Necessity of Formalism" (1971).

History has imposed upon the avant-garde the duty
not only of disinterestedly cultivating art and ideas
but of educating and leading an aimless body of
philistine taste and opinion. —Richard Chase, "The
Fate of the Avant-Garde" (1957).

All the accumulating avarice and repression of recent years
might be more defensible if cultural excellence needed protec-
tion at any cost from the challenges of unlettered hordes.
Although cynical rationalizations of that sort were often made,
especially in the course of decimating the young, the oppressed
were often less philistine and ignorant than their oppressors,
whose power corrupted intellectual discourse in more ways than
one. In retrospect, it is clear that ethical slack complements
declines in literacy and intellect, as the failure to acknowledge
the increasing corruptions in intellectual communication, for
instance, indicates certain perceptual insufficiencies, in addition
to moral ones. As literature's intermediary channels function
more and more as adjuncts to publishing publicity, another
inevitable result is the capitulation of both standards and objec-

tivity. These compounding declines have produced a paradox peculiar to post-World War II American culture: Although crucial developments in many scientific and artistic fields represent the best, most advanced, and most influential thinking in the world today, writing in supposedly literate publications has, on the other hand, remained abysmally uninformed. Thus, their writers and their readers remain generally unresponsive to these exemplary achievements in art and thought. In generalizing about American intellectual life or just recent literature and new art, commentators often reveal not only an indifference to elementary cultural values, but also a conspicuous ignorance of what they should know; and the more influential they become, the more ignorance does their insufficient commentary perpetuate. This predicament stems only in part from the fact, already noted, that behind much supposedly "serious" and "intelligent" writing are both rather unserious and unintelligent purposes and minds; but also at the root of current philistinism are certain intellectual flaccidities that have, alas, an increasingly deleterious influence.

Intelligent writing functions as an intermediary between advanced thinking or activity in one field and the general literate public (which may include advanced thinkers in other fields). As an intermediary, intelligent writing rarely makes primary contributions to intellectual history, which is shaped largely by individual initiative within a tradition of problems indigenous to a certain cultural domain. (Customarily, such innovations are initially presented in books and specialized journals.) However, since intelligent writing ideally forges a receptive cultural climate for the circulation and criticism of generally relevant ideas, it has the power to define intellectual history in its own time. In contrast to the genuine cultural achievements that are current in America, as well as the increasing size and intelligence of the literate audience, the qualitative decline of intermediary writing becomes more striking and all the more ominous.

The primary problem, in short, is the illiteracy of the intellectuals, or those who would call themselves "intellectuals," who simply do not know what they pretend or ought, their writing often displaying an inadvertent riot of ignorance. It seems that as an educated man grows older and more demands are made upon his time, to teach and to write and to attend to his growing fortunes and family, he is forced to reconsider how his available hours are apportioned. The first cuts are usually made in time devoted to reading, especially in areas outside his circumscribed "field." In my observation, this constrictive process begins to occur just past the age of twenty-five, and rare nowadays is the busy writer over forty who can even *read* a book not immediately related to his current projects—and just as rare nowadays is the "intellectual" over that age who is ashamed of that incapacity (or even criticized for it). Professionals in the humanities seem especially unable to acquaint themselves with any developments occurring (or coming to their attention) after they have ceased to educate themselves actively. Once they are no longer self-educative, their ignorance grows with the inevitable changes in pertinent learning, at worst making them increasingly anti-intellectual in time.

When success brings yet further demands upon one's output, a once-searching mind becomes tragically inclined to repeat the same ideas, if not the same phrases, over and over again. For this reason, many intellectuals famous for achievements realized over a decade ago seem to carry into the present a stunted literacy that, with the changing times, makes them progressively more defensive and conservative about knowledge, typically decrying as "faddish" or "irrational" anything they cannot, or would not, understand. If businessmen were half as arrogantly conservative in pursuit of their trades, they would soon go bankrupt; but the literary world is, by nature, conservative enough to keep many such has-beens permanently employed and, alas, in print. Furthermore, it should be obvious that no intellectual, no matter how honored and influential, has sufficient license to discuss things he knows nothing about. The fact that some of these "intellectuals" are much-praised does not lessen or rationalize their conspicuous illiteracy. Indeed, nearly all of the "critics" quoted in this chapter have not only published widely but collected their occasional essays into books, which stand as an elementary measure of professional eminence.

It is possible for ignorance to become institutionalized, so that a culturally-aspiring magazine would assuage, rather than rectify, the likely illiteracies of its regular readers. Instead of leading its audience as a cultural institution should, such a publication adopts the middlebrow strategy, more typical of *Time* and *Life,* of pandering to its audience's intellectual limitations. Although *Commentary*'s frequent advertisement for itself as "The World's Greatest Magazine" might be blamed upon an ebullient ad man, numerous statements by the magazine's chief editor, Norman Podhoretz, as well as testimonials by others (including his friend Willie Morris) suggest that the slogan has some serious "intellectual" currency. However, this boast simply will not stand up to objective scrutiny. In the 763 pages of *The Commentary Reader* (1966), which collects supposedly choice articles from twenty years' publishing, there is absolutely no awareness of numerous distinctively post-World War II intellectual and artistic accomplishments of both common relevance and the first rank—among them serial music, quantum physics, molecular biology, the theory of relativity, analytical philosophy, post-New Criticism, experiments in human perception, mixed-media art, and so on. No serious thinkers could possibly neglect these recent-vintage subjects. The criticism in *Commentary* takes easy shots at intellectual inferiors while exhibiting a philistine ignorance of its cultural betters; its pages exemplify that pernicious contemporary illiteracy which regards all knowledge too recent or too different from "the liberal arts" one assimilated as an undergraduate as unfit for the educated gentleman. "The writer who defines his audience by its limitations is indulging in the unforgivable arrogance," Trilling once wrote; a truly educated person, by contrast, knows what he does not know and remains humbled by his ignorance.

In *Commentary,* as in other New York literary-mob publications, nearly all contributors think within a frame of intellectual explanation established by Karl Marx and Sigmund Freud, the two patriarchs of the Jewish intelligentsia, both of whom belong to a cultural period that ended at the latest with the Second World War (and perhaps with the First). This limitation primarily explains the peculiar archaisms of the New Yorkers' typical modes of explanation and discursive vocabulary. The twentieth century of electronic technology, nuclear power, and mass production owes more to Thomas Alva Edison, Guglielmo Marconi, Enrico Fermi, Norbert Weiner, R. Buckminster Fuller, and Henry Ford than it does to either Marx or Freud. Few intellectual vaudevilles are more ridiculous than that of a musty mentality trying to confront the radical developments of the present. Such biases in literary criticism—a nineteenth-century concern with social-psychological meanings, coupled with a

218

neglect of formal invention—partially explains why its favored "critics" are both so obtuse about post-Joycean experimental literature and absolutely unable to understand the non-literary arts. In sum, one could hardly ever know from reading *Commentary, Modern Occasions,* or *The New York Review of Books* that the corpus and character of knowledge relevant to intellectuals has changed radically since 1920, and there is no reason to believe its editors have assimilated that truth either. Podhoretz's own writings, for instance, indicate little, if any, familiarity with new knowledge; and as Cyril Connolly once observed, "No magazine can be more intelligent than its editor, and the limitations of an editor will gradually impose a ceiling." Perhaps because, as Trilling once judged, "The class of New York intellectuals is not remarkable for what it originates," so they are predictably critical of whatever original art and thought happens to break through their barriers of ignorance.

If there are only two separate cultures today, the most distinct dividing line runs between the intellectual modernists and the conservatives, between those who think the present differs so radically from the past that equally new ideas and ideations are essential, and those who think the old notions and thought-patterns should still be our predominant guides. This bias toward the latter probably explains not only those intellectual limitations already noted, but why *The New York Review*'s survey of its readers revealed that less than one-half of one percent were employed in the distinctly contemporary trades of systems analysis and computer programming. By the seventies, intellectually conservative attempts to sustain the heritage of Marx-Freud generally define an intermediary channel as semi-literate, incapable (perhaps by design) of understanding contemporary life and literature. Mutual infatuation of mutual ignorance, not unlike that fostered by *The Daily News,* simply offers little hope for correcting such deficiencies.

Semi-literacy of this rank typically favors periodicals over books (thus neglecting the kinds of knowledge the latter contain), for only such a limitation could explain Irving Howe's erroneous assertion that, "Most of the intellectual figures in America have done their best writing in [periodical] essays." Critiques authored by such sensibilities usually reveal a sense of information and emphasis honed primarily upon newspapers, which are a very limited informational medium. Newspapers suffer not only from stylistic superficiality but also from incorrigible redundancy, as the stories in one paper duplicate those in another or already heard on radio or television (with "newsmagazines" repeating them all). Another reason is that journalism specializes, by definition, in what happened yesterday. This partially explains why the efforts of newspapermen to pose as pundits for the age, as do *The New York Times* "intellectuals," are usually short-sighted and monumentally embarrassing. However, as the most important changes in modern times—and intellectual developments especially—simply do not occur and cannot be perceived in a single day, the journalistic mentality is generally unaware of (or intellectually undone by) almost anything developing over a longer span of time; and it is indicative that the cultural domains ignored by *Commentary* are generally neglected by newspapers as well. Among newspapers, magazines, and, alas, too many "intellectuals," the most compelling vested interest is not knowledge but ignorance.

II

> Persons whose outlook and sensibility differ radically from what is current, or acceptable, within the establishment are unlikely to be understood by establishment members. They are automatically relegated beyond the pale. For them to be heard, published, read, understood, or appreciated according to their merits becomes very difficult. —Ernest Van den Haag, *The Jewish Mystique* (1969).

Nowhere is ignorance more smug, or in closer rapport with a philistine audience, than in discussions of both "the young," as in the infamous Howe essay quoted before, and avant-garde art—those two repeatedly stigmatized cultural classes. Regarding the former, no one who ever read it can forget Diana Trilling decrying, back in 1958 no less,

> the shoddiness of an audience in which it was virtually impossible to distinguish between student and campfollower [as if that should be necessary], the always-new shock of so many young girls, so few of them pretty, and so many blackest black stockings; so many young men, so

few of them—despite black beards—with any promise of masculinity.

Or that John Canaday, the principal art critic of *The New York Times,* called in 1960 for a Darwinian purge, mobilizing prejudices destructive of opportunity, his final three words betraying a reactionary desire to return to an earlier artistic condition:

> The assumption that young painters should be encouraged is absurd and in the end vicious. No one owes them a debt of gratitude for their adoption of a dubious profession; they should be cut down in battalions, on the principle of weeding and pruning, to allow the ones with the vigor to rise again.

Who can forget John Aldridge's pseudo-description in his hysterically conservative polemic, *In the Country of the Young* (1970):

> The new body style for men is neither tall nor short, fat nor thin. Classic Arrow Collar features have been replaced by the androgynous medieval squire or hairy simian look, ugliness now supposedly being suggestive of ferocious sexual vitality. Among male hippies this notion has been carried to the point where hair—usually of exactly the right color and texture—is worn like a pubic growth covering indiscriminately head, face, groin, and armpits; so that the entire person becomes a sex organ. Even the thighs exposed by miniskirts no longer seem to be the sexy upper parts of legs but interchangeable items of mannequin decor, purchased like wigs at boutiques.

Or Professor Philip Rieff's diabolical equation of initially separate antagonists: "All bohemians must be sociologically defined as young, for the essential and public form of bohemian activity is sexual exhibitionism." Or William Styron, a non-academic repository of literary cant, assuring his interviewer Philip Rahv, "to be sure, most of them [the young] don't read much of anything." Just as it is the radical literary entrepreneur's hypocrisy to advocate revolutions in all places except his own, so it is a typically conservative strategy to complain that the hierarchies are breaking down, while one's own position is either smug and secure or aggressively advanced.

It follows that similar ignorances riddle elder literary critics' remarks about writing and art that are radically new. Those who flatly assert, with George P. Elliott, that "there never was much of an avant-garde in America, and there is none now," are too thick-headed, too ignorant, or self-serving to recognize what a rich and valuable avant-garde there is, and has been, in America. (Anyone making such a blanket assertion also incapacitates himself for the experience of surprise, which is the initial indication of originality in art.) Indeed, the existence of new art seems to inspire a penchant for commenting upon work that the "critic" evidently has not seen or knows nothing about. Although a senior professor would unhesitantly flunk a student for submitting a review of a book that he had not read, the same professor suffers no qualms about criticizing artworks he has not examined at first hand. Thus does Professor Alfred Kazin, in 1971, dismiss John Cage as just a musician "whose well-known ability to sit publicly at a piano and *not* play anything is the greatest comic act in the music business." He is referring, apparently, to Cage's so-called "silent piece," officially entitled *4'33"* (1952), which rates as one of the most crucial works of recent art; anyone present at its only two performances in the fifties, or even familiar with the abundant secondary literature about the work, knows that *4'33"* was performed not by Cage himself but by the pianist David Tudor. And although it was not especially funny at the time (and has not been "performed" in the past dozen years), Cage himself often is, as well as being a far more serious thinker than Kazin's flippant and ultimately retrograde remark suggests. René Wellek, the Sterling Professor of Comparative Literature at Yale, joins Kazin in protesting Cage's "notorious piece of music in which three musicians did nothing," which he could not have experienced, because the piece he describes does not exist. Illiteracy of this sort makes the possible relevance of criticism dependent, like Cage's "aleatory" music, on pure chance or simply upon luck.

Some criticisms are so inappropriate that knowledgeable readers inevitably doubt if the work was actually seen. I doubt if anyone who attended the Performance Group's first-rate *Dionysus in '69* (1968), no matter how prejudiced or obtuse, could characterize it, as Irving Howe did, as "a theatrical grope-in" or complain that it used only one-third of the original text ("Why even a third? Who needs words at all?"); whereas the more common, more astute criticism made by those actually attending it was that declamation was less effective than choreography. No spectator who ever experienced *Paradise Now* (1968) could call The Living Theatre, to quote Howe again, "an institution in which hysteria has been elevated to the dignity of authoritarianism" (even though the exit doors were never locked!); one suspects that such characterizations could only be derived from a highly prejudiced reading of reviews (just as a dishonest student might forge his critique from a digest of plot summaries). Similarly epitomizing the disintegration of research standards and common critical courtesy, Benjamin DeMott based a derogatory essay on "Tickle-Touch Theater," reprinted in *Supergrow* (1969), not upon any evidence of personal participation in such works, but instead on statements by the practitioners and participants, his caveats avoiding the key issues posed by such performances and drawing in the end upon as much first-hand experience as a Hottentot's upon ice-skating.

Only the authority of ignorance could allow John Simon to call John Cage "a fey farceur and effete solipsist, . . . playing campy games with silence," even though no-sound is crucial to very few of Cage's compositions or performances; or to characterize Andy Warhol (always a facile obscenity in literary circles) as "a vulgar little window-decorator, . . . without a single idea or vision in his head," although Warhol's work reveals several clear and powerful ideas about repetition and the over-emphasis of one artistic dimension (usually coupled with the atrophy of another). The kind of "happenings" that Louis Kampf's *On Modernism* (1967) attributes to "Andy Warhol" would clearly be more characteristic of that art's inventor, Allan Kaprow; with equal ignorance Kampf, an M.I.T. "Humanities" professor (and past president of academia's M.L.A.), credits the composer Milton Babbitt with "mathematical procedures which will totally organize—indeed predict—the sounds of any musical composition." (Babbitt's response: "Would God they could.") Were he unfamiliar with Chinese, Kampf would scarcely comment upon an untranslated novel; but his ignorance of contemporary music's language makes him, curiously, more arrogant than modest. It is scarcely surprising that in book after intellectual book, article after literary article, *Finnegans Wake* is misspelled (e.g., Susan Sontag, *Partisan Review* [Summer, 1963], p. 262; Ralph Ellison, *Shadow and Act* [1964], p. 163; Morse Peckham, *The Triumph of Romanticism* [1970], p. 211; Cynthia Ozick, *American Journal* [Dec. 1, 1972], p. 26; Ann Charters, *Kerouac* [1973], p. 312). As anyone who has actually read it should know, there is no apostrophe!

It is vulgar as well as ignorant to dismiss LeRoi Jones "as a distinctively American success, the pop-art guerilla warrior" (to belabor Howe again), for there is no connection, beyond polemical assertion, between Jones and a respectable painterly style that Howe the "critic" obviously does not understand. (His subsequent reviews tend to judge not how much can be gleaned from the work at hand, but whether Howe himself approves of its position or it agrees with him—exemplifying the principle of ideological solipsism.) "It is, I think, exceedingly difficult to speak meaningfully of a Jackson Pollock painting or a composition by Stockhausen," writes George Steiner in *Language and Silence* (1967)—especially if the mid-Atlantic "critic" knows as little about music and painting as Steiner apparently does, or his critical equipment is linguistically inadequate. Some "literary" intellectuals are so shockingly illiterate, not only in books but in the other arts, that their ignorance of new theater, new painting, and new music should be no surprise; but their almost unanimous deprecation of work they have not personally examined or do not understand clearly reeks of outright fraud.

The congenital conservative seems to establish a double standard for dealing with new art, assuming that his criticisms of it need not follow the rules of evidence customarily accorded the classic texts; so that his erroneous remarks reveal not just personal (and editorial) ignorance, but a fundamental corruption of critical intelligence. In Leonard Meyer's much-acknowledged, but misleading essay on aleatory esthetics, "The End of a Renaissance" (1963), no single work is experienced or even described, let along analyzed in detail, although secondary texts of varying quality and authority are scrupulously quoted; and his conclusions about the formlessness of aleatory art reveal an easily remedied first-hand ignorance of its works. *The Jumping-Off Place* (1969), a thoroughly detailed survey of

224

recent drama by Professor Gerald Weales, devotes thirty-five unsympathetic pages to "The Other Theater," even though, as the author admits, "my own experience of the Happening is severely limited (to an occasional Environment and an evening at the Armory)." By relying instead upon secondary texts of varying value, Weales succumbs to an excess of error and critical misunderstanding—the principle apparently being that fashionable conservativism can rationalize an academic's ignorance. Gerald Sykes, in *The Perennial Avant-Garde* (1970), utters all sorts of conservative platitudes in the course of revealing absolutely no first-hand knowledge or experience with avant-garde art of the sixties. That such a book should be published, reviewed, and favorably blurbed by Alfred Kazin, Harold Clurman, and the like is itself dispiriting; the fact that it was even written suggests that the restraints of critical conscience no longer encumber reactionary ignorance.

In a particularly outrageous example of making a virtue of first-hand non-acquaintance, Professor Roger Shattuck asserts in *The New York Review* of a work "I have not seen":

> I am convinced that *Etant donnés* is Duchamp's ultimate and most daring art history hoax, perpetrated upon (and with the connivance of) museums, critics, art historians, book reviewers, stunned public and himself.

The fear is that criticism about art unseen could resemble debates about God, except that *Etant donnés,* unlike God, was open to the public. A recent issue of the conservative-academic little magazine *Salmagundi* contains an essay on new dance by a Buffalo English professor named Martin Pops who writes that:

> In [Merce] Cunningham's theatre the involvement of his audience has grown literal: he has been known to shine a spot-light at his patrons, and his dancers have chatted with their audience during (and as part of) a performance. Cunningham has also choreographed for conditions of darkness—one thinks of Ad Reinhardt's so-called "black" painting of the same period.

This brief passage about the world's foremost avant-garde choreographer contains four outright errors and one mistaken allusion. First, no Cunningham piece necessarily shines lights *at* the audience, though this may sometimes happen inadvertently in certain theaters (and other choreographers have intentionally done this). Second, in no piece do Cunningham's dancers chat with the audience; neither is the audience ever invited to participate in the piece. Third, the inviolable darkness of Ad Reinhardt's paintings scarcely resembles that of Cunningham's one dark piece, *Winterbranch* (1964), where the darkness is sporadically violated by beams of light. Fourth, those "so-called 'black' paintings" are in fact called Black Paintings (1960-66). However, the more appropriate analogy in painting, obvious to anyone familiar with the field, would be Robert Rauschenberg's light-reflective Black Paintings (1951) which subtly differ from Reinhardt's, especially since Rauschenberg happens to be credited, in the Cunningham program, with the piece's "decor" of darkness. (Why don't such authors and their editors ask whether they are sufficiently *qualified* to publish such an essay—not in an academic sense of sufficient degrees, but, simply, knowledgeable enough to judge whether its statements are right or wrong?)

Nonetheless, given the deleterious literalness that everything in academic print acquires nowadays, these Pops' assertions (along with his equally erroneous major thesis) will undoubtedly be quoted in subsequent academic essays on the new dance, further propagating the reigning misunderstandings. However, precisely because works of new art are so different, as well as so vulnerable to misrepresentation, they demand of every critic worthy of that title both a truly "liberal," open-minded, first-hand experience of the work itself, a perception fine enough to describe it accurately, a knowledge of the relevant comparisons and traditions, and then an intellect strong enough to define unusual forms or order. It is the critic's job to repair ignorance, not to perpetuate it.

III

> The academics, that is, have not changed their skins at all, merely camouflaged them. They still object, as they always have objected, to the practice of real literary criticism, which necessarily menaces their self-esteem and professional reputation. —Q.D. Leavis, "The Discipline of Letters" (1943).

In current criticism of new art is a catalogue of contemporary intellectual sins, representing in sum a betrayal of intelligence; for if "liberal education" is designed to open the mind, "philistinism" by definition advocates and exemplifies smugly conventional modes of comprehension, initially forbidding receptivity to even the most auspicious new art. More than one supposedly serious critic will confine a general discussion of, say, "the state of fiction" entirely to recent works of previously established novelists—or, even worse, just the highbrow best-seller list—rather than risking any interest in new or unknown figures. The range of accepted contemporary subjects is not only remarkably narrow—a literary canon established before its time has come—but it is also largely the result of publishing and literary-political promotions.

The new art is often condemned as "irrational" or "formless" or something similar, usually because its particular nature cannot be critically encapsulated; and only by ascribing such a false "destruction of coherence" could Erich Kahler, for one conservative, accuse new art of "the conscious destruction of consciousness." Nine times out of ten, however, the critic using such epithets simply lacks, as Kahler evidently does, the artistic knowledge, intelligence, and perceptual experience to discern the form (or "coherence") of anything so different from what he has previously known. Thus does George P. Elliott dismiss William Burroughs' *Naked Lunch* and *Nova Express* with: "The difference between these two non-books is slight beside their similarity. Neither has a form of its own." In principle, however, every creation of man that realizes any sort of distinctiveness, no matter how unfamiliar—that can be characterized or compared in any encompassing way, as Elliott inadvertently does—must also have some kind of perceptible and thus definable form. (And since the term "art" implies degrees of shaping coherence that differentiate such human creations from life, "formless art" is a contradiction in terms. So is "non-book" if the pages are bound together and the contents of one page relate to the others.)

Similarly, there is no such thing as a "boring work of art," though some temporal art consumes too much time for its content. When the word "boring" is used to characterize something that other people seem to find genuinely interesting, it is quite likely that the "bored" spectator suffers an incapacity, perhaps due to easily remedied ignorance, to perceive the work's particular artistic language or source of interest. (A conversation in Russian would, no doubt, be comparably boring to someone ignorant of the tongue.) Some reactionaries are forever ignoring the puzzles of new work to impugn the motives and personalities of its artists; Robert Brustein, for example, frequently discredits a work through inaccurate, if not libelous, characterization of its spectators: "The audience at *Gorilla Queen* is composed mostly of Madison Avenue queens on a slumming tour. . . ." "Miss McCullers' Gothic stories were modish twenty years ago, but since they were obviously written for the female reader, they eventually found their proper level among the pages of *Vogue* and *Harper's Bazaar*."

The new art is also criticized for attracting a large following (though this is rarely true) and for a fictitious commercialism (though the most profitable art today, as always, is conventional), and for swaying easily impressionable critics. John Canaday charges that "the bulk of Abstract art in America has followed the course of least resistance and quickest profit"—which is not true, as the bulk of abstract art never found any customers at all, especially in America. Brustein speaks of "the willingness of virtually everyone, and most especially the mass media, to welcome 'new works, new writers, new forms.' " In point of fact, most middlebrow magazines are far more receptive to an essay attacking vanguard art than anything favoring or explaining it; academic quarterlies are similarly prejudiced. Also, there are no reviewers predisposed to new art writing regularly for any American daily, weekly, or monthly—the only possible exception being Eric Salzman who sporadically provides short record notices to *Stereo Review*; so that established American "critics" actually do little, if anything, to help overcome the natural ignorance and fear of the new. Indeed, reviewers, as a rule, perpetuate accepted reputations and promotions most of the time. That is the principal reason why they are hired to write regularly. Thus, art in America continues its radical development in spite of the conservatism of criticism, until formerly avant-garde works are incorporated into the canonized culture or, perhaps, a new generation takes critical command within the intermediary media.

Because of its concern with novelty, the new art is equated with "advertising" or "marketing" even though its messages are,

228

by definition, not immediately comprehensible and its produce is not instantaneously commercial. (By similarly partial logic, the poetry of Alexander Pope could be equated with jingles—both favor couplets.) It is not avant-garde writing but rather old-fashioned works which make easy, unproblematic reading. Such works as *The Fixer, Herzog, The Confessions of Nat Turner,* or *Portnoy's Complaint* sway not only easily impressionable reviewers, but supposedly more serious "fiction critics" as well (some of whom would have piously charged, not too long ago, that no novels so popular could possibly be "serious" as well). The principal reason for this default is that nearly all American criticism functions instead to reaffirm a canon of established styles (and reputations), as well as conventional forms of reading. As Guy Davenport notes, an academic critical magazine "can be counted upon to welcome an essay wondering whether Bill Styron is truly a modern novelist or an old-fashioned novelist who passes for modern; it is embarrassed [by genuinely avant-garde figures] ." The analogous sin common in film criticism is writing about current films, whether as a regular reviewer or in a comprehensive survey, without even considering experimental works (that are customarily produced apart from the big studios and their promotional-distributional system); so that many superficially encompassing generalizations about "the state of film [or fiction] today" are made in total ignorance of some very relevant work.

"There is not a single artistic style, however, avant-garde, that does not sell [in America] ," declares Herbert Marcuse; but any overview of every art today shows quite clearly that only a few styles, which are usually behind the avant-garde, actually sell, and that most truly avant-garde art, like that discussed later in this book, is as neglected and unremunerative as ever. This charge, like so much else in Marcuse, would be more reassuring, if true; but by such prejudices does Marcuse join hands with Eric Hoffer, liberalism's oldest fogey, who smugly asserts:

> What needs explaining is the presence of a receptive audience [for "the contemporary explosion of avant-garde innovation"] . More significant than the fact that poets write abstrusely, painters paint abstractly, and composers compose unintelligible music is that people should admire

what they cannot understand; indeed, admire that which has no meaning on principle.

Such an illiberal mind will never learn anything from either the new art or those who genuinely understand it. Avant-garde artists are often dismissed as opportunists unable to create in conventional ways; yet not only is this more untrue than not, but many, many more conventional and commercial artists in any field can be classified as "failed avant-gardists." (It was Kenneth Burke who reported, refuting a comparable piety, that he knew more failed writers who became businessmen than vice versa.)

Another typical deceit is generalizing from inadequate evidence, if not from just one or two admittedly weak or untypical examples. A "critic" who demolishes in detail a particular experimental novel, or a single mixed-means theatrical performance, or just its articulated theory, will then eagerly draw untenable, often diametrically erroneous conclusions about a whole artistic enterprise. Benjamin DeMott's apparent inexperience of the new theater, for instance, does not prevent him from concluding that it inhibits "absorption, attentiveness and otherness," though those are precisely the processes that, in my own experience, are emphasized and enhanced in mixed-means performance. A more elaborate version of this conservative strategy was articulated in *The New York Review* by someone who should know better, Roger Shattuck, one of the artistic avant-garde's finest historians (though that is no necessary qualification for current critical acuity):

We also understand, though far less clearly, that over 90 per cent of [scientists'] experiments go unrecorded because they are uninteresting or unsuccessful. No one has ventured to say how large a percentage of the avant-garde artists of all time are alive and active today. Whatever the figure, however, they are rarely willing to work with the same margin of success. They insist on performing or publishing practically everything, hence the flimsiness [in, it is implied, all or nearly all avant-garde art].

However, percentages simply do not matter, for the most elementary rule of qualitatively generalizing artistic criticism is that *the bad ones do not count*—that the deficiencies of *King John,* say, are just not a viable measure of the general quality of either Shakespeare's plays or Elizabethan theater (and probably not worthy of sustained analysis either). In art, as in science, only the "successful" experiments count, though in art, unlike science, success cannot be instantly ascertained.

A weak instance or even ten duds cannot be validly used to discredit an entire cultural collection. Indeed, the presumption that a small sample can be turned to such general ends reveals, by itself, initially unsympathetic motives, as well as the condescending assumption that a whole artistic endeavor so judged is uniform in quality. (By the same false process could scholarship be called "hopelessly dull," even though professors write many lively books.) "But not all that is contemporary is genuine literature," writes Cleanth Brooks in an obvious conservative converse. "Some of it is trash and worse than trash"; but so was most Elizabethan writing and even most New Criticism. Similarly again, just as the existence of many bad paintings provides insufficient reason to question the efficacy of brushes, so examples of poor technological art do not, as is frequently charged, bring into doubt all the possible artistic uses of machinery. By the same false criterion—excess low-grade production—could iambic pentameter also be completely dismissed. In short, unless a critic fresh to a field has bothered to familiarize himself with the good ones and assimilated as well the prior advice of their most sophisticated advocates (no matter if he is talking about Shakespeare's plays or a new art), he is *not sufficiently literate* to draw such comprehensive conclusions.

A more subtle intellectual fault that plagues discussions of new art is a blinding allegiance to critical categories honed upon the experience of earlier work. In this instance, all new art which transcends the old formulations, or all in the new art that remains incomprehensible or undefinable to the critic, comes to represent, perforce, diametrically contrary qualities. If the old art were supposedly highly rational, then the new art must be "irrational"; or if once socially conscious, it now must be "estheticist." Or if the old art were "humanistic," then the new art is "dehumanized"—a sustained demonstration of this fallacy is Kahler's *The Disintegration of Form in the Arts* (1968). That last epithet, "dehumanized," also signifies, more often than not, that the "critic" is not sufficiently open-minded or humanly perceptive to locate the human being in the work of art. Unfortunately, those contrary terms are often applied in such arbitrary ways that anyone favoring such epithets will invariably use them indiscriminately to characterize and thereby dismiss everything in recent art he does not like.

Such derogatory terms, no matter how false or inept, also function to create a comprehensible negative category into which all artistic garbage may be unwillingly dumped, for the *dreck*-maker provides philistines with terms of ready dismissal. Conservatives also attempt to popularize a stereotype (i.e., "beat" or "literature of nihilism") as a prelude to the fallacy of dismissing one part with the whole (or the whole by a part), even though the stereotype may be inapplicable to the part at hand or the particular work may simply be deficient. The deceit of this approach lies in persistently denying the truth of individual differences in literature. An epithet like "beat" was popularized by "critics" before entering the popular press; and one sign of Allen Ginsberg's immense perseverence has been his success in overcoming the stereotype that once imprisoned both him and his poetry.

A limited critical vocabulary by itself usually indicates the writer's inability to comprehend specific works at hand; even a critic as once-brilliant as Harold Rosenberg, whose essays crucially defined "action painting," has rejected practically everything important in the art of the 1960s—all that successfully succeeded the decline of the advocacy that made him prominent—with a small repertoire of caveats. His essays predictably accuse each new development of being less new than it seems or than its advocates say; of selling out to the mass media and its machinery of promotion; of succumbing to technology rather than revealing humanity; of exploiting faddishness rather than transcending it. The polemic is the same, as are the derogatory (and ultimately censorious) terms; only the examples and names of increasingly younger artists are changed. To further compound his shortsightedness, Rosenberg shares Howe's penchant for ascribing positions which are often inaccurate, using qualifiers like "as it were" as a license for unironic exaggeration: "In contrast to the meagerness of art, the artist is blown up to gigantic proportions. . . . The artist has become, as it were, too big for art." (And Professor Wellek, sure enough, quotes Rosenberg as saying, "The artist has become too big for art.") Rosenberg talks primarily about the circumstances of today's art—the education of artists, the creation of new art, its acceptance, and its popularization—in lieu of any apparent interest in, or experience of, the works themselves.

A more congenital conservative, such as Hilton Kramer, adopts the disingenuous trick of forever decrying the most recent avant-garde as inferior to its predecessors whose achievements he then seems to acknowledge, whereas he has in fact previously condemned each of them as similarly inferior to *its* predecessor; but mindlessness of this rank need not have an eye to see. Leslie A. Fiedler, by contrast, is forever asserting that the avant-garde is dead and yet acknowledging the validity of every widely accepted innovator emerging from its tomb—Ginsberg, Barth, Hawkes, Burroughs. Finally, only a critic as reactionary as John Simon could write in 1972, without irony, that "I am neither against the innovative nor against the difficult in art. . . . My enjoyment of truly innovative theatrical works like Jarry's *Ubu Roi* or Apollinaire's *Les mamalles de Tirésias* is sweet and unalloyed," even though both these examples were written more than a half century before! All of these polemical strategies not only exemplify the growing distance between contemporary art and intermediary writing, but also represent a failure or perversion of critical intelligence. It is the defining mark of the middlebrow critic (and magazine) to favor the rote condemnation of truly new art, rather than the creation of a discriminating taste for it.

Perhaps the epitome of fallacies in confronting radically innovative art is Renata Adler's essay, "Selling an Enraged Bread Pudding," which first appeared in *The New Yorker* (Nov. 12, 1966) and was subsequently reprinted in her book, *Toward a Radical Middle* (1969). As the only American critic born after 1933 to win the long-sustained support of established institutions—not only *The New Yorker* and *The New York Times,* but also Random House (where one senior editor, Joseph Fox, published her books over reported internal protestations) and the National Book Award Committee which once made her a juror—Adler has always been more conservative than radical, the title of her book notwithstanding, and more comforting than controversial. She was sufficiently open-minded, however, to recognize critically some new art of the sixties and actually witness its works; but her straightforward remarks exemplify certain reactionary postures and anti-intellectual strategems. The occasion for her review was "9 Evenings: Theatre & Engineering," a series of mixed-means (or non-literary) theater pieces that was typically both different from literary theater and mixed in quality, as well as untypically (and inexcusably) sloppy in technological execution. Thanks in part to the eminence of certain participants, especially John Cage and Robert Rauschenberg, along with the efforts of a high-powered press-agent, this extravagance received far more attention than it deserved, drawing an audience as well as some critics (like Adler) whose previous experience of mixed-means theater was negligible. (In that respect, the poor quality of the performances may have discouraged many open-minded people who might have, in better circumstances, become new enthusiasts.)

Although Adler accuses the new theater of "blurring distinctions," the most conspicuous defect of her collective review is a reluctance to differentiate among the ten different performances; for it was the nearly unanimous opinion of the informed critics (as well as the participating artists themselves) that one work was superior and more successful than the others—John Cage's *Variations VII* (1966). Indeed, Adler's confession of frequent boredom *during* the pieces (rather than between them when the technicians took interminably long to set up) suggests, as noted before, that she might have lacked the experience necessary to perceive and comprehend them; and there is no evidence within the essay to suggest that she bothered to discover the articulate purposes of this new art or to inform herself about the previous works or characteristic concerns of the participating artists. Even worse, she resorts to the philistine fallacy of damning the artists by quoting their statements, as published in the theater program, without first considering (as should be clear) that some of these declarations were perhaps willful parodies or that "poetic" or gnomic assertions relate to the artists' works in various unliteral ways. (She even makes the ridiculous charge that "these statements actually *constituted* the works in question," which is completely untrue even in an ironic sense.) Adler freely draws assumptions about the participating artists which seem highly unjustified, as well as foisted ascriptions about the audience's experience which this member for one knows to be indisputably false. During Cage's masterpiece, for instance, she finds the audience lying "about the floor in a parody of sleep or catatonia." No, since there were no chairs, they were merely listening to the surrounding music in the most relaxed position possible.

It is typical for conservative critics to cast themselves in the underdog position even when addressing an audience far larger than the new art receives—an hypocrisy exemplified by the two conservative art critics of *The New York Times*. Adler has the audacity to pitch her lone self against "a permanent cadre of viewers, critics and collectors determined never to be caught again outside the swim of art. They are marked by a terrible anxiety to ferret out the New. . . ." However, this posture is essentially philistine because her essay implicitly congratulates its middlebrow audience for its neglect of vanguard art. In further fact, there is no "permanent cadre" of critics, and "9 Evenings" received all but unanimous unfavorable notice.

Upon this and only this circumstance, nonetheless, rather than the dozens of better examples she missed, Adler makes generalizations which, to judge internal evidence, she simply is not qualified to draw; to wit: "Mixed media were and are, in any case, better suited to propaganda than art; they do not enlighten, they incite or numb." Rather than conclude with that faux pas, she first equates "9 Evenings" with a sub-artistic celebration of "Krishna Consciousness" (on the falsely foisted Brusteinian ascription of "the same constituency, or an overlapping one") and then audaciously proceeds to generalize as well about the "deliberate combination of art and technology," all in apparent ignorance of any other contemporary artworks in that vein. "It is for selling something," her conclusion invalidly sweeps; "and that, of course, is the whole point." Critically this is disagreeable to me, no doubt in part because one of my own books deals favorably with *The Theatre of Mixed Means* (1968); but intellectually the essay is a wretched performance whose failures are more typical of conservative criticism than idiosyncratic.

In his book on *The Failures of Criticism* (1967), Henri Peyre enumerates several attitudes, all ultimately philistine, that have historically prevented the comprehension of new writing. First, whereas earlier ages were characterized by focus and unity, "today, however, confusion reigns supreme. No 'elite' imposes its views on the public; the field is surrendered to young upstarts and false talents." Second, "the same critics likewise remark that the present era is full of interest, brilliantly gifted, rich in intelligent attempts, but devoid of geniuses." (An extended illustration was Alfred Kazin's essay on "The Literary Sixties," originally in the penultimate *New York Times Book Review* of that decade.) Third, "a far more attractive excuse for the unproductiveness of their age, or for their own inability to discern its great men, the critics find in the magical word: transition. . . . How can art and literature flourish when the social state is chaotic and mankind haunted by unheard-of-problems. . . ." Fourth, the new writing is dismissed for its lack of acceptable technique, "the young writers do not know how to write; the young painters cannot draw," etc. "Or again, the innovators repudiate the principle of selection. They do not know how to choose, and merely accumulate a mass of disorderly material." Fifth, the new is dismissed *in toto* as inferior to the glories of the past, which by and large the new work is; however, by evading the crucial critical questions of current value, that charge is irrelevant. Despite the fact that advanced art and advanced thought are gaining an audience today, the critical powers-that-be are currently no more enlightened than the philistines who exiled Henry James, ostracized Baudelaire, rejected Joyce, neglected Faulkner—in sum, contributing to the end of intelligent writing.

Double Standards
12 and Pseudo-Culture

I

The sin of the double standard [comes from] applying a less rigorous code to myself than to my friend,
and a less rigorous code to a stranger than mine
enemy. —Wayne Booth, *Now Don't Try to Reason
with Me* (1970).

A peculiarity of the Communist wolf is that he exists
in a kind of double image—he snarls and shows his
fangs at the frontier, at the same time that he baas
close at hand under his false sheep's head. —Harold
Rosenberg, "The Heroes of Marxist Science" (1959).

The quality of a man's life nowadays depends largely
on the quality of what he reads . . . so a diet of the
second-rate blunts one's capacity for genuine feeling
and disables the mind for digesting new and invigorat-
ing ideas. —Denys Thompson, *Reading and Discrimination* (1934).

The decline of American criticism permits the easy establishment of double standards, not only to excuse the wholesale
denigration of certain artistic developments (such as the New
and the Young), but also to construct a contrary set of artificial
elevations. In practice, the double standard functions to excuse
what might otherwise be called weaknesses or defects in favored
writers and then to fabricate public interest in cultural produce
that would otherwise be outside the audience's concerns.
Double standards, when systematically applied, create a minor
league of touted figures who are primarily discussed with reference to each other (because comparison with big-league performers would be ludicrous); so that the virtues ascribed to an
individual work or writer exist in a less than universal (or even

237

national) domain. The increasing literary politicization of American writing means that discriminating readers of criticism must frequently distinguish genuinely disinterested appraisals from partisan puffs or hatchet-jobs, especially when reading coterie-dominated magazines or coterie-minded "critics."

Every minority literary clique of any ambition attempts to create special terms for discussing its colleagues' works, because the acceptance of these pet epithets will in turn help create a sustained interest in all of the clique's produce. Its publicists will also make special claims for its minority-based particularity, whether it be racial or geographic, ethnic or sexual, for by that enticing "handle" can the public comprehend the entire enterprise; and not until a cultural audience accepts that claim can its loyalty be won. For these reasons, most non-esthetic, sociological categories ("Jewish," "black," "feminist," etc.) ultimately are not just self-serving but detrimental to objective artistic scrutiny. It follows that the influence of a certain literary pressure group can best be measured by the general acceptance of its particular mythologies and double standards, and greatest success comes when its minor league ("New York Intellectuals" or "Agrarians") is widely regarded as equal to, even if still separate from, the majors. However, should the discrepancy between a group's claims and the worth of its members' work become too stark, the whole enterprise loses credence with skeptical readers, for one inevitable result of nearly all collective elevations is an equally collective descent.

The recent epitome of this last development, after the Jewish-American example, has favored a succession of black writers, such bias also reflecting extra-literary circumstances. Although the racial (or sexual) identity of the artist counts for little in most artistic communication, it is likely to determine how cultural institutions respond to the artist's work. Black writers have recently received more fellowships (in compensation for supposed cultural disadvantage) than comparably talented whites get—one sure sign of an established double standard—while their latest works are often praised by certain well-known black writers (helping their own) and white critic-publicists famously sympathetic to any and all black art. (One sign of the current efficacy of "Black Power" is that other, mostly smaller cultural minorities have not been so favored.) In example after example, "critics" of black-authored books reveal their racism or race-determined consciousness precisely as they try to deny it, for double standards based on skin color reflect white-authored racism even if articulated by a black man. However, as most reviewers currently seem unable to adjudicate, or even approach, black-authored books without presuppositions (usually based upon the ascribed "meaning" of race) detrimental to open-minded literary scrutiny, so are sophisticated readers of such reviews unable to escape other, negative kinds of unfortunate presuppositions—the suspicion, for instance, that the praise of the book is unjustified. For that last reason, no class of writers has been so detrimentally betrayed by ultimately counter-productive publicity which has as often been espoused among, or foisted upon, themselves.

A double standard is patronizing in the end, especially when established by outsiders (fawning favor being the cynical side of disfavor's coin), because the racial segregation of literature implies that black writers ultimately do not possess the education and talent necessary for the creation of books good enough to compete equally with those by whites. (Apologists for this position, whether black or white, are thus forced to ignore or dismiss the glaring counter-example of Ralph Ellison's *Invisible Man* [1952], which is customarily ranked among the six great postwar novels.) For these reasons, black-backers scarcely did young Cecil Brown a favor when they compared his fine first novel, *Life and Loves of Mr. Jiveass Nigger* (1969), to James Baldwin, Richie Havens, and others, because Brown's novel descends from, and belongs to, more august, integrated artistic company. Similarly, only a racial double standard would permit the circulation of such a kiss-of-death anthology as Clarence Major's *The New Black Poetry* (1969), where sixty contributors, each represented by a token poem, seem so similar (and similarly amateur) that one suspects a single fecund black poet authored every work. (And it is no surprise that a white publisher of very leftish leanings released so much dreadful black poetry.) Furthermore, unless the loyalty of an audience is assured in advance, usually on non-esthetic, socio-political grounds, possible readers are likely to discriminate against such promotions, sight unseen, as suspect or irrelevant to their interests. As a result, books of rare virtue are inadvertently buried by increasingly common platitudes. (Counter-examples include such superior, though racially segregated, anthologies as Ishmael

Reed's *19 Necromancers from Now* [1970] and Adam David Miller's *Dice or Black Bones* [1970].) Even as they are publicly praised, works by black writers must overcome extra hazards nowadays in making their critical way; not only are they neglected because of race, but over-zealous friends can sometimes be as destructive as enemies. Some U.S. review-editors play a similarly parochial game with new books by Canadians, assigning them only to their countrymen who thus find a negative notice unpatriotic and a platitudinously positive review counter-productive. Some reviewers in *Ms.* are fashioning a similar parochial predicament for books by women.

A further truth contrary to the double standard is that a great book is no easier to write because one is black (or Jewish or female), though it is far easier for either one's sympathizers or oneself to rationalize a bad one on minority-defined grounds. For artists, like athletes, there are no legitimate excuses for inferior performances, and no black sprinter worthy of respect ever acknowledged any racially-biased double standard or blamed his professional losses upon social disadvantages. Indeed, the deleterious influence of double standards, rather than discrimination in publishing or reviewing, may well be the primary reason why American Negroes have *not* been producing more first-rate books. "All you have to do," notes the black critic Albert Murray, "is compare the kind of encouragement given by the typical white literary patron with the aspirations of the managers and promoters of Negro prize-fighters. Financial double-dealing aside, the backers of Negro boxers are out to produce champions of the world." The impact of jazz and blues show that black artists need not depend upon double standards to win an audience. However, those that become popular with a large, interracial public are likely to inspire negative criticism, unless their advocates are powerful enough to keep such reactions out of public circulation. That last criterion remains a sure measure of the continuing strength of the Jewish-American literary movement, especially in contrast to the black.

Only a racist double standard could allow the publication and republication of this Nikki Giovanni poem which articulates a rationale for murder:

> Can you poison
> Can you stab-a-Jew

Can you kill huh? nigger
Can you kill.

Can we learn to kill WHITE for BLACK
Learn to kill niggers
Learn to be Blackmen

A further ridiculous development, scarcely worth refuting, is the attempt by a C.U.N.Y. literature professor, Addison Gayle, Jr., to base "a black aesthetic" on the utilitarian solipsism: "Not how beautiful is a melody, a play, a poem, or a novel, but how much more beautiful has [the work of art] made the life of a single black man?"

In applying the double standard, racialist critics display two different and somewhat contrary strategies, the first citing black skin per se as the primary credential for expertise on all Negro-American phenomena (even if the writer knows little about his ostensible subject, such as music or painting) and the second advocating highly defined (and thus limited) conceptions of "authenticity" and "honesty." The first leads to the illiberal segregation of art and culture (sometimes realized with white complicity), where black writers are regarded as completely isolated from white (and western) literature and only black critics are permitted to review books by Negroes. Thanks to this bias, reputations are established within a hermetic system, linguistic signs familiar only to blacks are cultivated, and a parochial "esthetic" is posited, all these processes further institutionalizing a double standard (invariably perpetuated in "black" anthologies). "Being black," notes Murray, "is not enough to make anybody an authority on U.S. Negroes, any more than being white has ever qualified anybody as an expert on the ways of U.S. white people." If more Caucasian authors tried to "pass" as black, as Dan McCall did in his fine neglected novel, *The Man Says Yes* (1969), and contributed as well to avowedly "black" magazines, this last bastion of lily-pure segregation, as well as its accompanying false criteria, might be ridiculed into extinction.

Indeed, precisely because self-segregation can finally be so self-defeating, it is surprising that black writers are not more suspicious of the white literary moguls who seem less eager to segregate authors belonging to other American minorities. It follows that anthologies of less-than-best "black writing," like those of less-than-best "women's literature," are deleterious, because weak writing from any discriminated-against group inadvertently confirms existing negative opinions. Indeed, while the favor of one's own kind and colleagues is gratifying, most American artists also want to win a larger integrated audience as well, in part because success with *them* also enhances prestige *within* one's own minority group. Neither James Baldwin nor LeRoi Jones became nationally famous among blacks because of publicity exclusively within the Negro press; as John A. Williams observed in 1967, "The Negro writer is accepted by the Negro community only after he has made it in the white community." For that reason alone, it is also tactically unwise for blacks to discourage respected white critics from the perusal of black writing (or to allow them to feel excluded) or to prevent white professors from teaching black kids; and it should never be forgotten that the cultivation of both esoteric lingo and parochial cultural allusions comes at the risk of a literary obscurity that only double standards can rationalize. Not even the prominent Scottish poet Hugh MacDiarmid became internationally renowned for the works he composed in Scots dialect. Only if an author thinks his work belongs with the masters, rather than the minors, does he have a chance of joining them. Perhaps the problem lies in using the word "literature," for if a disaffected group wants to play a separate game with bats and balls it would be wise not to undermine their separatism (and raise indivious comparisons) by calling it "baseball."

Secondly, the primary trouble with all narrowly-drawn conceptions of "authenticity" is that they change so drastically over time. What white intellectuals (and blacks influenced by them) now regard as "authentically black" scarcely resembles the predominant stereotypes of the thirties—those criteria now (or just recently) include such admitted superficialities as coiffure. In practice, these conceptions of exclusive "authenticity" stem either from highly reductive political ideologies or from the currently established sociological generalizations about Negro life; so that the measure of "authenticity" is how neatly an individual's behavior, appearance, or interpretation of his own experience jibe with the socio-psychological stereotypes. For this reason, critics, especially if Caucasian, are predisposed to praise as "real" those Negro-authored imaginative works that most conclusively (and vividly) illustrate the current theories,

242

even though such expertise is based largely upon bookish under-standings (abetted by vivid inventions and/or aspirations to empathy). The end result of much book-reviewing is not criti-cism and esthetics, but sociology and pseudo-psychology. In truth, as an author literate enough to write a book, as well as his publishing editor, have also been influenced by the same socio-logical theories, the affirmative review thus becomes a simple illustration of intellectual feedback. The impact of literary-sociological stereotypes also explains the limited repertoire of racist themes either in a single poet or an entire anthology. (Such stereotypes can also be exploited by a group's enemies who would like white Americans to believe that all blacks are incipient Panthers—the spectre against whom all repression is just and whose excesses are cited to excuse one's own sins against them.) Such politicized understanding implies, as Ish-mael Reed noted, that "Art is what white people do. All other people are 'propagandists.'"

It follows, in some minds, that if one (or another) personal-artistic style is authentically black, then all contrasts are non-black, or white, by default, even if its exponents are racially dark. Those blacks who disagree with what is asserted to be the majority racial opinion are sometimes dismissed as "white" (and thus, it is hoped, susceptible to Caucasian racial guilt by rhetori-cal equation). The emphasis upon minority-spokesmanship also means that the public "personalities" of black authors are judged more readily than their works (a critical confusion which also results from excess personal publicity—e.g., Norman Mailer and Jacqueline Susann). In addition, this quality of stereotype-consciousness tends to identify Martin Luther King or Malcolm X or someone else as "the voice of black aspiration" or simply "the Negro," presuming a kind of primitive unanimity about U.S. Negroes that is not only condescending but untrue. Nor, for the same reason, could any single individual be identified as *the* spokesman for white America or even "The American Jew." (Beware as well of any intellectual who speaks familiarly of "The Negro" or even "The Afro-American" because he prob-ably hasn't met any individuals recently.) Nonetheless, the speed with which "black" superseded "Negro" in common white-liberal discourse reveals the assumption of a similarly undifferentiated, herdish conception of black America, as well as signaling a rapid evolution in acceptable stereotypes.

Thirdly, double standards have always had such a determin-

243

ing effect not only upon what is praised but also upon what gets into print, whether in white-controlled magazines or black, that it is my considered hunch that much good writing by American Negroes has not been published at all. Scholars who generalize about typicality in past "Negro poetry" should also consider what *was not* getting into print at certain times and why. (Indeed, such considerations should probably inform *all* historical literary study by criteria other than race as well.) When a literary historian writes that "not a single Negro novel was written between 1914 and 1924," what he really means is that no novels by blacks were published in that decade. To say, for instance, that "black poetry became more militant in the sixties" really describes what the editorial establishments were then favoring, for few magazines of note would publish first-rate black-authored poems that were not avowedly militant, while such militant statements would, at earlier times, have encountered more resistance. Similarly, if European expatriation is unfashionable, as now, then the work of a black American writer living in Europe is not likely to be published at home. (All generalizations about artistic collections ought to reveal explicitly how the examples were chosen; and if the selection procedure is questionable, the conclusions probably are too.) The prevalence of stereotype-defined understanding also explains why some of the very best young black writers whose work is counter-cliché (e.g., Norman Henry Pritchard II and Robert Boles), or such older novelists as Paule Marshall and William Demby, or the critic Nathan R. Scott, Jr., have not gotten the critical attention or publication their works deserve. The fault lies less with minority authors, however, than with white America's control of the media stereotyping the minority's existence, for true cultural "power" in America includes the capacity to determine public dissemination of a particular definition of a less powerful group's experience, often with the assistance of the latter's appropriately attuned "spokesman."

Perhaps the most ridiculous illustration of the circular fulfillment of stereotype is Claude Brown's *Manchild in the Promised Land* (1965), a memoir about growing up in Harlem, which reveals the influence of its young author's social work and which was heavily pruned and shaped by a white Harvard-educated editor (its author publishing almost nothing since). Among those double-standard merchants who certified the supposed authenticity and typicality of *Manchild* were, in Albert Murray's summary, "a white Negro like Norman Mailer, a part-time Negro like Nat Hentoff, a non-Negro like Norman Pod-horetz, and a non-Jewish New York know-it-all like Tom Wolfe, [who] have all engaged in promoting *Manchild* as the raw truth and excusing its shortcomings." However, not even Brown's own racial duskiness can give much authority to his own testimonials, precisely because race is, alas, no barrier to his assimilating the same sociological ideas and processes of explanation that his white admirers display. Since Brown himself graduated not only from college but law school, he is scarcely a typical ex-slum child; and textual evidence in his memoir reflects, a bit naively, a literacy that includes precisely such sociology textbook schema. (As an intellectual rule, whatever is touted as "typical" or "representative" is likely to echo a stereotype.) Just as no one can tell "what it means" to be white or even to be a WASP in America, so no single book can perform a similar anthropological service for the epistemology of American Jews or American blacks, even just those residing within a single large city. Not only are racialist double standards humanly pernicious, but they also burden writers with too many false comforts and inapproachably high expectations and experiential cliches, on all counts raising the question of who is doing whom a favor.

II

In journalism, the reader finds what he is looking for, what the reader wants, whereas in literature he must find at least a part of what the author intended.
—Ezra Pound, "Summary" (1917).

The riot of double standards epitomizes even greater critical weak-mindedness, as well as contributing to the obliteration of many crucial distinctions that are essential for the future of art. Every critic of the current morass has his favorite example of recurring flaccidity. One of my own is the discriminatory rule that eminence is the prerequisite for criticizing another eminence seriously, even if the same criticisms are made, for it reduces "criticism" to the level of baseball backbiting. As Jim Bouton noted, "You have to be a Frank Howard to call [Carl] Yastremski a yo-yo, or you have to have a hot month or a hot week. You're only as smart as your E.R.A." Another favorite of mine is the widespread reluctance to distinguish art from pop. The past years have witnessed numerous "critical" essays about the Beatles and others, less by musicians (or at least not by first-rate ones) than by literary people who either imply or outright certify that the four Liverpudlians rank as major contemporary "composers." Art and pop have always inhabited separate domains, intending to reach audiences of different dimensions, extending from separate traditions, and seldom interacting (or resembling each other) at the creative level. Furthermore, the aural, visual, and literary arts each have their popular forms; as pop music derives from modern music, so do both journalism and pop song lyrics relate to literature, and commercial art stands to painting. Quite simply, all pop forms are more direct in their communication, more universally accessible, less innovative in form, less complex in ideas, more clichéd, more imitative in inspiration, more explicit in articulation, more conducive to collaborative production, more subservient to both recognizably transient fads and mediumistic conventions. Just as newspapers and magazines are meant to be quickly discarded, so, by design, are both the poster and pop records.

Art, unlike pop, is not limited by the demands of the mass market, or by established structural conventions, or by available materials (such as the talents of one's musicians, or collaborators in a design studio, or a magazine's available "space"); so that pop strives to emulate the creative freedom of art, rather than vice versa. All pop is by definition intended not for the few, as is most serious art, but for the many (which may, however, include "the few"); so that pop at its most successful is many times more commercial than art, the most successful pop musician earning, for one measure, much, much more from royalties than several major modernist composers combined. Just as it is culturally fallacious to compare critically the Beatles with Stravinsky, so it is wrong (or suspect) for an old critic to regard young journalists, rather than young poets and critics, as representing the new generation's literary talent (or the "new journalism" as epitomizing the "new literature"). The attempt to give rock lyrics the status of "poetry" corresponds to Norman Podhoretz's effort in 1958 to elevate the article into "art" (or Pauline Kael's attempt to find "art" in kitsch); and once journalistic values are confused with literary, more double-talk follows. Clear as these distinctions, once drawn, may now seem, they are largely lost to public criticism; and that development could have disastrous results, especially if talented people are persuaded to forsake their laudable cultural ambitions for more poppish ones.

III

> *Kurtz:* What would you say is the key moral problem in Rusia today?
> *Volpin:* It seems to me that the most important moral problem is that of lying. In Russia, lying is very widespread and the people are so accustomed to it that they are indifferent.
> *Kurtz:* Do the ordinary people lie to one another?
> *Volpin:* Very much so, but not only the ordinary people, even the intelligentsia. They lie whenever it is more convenient to tell a lie than to tell the truth. Generally, people prefer the truth, though in practice they prefer to lie. —Paul Kurtz, "An Interview with Aleksander Yesennin-Volpin" (1973).

Given the decreasing value of truth in these hypocritical times, it is probably inevitable that intellectual discourse in America should be riddled by assertions that are patently false. This is not a matter of mere differences in opinion or evaluation which are natural in intellectual discussion, but of grave failures in the processes of perception, analysis, and judgment, in addition to the articulation of statements that are demonstrably untrue. There is no credibility either in Ezra Pound's classically ludicrous assertions that both James Laughlin and Charles Olson were "Jews" or in denials of the New York literary mob's existence. Not only did Philip Rahv declare in 1967, "In point of fact, the American-Jewish writers do not in the least make up a literary faction or school," but he then reprinted it two years later. James Baldwin once declared, "It is still true, alas, that to be an American Negro male is also to be a kind of walking phallic symbol," though that is scarcely true of all or even most Negro men. (That imagery primarily characterizes those studs dressed for the kill, as it might also portray white dudes similarly attired; so that dress, not race, is the root of this symbolic phallicity.)

Some hoodwinkings are entwined in attempts at self-fulfilling prophecy (or statements designed to *become* true); but most seem, upon considered inspection, at the service of ulterior ends which supposedly justify the means. In the worst examples, the writer must know as well as his critical reader that his statement was not meant to be true, but neither is it obviously ironic. In an essay, "Is Poetry an American Art?", first published in *College English* and then reprinted in *To Abolish Children* (1968), Karl Shapiro asserts, "I cannot name five poets writing in the English or American language today who have enough individuality of style to be distinguished from one another." Robert Brustein, whose importance has stemmed from the power of his two positions—as former *New Republic* drama critic and dean of the Yale Drama School—is so obsessed with intellectuals genuinely more influential or popular than himself that he asserts, quite erroneously, that celebrityhood is available to Every Writer—that, to quote him, "Everyone who would hold a pen was in a position to be as famous as a movie star." Joseph Epstein noted in *The New York Times* early in 1971 that Saul Bellow "has come to his eminence not through the mechanics of publicity, self-advertisement or sensationalism, but through slowly building up a body of work, an *oeuvre.*" The epithet "New York Intellectuals" is itself such an obvious falsehood unless qualified by the adjectives "some" or "certain" that the integrity and intelligence of anyone using the term should be questioned. (The phrase "New York Poets" is a comparable lie unless it refers to every practicing poet living in New York.)

Facts and verities become so sabotaged by fashionable rhetoric that all kinds of curious incongruities creep into prominent channels. Certain wealthy writers are forever attacking their poorer brethren for their supposed enterprise. During the 1966 PEN Congress, Saul Bellow ridiculed literary people who echo modern culture's dislike of modern civilization and yet are "very well off. They have money, position, privileges, power. The send their children to private schools. They can afford elegant dental care, jet holidays in Europe. They have stocks, bonds, houses, even yachts." In truth, not more than fifty American writers, academic or otherwise, can live quite that well without an outside (i.e., non-professional) income; and Bellow as both a best-selling novelist and a full professor at the University of Chicago is clearly one of them. "Could anything be neater?" his critique ironically concludes. Similar rhetorical deceit permits a man of Bellow's income to attack the culture merchandisers "who have successfully organized writing, art, thought and science in publishing houses, in museums, in foundations, in magazines [etc.]. All these things have been made to pay and pay handsomely"—though not as handsomely, most of the time, as Bellow's own income. Any intellectual should think twice before ever accusing anyone poorer than himself of avarice.

Literary people are particularly susceptible to sins of untruth when they choose to write about politics, trying, like a Congressman's speechwriters, not to understand but to incite a particular, if not artistically predictable, reaction. Intellectual procedures are always corrupted by the rhetorical demands of politics, whether radical or conservative; as Renata Adler noted of the 1967 National New Politics Convention, where the participants included many influential writers, "being 'radicalized' meant having been persuaded of something by [self-defined] radicals." However, precisely because common political discourse is so riddled with lies, he who would call himself a *serious* writer must show more scrupulous devotion to the realities of evidence. James Baldwin recently told an interviewer that "when they killed Martin [Luther King], they killed hope"; but James Earl Ray, not white America, *killed* M.L. King, the rhetoric of culpability-extension notwithstanding. (And it is equally untrue to imply that most of white America, or the white "establishment," wanted King dead.) Militancy is simply no excuse for such poor thinking, no matter how sympathetic the author's purposes, politics, personality, or skin-color.

Some untruths come from the misuse of evidence, especially in drawing judgments; and literary people, accustomed as they are to reading meanings in (or into) surface phenomena, are particularly susceptible to the presumption of *knowing* a man by his surfaces, such as the content of his writings or the details of his body. Critiques of Herman Kahn and Marshall McLuhan are full of the former kind of presumption; this passage from Diana Trilling's "On the Steps of Low Library" (1968) contains an epitome of the fallacy of confusing physiology with psychology:

> I saw [Tom] Hayden in a television interview. His dedication is implicit in his appearance—were one not to know his profession one would still know that whatever he did he did with an extreme intensity. There is great nervousness in his face and body, but it is nervousness under practiced control, almost to the point of rigidity: he occupies a chair, he doesn't rest in it; he allows himself no freedom or forgetfulness within his lean frame; his head and neck are joined with his body as if by visible cords.

In a book on *The Black Aesthetic* (1971), whose Latinate title (and spelling) might be ironic, Addison Gayle, Jr. violates the Eighth Commandment with this apparently unironic assertion, "To be an American is to be opposed to humankind, against the dignity of the individual, and against the striving in man for compassion and tenderness," although all comparative cultural evidence suggests that Americans are no worse than other nationalities in this respect. Besides, an exclusively *black* "aesthetic" is impossible in the U.S.; for just as American Negroes are as many shades apart from pure *black* as Caucasians are from pure *white,* so nearly all American cultural artifacts are *mulatto* in various complementary measures. Professor Gayle has elsewhere written that, "The most reactionary institution in American society is the university, and the last place that one will find enlightenment, morality, or redemption is within its ivy-covered walls," though that assertion likewise fails almost every test of rigorous objective comparison; were it true, Gayle himself would be digging ditches instead of haranguing impressionable children.

The Greening of America's Charles Reich, a professor at Yale Law School, finds the U.S. teetering at "the brink of an authoritarian or police state [where] both dissent and efforts at change are dealt with by repression"; but this statement is self-refuting, as books calling one's host country a "police state" are not published in genuine police states. Nor do they become uncensored best-sellers. It is similarly false to characterize contemporary America as a fascist society (or spell it "Amerika") in

250

spite of certain resemblances; for as long as most, if not nearly all, of America's accusers remain out of prison, that statement is as demonstrably untrue as this from Herbert Marcuse's *One-Dimensional Man* (1964): "Not only a specific form of government or party rule makes for totalitarianism, but also a specific system of production and distribution which may well be compatible with a 'pluralism' of parties, newspapers, 'countervailing powers.' " This penchant for repudiating contradictions enables Marcuse to coin such epithets as "repressive tolerance" and "totalitarian democracy," or to conclude that "democracy would appear to be the most efficient system of domination," even though no previous totalitarianism permitted any semblance of political "pluralism" or "counter-vailing powers." The only operational rationale for such double talk would be a politically prejudiced double standard for measuring "totalitarianism" and thus "freedom" in capitalist and Communist countries.

Susan Sontag's following assertion in "What's Happening in America" (1966), first published in *Partisan Review* and then reprinted in her *Styles of Radical Will* (1969), is simply too exaggerated, too wilfully deceptive, too plainly unconsidered to inspire guilt (which I take, perhaps too generously, to be her self-excusing aim):

> The white race *is* the cancer of human history; it is the white race and it alone—its ideologies and inventions—which eradicates autonomous civilizations wherever it spreads, which has upset the ecological balance of the planet, which now threatens the very existence of life itself.

Thus is conveniently erased from history all the recent atrocities by Japanese, Arab, Indian, Chinese, and Vietnamese peoples. Another Sontag hyperbole inspires less outrage or persuasion than doubt, as well as revealing a debt to Norman Mailer's undiscriminating cancer metaphors: "What I'd been creating and enduring for the last four years was a Vietnam inside my head, under my skin, in the pit of my stomach." (A contrary strategy, more typical of the anti-Left, is making a key issue evaporate. Thus can the "sociologists" Nathan Glazer and Lewis

251

Feuer regard student protests as, respectively, attempts to destroy the universities and symptoms of exacerbated generational conflicts, as if the Vietnam War did *not* exist and college-age kids were *not* at the time being drafted!) Untruths of this order, when uttered by prominent "intellectuals," unfortunately function to stimulate similar statements by lesser minds.

Another peculiarly modern kind of error comes from dialectical understanding that insists that things must turn worse before becoming better, even if the indices and general mood gauge otherwise. C. Wright Mills once lamented, in a classic falsehood since echoed by many leftish polemicists, that "people experiencing such a history of increasing and uninterrupted material contentment are not likely to develop economic resentments that would turn their minds into political forums." Only a similarly dialectical sensibility would display great glee in "proving" with statistics that poverty is still prevalent in America, or that *more* than six million Jews disappeared during World War II, or that the police killed more Panthers than actually died, the numbers here becoming dehumanized counters in a polemical con game. Semi-literate "radicals" and congenital puritans usually fall for these dialectical fantasies and even attempt to popularize them; for as George Orwell once observed in another context, "You have to belong to the intelligentsia to believe things like that. No ordinary man would be such a fool."

IV

> Art in our society has become so perverted that not only has bad art come to be considered good, but even the very perception of what art really is has been lost. In order to be able to speak about the art of our society, it is, therefore, first of all necessary to distinguish art from counterfeit art. —Leo Tolstoy, "The Religious Function of Art."

Perhaps the most profoundly foreboding symptom of the disintegration of standards in American criticism is the widespread failure to distinguish between culture and pseudo-culture—between cultural materials which are truly important and stuff which, despite high-toned claims made on its behalf, is doomed to remain intrinsically trivial. The differences, as we shall see, are ultimately more definite than mere likes and dislikes, for fairly sharp critical distinctions can be drawn. Pseudo-culture is not necessarily a new phenomenon; it dates back to the discovery that high cultural achievement could in some circles be more respectable, if not more lucrative, than success at culturally middling or lower levels. Until recently, however, those higher circles have never been too large, nor that notion too popular, nor genuine culture so remunerative and prestigious. Pseudo-culture capitalizes not only upon the unprecedented prosperity of culture but also the recurring attacks upon "standards," often by people who should (or do) know better such as enthusiasts for popular music, literary-political publicists, or avant-garde apologists (who really favor new criteria in the place of archaic ones). What is unprecedented, however, is the dominance of pseudo-culture in the more respectable reviewing media and in more-or-less serious conversation sometimes to the exclusion of any interest in authentic endeavors. What is likewise new is the growing inability of many intelligent people, some of them in positions of eminence or power, to discern the necessary difference between spurious activity and the real cultural thing.

Pseudo-culture is best defined in contrast to genuine culture; for despite similarities on the surface, one delivers quality, while the other merely runs through pretentious motions. Pseudo-culture lacks the deeper penetration and import of genuine culture, its pioneering contribution, and more authentic conception. Pseudo-culture stems from culturally extraneous motives—to make money, to acquire professional reputation, to gain an academic position or promotion, to draw attention to oneself, or simply to make some current scene, all in contrast to culture which is created primarily for intrinsic reasons and merits. Most pseudo-culture is a notch above Dwight Macdonald's "midcult" as well, though it falls far short of intellectual history's domain. The critic John Simon once defined one aspect of it as "trash posturing as art." Pseudo-culture is the mass cult of the semi-educated.

If a society's culture is the reward of intellectual and artistic processes, pseudo-culture, by contrast, is artistic and intellectual processing for society's rewards. Edmund Wilson wrote significant criticism, while Norman Podhoretz, as he admits, writes primarily to be known as an important critic. William Faulkner

253

and Ralph Ellison wrote major fiction; Herbert Gold, for all of his dramatizing of his methods and motives, wants to be known as a major novelist. *Transition* was a first-rate little magazine that contributed to several revolutions in literary form and intelligent taste; but in *Paris Review,* the contemporary claimant to the tradition of Paris-based literary journals, the sole pioneering contribution is the extensive literary interview which rarely equals the expository essay for revelatory efficiency. As *Transatlantic Review* in the twenties published Hemingway, so did *Paris Review*'s editors sustain their imitative game by publishing an interview with their hero. Pseudo-culture usually acknowledges its derivations, frequently making deep bows towards its honorific models, thereby attempting to exploit with facility its predecessor's hard-earned prestige; yet its thrust is, by definition, present-minded and transient. Genuine culture, by contrast, originates with an awareness of posterity as well as the present; it usually assimilates a more eclectic set of influences.

Merchants of pseudo-culture often exploit the prevailing ignorance of genuine intellectual achievements, rationalizing illiteracy as *Commentary* does, rather than challenging it. Publicity becomes its ally in the relentless drive for success, and most of its purveyors are particularly adept at promotion, the absence of which would give the inconsequential no hope of gaining an audience. How else except by exploitative publicity could literary journalists, ever-responsive to "current interest" (which is to say *fad*), get themselves known as "the intellectuals," even though, as noted before, many of them have made no identifiable contribution to intellectual history? How else could "new journalists" become known as "*the* young writers" and their work classified (and even studied) as Literature? Pseudo-culture uses all means to deceive and seduce the judgment of "critics," any one of whom ultimately knows as well as the next that such spurious stuff has little value in the present and less in the future. More often than not, pseudo-culture makes great claims, publicizing its produce in proportion to the financial investment made (e.g., Truman Capote's "non-fiction novel"), while the creators of culture quietly go about their less remunerative work. (As Renata Adler reports, "There is nothing to match the high aesthetic indignation of people who have made a $15,000,000 extravaganza which they feel has not been received with sufficient critical warmth.") As culture is smothered by pseudo-culture, literary reputations today are forged not by critics but by reviewers, some of whom have, nonetheless, sufficient *chutzpah* to call themselves "critics."

Pseudo-culture seems to invade all domains of American life; no area is immune to its incursions. As Norman Podhoretz is to Edmund Wilson, so LeRoi Jones (as a poet) stands to William Carlos Williams, and Jones the polemicist to W.E.B. DuBois and Harold Cruse. As Addison Gayle stands to Albert Murray or George L. Kent, Lawrence Ferlinghetti or Gregory Corso compares with Allen Ginsberg, or James Dickey with Theodore Roethke; and the run of academic New Criticism relates to R.P. Blackmur and Kenneth Burke. Between culture and pseudo-culture lies the difference between Rudolf Carnap and Jacob Bronowski, between C. Wright Mills and Vance Packard, between Norman O. Brown and Herbert Marcuse, between Herman Kahn and Edward Teller, between Edwin H. Land and David Sarnoff, between Richard Hofstadter and Oscar Handlin, between the stuff of intellectual history and the scribbling of the New York literary mob—one is thinking, while the other merely imitates the procedures of thought. Although some genuine critical talents contribute to *The New York Review of Books,* it prints very little of first-rank intellectual importance; like most popular fronts, it is distinctly pseudo-cultural and proud of its worldly success. It is possible to build a fairly respectable cultural reputation entirely upon pseudo-culture. None of Mary McCarthy's several novels, whether popular or not, could possibly rank among the great or innovative recent works, while her "criticism" rarely rises above book-reviewing or debater's polemic on stale issues; yet she has relentlessly gone through the motions of being an important writer for so long that most everyone reckons her a major cultural pontificator.

Pseudo-culture is indubitably current, indeed priding itself on a close relation to both currency and latest fashion. Whereas the creation of culture customarily pays the greatest rewards to one's heirs, pseudo-culture is eminently profitable in the present. The most successful purveyors are invariably quite well-to-do and indubitably bourgeois. Pseudo-culture can also undermine the growing validity of an innovative style which emerges from genuine esthetic preoccupations and artistic exploration, merely by swamping the scene with a glut of profit-hungry derivatives. Pseudo-culture is not stylistically "new" but actually an imitation of the last hot item; if only to escape from the waves of pseudo-culture, the true avant-garde inevitably moves elsewhere. (That explains why few serious authors *today* can bear to write about sexual intercourse.) Mass magazines generally find pseudo-culture more congenial than the real thing, not only because pseudo-culture (like pop) is simpler and, thus, more comprehensible, if not more self-explanatory, but also because its creators usually know how to make good copy of themselves—how to exploit marginal eccentricity, how to appear in conspicuous places, how to make attention-winning assertions, and how to make personality more important than work, partly in a self-serving attempt to create public interest in one's work. However, like the stuff of slick magazines, pseudo-culture is (or was) doomed to be rapidly forgotten.

Many contributors to the genuine culture of our time dabble in pseudo-culture. James Baldwin's early essays stemmed from serious literary motives and achieved an indisputable niche, their deceptions notwithstanding; however, his vainglorious profile of Norman Mailer, first published in *Esquire* and reprinted in *Nobody Knows My Name* (1961), is distinctly pseudo-culture. It has so little pith to carry it beyond the present that even Mailer's future biographers will have few reasons to quote it. Mailer himself did not become truly famous or capable of making symbolic acts that a large audience found meaningful until he dabbled in pseudo-culture, for nearly all of the slick-magazine essays reprinted in *The Presidential Papers* (1963) or *Cannibals and Christians* (1966) have, even by now, no interest or importance beyond the fact that Mailer, a once-important novelist, wrote them. The fact that so many supposedly intelligent people consider these glib, hyperbolic pieces more important than *The Deer Park* (1955) or "The Man Who Studied Yoga" (1952) not only reflects the impact of double standards, but creates the real dilemma that Mailer, along with other writers, must face—that they are better known and often more lauded for their junkier work. Partly from this painful discrepancy grew Norman Podhoretz's specious contention that the magazine article could be "art," if not a surrogate for the novel as well; but this last point was based upon the erroneous assumption that the novel's primary purpose was more the journalistic function of "bringing the news," whereas every literate person knows, in contrast, that mediumistic qualities, rather than journalistic, make the greatest novels great.

Anyone who believes in the final efficacy of intelligence and good taste must, almost as a matter of faith, think that true culture will survive in the end. However, this familiar assumption is now facing an unprecedentedly severe test; pseudo-culture has all but superseded culture in the minds of too many people who should know better. Whereas the realm of art (and discourse about it) was once saved by the fact that popular art did not want to be "good" as well—that nothing but the real thing would care to be identified as highbrow—now rock lyricists and their publicists claim to be creating "the poetry" of our time while academics and critics, who should also know better, seem willing to go along. Indeed, precisely in its aspirations to cultural semblance and exploitation of double standards does pseudo-culture become a pernicious threat. The possible future of culture depends upon the fundamental discretion of intelligent human beings—that they will reject the less interesting for what is richer and more complex, the specious for the true, the transient for the lasting, the less significant for the more important. Whether that which is truly valuable can overcome the smothering deluge of producer-publicized tripe, whether perpetual culture can be separated from opportunistic fluff, whether objectively discriminatory standards can be restored, whether the rule of ignorance and philistinism can be overthrown—these are the issues that will crucially affect the future of intelligent writing.

PART II

13 New Literary Periodicals

I

This continuity of culture may have to be maintained
by a very small number of people indeed—and these
not necessarily the best equipped with worldly advantages. It will not be the large organs of opinion, or the
old periodicals; it must be the small and obscure
papers and reviews, those which are hardly read by
anyone but their own contributors, that will keep
critical thought alive and encourage authors of original
talent. . . . So far as culture depends upon periodicals,
it depends upon periodicals which exist as a means of
communication between cultivated people, and not as
a commercial enterprise; it depends upon periodicals
which do not make a profit. —T. S. Eliot, "A Commentary" (1938).

Now one of the things "little" magazines do, it turns
out, is not only to print things that can't be printed
in the big magazines, but to change the taste of the
big magazines and big publishers. . . . Little magazines
have traditionally fed talent to big magazines and
presses, opening up audiences for minority writers.
—Leslie A. Fiedler, in a symposium (1970).

Given the resistances of American literature's establishments
in addition to their general intellectual decay, emerging writers
should have recognized that new institutions were desperately
necessary; for unless the existing channels of literary communication were sympathetic to the best fresh work, the fate of
intelligent writing would obviously be jeopardized. However, far
too many writers coming of professional age in the sixties
tended to follow their immediate predecessors (those born

261

around 1935) in knocking on all the visible editorial doors until they got tired, bored, or clobbered, trying everywhere they could until they tried no more. Even those who were fortunate enough to pass through one or two of the doors subsequently found the others all firmly shut. Nearly every new writer who was not an exploited protégé encountered persistent obstacles (and needless paranoia at times) because, as everyone eventually learned, these doors were not meant to be opened too widely, if at all. There were no prominent literary magazines especially receptive to unknowns, no established book or periodical editors with decided enthusiasm for young writers and, in short, no place particularly open to even the possibility of publishing them. Decimation was the rule and the reality.

Many writers showing clear promise in the early sixties subsequently disappeared from print, perhaps the victims of the generally repressive situation—among them the novelists Leon Rooke (b. 1934), David Deck (b. 1934), Samuel Blazer (b. 1934), Ulli Beigel (b. 1935), Irving Rosenthal (b. 1936), Keith Lowe (b. 1938); the poets Robert Bagg (b. 1936), Frederick Seidel (b. 1936), and Tim Reynolds (b. 1936); the film critics Harris Dienstfrey (b. 1934, who reemerged as a publisher), Paul Breslow (b. 1934), Sheldon Renan (b. 1940), James Stoller (b. 1940), and Grandin Conover (b. 1937-70, by suicide); the playwrights Kenneth H. Brown (b. 1936) and Deric Washburn (b. 1937); the poet and jazz critic A. B. Spellman (b. 1936); the literary critics Alfred Sundel (b. 1931), Gordon Rogoff (b. 1932), Paul Levine (b. 1935), James Gatsby (b. 1937), and David Galloway (b. 1937). Two of the late fifties Harvard-educated Rhodes scholars abandoned their frustrated literary careers to reemerge as child-education polemicists—Herbert Kohl (b. 1936) and Jonathan Kozol (b. 1936). Many more examples could be cited and more personal stories told.

One reads books like *The Quixote Anthology* (1961), which collected some of the best fiction published in the quarterly *Quixote* (1954-61), or *Stories for the Sixties* (1963), edited by the novelist Richard Yates (and cosponsored by *Esquire*), with an increasing sense of distress—so few of their many promising contributors are known today. Frank Conroy (b. 1935) testified in 1968 that "those of us now in our early thirties were not a generation in any self-conscious sense. We had no leaders, no programs, no sense of our own power, and no culture exclusively our own." This generation's editorial exemplars were servants of pre-existing literary establishments rather than initiators of alternative directions—Willie Morrises, rather than Paul Krassners. Writing in 1969, Renata Adler (b. 1938) lamented the absence of a "generational voice": "Even now (and we are in our thirties), we have no journals we publish, no exile we share, no brawls, no anecdotes, no war, no solidarity, no mark." A generation that does not communicate with itself is inevitably victimized by its elders' ideas.

My own generation (those born around 1940) suffered the same misfortunes as our immediate predecessors, mostly because we repeated their mistakes and were not able to transcend their self-defeating limitations. As both literary life and academia became more "glamorous," as well as more remunerative, many more young people would seriously pursue their writing ambitions—perhaps twice or thrice as many as two decades before; yet the channels of communication did not expand concomitantly. The issue was not so much whether one could or could not get published—that remains a question of individual quality and taste—but whether anyone was publishing new and young writers while respecting the integrity of their work. And if no one was, what could and should be done?

Rather than consider the possibility of radical alternatives, my aspiring contemporaries tended to accept all the blockages of circumstance, blamed themselves for literary (rather than literary-political) insufficiencies, or devised superficially acceptable rationalizations for their failures. As a result, too many of them stopped writing, or scribbled primarily for themselves, or sold out to the nearest employer, or simply disappeared to points unknown (and by now forgotten). In spite of the growing sentiment toward radical politics, few young writers were able to challenge the corruptions and repressions of the literary world, partially because there was no American precedent for that kind of professional courage, but also because few prominent "radical" writers took any of the necessary risks (which might, after all, actually jeopardize their prosperous literary careers). Beyond that, too many rising stars were conned into believing that "writing had no future," or that no one read any more, or that "there were no young writers," in spite of so much real evidence to the contrary; and some were thus discouraged from taking the steps that would have refuted those dangerous pieties.

Most tragically, emerging intelligent writers failed to establish enough of their own institutions—not just to serve the surplus of available writing but also to forge both necessary links of generational communication and a truly alternative intellectual world. They made the tactical mistake of ignoring the oldest cultural truth—that it is far easier to found a new magazine or a new publishing house than successfully infiltrate or change a thriving one (or even an ailing one, for that matter). In Europe, whenever newcomers feel excluded, they unhesitantly create an appropriate new journal; but perhaps because American writers are such loners, regarding themselves in competition with everyone else, most of them seem reluctant to pursue even minimal collective action in a serious way, no matter how necessary or opportune such initiative might be. That failure explains not only why every attractive periodical receives more "publishable" material than it has space to print, but also how there could have been (and probably still is) enough unpublished but first-rate intelligent writing to fill a new literary monthly as creamy as *The Dial* (1920-29) or a quarterly as awesomely excellent as *The Little Review* (1914-29). And such magazines, had they existed, would have succeeded in every way, in part because all the good new writers would have submitted their best work with the confidence that it would receive serious editorial consideration, but also because the very best readers would have subscribed. Nonetheless, no one, it seemed, had sufficient initiative and ideals to found a journal that would realize such optimal conceptions. How many current cultural periodicals could dare claim, like *The Dial*, for instance, "to serve American letters by publishing the best work of known or unknown Americans expressed in new or traditional forms, together with the best work of the same type produced in Europe."

From editing anthologies of avant-garde writing, I personally know of enough innovative work to fill the equal of *transition* (1927-38), say, or early *New Directions* (from 1936 to about 1949), but no outlet eclectically predisposed to experimental writing has recently appeared. I also see enough literature in all modes by young Americans to exceed the annual *American Caravan* that Lewis Mumford and Paul Rosenfeld coedited from

1927 to 1936, though nothing like it exists today. The absence of prominent American writers younger than Updike, Roth, and Sontag is not the result of any lack of talent, but old-boy resistances on one hand and the absence of appropriate literary institutions on the other. Even worse, whole levels of intelligence remain uncommunicated and, thus, unavailable.

The young in the pop music business produced the consequential records and originated the new companies. If previous chiefs had remained in power, both the art and the scene today would be drastically different; however, not even this example of the young communicating with each other through their own media could set a convincing precedent for the literary young. So discouraged and demoralized were we (and perhaps too needlessly awed by successful finks) that these alternatives were not pursued frequently or doggedly enough, nor were they adequately supported from either within or outside. "Prudence is a hateful thing in youth," noted Randolph Bourne. "A prudent youth is prematurely old." In fact, too many new institutions were abandoned too soon, as often because of prudence or insufficient energies as insufficient funds. Too many admirable efforts went unrecognized, while others were undermined by patently self-serving or coterie-serving compromises with excellence or intention (constituting yet other forms of prudence).

In retrospect, all these little steps, some of them quite marvelous, seem tragically inadequate in sum, in part because neither the young nor the new was adequately served, the best writing was diffused, too much got lost in esoteric channels, ambitions were unnecessarily compromised, and promises were disappointed, but also because certain larger strides were not taken. In addition, the energies behind all these rising forces did not powerfully coalesce into cooperative realization of common literary-political goals. As James Aronson pointed out in another context, the sixties "saw a remarkable increase in radical *activity* without the necessary concomitant of radical *organization*." Behind all the isolated initiatives were certain pervasive failures.

II

One of the most depressing facts [is] that the channels for disinterested criticism of any kind are rapidly

> being closed, if indeed any remain. One after another
> the serious politico-literary periodicals have disap-
> peared or lowered their colours, and there is scarcely
> one left whose liberty of speech has not been sold to
> the advertiser or mortgaged to vested interests. —Q.
> D. Leavis, *Fiction and the Reading Public* (1932).

The most practical outlet for literary radicalism now is the
founding not of a publishing house, which demands the investment of considerable time and money, but of a "little magazine," the adjective referring less to its possible significance than
the numerical amount of its typical printing. The initial audience for such journals is inevitably small, consisting at its base
of universities and other writers, along with teachers of literature and very sophisticated readers. While the optimal little-
magazine circulation is probably 15,000 (in contrast to the
100,000 subscribers to *The New Republic* or *The New York
Review of Books*), some of the more eminent little magazines,
such as *Hudson Review,* circulate fewer than 4000 copies.
According to a 1972 survey that The Committee of Small
Magazine Editors and Publishers (COSMEP) made of its membership, 22 percent distributed less than 500 copies, 28 percent
between 500 and 999, 37 percent between 1000 and 4999, 9
percent between 5000 and 20,000, and only 1 percent above
that. Most report that their biggest problem is distribution,
which includes not only soliciting subscribers but depositing
copies in outlets where they might be bought; and it is nothing
short of scandalous that an annual as substantial as *December,*
say, has less than 250 subscribers.

Partially because a new journal is easily begun, there are
hundreds in North America with varying degrees of viability;
this sheer abundance is per se an index of literary opportunity
and cultural health. Some have academic sponsorship or subsidy, a university wisely deciding to exchange a modest amount
of support (the cost of a full professorship or two) for the
honorific publicity accrued by a well-known publication. (If not
for *Kenyon Review,* for instance, far fewer people would have
heard of Kenyon College; now that the magazine is gone, the
college is fading from public view.) This form of support accounts for why academic literary periodicals often receive their
budgets through a university's public relations department.

Some little magazines offer full-time jobs for their staff, others are part-time endeavors incorporated into a full-time academic position, while yet others are just unremunerative hobbies. Though most have "editorial boards" and "advisory committees," one person is usually in charge; and the magazine will probably reflect both his enthusiasms and limitations. If he moves to another place, the magazine customarily moves with him, echoing the strategic mobility of a guerilla. "Freedom of the press," according to A.J. Liebling, "is guaranteed only to those who own one."

The minimal costs of producing such a periodical put a low ceiling upon its founder's financial investment (and ought to encourage, as well, some modest patronage); so that small literary journals, unlike commercial magazines, can *afford* to print innovative writing and unknown writers. (By contrast, an excess of literary celebrities, especially in a new magazine, usually indicates that the editor-publisher wants to impress not particular readers but academic sponsors, both current and potential.) In spite of laudable intentions, most little magazines seldom provide financial gain to anyone associated with them; by and large they are ignored, not only by potential subscribers but by cultural philanthropy, perhaps because little magazines have never been too fashionable. Most are unable to qualify for the comparatively low postal rates granted to slick periodicals. The survey mentioned before ascertained that 84 percent of them "lose money" while 7 percent "break even." The most immediate benefit of The Coordinating Council of Literary Magazines (CCLM) is a modest amount of government-funded beneficence which helps, even if thinly distributed. Deficits are currently handled in the following ways: "Out of publisher's pocket—58 percent; college or university subsidy—14 percent; from grants—19 percent; private contributions—8 percent." Another appropriate term for them is non-commercial magazines.

Most little magazines "pay" their contributors only with copies in lieu of money; and a few distribute more copies to their contributors than to paying subscribers. (However, from the perspective of readership, no circulation could be better in quality.) Since even the best of them are also handicapped by insufficient publicity, their genuine achievements, if any, generally go unrecognized until long after the publication has folded, its editors customarily both disillusioned by the lack of adequate response and relieved to be rid of all the corresponding nuisance. Nonetheless, precisely because their mission is so specific and their financial base so precarious, such periodicals were not meant to last forever. A few, indeed, persist too long.

Little magazines serve literary purposes, or at least literary writers, in contrast to slick magazines which are editorially enslaved to their advertisers or a circumscribed concept of their audience (or an imagined phalanx of the two). Like *The Little Review,* to quote its motto, they can afford the boast of "making no compromise with public taste." As commercial periodicals are obliged to provide profits, little magazines are, by birthright, obliged to sustain intelligent writing, making visible much literature that might otherwise remain invisible. Some of them also represent those literary classes that, for reasons of prejudice, found other avenues closed—all the ethnic, geographical, racial, and sexual minorities mentioned before.

New writers are likely to find short pieces more feasible than longer works, not only because periodical outlets are more plentiful than book publishers, but also because the editorial loyalty of a magazine can provide continuity of communication. Much as law reviews give students the semblance of professional opportunity, so little magazines give new writers the benefits of public exposure. "Our intellectual marines," runs W. H. Auden's aphorism, "landing in Little Magazines." To a new writer, appearance in cold print can, much like initial combat, be a shocking experience conducive to further maturation. Reputations can be made entirely within the world of little magazines, the writers never surfacing in the slicks or the academic quarterlies or on New York publishing lists. Charles Bukowski and Douglas Blazek, for two, owe their fame exclusively to this underground, and their kind of poetry, familiarly known as the "meat school," is still *infra dig* to the established literary world. Since there are so many talented young writers in America, it is not surprising one frequently picks up a new magazine which is filled with interesting work even though the names of its authors are unfamiliar.

All new directions in serious writing first appeared in small-circulation journals; so have all of American modernism's major writers. Indeed, the most admired American poets of this century published all but exclusively in little magazines for their entire lives. Given the closures elsewhere, it is clear that literary initiative of all kinds will continue to depend upon little magazines. The most consequential journal will eventually influence many more readers than its original circulation—T. S. Eliot's legendary *Criterion* (1922-39), for instance, having less than a thousand—in part because they are usually saved, much like books, by their subscribers. For that reason, the best of them are destined to remain currently important, so to speak, long after their official demise.

Recent little magazines have come in several stages of opulence, ranging from such glossy-papered, spine-bound occasionals as the original *Ramparts* (1962-64), *Location* (1962-63), and the elegant type-setting on laid paper of *Prose;* through such thick and paperbound ersatz "books" as *Stony Brook* or *Tri-Quarterly;* to mimeographed journals both typed and stapled together by the editor's own hand. Whereas literary magazines of the fifties were produced by either letterpress or mimeograph—the first being considerably more legible and expensive than the latter—the sixties witnessed the development of offset printing which, though rarely as distinguished as letterpress, was far cleaner than mimeograph and nearly as cheap. Some culturally American little magazines have been published abroad such as *Transatlantic Review* or *Paris Review,* but since literary expatriates are now comparatively few, most are published here. The majority of these, unlike publishing houses or slick magazines, have their editorial offices outside New York City.

Small-scale literary journals can be divided into two groups—coterie and diversified, which are, respectively, those founded by a tightly-woven group, primarily to print each other (and intended for an audience composed largely of themselves), and those founded for less exclusive, more generously eclectic literary purposes. As these characterizations make clear, coterie magazines generally serve gods no greater than themselves, necessities no larger than their own; they could not possibly survive tests of "open admission" or "unbiased discrimination." (Some are founded by a professor, particularly to publish "my students.") Although rewarding their contributors with editorial comfort, perhaps to degrees detrimental to excellence or further growth, coterie magazines neglect the literary-political predicament. The exception to this stricture would be those that manage to generate some contagious ideas that affect a larger readership such as *The Radical Therapist* (established in 1970), or successfully enlarge their base of contributors.

Clayton Eshleman's *Caterpillar,* for example, was founded in 1967 expressly to publish a select group of New York-based poets, most of whom had previously contributed to David Antin and Jerome Rothenberg's *Some/thing* (1964-65), and who are also fairly close personal friends. In an epitome of collective narcissism, the opening issues of *Contact* (est. 1972), a Philadelphia magazine, printed only six rather pretentious male writers who also publish their collaborations with each other, review each other, interview each other, and even take photographs of each other. Not only kid poets but academics are susceptible to such collective narcissism. In the Winter 1972 issue of *Diacritics* (est. 1970), published by the Department of Romance Language and billed as "a review of contemporary criticism," Professor Robert Martin Adams, who once taught at Cornell, reviewed a book by Angus Fletcher, who also once taught at Cornell; an outsider reviewed M. H. Abrams, who has long been a Cornell professor; Fletcher wrote on Paul De Man, who recently moved from Cornell to Yale; Jeffrey Mehlman, identified as a French teacher at Cornell, contributed an essay; and De Man contributed a "Work in Progress." (The sixth and last essay is contributed by a ringer teaching at Johns Hopkins.) Other coteries are confined to the editor's own body or just his head. Tom Veitch told a surveyor that his *Tom Veitch Magazine* (est. 1970) is "Tom Veitch's personal ego-blast. It doesn't accept submissions but does print collaborations between the editor and his buddies." Another kind of coterie has a more esthetic base—an exclusive commitment to a particular style. Although Robert Bly's *The Seventies,* founded in 1958 as *The Fifties,* initially had a liberating effect, the magazine became, by the later issues of *The Sixties,* just another establishment. "Editorial range is narrow," its spokesman told the *Directory of Little Magazines.* "We try to encourage the poem composed entirely of images."

In the worst of the coterie magazines, the contributors are all so similar that attempts at realizing an individual voice are defeated. An excess of cozy outlets within a cozy group is likely to inspire a decline in quality. The history of the "New York School" exemplifies this last process—not only with *The*

World, Angel Hair, and several parochial anthologies, but also *Lines, The Genre of Silence, Clothesline, Mother, Adventures in Poetry, C., Elephant, Columbia Review, Unnatural Acts, Sundial, Sun, Chicago;* the poems becoming progressively less purposeful and more forgettable with each issue, further trivializing an already self-consciously trivial poetics. Most coterie magazines survive only as long as the group's alliances prosper—*City Lights Journal* (1963-66), for instance, disintegrating when the hip movement superseded the "beat," and nearly all of the "New York Poets" magazines falling apart when most of the group left New York. Sometimes, too, a magazine is so deeply personal that everything in it reflects the unalloyed enthusiasms of a highly idiosyncratic editor, such as Donald Phelps in his *For Now* (est. 1965) or Coburn Britton in his *Prose* (est. 1970), so that the semblance of an exclusive coterie is more imaginary than real. A further trouble is that any literary magazine established for any length of time tends to create and perpetuate its own circle. Literary ego-tripping, whether individual or collective, should be discouraged, for magazines which are run in that spirit do little, if anything, to alleviate larger predicaments.

It would be in new diversified magazines that intelligent writing would have its more likely future; and if the inconsequentiality of coterie journals was probably predictable, the disappointing careers of these more eclectic magazines offered more cause for alarm. The mere founding of a new, editorially open, literary institution clearly represents an admirably radical action in cultural politics, implying that the world of writing needs to be changed to some degree and that new opportunities should be forged. For that reason, all the editors discussed in the following pages are, or were, generous people who have overcome the trials besetting non-commercial cultural enterprises. The quality of their evident ambitions places them above the quietist or the congenital sellout. Nonetheless, good intentions and intelligence can be compromised by exclusively personal ambitions, outside pressures, or so much overburdening work that a periodical's original designs are smothered. More than one editor boasted at the beginning that he would not allow his fresh journal to last more than a fixed number of years, only to let this vow disintegrate before the tokens of prosperity; but sins of that order are, in the final judgment, comparatively minor.

It is a greater fault that nearly all of the new diversified journals suffered compromise or suspicious decline in the quality of work published (especially if one considers what has been available) and then physical disintegration or premature demise, as much because of their own insufficiencies as because of public-financial neglect, both support and effort dwindling together. They have not been as good as their best writers, not as good as, for the sake of writing, they should be. Few, if any, are so consequential that their readers, upon getting a new issue, feel compelled to read it at once; few, if any, are so mind-bending that they can change the reading preferences of their audience. Few are so essential that their disappearance would leave a perceptible hole in cultural communication. They have also failed the larger problem of establishing alternative distribution systems and making the literate public aware of the essential function of little magazines. A further related, recurring deficiency of little magazines is unashamed small-mindedness which can be attributed, perhaps, to the perils of small-scale power apart from larger responsibility—ego without superego; and this in turn can be attributed, perhaps, to the predominant psychological bias of recent poetry—egotism verging on egomania. As a result, the great tradition of little magazines has in many ways been betrayed.

In characterizing a literary institution (or literary produce and even literary people), let me propose three sets of relevant issues—its politics, its esthetics, and, most crucially, its literary politics—that are subject to familiar left-right categories. Whereas nearly all long-established magazines or publishing houses tend to be conservative in their literary politics, new institutions reveal a spectrum of literary-political biases. For example, Philip Rahv's *Modern Occasions,* first founded in 1965 and revived in 1970, is radical in its politics, conservative in its esthetics, and conservative in its literary politics. Theodore Solotaroff's *New American Review* (est. 1967) is liberal, liberal, and liberal-conservative on these respective issues; Richard Goldstein's *US* (1969-70), by contrast, was respectively radical, radical, and liberal. One key question, never to be forgotten at the current time, is whether a new institution (or even a writer) encourages, opposes, or ignores the growing forces of literary-political repression. It follows that the neglect of young writers defines a literary institution as conservative, if not reactionary, no matter how "radical" its "politics" might be. Our current predicament, in brief, stems from the lack of new literary institutions whose professional politics are sustainedly radical.

As the following critical survey will evaluate a large number of titles, it should be understood at the beginning that my remarks are based to different degrees upon reading their issues, plus conversation and correspondence with their editors which produced tentative judgments that have, in turn, changed in response to new evidence over the years. (Further changes may also make some of the following remarks obsolete.) Since little magazines are rarely written about, particularly when they are still alive, their editors are unaccustomed to attention or criticism which, because of inexperience, they sometimes take immaturely. The survey includes Canadian magazines because I regard them as integral parts of North American culture. Though I have at various times contributed to many of the following journals, I trust my judgments are intentionally clear of petty feelings. With none of them, except *Arts in Society, The Humanist, The New York Ace,* and perhaps *Panache,* am I currently affiliated.

III

> He began to see in the new class-consciousness of poets the ending of that old division which "culture" made between the chosen people and the gentiles. We were not to form little pools of workers and appreciators of similar temperaments and tastes. The little magazines that were starting up became voices for these new communities of sentiment. —Randolph Bourne, "The History of a Literary Radical" (1919).

I noted in *The New American Arts* (1965) that the years 1958-59 represented the beginnings of a revival in American culture; for by that time, the repressions of the Eisenhower-McCarthy years subsided enough for previously demoralized intellectuals to exercise imprudent initiative again. Thus, it is not surprising that some of the potentially important, new, eclectic quarterlies made their debuts in that season—*Contact* (1958-64), *Columbia University Forum* (est. 1958), *Big Table* (1954-61), and *Transatlantic Review* (1958 to the present). The first was founded in San Francisco by the novelists Calvin Kentfield and Evan S. Connell, along with a peripatetic cultural entrepreneur named William H. Ryan (all then in their middle thirties). Un-New Yorkish without suffering from provinciality, more open to young writers (even those living on the East Coast) than to innovative literature, *Contact* became progressively thicker and glossier, until it jumped from its original 6" x 9" size to a larger 8" x 11" format and aimed to become semi-monthly. It even issued a few books, including S. P. R. Charters' highly prophetic ecological essay, *Man on Earth* (1962). However, *Contact* also suffered from excessive entrepreneurial ambition and perhaps some mismanagement as well, investing too much money and energy in peripheral, ultimately sub-literary activities that drove the enterprise bankrupt much too soon. Its West Coast commitments to imaginative literature were extended by Jeff Berner's awesomely prophetic, three-shot *Stolen Paper Review* (1963-65) and Gordon Lish's six-shot *Genesis West* (1962-64) which introduced some modestly avant-garde fiction before its similarly premature death. (In 1969, Lish became *Esquire*'s fiction editor, publishing the same kinds of writing he favored before. Although this taste represented an advance over his editorial predecessor, *Esquire* typically ignored the yet more advanced fictions of the seventies.)

The most successful West Coast periodical, *Ramparts,* began in 1962 as a large-format, editorially-diverse Catholic quarterly (with an ecumenical editorial board) that published long, liberal, and intelligent articles on both social and literary subjects. Responding, it seems, largely to the growing influence of a young managing editor named Warren Hinckle (b. 1939), *Ramparts* gradually neglected both its Catholic origins and cultural interests to become, by 1964-65, a slicker monthly with a tighter editorial policy and a more iconoclastic stance. Having become a West Coast *Harper's*, so to speak, it then forged an identity largely of its own invention—the first incorrigibly slick, radical, mass-circulation magazine. After much similarly unjustified extravagance, *Ramparts* went bankrupt, another victim of needlessly excessive ambition. Another new corporation was formed in its wake, assuming publication of the magazine, while Hinckle moved to New York to found *Scanlan's Monthly* (1970-71) which tried to reinvent the identity in the face of increasing difficulties and *de facto* censorship. Whatever intention to publish intelligent writing that *Scanlan's* or a resuscitated *Ramparts* may have had were by now largely superseded by policies conducive to overshadowing graphics, interchangeable contributors, and slickly written reportage—the sins more typical of a mass magazine. *Columbia University Forum,* though founded on the attractive concept of a general quarterly for over 100,000 alumni, was too academic and subservient in its origins and editorial policies to be open to the new or the young. Indicatively, an unusually large percentage of its pages were preprints from forthcoming books (or material already certified, so to speak, by the editorial-industrial complex).

Transatlantic Review, founded in Europe by Joseph McCrindle (still its editor and primary patron), has followed *Paris Review* in publishing only fiction, poetry, and interviews, thus avoiding criticism entirely. Modestly devoted to its superficially modest business, *Transatlantic* has remained more persistently open to the young (and some of the new) than any other established literary quarterly. This fact is somewhat obscured by both the conservative appearance of the magazine, its undistinguished choice of poetry, and its apparent commitment to certain authors (mostly British) of mediocre interest and reputation—its anthology, *Stories from the Transatlantic Review* (1970), documented this predominant bias; but nearly every issue contains a few fine, fairly innovative works by promising unknowns. *Big Table* (1959-61), by contrast, had more radical and coterie origins; an issue of *Chicago Review* compiled by Irving Rosenthal was foolishly censored by the university's administration. Under the editorship of Paul Carroll (b. 1928), *Big Table* continued to specialize in the "beats," becoming the first periodical in America to publish parts of William S. Burroughs' highly controversial *Naked Lunch* in America, along with Allen Ginsberg's greatest single poem, "Kaddish." Although this clique became even more famous, the magazine lamentably failed to survive beyond its fourth issue. Paul Krassner's *The Realist* also emerged in 1958, quickly becoming a spunky satirical magazine that both reflected *Mad* (established in 1952, perhaps the first mass magazine of the counter-culture) and subsequently influenced the "underground press."

The Drama Review began in 1955 as *The Carleton Drama Review,* thanks to Robert Corrigan (b. 1929), who was then teaching at Minnesota's Carleton College. It followed Corrigan to New Orleans' Tulane University, becoming in course the *Tulane Drama Review*. Receiving an attractive academic offer from Carnegie Mellon University, Corrigan in 1962 entrusted the magazine to a graduate student, Richard Schechner (b. 1934). He gathered around him several equally young associates, and the *Tulane Drama Review* began to pursue a more radical course. At first rejecting the Broadway theater for provincial alternatives, it then surpassed an older post-Eric Bentley commitment to European dramatic literature to support the non-literary theater of happenings and guerilla street events. When Tulane University became less sympathetic, Schechner took the magazine to New York University (where Corrigan had transiently become a dean). Obtaining a full professorship for himself, he changed the title to *The Drama Review* which was then shortened, if only to preserve continuity, to *TDR*. However, by the time Schechner relinquished the editorship to his long-time managing editor, Erika Munk (who had previously worked for *Partisan*), not only had *TDR*'s reputation for editorial high-handedness alienated many possible contributors, but it had become another academic journal filled with heavily documented, professorial essays on a limited range of subjects. In 1971, a split ensued, Michael Kirby becoming editor of *TDR* while Erika Munk founded the quarterly *Performance,* two rather similarly-declining magazines emerging from one, with nothing new to fill the slack.

As in the example of *TDR* or Jonas Mekas' *Film Culture* (est. 1955), a decisive change in criticism often accompanies, and ideally complements, a revolution in art, the new little magazine preceding critical books as the most effective disseminator of hypothesis and debate about artistic change. *Artforum,* a monthly founded in Los Angeles in 1962, became the most influential American art periodical by publishing the most extended and intelligent essays on the new, post-Abstract Expressionist visual art of the middle sixties. Its success capitalized upon the decline of earlier art journals, most of which were still detrimentally married to earlier enthusiasms. The great achievement of *Perspectives of New Music,* also founded in 1962 and subsequently edited primarily by Benjamin Boretz (b. 1933), was the development of an intentionally empirical, analytical criticism that was particularly useful in elucidating those new works composed in post-Schoenbergian traditions. It was not

276

until the middle sixties that the dance critic Arlene Croce, approximately the same age as Schechner and Boretz, founded an equally necessary new dance magazine, *Ballet Review;* but both a persistent lack of financial and academic support plus philistine inattention have stymied this persisting labor of love, if not the probable maturation of the young dance critics gathered around it.

What is remarkable, by contrast, is the comparative absence of notable new critical journals in literature. New magazines devoted entirely to criticism, such as *Novel* (est. 1967) or the *Journal of Modern Literature* (est. 1970), followed the example of *Wisconsin Studies in Contemporary Literature* (est. 1958) or *Critique* (est. 1958) in favoring single-theme, non-controversial investigations of critically precertified authors. Not only was such criticism invariably dull and inconsequential, but such magazines completely neglected the various strains of experimental writing that had emerged during the sixties. Such magazines could scarcely serve those new critical intelligences especially interested in new writers, or young critics whose concerns transcended the academic pigeonholes of a single art or even a single genre. What these new critics needed was more comparably polyartistic and adventurous critical journals like Ralph Cohen's *New Literary History* (est. 1969), Stephen Goode's *Studies in the Twentieth Century* (est. 1969), Frank Davey's *Open Letter* (reestablished 1971 in Canada). The scarcity of critical interest in experimental literature meant that the new work would be less adequately understood and that the current morass of indiscriminate confusion might continue indefinitely.

IV

> But were it not for the plethora of little-mag outlets, American culture would likely become stultified. Writings that are new (in the sense of innovation) would find almost no print. Without need for documentation, it can be stated that this is a period of cultural crisis and that outlets are demanded for declarations of anti-establishment movements of all types. —James Boyer May, "Toward Print" (1971).

Of all the new primarily literary magazines, the most heavily endowed, at least on appearance, was *Tri-Quarterly,* initiated in the late fifties at Northwestern University for the coterie pur- pose of printing its faculty and students. However, after a young novelist named Charles Newman (b. 1938) took com- mand in 1964, it started to issue strikingly large (7" x 10") and fat issues full of all kinds of literary work, clearly overcoming its parochial beginnings. With its large staff and contributors' payments running several thousand dollars per issue, *Tri- Quarterly* may well be the most expensively produced little magazine in America. There have been several special issues, each devoted to a featured subject of hugely varying impor- tance, some of which are delivered by sub-contracted subedi- tors. Some of them are encomiums to septuagenarians (Dahl- berg, Borges, Nabokov); another entitled "Under 30" was edi- torially pointless and suspiciously mediocre. However, precisely by bowing in all directions, impressing a variety of existing powerhouses, the magazine has forged an identity mark primar- ily by opportunism and evasion, accomplishing far more at impressing its academic sponsors than carving a future for intelligent writing (or Newman's own literary generation). In short, although there is no future, either literary or commercial, in duplicating what has already been done, academic philan- thropy invariably finds such safe activity preferable to adventur- ous intelligence.

Salmagundi (est. 1965) had more modest and independent beginnings on a few hundred dollars amassed by three friends then in their early twenties; its open editorial policies initially showed the genuine advantages of freedom from academic spon- sorship. Although founded upon a sense of generational neces- sity, it was nonetheless awed by the reputations and promotions of literary establishments, publishing such veteran fellow travel- ers as Lionel Abel, Martin Greenberg, and Stanley Kauffmann, in addition to devoting its first special issue to several essays on Robert Lowell. *Salmagundi*'s editors are fairly literate, high- minded, and perhaps too naively "intellectual," explaining in part why they should be so easily conned by disingenuous myths detrimental to the New and the Young; so that the magazine has come to exemplify the cult of cautiousness, win- ning establishment prizes and making the curious boast, re- corded in a questionnaire distributed by the *American Literary Anthology,* that *Salmagundi,* "chiefly directed toward the liter- ary community, . . . is in no way limited to the discovery and encouragement of new talent." By 1968, the magazine had sold its title to Skidmore College, its chief editor Robert Boyers (b. 1942) becoming a professor there. In the fourteenth issue, dated Fall, 1970, more than half of its available space was devoted to a newly translated and uninteresting play by Alberto Moravia (which Farrar, Straus & Giroux would publish the following year); of the remaining contributors, all but one (with only two poems) were over forty, all but two were academics, most were safely established, in sum delivering a telling blow to the magazine's original purposes. New magazines and young writers are so clearly destined for each other that the disintegration of such relationships is wrong and tragic, as well as culturally deleterious. There are several reasons why magazines open at one time to the young might so quickly close down, but these rationalizations do not survive historical scrutiny with honor.

Other new and diversified little magazines begun during this period were disappointing in various ways; none were fractionally as important to the emerging generation as either *The Dial* or *Partisan Review* or *Kenyon Review* were in their respective primes. *Arts in Society,* founded in 1958 at the University of Wisconsin, could have become an important polyartistic critical magazine; but various factors, such as academic conservatism, a physical-psychological distance from artistic developments, and continuing pedagogical concerns has kept its contribution minor. *Studies on the Left,* founded the following year, also at the University of Wisconsin, served the crucial function of publishing those extended political and cultural analyses too radical or too young (or too female) for *Dissent,* and too scholarly for Marxist newspapers. It became the best and most persistent of several new radical quarterlies initiated about that time; but its academicism (and precious inattention to literary politics) led to its premature demise, which unfortunately contributed in turn to the subsequent intellectual confusions and immaturity of the "New Left." *Noble Savage* (1960-62), co-edited by Saul Bellow and various associates, had a consistently high literary taste, exemplified in a stunning opening issue and then enough editorial generosity to include an early Thomas Pynchon piece; but along with succumbing to Bellow's idiosyncratic alliances, this bi-annual declined over its five issues.

It is indicative that remarkably few little magazines new in

the sixties have developed genuinely avant-garde and open editorial positions from their beginnings—Wally Depew's *Poetry
Newsletter* (1964-1967), Clark Coolidge's *Joglars* (1964-6), Jan
Herman's *San Francisco Earthquake* (est. 1967), Joachim Neugroschel and Suzanne Zavrian's *Extensions* (est. 1968), and
George Drury Smith's *Beyond Baroque* (est. 1968). Though this
factor makes all those journals consistently interesting, their
particular inclusions have generally been less distinguished than
their aims. R. B. Frank's *Panache* (est. 1965) has, by contrast,
evolved toward a similar adventurism, partially because of (or in
spite of) my own 1971 issue devoted to "Future's Fictions";
and John Logan's *Choice* (est. 1958) has the rare distinction of
a rich diversity that simply has not appeared often enough.

Among the even newer poetry magazines that incorporate
advanced developments along with an *expanded* sense of the
surviving traditions are Michael Andre's *Unmuzzled Ox* (est.
1971), Charles Haseloff's *Penumbra* (reest. 1970), Albert
Drake's *Happiness Holding Tank* (est. 1970), Ron Silliman's
Tottel's (est. 1971), John Taggert's *Maps* (est. 1971), John
Friedman and Irving Gottesman's *Shantih* (est. 1970), Jerome
Rothenberg's *Alcheringa* (est. 1971), F. A. Nettelbeck's *Throb*
(est. 1970), Karl Young and Jim Spencer's *Freek* (est. 1970),
White Pelican (est. 1970) in Edmonton, Alberta; Robert Grenier
and Barry Watten's *This* (est. 1971), Richard Mathews' *Kon-
glomerati* (est. 1971), Tom Ahern's *Diana's Bi-Monthly* (est.
1971), Harold Norse's *Bastard Angel* (est. 1972), Bill Berkson's
Big Sky (est. 1971), Michael Wiater's *Toothpick, Lisbon & the
Orcas Islands* (est. 1971), William Mohr's *Bachy* (est. 1972),
David Uu's *Lodgistiks* (est. 1972), Bob Heman's *Clown War*
(est. 1972); the disparate unbound mailings of the Mikolowskis'
Alternative Press in Detroit; *Box* (est. 1971) which emerged
from students at the California Institute of the Arts; Joyce
Holland's *Matchbook* (est. 1972), subtitled "a magazine of
one-word poetry," whose 1"-square pages are stapled into a
matchbook; and Gerard Dombrowski's *Abyss*, rejuvenated in
1971, after desultory beginnings a few years before. By contrast, the conservatism of such new magazines as X. J. Kennedy's *Counter/Measures* (est. 1972) or Daniel Halpern's
Antaeus (est. 1970) seem especially archaic, if not embarrass-
ingly pretentious.

Of the periodicals founded in the late sixties by paperback

publishers, the best of the lot, Samuel Delany and Marilyn Hacker's *Quark/* (1970-71) died much too soon after auspiciously introducing not only several good young writers, but a valid new development in science fiction that combines modernist literary virtues with speculative intelligence. (Now that it has disappeared, such innovative writing will probably be lost and the fortunes of the new sci-fi, customarily called "speculative fiction," will be no better than those that demoralize other forms of innovative writing.) In contrast to *Quark/*, Theodore Solotaroff's *New American Review* (est. 1967) has favored familiar strains, prepublishing the forthcoming super-promotions of the literary-industrial complex. Richard Goldstein's *US* (1969-70), though open to unusual fiction, largely published, as noted before, rock critics dealing with non-musical subjects and expressed an editorial bias against more intelligent writing (ignorantly dismissed as "academic"); Dotson Rader's *Defiance* (1970-71) dealt mostly in "radical" attitudinizing and self-hyping. Nearly all of Doubleday's *Works in Progress* (est. 1970) come from rather conventional books on the verge of publication, while the first issue of *Dutton Review* (est. 1971) flunked on several counts.

By the seventies it became clear the new fiction was suffering even more neglect than new poetry, primarily because fewer periodicals were receptive to it. As the novelist-critic-teacher Harvey Swados observed in 1972, "But we have more young people writing short stories right now, I suspect, than at any time in our history—and less possibility, as they mature, of their work seeing the light of day." Responding to this predicament, older magazines like *Tri-Quarterly* began to favor fiction; new outlets were founded like Carol Bergé's *Center* (est. 1971) and Mark Mirsky's *Fiction* (est. 1972), which added a midwestern supplement in 1973. However, in spite of rhetoric promising "the new," the truth was that genuinely avant-garde fiction remained as invisible as ever.

This sense of multiple disappointment was compounded by the absence of heirs to earlier kinds of necessary magazines, such as a highly prophetic and nonsectarian intellectual journal like Gershon Legman's *Neurotica* (1949-51) or Marshall McLuhan and Edmund Carpenter's awesome *Explorations* (1955-59); or a periodical as full of advanced speculative thought about art and culture as *Trans/formation* (1950-52). The closest semblances to such periodicals are *The Futurist* (est. 1967), whose avowed subject overcomes rather desultory editing and writing, and *Radical Software* (est. 1970), which specializes in radical proposals for electronic art. There also should be a new critical weekly to serve the new intellectual generation as well as *The New Republic* (est. 1914) provided communication to those born around 1890, for the established weeklies have been far too compromising and intellectually archaic for educated younger readers. And writers outside New York rightly wonder why there has not been a literary weekly or fortnightly comparable to William Marion Reedy's *Mirror,* published in St. Louis from 1891 to 1920. (The closest semblance in this respect might be the *Fault,* published in San Francisco in 1972-73.) Needless to say, little magazines could also use a selective annual with more editorial integrity than the *American Literary Anthology* (1967-69) in order to disseminate the most reprintable contributions to a larger literate audience. One esthetically conservative foray has been Curt Johnson's annual anthology, *Best Little Magazine Fiction* (est. 1971).

Few new American journals were receptive to visual poetry, although advances in offset printing make publication of such work more feasible than before; even fewer were open to other developments in avant-garde writing. There were no American magazines comparable to such recent European literary periodicals as *Approches* (Paris, 1966-68), Paul de Vree's *DeTafelronde* (est. Antwerp, 1953), Jean-François Broy's *L'Humidité* (est. Paris 1970), David Byers' *Pages* (est. London, 1970), *Crab Grass* (est. Belfast, 1970), and Sarenco and de Vree's *Lotta Poetica* (est. Italy, 1971). The closest semblance, in this last respect, would be the few issues of *Dust,* now defunct, that Wally Depew edited in the early seventies, while vanguard poetry sometimes sneaks into post-painting art magazines such as Willoughby Sharp's spectacularly produced *Avalanche* (est. 1971) and graphic collaborations like Ely Raman's *8 x 10 Art Portfolio* (1971). The opening issue of Barry Callaghan's *Exile* (est. Toronto, 1972) includes, along with more conventional works, an extended visual fiction—Robert Zend's "OAB"—of a kind and quality rarely, if ever, seen in U. S. literary quarterlies.

The few North American periodicals of sound-literature—the Harlemans' pioneering *Poetry Out Loud* (est. 1969) which is issued on records, and Lawrence Russell's *DNA* (est. 1971) which is published on tape in British Columbia—have so far exclusively featured their rather conventional founders (along with their friends); while both Alan Austin's *Black Box* (est. 1972) and Dennis H. Koran's *Panjandrum* (est. 1972) favor straight declamation, sometimes accompanied by music, in lieu of more experimental efforts, all of them thus short-changing the more radical possibilities of aural literary art. (*DNA* sets an eminent example, however, by going free to anyone who submits a blank stereotape or cassette of appropriate length.) These general omissions partially explain why visual poetry is rarely seen in the U. S. or native sound poetry is so rarely heard, or why, to cite a personal example, more of my own experiments in poetry and fiction have, until recently, appeared in European journals and anthologies rather than U. S. magazines. It is also indicative that of all the new periodicals only Larry Austin's *Score* (est. 1967), Phyllis Johnson's *Aspen* (est. 1967), and William Copley's *S.M.S.* (est. 1968), which are avant-garde art and music magazines, have risked much experiment (and expense) with innovative design and presentation.

All this activity creates the necessity for new periodicals about new literary periodicals; but these, too, are likely to reflect the limitations of the scene. One key weakness of Len Fulton's *Small Press Review* (est. 1967), Noel Peattie's *Spiapu* (est. 1969), and Richard Morris' *COSMEP Newsletter* (b. 1969), as well as the reviews in Peter Finch's *Second Aeon* (est. 1967, in Wales) and the *Alternative Press Index* (est. 1969), is a trade magazine-mindedness that avoids, by default, any head-on confrontation with the larger literary-political predicaments. Harry Smith's *The Newsletter* (est. 1969), by contrast, is a gossip (and promo) sheet that broaches problems without making connections or drawing conclusions, partly because comprehensive radicalism is beyond its gossipy style.

Once the Nixon depression swept in, many little magazines began to disappear while others produced belated "combined" issues that usually forecast their demise. In 1970, Rich Mangelsdorff, perhaps the most sophisticated critic of this material, could lament the end of the mimeo-press resurgence of 1965-68. By the early seventies there were probably a few more good and open outlets for intelligent writing than had existed a decade before; yet their efforts were diffused and irregular and sporadic as literary periodicals collectively neglected the necessary literary-political tasks, thereby creating the paradoxical impression, still current, that there were at once too many of them and yet far too few.

V

> Why an underground newspaper? Because the truths they tell cannot be told in the mass media, because they serve needs that are not being served, because a generation in rebellion and facing repression needs a voice. —Lincoln Bergman, in an afterword to *The Underground Press in America* (1970).

One familiar argument holds that since literature has gravitated into journalism and the slicker periodicals, it is there, rather than in little magazines, that the supposedly promising young writers are to be found. However, both these points depend, as noted before, upon debased notions of literary value, in addition to ignorance of both genuine contemporary achievements and the current literary-political predicament. First of all, journalism, unlike literature, is not intended to survive (or to be read) beyond its immediate publication; the journalistic virtues of relevance and impact have little currency in literature. Though the application of certain novelistic techniques to the writing of articles made the "new journalism" new to its periodical contexts, these styles were scarcely radical within the more inclusive traditions of modernistic writing.

Secondly, any little-magazine contributor who has also written for mass-circulation journals knows that their editorial conventions and limitations not only *care* less (if at all) about posterity, but are also scarcely conducive to one's best, freest, or most personal writing. Their editorial committees also take an extremely proprietary interest in the writing they commission (reducing, revising, rewriting); and, much like the "new journalism," such magazines tend to exploit styles, subjects, and attitudes that have already been established rather than risking innovation and discovery. A further fact contradicting the slick-magazine thesis is that *The New Yorker,* for instance, has not "discovered" a good critic younger than Renata Adler (b. 1938), or a good fictionist since John Updike (b. 1932), or a possibly avant-garde writer since Donald Barthelme (b. 1931), or a young poet since—? *Esquire* and *Playboy* score even less impressive records with the New and the Young. The final truth, never to be forgotten, is that slick mass-magazines, unlike the littles, are fundamentally uninterested in literature, although at times responsive to the growing public that is; so that without little magazines, the genres of both poetry and short fiction would certainly die of neglect.

Sophisticated magazine publishers know that the sixties witnessed the emergence of a large audience in its twenties and thirties that is too literate for the underground press, too young for *The New Yorker* and *The Atlantic,* too intelligent for most of *Esquire* or *Playboy* (although one article in each can capture their attention). Already middle-class, upwardly mobile, incipiently powerful, liberally knowledgeable, this is an audience that advertisers would like to reach, though no one yet has successfully created a large-circulation magazine especially for them. Ralph Ginzburg's misnamed *Avant-Garde* (est. 1968) probably had such people in mind, but it lacked the editorial taste to get their subscriptions. Clay Felker's *New York Magazine* (est. 1968) captures some of them, especially if they live in and around Manhattan, as does a somewhat rejuvenated post-Willie Morris *Harper's*; and with each publishing season comes gossip of yet more proposals for media aimed at this audience. Not until recently, however, did I believe that this obvious opportunity would go unexploited, both the audience and its writers thus suffering detrimental neglect.

Late in the sixties emerged the "underground press," a term which classifies periodicals, most of them intending to be fortnightly, that were printed on newsprint by a new offset process that is much cheaper than the old letterpress. Most of their contents were based upon the formula of three P's—pornography, protest, and pop. Usually founded with idealistic motives—to disseminate messages rather than make a profit—these papers enabled radical young newpapermen to avoid not only the conservative establishments, but the traditional procedure of starting humbly at the bottom. In this respect, along with the development of cheaper means of production, the underground press represents the initiative of young writers at its very best. However, in contrast to the new literary journals, these underground papers aim to compete against established newspapers and news magazines, replacing their conventional views of politics and social affairs with those of a radical generation. These new papers typically display a polemical courage that makes the "journalism reviews" (sprung up in several cities) seem, by contrast, much too timid. Given its context, it is not surprising that the language of the underground press, differences in vocabulary notwithstanding, is basically journalistic, as are its layouts, its emphases, its illiteracy and superficialities, its deference to its readers' suspected prejudices, its scheduling, and, alas, the mentalities of its editors. (The counter-cultural motives of such periodicals are generally more laudable than their collective intelligence.) The differences between smart writing and dumb clearly involve more than esthetics—the former has something important to communicate whereas the latter obscures by posturing and using clichés excessively. The best solution to academic hauteur is not anti-intellectualism, which is ultimately counter-productive, but more fundamental kinds of intelligence.

Underground papers rarely publish writing capable of influencing a discriminating mind (except perhaps as pure information), as underground publishers tend to want *everything* to "appeal to the kids"—a common denominator that is both insulting and condescending. One true contrast in political writing, say, is the extended muck-rake that appears in *Mayday* (est. 1969), the James Ridgeway and Andrew Kopkind paper that was retitled *Hard Times* (and later incorporated into *Ramparts*), or in *The Washington Monthly* (est. 1969), or in the books that young researchers produced for the Center for Study of Responsive Law whose well-publicized umbrella of "Nader's Raiders" gets into print lots of investigative reporting that might otherwise be trashed. Furthermore, even though the underground press sometimes publishes post-Poundian poetry, they remain newspapers, just as subversive "comix" are still essentially funnybooks. Book reviews, for instance, are as scarce in underground press pages as intelligent book critics (Rich Mangelsdorff and Michael Perkins being two who persist); and the movies reviewed, if ever, come not from the counter-culture but the post-Hollywood mainstream.

Subliterate at base, underground papers have not produced many respected *writers*. The most prominent sheets have more circulation than literary magazines for many of the same reasons that *The Daily News* has more readers than *The New York Times;* but these counter-intelligent reasons would also account for the underground press's (and *The Daily News's*) lack of consequential influence. (Exceptions to these caveats include Walt Shepperd's *Nickel Review* in Syracuse [1967-71] and, to a lesser extent, *Woodwind* [est. 1969] in Washington—two fairly intelligent cultural reviews published on newsprint.) "The greatest thing the underground press has done," in Ed Sanders' judgment, "is to help other publications have a more healthy and liberated prose style." Beyond that, it should be noted that though their editors are nearly all young, such papers are no more "typical" of the young literate generation than corporate house organs (whose editors are largely in their forties) represent anything about *that* age group, much as the spokesmen of each generation may wish such generalizations true of the other.

The pioneering success of underground newspapers in the late sixties inspired another, classier kind of youth magazine based upon the massive interest in popular music and characterized by more intelligent, extended, and discriminating prose (closer probably to *Newsweek,* if not to the middlebrow magazines). This group includes not only *Cheetah* (1967-68), perhaps the most literate of the lot, and *Rolling Stone* (est. 1967), the most successful, but also *Eye* (1968-70), *Crawdaddy* (1966-70, especially in its second metamorphosis), *Fusion* (est. 1968), *Changes* (est. 1969), and *Rock* (est. 1970). The seriousness behind their interest in rock reveals both genuine literacy and critical sensitivity that extend at times to certain other generational concerns and cultural phenomena. Although their editors often treat cultural material (and its writers) as cavalierly as the slicksters do, reviewing, for instance, the same new books covered in the more massive media, such intelligence about the latest pop enthusiasms could conceivably forge a comparable cultural taste, as well as underwrite more substantial interests. By 1973, however, this desirable maturation had scarcely begun. In 1971-72 emerged several more impressive papers which published some of the better counter-culture writers in a creamier mix—*The New York Ace,* the *Staff* in Los Angeles, and *Sundance* in San Francisco. The fact that all these papers have exhibited so much directed energy, especially in comparison to more literate publications, in forging a genuine counter-culture suggests not that literary activity is dead, as some would have it, or that everyone under thirty is illiterate, but, to repeat, that a generation of literate young people have, quite simply, shirked the literary-political tasks that still need to be done. Unless good little magazines are founded and supported, a lot of consciousness will remain inarticulate and intelligent writing will have no future.

14   Alternative Book Publishers

I

It is a higher degree of freedom when thoughtful and independent individuals have the opportunity of addressing each other. If they have no vehicles by which they can express opinion, then for them the freedom of the press does not exist. —T. S. Eliot, "A Commentary" (1938).

The young need the young more than they need the old and honored; great writers take care of themselves and don't need monuments and schools since their influence is always present; but the brilliant kid writer can be crushed or turned into a foolish acrobat unless he gets an enthusiastic response from his own contemporaries, not elders whom he has sensible mixed feelings about, no matter how concerned they are. —Seymour Krim, "What's This Cat's Story?" (1961).

There were now also quite a few young publishers and young publications devoting their energies, whether practical or spiritual or both, to the competent housing and exploitation of the men and women and movements expressive of the time—and in rare instances, beyond the time. Visionary fellows like Huebsch, Liveright, Knopf, Selzer, Harcourt, Brace, and Howe, with excellent sense in their veins, were performing an artistic and comparatively lucrative service in bringing writers and their public together. —Alfred Kreymborg, *Troubadour* (1925).

As the large North American publishers are less and less able to issue the manuscripts essential to the survival of intelligent writing, the need for new and independent book-making enterprise becomes greater and more urgent; yet the natural cycle of decay and rebirth has not progressed with enough deliberate speed. Though many new firms were founded in the past decade, not all of them were particularly interested in young writers or radically different books; and none, in the end, served emerging writers as nobly as, say, Bennett Cerf (1898-1971) and Alfred A. Knopf (b. 1891) supported some of their respective contemporaries. Not only did alarmingly few of the new houses risk that kind of eclectic literary publishing, but few of the affluent or entrepreneurial young founded new publishing firms; and given the growing expenses and hazards of the business, those that were successfully launched subsequently encountered considerable difficulty staying alive. Truly alternative publishers must be distinguished from both sectarian houses and the carbon copies of commercial publishing (as well as those specializing in pornography). Sectarian publishers were founded to print books by, for, and about a certain faith, ethnic culture, esoteric enthusiasm, or political persuasion, such as Catholicism, Armenians, astrology, and Communism, respectively; and none of these publishers are, by definition, at all interested in anything outside their initially circumscribed orbit. Other new imprints grew out of successful periodicals, such as *Playboy* and *Psychology Today,* largely to provide books of material similar to that featured in the magazine (and probably destined for precisely the same audience).

Other new imprints were started by experienced commercial publishers, some of whom had resigned from (or had been fired by) the larger corporations to which they had previously sold their stock. Victor Weybright, for instance, built up the New American Library before selling it to the Times-Mirror, Inc.; and their mismanagement of the paperback firm, as he tells it, led to his resignation (and the subsequent decline of NAL). In 1966, he joined his son-in-law, Truman Talley, in founding Weybright & Talley, which floundered aimlessly before they sold it to David McKay, Inc. Richard Baron sold 60 percent of the Dial Press, which he once solely owned, to Dell before departing to found an imprint under his own name in 1968. Seymour Lawrence, a new publisher (est. 1965) affiliated with Dell, was a long-time senior editor at Little, Brown; the proprietors of Gambit (est. 1968) in Boston had long labored for Houghton-Mifflin; Richard Kluger, the founder of Charterhouse (est. 1971), had previously been a top editor at Simon & Schuster and then at Atheneum; and Peter Weyden had been executive editor at *Ladies Home Journal* before founding a press under his own name. All of these new firms were replicas of the larger outfits with offices in midtown Manhattan or mainline Boston; the books they published plainly revealed their founders' devotion to the myths and aspirations of the literary-industrial complex.

The mark of truly alternative publishing, by contrast, is books that long-established houses would not do; and all of the new publishers discussed in the following pages exhibit, at least in part, the kinds of commitment conducive to the future of intelligent writing. They tend to favor not only classes of writers, but kinds of writing ignored by the literary-industrial behemoths. One or another of these new presses has been particularly open to black writers, women writers, post-Black Mountain poets, Canadian writers, young writers, and experimental writers. Had the manuscripts published by these alternative presses actually been submitted to the commercial houses, they would surely have been declined as "too incoherent," "too religious," "too esoteric," "too provincial," "too peculiar-looking," "too personal," "too idiosyncratic." Given conditions elsewhere, it is not surprising that most of the decade's most consequential books of poetry came from small presses.

Most alternative presses have been founded by writers who realized the larger meaning of their own predicament; and these alternative writer-publishers draw upon income gained from outside sources—usually a teaching job, though few would regard either themselves or their work as "academic." Most remain one-man operations where the "publisher" functions as editor, designer, secretary, and delivery boy, if not the printer as well. As loans for this kind of venture are not easy to come by, most alternative publishers are self-financed, their founders scarcely compensating themselves for their working time. Only a scant few, unlike little magazines, are currently subsidized by universities or other cultural institutions. If only for the quality of their intentions, nearly all alternative pressmen are as personally laudable as other literary servants; the best of them print serious writing that would otherwise be lost.

Lower operating costs also enable them to do first editions in smaller numbers than commercial firms would find feasible—less than 5000 copies—and to keep the book "in print" until all of the available copies are sold. Some publish strictly limited editions, customarily done by the publisher himself on a hand-press and signed by the author (along with any collaborating artists), all of which hopefully give the book the aura of a treasured "art" possession—an aura comparable to that of a graphics portfolio. Others use the cheapest available offset processes to print more copies than they can possibly sell. Some alternative-press books have spines with the title and the author's name, while others are simply stapled down the middle and folded over. Most issue only paperback editions, in sharp contrast to the commercial replicas, not only because the small press's likely customers rarely buy hardbacks, but also because "subsidiary rights" are not a primary part of their business.

Books issued by alternative publishers are not necessarily better or worse than those of commercial houses; in practice, each is editorially selective in different ways. However, just as certain kinds of badness are more typical of one kind of publishing, so certain kinds of excellence are available in the best small-press books, such as realized formal invention which scarcely turns up in literary-industrial produce. One by-product of alternative publishing is the possibility of alternative reading.

The biggest problem that these publishers have in common, after the acquisition of operating capital (politely called "seed money"), is distribution. Most place their books in those nearby bookstores already sympathetic to literary ventures. Some use national distributors to reach outlets beyond their immediate milieu, while others mail copies to selected retailers across the country. Some new presses have tried to develop a list of regular subscribers who, much like magazine subscribers, pay in advance for whatever is published. As most small presses fail to turn an immediate profit, and their proprietors find that their venture consumes increasing amounts of time and money, only a few survive more than a decade. However, if they pick good writers who are subsequently acclaimed, the unsold copies will fetch surprisingly high prices on the rare-book market. Kenneth Rexroth quotes a book dealer who noted, "Any book of poetry which isn't complete vanity publication trash will double in price three years after it goes off the market."

Some small presses bring out as many as twenty new books a year while others print only one book, such as X-Communications for Liam O'Gallagher's *The Blue Planet Notebooks* (1972), or only one author, such as the Turtle Island Foundation for the works in various genres by the late Jaime de Angulo, or Emil Antonucci's Journeyman Press for the otherwise neglected minimalist poetry of Robert Lax. Writers whose books are ignored completely by the big houses can gain a certain celebrity entirely from small press publications—for example, the poet Doug Blazek, who placed the first 17 of his books with a dozen different publishers, and the man-of-letters, Hugh Fox, whose 18 books were done under nine imprints. Some of the new book publishers grew out of literary magazines, the editor deciding that a single writer could fill an entire issue. *Quixote, The Sixties, The Smith, Tri-Quarterly, Intrepid, Elizabeth, Abraxas, Assembling, Lillabulero, Genesis:Grasp, Mulch, Caterpillar, Radical America, Ann Arbor Review, Cotyledon, White Pelican,* among other periodicals, have also published books. Approximately one-fourth of the Committee of Small Magazine Editors and Publishers, according to a 1972 survey, published both books and magazines. George Chambers' *The Bonnyclabber* (1972), a first-rate experimental fiction, was put out by two little magazines, *Panache* and *December,* collaborating for a single shot. (Each had previously published another book wholly on its own.) One new imprint, Douglas Books, evolved from a New York record company of the same name; another, Links, grew out of a successful pop music songbook publisher. Small presses in all sizes are so numerous by now that the following survey, though superficially compendious, is certainly incomplete; yet for all kinds of obvious reasons, there are fewer new small presses than literary magazines.

Several of the larger new firms were full-time ventures founded independently of magazines by young editors who had previously worked for the larger houses. The first and most obvious advantage of having one's own firm is editorial autonomy. The same editor who previously had to convince his firm's president, sales manager, and others could now make crucial editorial decisions on his own. The author could have the comparable pleasure of. dealing directly with the chief, instead of an underling (who invariably must "ask someone else"). One experienced writer I know was so surprised and pleased to hear an editor say, immediately after examining the manuscript,

"We'd like to do it now," that he never got around to asking for any advance money.

II

> If any companies get too big and become too commercial, there will always be newcomers ready to snatch the good manuscripts that they turn down.
> —Bennett Cerf, in a lecture (1960).

The oldest genuinely alternative publisher in New York, if not in all North America, is James Laughlin's New Directions, founded nearly forty years ago and (unlike Grove Press) still issuing many books that no one else would even consider—Jesse Reichek's totally visual fiction, *etcetera* (1965), Jean-Francois Bory's post-concrete pastiche, *Once Again* (1968), and Marvin Cohen's *The Self-Devoted Friend* (1968), among others. It has also displayed an exemplary loyalty to its best American authors—Kenneth Rexroth, Kenneth Patchen, Gary Snyder, Denise Levertov, most of whom had previously been ignored by New York publishers. However, even though its founder scarcely qualifies as a pensioner, the firm has lost its earlier initiative, never, in recent years, publishing books by an American writer currently under forty. Its most prominent successor, particularly in poetry publishing, was City Lights, the first San Francisco literary firm ever to win a national audience. (Precursors failing to survive include the Colt Press and Circle Editions, both of which did several good books in the forties.) Since there were no local publishers predisposed to literature, even Rexroth, the putative dean of the San Francisco poets, had, like Robinson Jeffers before him, published most of his books in New York. Younger West Coast poets like William Everson (a.k.a. Brother Antonius) and Robert Duncan also published their own earliest books.

Founded in 1955 by Lawrence Ferlinghetti, a New York poet (b. 1919), City Lights took its name from a short-lived San Francisco critical magazine (1953-54) edited by Peter Martin, who was also Ferlinghetti's partner in founding the popular City Lights bookstore. This imprint published a pioneering series of inexpensively produced poetry pamphlets. As the first was Ferlinghetti's own *Pictures of the Gone World* (1955) and the fourth was Allen Ginsberg's *Howl and Other Poems* (1956), the imprint thrived on the "beats'" notoriety and subsequent popularity. City Lights also published other anti-academic poets who were then ignored by the eastern houses—Patchen, Bob Kaufman, and Gregory Corso (all of whom later passed on to New Directions). Other new San Francisco poetry presses such as White Rabbit and Auerhahn, no doubt impressed by City Lights' example, emerged from nowhere; and publicists spoke of a "Renaissance."

However, as the sixties brought a new literary culture, City Lights appeared tied to an earlier position, along with its kind of poetry, all but completely neglecting the newer writers. It published fewer new books in the seventies, and nearly all of these were prose. Though City Lights had functioned as a distributor for other West Coast poetry publishers, that service was terminated by the late sixties; and until new channels of distribution emerged, Oyez and other California imprints were scarcely seen in eastern bookstores. The unfortunate truth is that a small publisher's success, rare though it is, can have the negative effect of undermining the purposeful energy necessary for continuing editorial adventure; so that, in its literary politics at least, City Lights became the first conservative establishment ever ensconced in California. Small-mindedness, in one form or another, tends to be a recurring fault of alternative publishing.

The past decade's most prominent avant-garde publisher has been the Something Else Press, founded in 1964 by Dick Higgins (b. 1938), himself a sometime poet, composer, printer, film-maker, mixed-means theatrician, and scholar with both diverse avant-garde interests and an energized sense of historical necessity. All these other activities notwithstanding, book-publishing has been the most substantial of his achievements. The press's first venture was, like City Lights' opening book, a collection of the proprietor's own work, *Postface/Jefferson's Birthday* (1964), his personal predicament as an experimental writer and critic inspiring the creation of a necessary enterprise. The firm's founding manifesto included this appropriate declaration:

> When asked what one is doing, one can only explain it as "something else." Now one does something big, now one does something small, now another big thing, now another little thing. Always it is something else.

The firm's opening lists revealed, nonetheless, more particular commitments to the international musical-artistic avant-garde that Higgins had discovered in the early sixties; and among the Press's most important publications are books by an older generation of influential non-literary artists: Ray Johnson's *The Paper Snake* (1965), Claes Oldenburg's *Store Days* (1967), John Cage's elegant anthology of *Notations* (1968), Merce Cunningham's *Changes: Notes on Choreography* (1969), all of which are extremely imaginative—quite "something else"—in conception, content, and design.

These titles defined a kind of publishing previously rare in America—different in experimental seriousness from the glossy picture books of the art publishers, and different as well from both the extravagant hand-printed poetry books and the more spartan productions of City Lights and New Directions. Perhaps the closest American precursor to Something Else was Wittenborn, Schultz, Inc., a New York art-book retailer who issued an impressive series of "Documents of Modern Art" in the late forties and early fifties, or Paul Theobald, a Chicago art-bookstore that published Moholy-Nagy's *Vision in Motion* (1947), among other similarly post-Bauhaus titles, in the same post-World War II decade. One auspicious successor in this tradition was George Maciunas' Fluxus, essentially a graphics firm that issued printed packets along with other "multiples"; a more recent semblance is the Press of the Nova Scotia College of Art and Design which opened in 1973 with *The Architecture of Ludwig Wittgenstein.* Art galleries and museums that occasionally publish books also fall into this tradition. It was the Whitney Museum of American Art, rather than a commercial firm, that produced *Samaras Album* (1971), an awesome visual-verbal essay on narcissism by the sculptor Lucas Samaras.

In addition to its books by artists, the Something Else Press brought out a series of invaluable, and otherwise unavailable, pamphlets by allied and precursor figures, many of them European. It reprinted the most eccentric books of Gertrude Stein (for example, the full-length *The Making of Americans,* and *Geography and Plays*) and Henry Cowell (*New Musical Resources*). Responsive as well to neglected older experimentalists, Higgins published unprecedentedly large collections of poetry by Bern Porter and Jackson Mac Low—respectively *Found Poems* (1972) and *Stanzas for Iris Lezak* (1972). The Something Else edition of Emmett Williams' *An Anthology of Concrete Poetry* (1967) became the firm's best-seller (over 15,000 copies), if not its most influential book; and Williams' own novel, *Sweethearts* (1967), was also far beyond the bounds of conventional publishing, as well as the best of its author's several works. Something Else also published one of my own books, *Breakthrough Fictioneers* (1973)—an anthology that was declined as "something else" by the larger publisher who initially contracted it. At least half of its nearly hundred titles are distinctive and individually memorable. "A good newspaper," in A.J. Liebling's aphorism, "is as truly an educational institution as a good college"; so is a substantial avant-garde publisher.

In spite of such intentions and achievements, Something Else's books suffered from insufficient notice even from those media commonly regarded as "crazy about the New"; and those critics who tried to review its titles for the established media invariably encountered resistances and rebuffs. It is indicative that neither *The New York Times Book Review* nor *The New York Review of Books* has *ever* singled out a Something Else title for individual review. However, since the press's prominence in avant-garde circles was undisputed, Higgins received and rejected many manuscripts that could (and should) have been published as "something else," but, since the gap between Something Else and everyone else was so great, these works would probably not appear at all. By superintending the most propitious channel for a certain kind of book-writing, Higgins assumed a power whose form was not unlike Jason Epstein's over radical criticism, though different, of course, in quality and operation, for Higgins himself recognized the dangers implicit in such a concentration of editorial authority due to the absence of substantial competitors. Partly because the New York reviewing media were so unresponsive, Higgins moved the business first to California and then to northern Vermont.

The default of New Directions and then Grove, as well as City Lights, created large gaps in the publication of counter-academic poetry; and one of the first to fill this vacuum was Corinth Books in New York. Founded in the late fifties by Ted Wilentz, then a prominent Greenwich Village bookstore proprietor in close touch with its literate community, Corinth issued a volume of Allen Ginsberg's pre-*Howl* poetry, *Empty Mirror: Early Poems* (1961), and Charles Olson's *Maximus*

Poems (1960), as well as reprinting, in 1959, Bob Brown's pioneering collection of visual poetry, *1450-1950,* which was originally published thirty years before. Pursuing the kinds of previously neglected work gathered together in Donald Allen's counter-establishment anthology, *The New American Poetry* (1960), Corinth published "San Francisco" poets, such as Gary Snyder and Philip Whalen; "Black Mountain" poets, such as Olson and Robert Creeley; "New York" poets like Barbara Guest and Frank O'Hara; black poets, such as LeRoi Jones, Clarence Major, Tom Weatherly, and Jay Wright; and then, unlike City Lights, an even younger generation of poets, mostly associated with the "New York School"—Lewis Warsh, Anne Waldman, Peter Schjedahl, and Ted Berrigan—in addition to Brenda Herold, a talented teenager from New Orleans. Sustaining the press through personal adversity while he moved through a succession of other jobs, Wilentz has kept everything in print (unless the author wanted to incorporate his Corinth book into a larger subsequent work), and the press slowly but surely became one of America's most substantial poetry publishers whose success was based not upon capital or celebrity-chasing but tasteful perseverence.

By incorporating counter-conventional work into more general aims, a few other recently founded New York publishers have put alternative work into print. Grossman Publishers, set up in 1962 (and now a division of the Viking Press), has mixed much undistinguished fiction by alumni of creative writing schools with such truly alternative titles as Madeline Gins' *Word Rain* (1969) and M.D. Elevitch's *Grips* (1972), as well as importing books of American poetry—mostly post-Black Mountain, varying greatly in quality—originally published by Cape Goliard in England. Grossman's Orion Press subsidiary under separate editorship did one of the best novels of the late sixties, Kenneth Gangemi's scrupulously uninflected *Olt* (1969). Another New York firm, Outerbridge & Dienstfrey, established in 1969, issued such unusual titles as Edmund Carpenter and Ken Heyman's *They Became What They Beheld* (1970), a profound verbal-visual essay that many other publishers had rejected, plus G.S. Gravenson's *The Sweetmeat Saga* (1971), a novel so typographically eccentric that its manuscript had to be photo-offset (rather than typeset). Once Dienstfrey departed, however, the firm's lists lost their literary edge.

Among the other smaller New York publishers doing important alternative literature are Lita Hornick's Kulchur Foundation whose two books a year have included Charles Henri Ford's *Silver Flower Coo* (1968) and David Antin's *Talking* (1972); Ralph Gibson's Lustrum Press is revolutionizing the publication of book-length photographic essays; 1st Casualty Press in Brooklyn opened with a much-rejected anthology of war poems by Vietnam veterans, *Winning Hearts & Minds* (1972), which, after it won acclaim, was reprinted by McGraw-Hill; Lawrence Dent's Winter House, whose most unusual book has been Frederick Barthelme's indescribable *Rangoon* (1970), has also issued collections of young dramatists' plays; Harold Witt's Croton Press did Michael Disend's unforgettable novel, *Stomping the Goyim* (1969), and collected Donald Phelps' much-admired essays into *Covering Ground* (1969); C. W. Truesdale's New Rivers Press specializes in handsome editions of poets not collected before; John Bernard Meyers' Tibor de Nagy Editions has selected the best of the early "New York School"; Vito Acconci's 0 to 9 did its founder's early books; Larry Fagin's Adventures in Poetry has mimeographed lots of second-generation "New York School" trivia, along with inarguably innovative texts by Clark Coolidge and Jennifer Bartlett; the Vanishing Rotating Triangle, founded by Leandro Katz and Ted Castle, is devoted to the confluence of Latin-American literature and avant-garde art; George Wittenborn, the art-book dealer mentioned before, though no longer publishing art books, has continued to issue the rigorously difficult fictions of Arlene Zekowski and Stanley Berne; Johnny Stanton's Siamese Banana put out Keith Cohen's *Madness in Literature* (1970); Ray Freed's Doctor Generosity Press was founded in a New York bar that also presents poetry readings; Barlenmir House does collections of otherwise unfavored poets; the Eakins Press, Johanna Gunderson's Red Dust, and George Koppelman's Seven Woods are still other alternative publishers issuing important work. Perhaps because writers living in New York are more immediately aware of the failings of big publishers, they are less likely than provincials to bang their heads forever against literary-industrial walls.

III

The other part must be the small publisher devoted to bringing out works of quality which do not have a

> chance to make their ways in commercial publishing. My feeling was that book publishing needed the "little publisher" the same way that the world of magazines needed the "little magazine."—Alan Swallow, "American Publishing and the American Writer" (1960).

Distance from New York, or at least from midtown Manhattan, may be prerequisite for truly alternative publishing so that independent editorial taste can remain less awed by both transient fashions and exclusively New York pressures. Editors in the provinces might also avoid the European influences that afflict not only a fairly serious midtown publisher like George Braziller, say, but even the Something Else Press (during its Manhattan period). However, unless the provincial firm is wealthy enough like Houghton Mifflin or the University of California Press to establish a "New York office," the primary peril of publishing outside New York is even less proximity to the most powerful media of review and publicity. This ineluctable lack of media interest, even if expected, inevitably puts a damper on aspirations, in addition to causing needless neglect in their immediate milieus. "We do better in N. Y. and L.A. than we do at home," one San Francisco editor complained in a letter to me, "where a mixture of paranoia and provincialism make people deathly scared to admire anything that doesn't come out of New York." As provincial writers are a severely neglected literary class, small presses outside New York are eminently necessary; but they *never* get the benefits and attention that, for the sake of literature's future, they deserve. As a result, not only do they rarely develop a larger, unparochial vision of literary necessity, but so much of their very best intentions go to waste. (A lesser disadvantage is a distance, both physical and psychological, from the new intelligence continually generated by New York's artistic change and exchange.)

The historical epitome here was Alan Swallow (1915-66) who operated a one-man firm out of his own house in Denver, Colorado, publishing small editions, cheaply printed, of largely forgotten poets (and some better-known, commercially-abandoned, older, mostly western writers) to a negligible amount of sales and even less reviewing response. A former football player, he worked around the clock and for a while also taught at the local university. "For many of us in publishing,"

300

he wrote in a classic statement, "the chief concern is less that of seeing important work of the past continue to be available than it is the situation for the talented new writer. We are concerned with the poetry, the fiction, the literary criticism of inherent significance." Nonetheless, rare is the small publishing enterprise outside New York that lasts as long as Swallow's press did—twenty-five years, until his premature death. "He never published a book he didn't like," the novelist Mark Harris explained. "Thus, he never fell into self-contempt."

Another exemplar of sorts has been Bern Porter (b. 1911), a peripatetic poet and physicist, who issued numerous books that were then otherwise unpublishable: Philip Lamantia's *Erotic Poems* (Berkeley, 1946), Kenneth Patchen's *Panels for the Walls of Heaven* (San Francisco, 1947), several volumes of Henry Miller's essays, and even Dick Higgins' *What Are Legends?* (Calais, Maine, 1960). In 1939, August Derleth, better known as a prolific novelist, founded Arkham House in his native Sauk City, Wisconsin, to publish both regional material and literary fantasy (especially the otherwise abandoned fiction of H.P. Lovecraft); for nearly as long, Harry Duncan's Cummington Press has published a steady stream of exceptionally well-printed books of excellent poetry, including Robert Lowell's first book, *Land of Unlikeness* (1944), and the first edition of Armand Schwerner's *The Tablets I-VIII* (1969). In the forties, James A. Decker, also operating in the Midwest, issued numerous collections of otherwise unavailable poets such as the first book of David Ignatow. City Lights, of course, represents yet another historical step in the necessary decentralization of American publishing.

Capitalizing upon its decline, other California firms have filled the breach in poetry publishing. The most prolific has been Black Sparrow Press which John Martin started in Los Angeles in 1968, initially printing limited editions of younger American poets, many of whom had not previously appeared in book form—David Antin, Kenneth Gangemi, George Econo-mou—in addition to older, mostly West Coast poets descending from Black Mountain traditions. Currently doing about twenty books a year plus a modest monthly magazine, Martin generally prints around 1500 copies, nearly all of which are bound in cardboard and sold for four to six dollars. The remaining two hundred or so are bound in harder covers, signed by the author and sold for a higher price. Unlike small publishers who depend upon grants or private beneficence, Martin survives on sales alone. "I'm doing well (enough)," he recently wrote me, "making expenses and a kind of living (I have no other income except what the press gives me); but to accomplish all this, I have to do *everything* myself: editing, mailing, ad copy, shipping, bookkeeping, correspondence, etc. It means a 70-hour week. And my wife designs the books, which saves a big expense. I'll continue as long as I can, publishing what I want the way I want to do it." Martin reports that, like other serious small publishers, he cannot do all the titles he would like, estimating that "each year I must send back 20 books I'd love to publish, but I can't." In 1972, Corinth found itself in a similar predicament, telling the *Directory of Little Magazines* that, "We are not considering unsolicited manuscripts, because of present commitments."

Another West Coast publisher, Donald Allen's Four Seasons Foundation, favors poets he has previously anthologized—Creeley, Olson, Philip Whalen, and Michael McClure; it scored a commercial coup by publishing the original editions of Richard Brautigan's much-rejected *Trout Fishing in America* (1967), *In Watermelon Sugar* (1968), and *The Pill Versus the Springhill Mine Disaster* (1968). Robert Hawley's Oyez Press did Philip Lamantia's *Touch of the Marvelous* (1966), the best book by a poet who, though famous for nearly 30 years, has never been published in the East. Dave Haselwood issued Allen Ginsberg's *Indian Journals* (1969), while Grey Fox in Bolinas published the first edition of Ginsberg's long-lost rhymed poems, *The Gates of Wrath* (1972). Glide Publications, the book-making arm of a San Francisco activist church, did *Mark in Time* (1971), an opulently produced anthology of local poets (and their photographs); and clearly in response, Paul Foreman's The Throp Spring Press, across the bay in Berkeley, issued the *San Francisco Bark* (1972), a more modestly produced selection of totally different poets, many of whom teach at the local university.

Among the other West Coast alternative publishers are Doug Blazek's Open Skull whose stellar production was Lyn Lifshin's first collection, *Why Is This House Dissolving?* (1968); Unicorn Press, founded in Santa Barbara by Teo Savory and Alan Brilliant, which offers a large and eclectic poetry list; Noel Young's Capricorn Press, a Santa Barbara fine-book printer, who did the original edition of L. Clark Stevens' *EST: The Steersman's Handbook* (1971); George Hitchcock's Kayak Books which moved from San Francisco to Santa Cruz; Ramparts Press, a spin-off from the magazine, which issued Dave Meggyesy's consciousness-changing *Out of Their League* (1970) and Murray Bookchin's *Post-Scarcity Anarchy* (1971); Jan Herman's Nova Broadcast Press, established literally within City Lights offices, which issued Liam O'Gallagher's one-man collection of visual poetry, *Planet Noise* (1969); The Futharc Press in Chico; John Oliver Simon's Galactic Approximations Press in Berkeley; Doug Palmer's Peace & Gladness; Don Gray's Two Windows, Dennis H. Koran's Panjandrum, Stephen Levine's Unity Press, Coyote, Beach Books, Cranium, Klonk, Black Dragon, Cloud Marauder, Kingdom Kum, Grape, Stolen Paper, all of which have also resided in San Francisco.

Up in Bolinas is David Meltzer's Tree Books, while down in Santa Barbara is Graham Mackintosh's Capra and Melissa Albers' Christopher Books; Great Balls of Fire in Santa Monica does photography books. Out in Sacramento was D. r. Wagner's Runcible Spoon; in Oakland is Oneiric Press; in Paradise, California, is Len Fulton's Dustbooks which issued Wally Depew's totally abstract short fiction, *Once* (1971), along with the annual, indispensable *Directory of Little Magazines, Small Press & Underground Newspapers* (1965 to the present). Up in Oregon is Bill Thomas' Toad Press which did a book of Ruth Krauss' striking poetry, and Don Cauble's Dead Angel which does some of the handsomest hand-press book-making in America. David Kherdian's Giligia Press (in Fresno before it moved to New Hampshire) issued *Down at the Depot* (1970), an anthology of Fresno poets that is the first in a series of comparable collections from other American cities. In Fairfax, the Red Hill Press did *An Anthology of L.A. Poets* (1972), and Ben L. Hiatt recently moved his Grand Ronde Press along with the *Grand Ronde Review* (est. 1964) from Sacramento to Folsom. Many of these smaller California presses are distributed by Serendipity Bookshop in Berkeley which, in addition to issuing its own titles, has also assumed the distributorship of certain books that were abandoned by their original (commercial) publishers.

Not all of the new West Coast publishers, however, are primarily literary. Straight Arrow, founded by *Rolling Stone* magazine and headed by a literary-industrial refugee, has

303

THE END OF INTELLIGENT WRITING

specialized in pop publishing—books designed to exploit faddish enthusiasms and personalities—and that orientation informs their few forays into literary publishing, for example, Richard Meltzer's *Gulcbur* (1972) and Ann Charters' *Kerouac* (1973). The most famous of the new Bay Area publishers, the Portola Institute, scored on a self-help book intended for practical usage—*The Whole Earth Catalog* (1969-72). Its other publications, such as the educational periodical *Big Rock Candy Mountain*, continue in this vein. Other new California publishers favor spiritual self-help (Shambala), nature books (Sierra Club), photo books (Scrimshaw), cookbooks (Nitty Gritty), psychological self-help (Real People), and comix. It is books of these kinds, rather than poetry and fiction, that New York publishers hope to find when they "scout" in California.

After Alan Swallow's death, his press acquired new owners who moved it to Chicago. It has since issued several major alternative books such as Raymond Federman's typographical novel, *Double or Nothing* (1971), and Eugene Wildman's *Nuclear Love* (1972), as well as the latter's path-breaking anthologies of *Concrete Poetry* (1968) and *Experiments in Prose* (1969). The poet Paul Carroll persuaded Follett, a Chicago text-juvenile house, to sponsor a literary list called Big Table Books after the magazine he had edited a decade before. It began auspiciously with his anthology, *The Young American Poets* (1968), and subsequently issued, among other titles, two volumes of Bill Knott's extraordinary poetry and prose; but a dispute with Follett's senior management led to Carroll's bitter departure and the disintegration of the list. Another Follett executive, J. Philip O'Hara, recently started an imprint under his own name, while a fourth Chicago firm, Traumwald Press, was founded to publish only one author, Dorothy Langley; but it is odd that America's third largest city, with all of its cultural resources, should have so few literary publishers.

As New York has its small presses, so does U.S. publishing's second city, Boston; and among the more prominent are Gerard Dombrowski's Abyss in neighboring Somerville which did Bern Porter's *The Wastemaker* (1972) and Hugh Fox's pioneering *Charles Bukowski: A Critical and Bibliographical Study* (1970); James Randall's Pym-Randall in Cambridge whose most auspicious effort has been CPGraham's book of related poems, *ime* (1969); Joseph Wilmott's Barn Dream, also in Cambridge; and

304

Ottone Riccio's Hellric Press in suburban Belmont. Milwaukee, of all places, has produced a spate of alternative publishers, including James Sorcic's Gunrunner, Karl Young's Ziggurat/ Membrane, David Burge's Harpoon Press, Morgan Gibson's Morgan Press, Tom Montag's Monday Morning, Martin J. Rosenblum's Albatross, among others. Not only does the most persistent small-press reviewer, Rich Mangelsdorff (b. 1943), live there, but Montag and Burge have combined to publish *Margins* (est. 1972), a monthly review of alternative publications. A Milwaukee refugee living in New York, the Reverend Frederic A. Brussat (b. 1942), started *Cultural Information Service* (est. 1970) which, though supported by the Lutheran Church of America, is responsive to the intelligence of the counter-culture.

Perhaps the oldest major rural literary press is Jonathan Williams' Jargon Society which follows its founder-poet in commuting between North Carolina and Lancashire, England. Its distinctions include the first edition of Buckminster Fuller's long-unpublished *Untitled Epic Poem on the History of Industrialization* (1962) and a pioneering collection of Russell Edson's much-admired fables, *What a Man Can See* (1969). Sumac Press, which emerged from a defunct northern Michigan magazine, has published a series of fine poetry books that includes Michael Heller's especially impressive *Accidental Center* (1972), and Ithaca House has put out a conceptually comparable series of handsome paperbacks of previously uncollected poets. In Ann Arbor, Carl R. and Ellendea Proffer's Ardis Publishers has produced impressive books of Russian literature and criticism in both the original language and English translation, in addition to an awesomely hefty periodical, *Russian Literature Tri-Quarterly* (est. 1971).

Among the other notable U.S. small presses are Stone Marrow, also in Ithaca; Times Change in Washington, New Jersey, which has an ecumenically radical outlook; Artists' Workshop in Detroit which was run by John Sinclair before his unjust imprisonment; John Gill's Crossing Press in Trumansburg, New York; Gregory Smith's Atom Mind in Syracuse; the Institute of Further Studies in Canton, New York; Robert Bly's The Sixties Press which has concentrated upon translations; Harvey Brown's Frontier Press in West Newbury, Massachusetts; Burning Deck in Providence, R.I. whose key work is Rosmarie Waldrop and

Nelson Howe's *Body Image* (1970); Alan Sondheim's Ppress, also in Providence; Stephen Goode's Whitson in Troy, N.Y. which did Hugh Fox's critical book on *The Living Underground* (1970); Charioteer and Some of Us, both in Washington, D. C.; Ernest and Agnes Tedlock's San Marcos Press in Cerrillos, New Mexico; Albert Drake's Stone Press, in Oskemos, Michigan; Jonathan Greene's Gnonom in Lexington, Kentucky; the Ashland Poetry Press in Ashland, Ohio; Richard McConnell's Atlantis and Andrew Wylie's Telegraph Books, both in Philadelphia; Georgakas' Smyrna Press in Glen Gardner, N.J.; Zeitgeist in Saugatuck, Michigan; Jerry Patz's Despa Press in Northampton, Massachusetts; John Jacob's Two Bags Press at various midwest addresses; and Eric Grienke's exceptionally prolific Pilot Press in Grand Rapids, Michigan. Among the foreign publishers issuing American works, mostly avant-garde, are Beau Geste Press in Devon, England, which is run by graduate students in American studies; various European art galleries which have a book-publishing tradition scarcely imitated in America; and Centro de arte y communicación in Buenos Aires.

Also in the cultural hinterlands are university presses which, recognizing both the opportunity and the need, have published poetry and sometimes fiction. Wesleyan University Press has been the pioneer here, building up one of America's most substantial poetry programs in less than fifteen years; and this success has perhaps persuaded the book editors at the universities of Massachusetts and Pittsburgh to field more modest poetry lines. The University of Illinois Press has issued new fiction as well as poetry, including Paul Friedman's first-rate collection of stories, *And If Defeated Allege Fraud* (1971). The University of California scored a commercial coup not only by reviving all of Kenneth Burke's books into a uniform paperback series, but also by publishing the initial edition of Carlos Castaneda's *The Teachings of Don Juan* (1968) which its author, then a graduate student, reportedly felt would be too esoteric for a commercial house and too unscholarly for a standard university press.

Since university presses have tax-exempt status, they are a public trust whose cultural responsiblities ought to include the decentralization of book publishing and, thus, the issuance of regional, if not local, writers whose works are ignored by the metropolitan firms. For one thing, regional publishing—books

306

written by *and* for members of a non-cosmopolitan community—remains one of the biggest gaps in the spectrum of literary-intellectual communication. Indeed, since the network of American universities rather than New York or Boston is paradoxically the closest semblance of "an intellectual center" that this country has, book publishing ought to emulate American cultural reality rather than the reverse. Nonetheless, as Charles Newman has observed:

> The university press, as a countervailing institution, has failed utterly to provide a genuine alternative press or distribution system. It has favored exegesis over art, and generally ignored the culture of its time. It has not created a single innovation in production or distribution technology, despite massive subsidy and proximity to all the research facilities necessary. It has been timid editorially, conservative politically and esthetically. It has failed to serve even the day-to-day educational needs of its own community (except to certify certain academic hiring and promotion policies) and ignored any audience beyond its narrowest constituency. It has passed its costs, in the form of outrageous cover prices, on to its basic consumer, the library, which in turn has passed them on to the government. And when the economic crunch comes,...the first things to go are the poetry series, the literary reviews, the search for the unexpected imagination, all these "luxuries" whose constituency is never represented on policy-making boards.

IV

> I've declined partnerships, mergers, and incorporations, as I want freedom and flexibility of action; want to devote the press to poetry. . . . Income from the press goes into publishing new books in an attractive and inexpensive format. I pay royalties to other poets, but royalties on my own books go back into the press. —Dudley Randall, "The Poets of Broadside Press: A Personal Chronicle" (1970).

Many alternative publishers, like little magazines, gather the work of minorities that have found the larger houses unresponsive to their work. In this sense, the avant-garde constitute one literary minority; the young, as noted before, comprise another neglected class. Black writers, a third, have founded several literary presses, including Joseph Okpaku's Third Press in New York; the Third World Press in Chicago which issued the especially perspicacious essays of the scholar-critic George L. Kent, *Blackness and the Adventure of Western Culture* (1972); Alfred E. Prettyman's Emerson Hall in New York; Jihad Productions which Imamu Amiri Baraka (né LeRoi Jones) founded in Newark, N.J.; and Yardbird Publishing Co. which opened with *The Yardbird Reader* (1972), an exceptionally fine anthology compiled by Ishmael Reed. Perhaps the best-known of the black literary publishers has been Dudley Randall's Broadside Press in Detroit which has put out Gwendolyn Brooks' most recent large collection, as well as pamphlets by Don L. Lee, Etheridge Knight, and Sonia Sanchez. Enterprising in other dimensions as well, Broadside has issued both poster poems (at fifty cents apiece) and a series of poets' tapes, along with distributing the booklets of American black poets that Paul Breman publishes in England. A sometime librarian and factory worker, Randall was a literary late bloomer, starting Broadside at the age of fifty in 1964, and he continues to run it out of his own house. Johnson Publishing Co., with its base in *Ebony* and related magazines, has published more popular books which are, like its magazines, destined for a large black audience; but in its avoidance of literary publishing, Johnson's book division, again like its magazines, imitates the white literary-industrial complex.

Chicano writers have founded their own publishing houses such as Quinto Sol in Berkeley which did Nick C. Vaca's particularly literate book of fiction, *El Espejo* (1969), and Mictla and Barrio, both of which are in El Paso, Texas. Activist women have founded several companies: The Feminist Press at S.U.N.Y.—Old Westbury, Long Island; Know, Inc., in Pittsburgh; Shameless Hussy, run by a woman known only as Alta in San Lorenzo, California; and Adele Aldridge's Magic Circle in Riverside, Connecticut. The success of the Jewish-American movement suggests that a once-excluded group can be only as strong as its literary organizations.

Canadians constitute another discriminated minority in the

North American literary scene because their writings have always suffered neglect. Since nearly all major Toronto publishers are subsidiaries of American firms, they operate largely as extensions of the U.S. literary-industrial complex, importing books from south of the border rather than initiating their own. As J. Michael Yates observed:

> It is virtually impossible to find a Canadian paperback on a Canadian newsstand [because] newsstand distribution in Canada is exclusively American-owned and controlled. The only way a Canadian book can discover itself on a Canadian newsstand is via New York, where it would have to come out as a newsprint paperback from one of the big paperback houses.

Even in commissioning Canadians to do books for themselves, the editorial-industrial subsidiaries betray their immediate culture. David Godfrey and James Lorimer noted that,

> The main impact of foreign ownership upon a Canadian subsidiary seems to be that all the Canadian employees become fixated, nervously guessing at what it is that head office would like to see them doing, and then nervously trying to do it. Their main reference point becomes the big-time U.S. head-office people. . . . Occasionally, of course, the control with ownership is not so gently exercised.

For several reasons, then, those Canadian writers who did not expatriate to the south or to England have long been founding their own firms; and that probably explains why Canada has more small presses per capita than the United States. According to Wynne Francis, the earliest notable Canadian small press was First Statement, established in the forties by John Sutherland in Montreal; and its successor there in the fifties was Louis Dudek's Contact Press which was far more prolific and ambitious, surviving well into the sixties. The Fiddlehead Press, also established in the fifties in New Brunswick, set a precedent for subsequent regional publishing; it remains a prolific publisher of English-speaking poets residing in the Maritime provinces. The consequential Canadian small presses of the early sixties included John Robert Colombo's Hawkshead, James Reaney's Alphabet, Nelson Ball's Weed/Flower (which continues to publish Americans as well), Seymour Mayne and Patrick Lane's Very Stone House in Vancouver, William McConnell's Klanak, also in Vancouver, Ganglia and Gronk in Toronto, and Upbank in Quebec. "Most of the books privately printed or published by the little or private press," Francis testifies, "are not reviewed in [Canadian] newspapers and magazines." And that, of course, is scandalous.

Nonetheless, younger Canadians, recognizing that necessity is more inspiring than practicality, have recently established several important book-publishing ventures, all of which are open to young writers, some of which are hospitable to experimental works as well, most of which also belong to the recently founded Independent Publishers Association. The most striking books have come from The Coach House Press, now run by a cooperative (which had assumed Stan Bevington's Coach House print shop). Known as a "printer's press," Coach House publishes books in an incomparable variety of formats, in sum suggesting that each text was individually designed rather than fit into a pre-determined mold. Back in 1967, it broke new terrain with bpNichol's *bp*, whose three parts are a forty-eight page booklet with a long poem, a phonograph record of Nichol declaiming two extended sound poems, and fifteen "visual concrete poems and objects." Coach House has since done Bill Hutton's *A History of America* (1968) which Leslie A. Fiedler singled out as his favorite work by a young American; M. Vaughn-James's book-length surreal fiction, *The Projector* (1971); and Nichol's *Two Novels* (1969). It also prints *Image Nation*, an especially elegant photographic periodical.

The House of Anansi in Toronto was set up by David Godfrey and Dennis Lee, respectively a novelist and poet, and its earliest titles included their own books. It has since issued several anthologies of new writing each selected by a different editor (a wise policy); a series of inexpensively produced first novels; fine book-length poems by George Jonas and Margaret Atwood; the first large collection of Bill Bissett's experimental poetry; critical books on Canadian writing by both Atwood and Northrop Frye; and a long, awesomely complex first novel by Chris Scott, *Bartleby* (1971), that I regard as one of the very

310

best fictions of recent years. Also in Toronto are The New Press, which published Vaughn-James's earlier visual fiction, *Elephant* (1970); Peter Martin Associates; Griffin House, which did an especially brilliant record of Canadian sound poetry, the Four Horsemen's *Canadada* (1972); James Lewis & Samuel, which issued *Read Canadian* (1972), a polemical bibliographical guide; Neewin, which publishes "on Indians by Indians"; and the Playwrights Co-op, founded early in 1972, whose cheaply printed scripts cope with the fact that shockingly few new Canadian plays have previously been available in print. David Godfrey, having sold his share of the House of Anansi, recently founded Press Porcépic in rural Erin, Ontario; and Oberon Press, established in Ottawa, filled a need by issuing bpNichol's *The Concrete Chief* (1970), an intelligent anthology of Canadian experimental poetry.

Delta Canada, founded in Montreal in 1965 also by Louis Dudek, has since moved to La Salle, Quebec, where Glen Siebrasse currently directs it; and the best books of Ladysmith Press, also in Quebec, are those of its proprietor, Sean Haldane. Disposable Paper Press, also in LaSalle, Quebec, recently founded a mimeographed periodical devoted to *Little Magazines/Small Presses* (est. 1973). M.G. Hurtig Ltd., an Edmonton bookseller, did Al Purdy's *The New Romans* (1968), an influential anthology of anti-U.S. diatribes (which, it seems, Toronto publishers avoided like the plague); Talonbooks in Vancouver is a cooperative society specializing in experimental Canadian west coast authors. Sono Nis, founded by an American expatriate who has since become a Canadian citizen, J. Michael Yates (b. 1938), grew out of the writing programs at the University of British Columbia. Initially favoring local writers, it has published anthologies of British Columbian writing, along with several of Yates's own works, including his best fiction, *Man in the Glass Octopus* (1968), and books of poetry and fiction by several other recent immigrants to Canada. The most striking of its recent anthologies has been *VOLVOX: Poetry from the Unofficial Languages of Canada* (1972), which is to say languages other than French and English. (Similar collections of literature in America's "unofficial languages" could also be compiled, but U.S. publishing has so far neglected this opportunity.) Recently retiring from academia, Yates moved his press to the Queen Charlotte Islands off the coast of northwestern

311

Canada. It is unfortunate that neither Sono Nis books nor those by other new Canadian publishers are ever reviewed south of the border because most of these authors, like those in the States, write for *all* of North America.

V

> Poverty is a lack of power to command events. ...Any serious attack on poverty, then, is an attack on the *discrepancies* among men in their power to command events, and, principally, one another. —John R. Seeley, "Progress from Poverty?" (1966).

Another kind of book publishing necessary now is an authors' collaborative where risks and costs are spread among the participants who then constitute its board of directors. Though much discussed, usually with reference to the success of the Magnum group in photography or certain European cooperatives, this has never been tried in any substantial way in America. One explanation is that U.S. writers, unlike European, are unaccustomed to collaborating with each other, partially because each regards himself as being in continual competition with *all* of his peers. A more modest analogy in this vein is the anthology that makes a book out of the best work done by artist-writers of similar commitments, or with comparable problems, or by a circle of friends, or by members of a long-term class in creative writing.

Particularly to cope with the pervasive neglect of experimental writing, I cofounded (along with the writer Henry James Korn, later joined by the designer Michael Metz) an annual *Assembling*, as we call it, which we designed as an open format for "otherwise unpublishable" creative work. We realized that since the principle of editorial authority per se has been the primary obstacle of expressive freedom, our first radically purposeful move was the elimination of our own discriminatory prerogatives. Where other editors seem to have trouble relinquishing authority, we found it easy; instead of soliciting manuscripts for editorial decision, we have asked writers and artists known to be doing unusual or otherwise unpublishable work to contribute 1000 copies, 8½" by 11", of no more than four different pages of whatever they wanted to include. In this instance, "publication" consists of binding all the submitted sheets into a thousand finished books.

Since innovative writers in particular will, under current circumstance, need to learn publishing from the beginning, it seemed a good idea to ask each *Assembling* contributor to be responsible for the printing of his own work—to become his own self-publisher, so to speak. This has been easier than it seems, for not only do academics have access to xerox machines, but certain offset and Itek processes can commercially print one side of a thousand sheets for less than ten dollars and both sides for less than fifteen. In return for their contributions, *Assembling* agrees to give three copies to each collaborator (forty-two in the first issue, ninety in the third), and we sell the rest to reimburse our expenses. Simply by its compositional process, *Assembling* realized a commitment to unhindered communication, creative possibility, and artistic seriousness similar to that instilled by other comparably composed volumes, such as Dana Atchley's *Notebooks,* done in 1970 and 1971 in Vancouver, and Jerry Bowles' one-shot *Art Work, No Commercial Value* (1972), both of which, unlike *Assembling,* tend to print more graphics than literature. Not only do such easily imitated enterprises implicitly render editorial authority obsolete, but the whole book represents what artists and writers can realize if granted genuine expressive freedom.

The existence of so many new publishers is just one reason why we need new reviewing media; but not until the late sixties did they appear. *The Book Review,* founded by Jay Bail in San Francisco, started auspiciously, expanding steadily for two years, refusing advertisements, ignoring the hyped-up trash, reviewing small-press publications, attacking the cultural establishments. However, by the following year, both it and its editor disappeared as mysteriously as they arrived, and the review did not reemerge for another year, a ghost of its former self. *University Review,* founded in New York by Steve Roday, was designed to be a monthly supplement inserted free in university newspapers. However, since the magazine drew its income not from sales but from publishers' advertisements, its editors felt obliged to riddle its issues with hyper-fashionable names in order to impress not potential readers but literary-industrial advertising managers; unfortunately, the superstars' slick words

313

provided a peculiar contrast to the predominantly undergraduate reviewers. With editorial offices in the shadow of Columbia University, *University Review* was also responsive to the winds of classroom fashion, as well as pressures from an older generation, represented more immediately by local professors. In spite of all this Podhoretzian ambition, the review declined until 1972 when it disappeared for a six-month vacation. Reemerging the following fall as a tabloid that sold on newsstands, *UR,* as it was now called, discovered Radical Chic several years too late, at the price of ignoring books several years too soon.

University Review, like *The Book Review,* is a good idea that was unfortunately mismanaged. The losers are not only their editors, but those readers likely to be interested in alternative books. Until better critical media emerge, the best way to learn about small press books is through the annotated catalogs regularly issued by their distributors—the Book People and Serendipity, both of which operate out of Berkeley, and the Book Organization in Millerton, New York.

There will surely be more alternative publishers in North America as more and more literary people realize the exigencies of necessity. This survey scarcely mentions all the new imprints that currently exist. Some are omitted because of my ignorance; others because their output strikes me as subliterate or thoroughly coterie—small editions issued less out of any pressure of quality or esthetic principle than strong fellow-feeling. One outlet of this sort, the Tyndall Creek Press of Allston, Massachusetts, told the Fulton-May *Directory* that, "Our editions to date have been poems by members of our own editorial circle." Coterie presses rarely have more impact than coterie magazines, unless they publish a writer whose work transcends their mass; but rare in practice is the coterie press that has any impact at all.

Substantial books—those that present good writing; those that would change a reader's intelligence—are more commendable than those that do nothing either for their publisher or their readers. It was the English poet-designer Eric Gill who distinguished private presses, those that print what their editors choose, from public presses, which by definition publish what their audiences seem to demand. However, between these two criteria stands a third measure—what the literary situation requires. In my judgment, even a publisher as superficially narrow as Something Else becomes, by virtue of what it does, a sharper cutting edge for the future of intelligent writing. One trouble common to many other new publishers is that the kind of anti-establishment courage which must have informed their initial purposes does not govern their current editorial decision-making which tends to be safe and circumscribed.

All this activity is good and necessary; and if only because the habits and economics of this literary-industrial "closed enterprise system" are so cruelly contrary to their heroic efforts, all new publishers deserve a hero's support from everyone concerned with the future of writing and reading. Serious young authors would naturally prefer a similarly new publisher sharing the risk and whatever profits with a true extension (and equal) of themselves; and more than one I know gladly took no advance for a new book, try as they otherwise might to fleece a conglomerate. Many poets published by large houses also allow small-press editions of their new work, in part because certain care and freedoms are available in smaller editions, but also because their presence on a new firm's list bestows a sense of solidity. As every small publisher is offered more good books than he can afford to do, the success of his current production brings a further loosening of the bulging dam, and perhaps enough favorable precedent to inspire yet another imprint. The survival of more avant-garde publishers would insure that the public fate of writers working in experimental ways will not depend upon one firm (or only one man). In this example, as in others, small publishers bring diversity, regionalism, and decentralization to the channels of literary communication; and these principles demand, in turn, a succession of modest, though interlocking initiatives. Now is the time, let it be commonly understood, for alternative publishing.

Even though small presses have carved a distinguished tradition, their achievements are scandalously omitted from the standard, institution-minded (rather than book-minded) histories of American publishing whose authors overlook as well the reasons why small presses might ever exist. (Indeed, it seems odd that several histories of little magazines have appeared while the small presses are still disregarded.) The first volumes of most of this country's major poets were issued by small firms which continue to bring out more consequential poetry (and experimental writing) than all the larger firms combined; and unless the literary-industrial complex changes its present policies on fiction publishing, the impetus on this genre will probably also shift to smaller firms. Now is the time, to repeat, for alternative book-making.

Not only do the achievements of alternative publishers deserve more scholarly-critical recognition, but their publications must be bought and read. Unless certain cultural enterprises get sustained support, they simply cannot survive; and the changes implied by their existence surely will not happen. When one of them dies, we cannot forget, some of the circumstances prerequisite not only for the articulation of minority consciousness, but also for the survival of literature, pass away too.

15

The Nature
and Fortune
of Newcomers

I

Vasari, who had seen a great deal of misery among his
friends, both "freelance" and court painters, was
appalled by the descrepancy between "the extraordinary rewards" bestowed on the "most famous masters" and the plight of "those rare intellects who not
only without reward, but in miserable poverty, bring
forth their works." He firmly believed that, "If there
were remuneration in this our age, they would without doubt, produce greater and better works than the
ancients; but since they have to face famine rather
than fame, these hapless artists remain ignored and
unrecognized to the shame and disgrace of those who
could raise them from obscurity and yet do not lift a
finger." —Rudolf and Margot Wittkower, *Born Under
Saturn: The Character and Conduct of Artists* (1969).

Perhaps there is no such thing as an *avant-garde*, only
a few uncorrupted sensibilities who cling together in
times of rampant militarism or commercialism to
challenge their elders. —Cyril Connolly, *Previous Convictions* (1963).

No large group of North American writers today is as neglected as the young who are less organized and collectively less
powerful, as well as receiving proportionately less favor from
established publishers and reviewers, than literary blacks, or
literary Jews, Catholics, or women, and even literary WASPs.
At a time when cultural conflicts are more generational than
anything else, writers under thirty-five have suffered as well
from the discomforting confusion of hearing on one hand that
"no one young seems to write much nowadays" and, on the
other, that the publishing world is eager to have and hear them.
However, both these common assertions are untrue. First of all,

there are literally hundreds of practicing young writers in North America, scores of whom are discernibly promising, dozens of whom have already produced excellent work. However, suppressed by their professional elders, drowned out by their more poppish contemporaries, victimized by the increasing commercialization of literary publishing, disillusioned by recurring disappointments, and handicapped by their own ineffectuality as literary citizens, they are nearly all unknown, not only to each other but also to the larger public of equally young and literate readers.

Most find it hard to get their manuscripts published, especially if these run longer than magazine pieces; and those books by young writers that do get into print usually go unreviewed and, in too many cases, lamentably unread. That young writers should have trouble getting published or reviewed is no surprise, as individual rejections are to be expected, even for the best of any emerging generation. However, what is unprecedented and quite ominous is the almost total non-acceptance of both an emerging body of writing and a class of writers at a time when the conflicts of American intellectual society are divided along lines more generational than anything else. In this case, the resistances of the establishments are decimating their most likely heirs who are in turn becoming justifiably less inclined to honor even the genuine achievements of their predecessors. Neglects on one hand complement oppositions on the other, producing a generational conflict without precedent in modern American literary history; and that in turn indicates what is the most pressing literary-political issue of our time.

Although disorganized and distraught, young writers manage to exist, study, write, and occasionally publish, their works getting some circulation; and though their impact is far smaller than either the quantity or the quality of their numbers, it is clear that literate and imaginative young people have not all become journalists and film-makers, as the old-boy exclusionists would sometimes have it, but novelists, poets, playwrights, and critics, too. In sensibility, they differ from those who came of age in the middle fifties and who suffered the repressive atmosphere associated with the epithets "McCarthyism" and "conformity" (already an archaic word). As the most impressionable beneficiaries of the post-Sputnik educational renaissance and then the Kennedy radiance, young writers assumed attitudes of honest idealism and innocent, pre-drug optimism, not only about their personal talents but also about their professional fortunes. Some of them were among the first to exploit and pursue behavioral eccentricities that now seem quite typical—long hair, beads, "dropping out."

Even now, the best of these new writers seem disinclined to emulate the self-promotional and organizational vulgarities of certain predecessors, perhaps because they sense their talents are growing rather than shriveling; and most seem far more interested in producing good work than in generating literary-political prosperity. As writers in America have rarely formed cliques after the age of thirty, it is my suspicion that pluralism and fluidity might remain. "Community of date and space are," notes José Ortega y Gasset in *Man and Crisis* "the preliminary attributes of a generation. Together they signify the sharing of an essential destiny." By such criteria can young Canadian writers be discussed along with those in the States, as both inhabit a common cultural space.

Young writers also expected that, were their writing superior enough, it would be recognized, but experience has shown this idea to be illusory. Instead, those literary activities reflecting independence, genuine originality, or uninstructed achievement have encountered especially strong and persistent opposition. A few succumbed, alas, becoming "fair-haired boys" whose heads were patronizingly patted for a while (and pockets were lined in the middle sixties with a protégé-channeled Rockefeller fellowship). However, as Joanna Russ noted of a comparable situation, "Those who don't want to be that radical are finding themselves outstripped or ignored; they become (sadly) the darlings of an Establishment which likes them for all the wrong reasons." For much the same reason that the American military today has trouble keeping its brighter officers, literary establishments have discovered that "our young people" would sooner avoid such self-deprecating trips in order to cultivate openness and integrity, if not generosity and excellence. However, recurring misfortunes made them, in Jack Newfield's phrase, "the first generation that learned from experience, in our innocent twenties, that things were not really getting better, that we shall *not* overcome."

Nearly all young writers are still "underground," whether they want to be or not, because they lack free access to the aboveground media; and though most of them were temperamentally (if not economically) unprepared for this disillusioning reality, the fact that so many should remain independent, uncynical, and productive is amazing as well as gratifying. Lack of literary talent or achievement has never been their problem, though the obstacles of literary politics and literary business are and will continue to be. (It is also my suspicion that my own contemporaries, those born around 1940, may differ in this respect from even younger writers, those born after 1945 who matured into LBJ and the Vietnam War and, thus, into an articulate tradition of establishment-opposition; so that not only do they seem instinctively more militant, if not less liberal, but they also seem more inclined than we have been to organize their own institutions. A few decades ago, Ortega y Gasset estimated that fifteen years separate the generations; given the pace of recent historical change, that figure should now be smaller.)

II

> The republic of letters is in some ways desperately snobbish, but nobody is excluded from it because of his family background; in that respect, it is a true democracy. —Malcolm Cowley, *The Literary Situation* (1954).

Writers of these new generations have nearly all attended college which probably remains the most universal element in their otherwise diverse individual experiences. Most of them suffered rather than learned through courses in "creative writing," which are intended not to teach fundamental technique or even stretch the imagination but to inculcate a particular style and produce promising protégés. Many of the male writers also went to some sort of graduate school, which provided the most convenient military deferment during the sixties, although post-graduate education was generally an even less enlightening, if not more dispiriting experience. Graduate work in "creative writing" was especially restrictive and deleterious; for those who were terrifyingly adept at learning their lessons have since nearly all disappeared, along with all but a few of those chosen by teachers (rather than fellow students) to be in anthologies of university writing.

Since they come from everywhere in America and from nearly every kind of sociological background, there appears to be no special form or "formula" for producing young writers. Not only do the so-called "good schools" have no monopoly over the nurturing of literary talent, but a college education itself is scarcely a prerequisite for professional writing. Several notable new writers either did not matriculate or had undergraduate experiences too transient to note. The general truth is that most became writers in spite of (rather than because of) their education (or lack of it), for it is nothing less than marvelous that so many isolated young Americans get into their individual heads the idea of writing seriously. In general, they are literate though unacademic; their respect for books and book-writers notwithstanding, most of them preserve a marginal relationship or skeptical attitude toward academic rigmarole. For instance, although many young writers now teach in universities, less than a dozen of note had sufficient academic piety to finish their doctorates (and these were often done under untypically favorable circumstances). In brief, American writers, unlike European, probably did not descend from literary families, or learn much in the classroom, or go to school with other budding writers, or subject themselves (as, say, most musicians or dancers do) to a pedagogical process carefully designed to produce a mature talent. In America, rather than depend upon fortuitous background or training, the individual primarily makes himself the writer.

Contrary to much publicized opinion, young Americans are able to become more literate than their predecessors, not only in books but also in the other arts and the new media; and many of them, especially the incipient writers, have capitalized on the available opportunity. Some of this progress can be traced to the increasing sophistication and liberalism of educated parents, especially regarding the developing cultural habits of their children; and in spite of the low quality of typical American television programming, the tube nonetheless serves to accelerate the informational and emotional development of nearly all American youngsters. "Post-literate" is not by any interpretation synonymous with illiterate; for people raised in post-literacy are often as familiar with print as other media. The fact of earlier physical maturity has been empirically documented, but it is less well-known that reforms in education, along with general liberalization and the decline of censorship, have introduced adult cultural materials with all their embodied perceptions at a far younger age.

It also appears that the emerging generations have consumed progressively more print, reading not only more "juveniles" whose sales doubled (in number of copies) during the fifties, but also certain kinds of "mature" writing that were unavailable to their predecessors at a similar age. (All of us have met, if not sometimes envied, a seventeen-year-old who knew awesomely more about both literature and life than we knew at twenty, even though we then thought ourselves precocious!) Perhaps the strongest evidence of this increasing cultural awareness is the fact that high-school students have recently become a coherent book-buying public; and the less-than-best quality of certain enthusiasms notwithstanding (e.g., Hermann Hesse and also Jerry Rubin, whose *Do It!* sold over 200,000 copies in paperback, though less than 5,000 in hardback), this still represents a cultural advance. Indeed, the increasing radicalization of the young depends largely upon their passion for print, rather than upon electronic media that are, by custom, more easily censored; and it is indicative that even among teenagers this protest frequently takes such print-age forms as an "underground" newspaper!

The reading habit is continued in college where, thanks to both affluence and the paperback revolution, many young people amass substantial personal libraries. The general level of university education is also improving, especially in "modern" subjects; so that many university teachers have observed, along with Simon O'Toole, that "every college program I have taught in has been better than the one before it." Whether a smaller or larger percentage of the young are more avid book buyers than their predecessors seems statistically unclear, but there is no doubt that students comprise the strongest reading public and that more young people buy more books and better books (and perhaps read them better, too) than ever before in history. Quality paperbacks by their mere existence, as the publisher William Jovanovich observes, "have advanced education to a degree that is still incalculable." (Who else buys all those high-class titles? All those classics in the bookstores? Good poetry? Quality fiction?) *The New York Times Book Review* reported in 1970: "Ten years ago, less than 5 per cent of paperback sales

322

were to the school and college market. Last year the figure was 25 per cent. Thus, it appeared that the general public is actually buying fewer paperbacks today than it was in 1959."

Affluence, along with both increased fellowships and unemployment benefits, have given many young people more time to read, especially after they have spurned the hyper-involving temptations of the organizational society. Also, those courses in creative writing are filled with thousands of young people interested in contemporary writing—and they represent thousands more than there were two decades ago—while the population of American scholars and teachers continues to increase, having doubled over each of the last three decades. Young people are predominant in the new poetry audience and the audience for the new science-fiction, as well as in many other identifiable readerships that have emerged in recent years. It seems, however, that their numbers and tastes are rarely considered in publishing's editorial decisions. (Indeed, most decisions based upon the expectation that "the kids will love it" imply a condescending, almost insulting, and fundamentally inaccurate assessment of American young people. In fact, books narrowly aimed in their direction usually fail.) There is no doubt that young people are also more *diversely* erudite, especially in contemporary materials, again thanks in part to educational reforms. Reflecting those increasingly persuasive critiques of both specialization and "irrelevance," many of them are also more polyliterate, polymathic, and perhaps more inclined to act upon their knowledge. Indeed, the classical ideal of the variously educated man, dead in anti-dilettante recent generations, has been revived among the young.

It is especially lamentable, in this respect, that many young people have so easily accepted false characterizations of themselves as anti-intellectual, just as too many blacks and orientals have been conned into accepting negative, limiting stereotypes of themselves. Those supposedly self-conscious writers in each minority who reiterate or, even worse, embody such images, while often eliciting praise from the appropriate authorities, nonetheless evoke imaginary symptoms of their group's deficiencies. However, rewarding the young for their juvenility is also a way of segregating them out of adult society. The sociologist Herbert J. Gans has noted "how a stereotype which is only partially true becomes the basis of people's behavior and

323

is thus made all too true as a self-fulfilling prophecy." The worst sinners on this count have been young writers who should know better—mostly self-appointed "experts" on "youth culture"—as they have been caught in the condescending cliché of finding semblances of wisdom in stupidities they would not emulate .themselves. What they regarded as "truths" about the young were really just misunderstood deceptions and transient fashions; what remained untouched were the real problems.

All this educational progress explains why so many young people displayed precocious literary talent and why some of them are approaching stylistic maturity at an earlier age than their predecessors did. Not only can hundreds of them handle competently the problems of Yeatsian meter or post-Poundian structure in poetry, ironic narrators or multiple points of view in fiction, but others realize that imitating established formulas, though sometimes commercially or academically useful, is artistically a bust. Indeed, some writers still in their early and middle twenties have written stylistically inventive fiction, or extremely experimental poetry, or discriminating and personalized criticism. Literary talent in America has often been precocious, as many of our greatest novels were written by men around thirty—*Moby Dick, The Great Gatsby, The Sound and the Fury,* and *The Sot-Weed Factor*—while a few masterpieces were produced by writers even younger—*The Sun Also Rises* and *Lie Down in Darkness;* but never before have so *many* young writers seemed so professionally mature.

For that reason alone, it is simply false to say, as James Dickey did in his introduction to Paul Carroll's anthology of *The Young American Poets* (1968), that, "Most of these poets do not seem to be as informed or well-read as some of the best poets who immediately preceded them. Not one of them [the young] has the sheer amount of information that Randall Jarrell had when he began writing." One wonders whether Dickey has done sufficient research either in printed sources or personal interviews to support such a judgment; his assertion will not hold against Jonathan Cott, Vito Acconci, or (immodestly) myself—to cite poets included in Carroll's anthology; or Alan Sondheim, Dick Higgins, and Bruce Andrews—to name three original and spectacularly erudite young poets whom Carroll missed. (Such novelists as Thomas Pynchon and Ishmael Reed, for two, also refute Dickey's caveat, while few American

324

book reviewers are as exceptionally literate as John Leonard.) It is not surprising that older intellectuals should regard the young as non- or anti-intellectual, typically missing or ignoring signs of their genuine intelligence and literacy; but it is erroneous not to regard the literate poets as more representative of a generation's intellectual quality than the sub-literate or illiterate.

It should also be noted, partially in Dickey's defense, that the criteria for measuring literacy change with time so that the body of information and ideas that seemed "literate" in the forties may, because of the sheer increase of knowledge, seem only semi-literate now. Moreover, unless older writers' minds are open enough to recognize that what a young poet learns today may thus be quite different from what his predecessors know, they may miss evidences of his learning especially if it reflects new areas of knowledge. Very rare is the literary pro over forty who can recognize such recent-vintage ideas as feedback, intermedia, information theory, and related cybernetic concepts. (This deficiency partly explains why younger writers often find it frustrating, if not impossible, to conduct an intelligent dialogue with older writers, the most dogmatic and semi-literate of whom are simply unable to transcend their closed and hardened ways of thought and learning.) Not only do the best educated young minds seem much better educated than older intellectuals were at comparable ages, but also what a well-informed young writer now knows is likely to be more relevant not just to contemporary understanding but to the problems of artistic creation today.

III

By the term "historical pseudomorphosis" I propose to designate those cases in which an older alien Culture lies so massively over the land that a young Culture, born in this land, cannot get its breath and fails not only to achieve pure and specific expressive forms, but even to develop fully its own self-consciousness. All that wells up from the depths of the young soul is cast in the old molds, young feelings stiffen in senile works, and instead of rearing itself up in its own creative power, it can only hate the distant power with a hate that grows to be monstrous. — Oswald Spengler, *The Decline of the West* (1922).

The professional fortunes of the younger generation's intelligence have been, needless to say, more problematic; for nothing seems to antagonize older writers and editors more than the precocious maturity of the literate young. Though amazed, they put the newcomers down, biological envy complementing intellectual jealousy in predominantly middle-aged milieus. No young writer has had as facile a career with reigning establishments as John Updike (b. 1932), Philip Roth (b. 1933), Susan Sontag (b. 1933), or Willie Morris (b. 1934)—that fact alone indicating a lowered ceiling of conventional possibility. Indicatively, although young American writers are far more numerous than Englishmen of comparable age, many of the latter are now better known (and more optimistic about their professional fortunes); proportionately, the same is true of young Canadian writers. All this may partially explain why young American writers find literary people over sixty more sympathetic than those in their forties and fifties who capitalized on post-World War II prosperity and are now in the institutional saddle. It may also account for why some of them identify with older writers who are undeservedly neglected or forgotten—in short, why they are not likely to trust writers over forty and still under sixty-five.

The most successful young writers have probably been Thomas Pynchon, Renata Adler, and Joyce Carol Oates, the first born in 1937, the other two in 1938; and behind every exception to the rule of neglect is an idiosyncratic explanation along with a modicum of typicality. Pynchon, raised in suburban Long Island and educated at Cornell (with two years out for the Navy), started to publish soon after his graduation in 1959, placing stories in not only Cornell's *Epoch* but also *Noble Savage* and *Kenyon Review.* Attracting the notice of Candida Donadio, a literary agent who was particularly influential in the early sixties, Pynchon placed his first novel with Lippincott which then took the risky investment of circulating prepublication copies to probable reviewers. As *V.* (1963) was clearly an erudite and serious work about the absurdities of contemporary history (and man's inability to comprehend it), the book received several highly laudatory notices. Its successor, *The Crying of Lot 49* (1966), an apocalyptic novel about Southern California, was fairly well-received, though slighter than its predecessor. Not until 1973 did he publish a third, *Gravity's*

Rainbow. In spite of the fact that he scarcely appears in public or cultivates literary people, Pynchon has been the last young male novelist in America to receive abundant praise from older writers.

Adler, born in Italy and raised by German-speaking refugee parents in Danbury, Connecticut, was a graduate student at Harvard about 1960 where she studied with Edmund Wilson. It was largely through the intervention of S.N. Behrman, whose secretary was a friend of Adler's, that she was invited to become a staff writer on *The New Yorker* in 1962. Except for a few forays into other journals as well as a fourteen-month extended leave as film critic on *The New York Times,* she has had an entirely circumscribed career, writing entirely for *The New Yorker* and respecting that magazine's highly defined conventions and stylistic pieties; and the quality and loyalty of her patronage are both enviable and unparalleled. (The fact that she never needed to submit her work on speculation to disinterested editors separates her from nearly all other young writers.) Personally more hesitant and retiring than her spiky, sophisticated prose suggests, Adler has suffered periods of extended inactivity, producing remarkably little over the years, only a portion of it being especially good. (Even the fourteen essays she collected in *Toward a Radical Middle,* all of which were previously published in *The New Yorker,* are strikingly unequal.) Thanks to the huge circulations of her two employers, her best pieces—those on the New York literary mob, group therapy, new movies, Biafra (as yet uncollected), and the Conference on New Politics—reached a large audience of literate people, giving her some celebrity as well. Although her conservative attitudes ally her with an older generation (as she would concur), her courageous forthrightness and intellectual versatility are more characteristic of her juniors.

Joyce Carol Oates has pursued a far more independent and various career, from obscure working-class beginnings in western New York to Syracuse and Wisconsin universities where she married Raymond Smith, who came to teach at the University of Windsor in Canada, just across the river from Detroit. Of Catholic background, she taught first at the University of Detroit, a parochial institution, before joining him at Windsor. Her stories began to appear in the early sixties in numerous little magazines, her efforts exemplifying the honorable principle of trying everywhere she could and eventually accumulating a legion of minor-league supporters. Some of these artistically conservative pieces, indebted largely to Flannery O'Connor and John Updike (not only for style, but for kinds of moral sensitivity), were regularly selected for both the *O. Henry* and the *Best Short Stories* annuals. The odd break in Oates's career has been the persistent support of Vanguard Press, a publishing house run by older women not otherwise committed to notable young writers or known, since the forties, for especially good books. Since 1962, Vanguard has published one of Oates's works nearly every year, often honoring them with full-page advertisements in the reviewing media, making her its most-publicized active property.

Admirably persistent and prolific, Oates has published innumerable short stories, most (though not all) of which have been collected into her books; several novels; many less distinguished poems, so far gathered into three books; a few plays; and both critical essays and reviews (sometimes under her married name of "J. Oates Smith"). Except for a few highly inventive stories published around 1968, she represents an honest conservatism that could well become as popular with a mass of readers as Updike and Roth who are likewise more concerned with plot and character than structure and style. Oates's novels are becoming better, which is to say more ambitious in scope and complicated in language (though never stunning and rarely distinguished). *Them* (1969) is probably the best; and not only did she win the 1970 National Book Award for it, but her stories are now piously included in nearly every anthology of short fiction. The conventional quality of her work, let me conjecture, makes her reputation vulnerable to the disrepute that usually follows increased popularity. Precedent suggests that her high reputation will not survive the kind of artistic cautiousness more typical of the second-rate unless a literary-political machine (probably feminist) supports it against likely efforts at critical deflation. Beyond that, she has also had the damning misfortune of becoming that genuinely young token exception whom older literary politicians regularly cite as evidence of "our openness to young writers." Or she is characterized as surprisingly "old-fashioned" (by Alfred Kazin), rather than, as she is, a fine example of literary intelligence and creative persistence not untypical of her literary generation. As

328

each of these personal sketches makes clear, even the most successful young writers have been victimized, albeit in different ways, by the unfortunate situation—Oates writing too much and too repetitiously, Adler writing sporadically and rarely venturing outside a safe circle, and Pynchon chronically disappearing from public view.

Other untypically conspicuous young writers include the athletes and pop stars speedily exploited for their transient fame (rather than nurtured as professional authors): Richard Goldstein (b. 1944), perhaps the best-known and most successful of the sometime rock critics and anti-literary young magazinists (whose two books and three-shot periodical have been more typically neglected); Ed Sanders (b. 1939), a good post-Ginsbergian poet and sometime scatological novelist who, until he wrote *The Family* (1971), was more renowned first as an East Village bookstore proprietor and then as the chief lyricist and lead singer of a rock group called the Fugs; Michael Crichton (b. 1944), a sometime medical student whose hacked-out *The Andromeda Strain* (1969) became a surprising bestseller; Tom Clark (b. 1941), who parlayed his position as poetry editor of the *Paris Review* (inherited from his former teacher, Donald Hall, the prime poetry-entrepreneur of an earlier generation) into innumerable publications in other poets' magazines and anthologies, poetry-reading tours, several volumes of largely trivial verse, at least two anthologies, and other contracts; and Rex Reed (b. 1938), a theatrically knowledgeable and slick gossipist, occasionally doubling as a forgettable movie and pop-music critic, who owes his success not to his own generation but to his elders because he likewise expressed, as the critic Robert Christgau perceived, "an almost pathological distaste for his own contemporaries, especially the arty and rebellious ones, and showed an unnatural affection for women older than himself." In the end, however, not even the most conspicuous of the young writers have gained (or been offered) enough celebrity ever to make, say, those symbolic public acts that have imaginative meaning to a larger public.

Nearly all others remain unknown, their professional investments sinking unhindered to distant bottoms. Several young book critics have been willing to write about the literature of our chronological contemporaries; however, not only have the established periodicals shown no interest, but the newcomers have not been assertive enough in insisting upon the right to recognize each other in public print. The several selective anthologies of young (or mostly young) writers have, as noted before, gone scandalously unreviewed—my own first, for instance, getting less than a dozen notices in sum, only one of which appeared in a medium many of us see; my second collection receiving even less attention. Paul Carroll's equally overlooked anthology of *Young American Poets* (1968) remains, incidentally, the only one edited by a writer too old to contribute himself, exemplifying a genuine generosity rare in his over-forty literary generation. The only critical book on young writers, Hugh Fox's *The Living Underground* (1970), went similarly unnoticed. One of the strongest collections of recent short fiction, James Sallis' *A Few Last Words* (1970), published by a conglomerate, received only two reviews in the entire U.S.! The most brilliant of the recent feminist polemics, *The Dialectic of Sex* (1970) by Shulamith Firestone (b. 1944), did not get half as much attention as some of its inferiors. Canadian writers younger than Leonard Cohen (b. 1934), even the best of them, are all but totally unknown south of the border. It is frequently noted that there is no critic today comparable to Edmund Wilson in the twenties when he "discovered" Hemingway, Eliot, and Fitzgerald, in addition to writing *Axel's Castle* (1930); however, not even Wilson, if he were alive today, could survive the current morass.

Critical omissions complement other forms of neglect. Only one of Jerome Charyn's half-dozen books of fiction, some of them quite good and favorably reviewed, have appeared in paperback; none of Nicholas Delbanco's four novels or Heather Ross Miller's three have been given an invitation to mass readership. Only three younger critics have ever published collections of their essays, Renata Adler, John Lahr, and Lucy R. Lippard, the first two drawing upon pieces published in one and only one periodical—just *The New Yorker*, for one of Adler's two books, and just *The New York Times* for the other, and Lahr's just *Evergreen Review*; and these two have also been the only young critics to get principal positions in powerful media. One reason why other good young critics are overlooked is that they tend to be formalists, more attuned to mediumistic qualities than those of content, all in sharp contrast to an older generation; yet few critical books on modernist art are as brilliant as Gene

Youngblood's *Expanded Cinema* (1970), Rosalind E. Krauss's *Terminal Iron Works: The Sculpture of David Smith* (1971), and Bruce F. Kawin's *Telling It Again and Again* (1972). Merely in the course of doing research for this book, I discovered over four dozen young writers whose names were previously unknown to me, even though *all* of them have published not just stories or poems but full-scale books (mostly, to be sure, with smaller presses).

For nearly every individual of great talent there is a scandalous absence of recognition. The playwright-poet-novelist Ronald Tavel has not received half the respectful attention that the author of *Gorilla Queen* (1967) and *Street of Stairs* (1968) deserves, nor has the novelist-editor Eugene Wildman (b. 1938), the novelist-poet Kenneth Gangemi (b. 1937), the playwrights Richard Foreman (b. 1937) and Robert Wilson (b. 1943), the poets Diane Wakoski (b. 1937), Clark Coolidge (b. 1939), and William Knott (b. 1940)—to name several unquestionably first-rank figures. Nor have such nearly first-rank poets as Hugh Seidman, Norman Henry Pritchard II, Margaret Atwood, Louise Glück, bpNichol, Lyn Lifshin, Bill Bissett, all of whom have published stunning retrospective collections. Furthermore, no one seems to have critically noticed the following extraordinary full-length poems: Diane Wakoski's *The George Washington Poems* (1967), Joe Brainard's *I Remember* (1970), Charles Levendosky's *Perimeters* (1970), Margaret Atwood's *Power Politics* (1971). And nowhere have I seen in print much praise for any of these excellent long poems: Allen Planz's concisely rendered fifteen-page, "A Night for Rioting" (1969), Clark Coolidge's remarkable "A D" (1970), Norman Henry Pritchard's "L'Oeil" (1970) and "Via" (1971), David Shapiro's "A Man Holding an Acoustic Panel" (1971). This complaint about critical neglect could be extended almost interminably.

In fiction, few of any age can write as strikingly as Eugene Wildman in this opening paragraph of *Montezuma's Ball* (1970):

Montezuma dribbled the ball. It was with his elbow. He dribbled with his foot and kicked it. You could kick it. Nezahualpilli blocked it. Nezahualpilli bounced it once and hit it with his elbow. You could hit it with the elbow. Tenochcan Montezuma jumped high and stopped it. Head bounce to elbow bounce to head and Montezuma went again for the basket. They were playing on top of a pyramid. There was an altar. There were two hundred and seventy seven steps.

Or as coherently acoherent as this pastiche from Tom Veitch's *The Luis Armed Story* (1969):

In the dimness of the cage, the manager is arranging the tables and chairs, the ashtrays, the siphons of soda water; it is six in the morning. I awoke early, shaved, dressed, draped myself with cameras and equipment, and went on deck to record our entry into the port of Gothenberg. In the beginning was the Word, and the Word was with God; and the Word was God. The Agon, the. In her tight fitting Persian dress, with turban to match, she looked ravishing.

Or as originally as Toby MacLennan in this passage from *1 Walked out of 2 and Forgot It* (1972):

He was bombarded by various memories. An A and an Of, the toe of a shoe, a half of an apple. That night as he sat down for dinner, a stone dropped out of his ear.

Or with the perfect elegance of this opener from Dan McCall's *The Man Says Yes* (1969):

My uncle's PR Man was laying for us in the Dallas Airport. His domed straw hat sat very quietly on top of his big black head, and he had cultivated suggestions of a cool mandarin beard. As we followed him, poppidy-plop, his massive hindquarters boomlayed out from under his double-vented Madras tail like two squarish sofa pillows. Habitually pleasing the dignitaries, double-taking my wife's whiteness without a sound, Homer Brown put our matching bags in the back of a Chevy station wagon, bullet-green under its thick coat of dust. And we moved on out.

Nonetheless, all these books, as well as their authors, have gone scandalously unrecognized. In fact, Veitch's novel, which has appeared in a German translation, parts of which have been anthologized, remains unpublished in his native America! There is no doubt that future scholars will regard this period as one like 1910-20 in which the neglect of important new American writers was more characteristic than their recognition. Many, to be sure, will be belatedly "discovered."

Of very few independent young writers could it be said that premature success has instilled a false sense of professional confidence; instead, neglect nags at their spirits to varying degrees, leaving a good many embittered beyond the turning point of compensatory energy. All pieties about the integrity of unsuccess notwithstanding, recognition is better for the future of art (and the artist) than disfavor. "If success is corrupting," Stephen Spender noted long ago, "failure is narrowing." One widely published, thirtyish writer I know in New York avoids literary gatherings rather than suffer the humiliating experience of discovering again how unknown his name is—not among ignoramuses, after all, but among precisely those people who should read and know his work. Another potentially prolific young writer has become known mostly as "an editor," even though that work demands little of his time and thought, because no one has asked to publish any of his completed books. Elia Katz's slick report on communes, *Armed Love* (1972), can scarcely be compared with his extraordinary short stories; yet the former is available in a much-publicized mass paperback, while the latter are either unpublished or scattered through small-circulation journals. Since persistent adversity, weighed against the rhetoric of opportunity, inevitably produces bitterness which lapses at times into unjustified self-deprecation, negative feelings come to haunt the newcomers' conversations more often, alas, than plans for necessary action. Incredible determination, as noted before, seems, after sheer talent, the quality most common in those who survive; and for now, the greatest frustrations, to put it most moderately, come from not being read.

As it was naive for young writers to expect establishments to be open, so only an equally naive elder could believe that such pervasive resistances would leave the emerging writers amicable. Only an equally innocent or cynical "critic" would expect the writing of the young to mask completely the strains of their predicament. (Only those who are smugly ensconced can afford unalloyed chatter about Art!) The obstinate obstacles that have silenced many of them have also driven a few to excessive abundance—Douglas Blazek, Dick Higgins, David Shapiro, Joyce Carol Oates, Lyn Lifshin—in the effort, usually vain, to do in many pieces what might, in more fortunate circumstances, be more effectively accomplished by more concentrated shots. Three of them, along with others, have also responded to the collective predicament by becoming editors of modest magazines and anthologies that are largely by (and for) their contemporaries.

Nonetheless, young writers have failed each other by not founding enough new literary institutions as the situation required; and many have wasted too much time and energy (if not integrity) on finding the channels of communication rather than creating new ones, and upon soliciting the support (and endorsement) of established writers and editors. Young writers have also hurt each other by not presenting themselves at their very best, as in such patently (and suspiciously) second-rate anthologies of "young" writing as Geof Hewitt's *Quickly Aging Here* (1969), Charles Newman and William Henkin's *Under 30* (1969), Anne Waldman's *The World Anthology* (1969), or Jean Malley and Halé Tokay's *Contemporaries* (1972); for anything less than the best finally functions, when read, to confirm inadvertently the currently dominant criticisms of supposedly "talentless young." For similar reasons, an avant-garde composer I know always gets especially upset when a bad "modern" composition is performed on television—not only because the piece itself is so dreadful but because many viewers, innocently thinking that television producers like anthologists select only the best art, will take its dreadfulness as confirming their prior prejudice against "modern music"!

As children of a false prosperity, the new generation innocently thought that serious writers were not necessarily condemned to poverty—after all, their predecessors weren't—which left them ill-prepared for the subsequent devastations of the seventies. Though aware of selling themselves and each other out, young writers and editors discovered with the economic downturn the sheer precariousness of their bottom-rung position in the literary enterprise. Amazingly few live entirely off their writing—even among those who publish frequently—as most supplement their incomes with unemployment-welfare,

334

part-time jobs, or an organizational position that usually extracts its toll in time and spirit. (Less than one-half, contrary to popular assumption, teach for a living, in part because academic positions have not been plentiful recently.) Poverty, or the threat of it, especially in the midst of an established generation's continuing prosperity, is especially disheartening; recessions are less conducive to creative activity than pervasive depressions—so long as good fortunes seem possible (and are thus sought), counter-productive disappointments and demoralizations become far more frequent.

16

Young Writers in North America

I

The young should be an audience for one another. . . . The interest that [young readers] can give to the writer who is going to be outstanding among you is the equivalent, at this stage of his development, to a blood transfusion. And it is blood which only the young can give to others who are young. —Stephen Spender, "The Young Writer, Present, Past, and Future" (1953).

The ideas of the young are the living, the potential ideas; those of the old, the dying or the already dead. This is why it behooves youth to be not less radical, but even more radical, than it would naturally be. It must be not simply contemporaneous, but a generation ahead of the times: so that when it comes into control of the world, it will be precisely right and coincident with the conditions of the world as it finds them. —Randolph Bourne, "Youth" (1912).

The best work is always neglected and there is no critic among the older men who has cared to champion the newer names from outside the battle. The established critic will not read. So it is that the present writers must turn interpreters of their own work. —William Carlos Williams, "Marianne Moore" *The Dial* (1925).

Generalizations about young writers defy certain categories that were dominant a decade ago. The distinction between academic and nonacademic, the most common currency of early sixties' criticism, does not successfully divide these writers, as the works of those who never finished college (or graduate school) scarcely differs from the works of those who did. Likewise, Jonathan Cott's writing and Renata Adler's, as well as Thomas Pynchon's and Richard Meltzer's, may seem more "intellectual" and pedantic than David Henderson's and Richard Goldstein's, Jerome Charyn's and Michael S. Harper's; yet those in the latter group are (or have been) professors and the first four have not yet taught at all. That adjective "academic" best characterizes, instead, essays that scrupulously pursue a single thesis, or literary works that fulfill a formula which was learned, customarily, in a classroom (i.e., creative writing courses), regardless of whether or not their author is now (or ever has been) a university teacher.

All expressions from their speech to their doodles suggest that everyone growing up in America today is enormously affected by popular culture. Nonetheless, what separates serious writers from commercial is that the former usually turn this influence, or allusions to it, to non-poppish artistic ends. The sensibility of *Mad* magazine, for instance, has affected both Richard Meltzer and *The National Lampoon;* but the latter publishes cartoons, while the former is a writer, whose ironic essay, *The Aesthetics of Rock* (1968), brilliantly mixes (and subverts) both Plato and pop in adjacent phrases. The influence of mundane culture may account for why young American writers tend to avoid the pretentiousness of both style and thought more typical of European (i.e., Parisian) literati, for one benefit of pop is a salutary corrective to the "elitist" inclinations perhaps intrinsic in the profession. This last factor may partly explain, in turn, why few young writers of note currently live abroad or especially reflect the influence of contemporary European culture, or why few have established any personal contact with comparable Europeans. (The principal exceptions to these generalizations are those artist-writers involved with "concrete" and other internationally defined avant-gardes.) Although the literary young slightly overlap with academic youth, they are hardly synonymous with either the young political activists (and writers) or post-acid hippies, both of whom emerged from predominately separate traditions and are largely motivated by different aspirations and stimuli.

Nonetheless, like their more political and disaffiliated peers, young writers advocate the redistribution of social power and the creation of alternative cultures. They also place a high value upon honesty and openness, as well as freedom in both action and thought; and they show a moral sense that is generally finer and less compromised, making them unashamedly disgusted with those corruptions and hypocrisies that went largely unprotested before. It was a young former employee of the Famous Writers School, the novelist Cecelia Holland (b. 1943), rather than an old pro, who confessed, "I'm guilty of encouraging people who could barely read to think they might someday write the great American novel. By comparison, crookery is moral." The young black novelist Cecil Brown once suggested that, "If black means anything, nowadays, it means living honestly," and much the same could be said for being young and a writer, too. (It is significant, I would think, that no writer born after 1939 has been an initiator of the type of literary scandals this book describes). However, young writers have not been as willing as their political brethren to act upon their alienation or to risk themselves for a cause greater than their personal (bourgeois) fortune.

Older readers (and critics) especially sensitive to the minority backgrounds of writers they read will have trouble distinguishing the young Southerners from the Northerners, the homosexuals from the heterosexuals, the gentiles from the Jews (although probably not those orientals, blacks, and women whose self-segregation is untypical), perhaps because the imagination of nearly every intelligent young American today owes more to common national experience than to the parochial influence of a particular ethnic subculture or geographical area. Closer scrutiny suggests that the social life of the younger literary generations is divided largely not by religion, class, or ethnicity, as in an earlier periods, but by drugs, the "heads" generally inhabiting social worlds quite separate from those who are predominantly "straight"; and the general neglect of alcohol, needless to say, separates the younger literary generations from their elders. These genuine differences, involving not only life-styles but mental orientation, too, are revealed in their writings, such as those fictions, invariably quite striking, intended to reflect post-hallucinogenic consciousness—for examples, Michael Disend's *Stomping the Goyim* (1969) and G.S. Gravenson's *The Sweetmeat Saga* (1971). Nonetheless, no imaginative work I know has yet "done" the drug experience as definitively as Malcolm Lowry's *Under the Volcano* (1947) treated alcoholism.

(It is nonetheless quite possible, given the current situation, that some young writer has, though his book has not been published or sufficiently noticed.)

Every artist draws upon his "personal experience," to be sure; but the experience of most young writers includes not only his university education but a goodly number of books, some of which provide him with the intellectual and imaginative tools for comprehending the world around him. "All art originates in the human mind," notes the art historian E.H. Gombrich, "in our own reactions to the world, rather than in the visible world itself." Precisely by that process is all art ultimately (even if circuitously) indebted to selected examples of previous art, each work of literature, in every respect from its over-all form to the structure of its sentences, eventually revealing certain earlier readings. The crucial observation for now, however, is that the best writing of the new generations reveals a literacy as diverse and individual and yet predominantly American as its background. Not only is it difficult to detect any single seminal influence—the era of Faulkner's overwhelming example is long past—but the echoes one hears in individual works are usually quite various and idiosyncratic.

Moreover, the absence of self-obsessed writings indicates that this may well be the first literary generation to know—to acknowledge in both precept and practice—a previously submerged truth: that literature (unlike journalism) comes largely out of cultivated imaginations. Unlike the novelists of "experience" who tend to tell the same story over and over again, the works of young Americans reveal self-critical sensibilities that transcend all dominating obsessions in favor of continued experiment and creative adventure. On the other hand, those novelists who are experience-oriented fulfill the reportorial function, exemplified by Philip Roth, of revealing social truths that were previously hidden—not only Cecil Brown and Frank Chin, but Dan McCall and Norman Fruchter, among others. Even the most notable playwrights are not "realists" but anti-realists, absurdists, abstractionists, and fetishists—sometimes to an extreme; and that mid-sixties movement called "The Theatre of the Ridiculous" revealed that even European "absurd theatre" suffered from stylistic conservatism. By and large, the young writers are artistically conscious and intelligent, very much

340

aware of what they are doing (as well as what has been done) and willing to discuss it openly and truthfully.

As the old molds have disintegrated, emerging writers confront their creative tasks with fewer intimidating restrictions than any previous literary generation; and this sense of unprecedented freedom informs not only what they write but, perhaps more important, how they pursue their professional lives. For one thing, they have no use for old-fashioned restrictions upon the scope of their literary activities; so that whereas writers of earlier generations usually forged narrow definitions of themselves, endeavoring to become "novelists" or "poets" or "critics" or sometimes just "drama critics," one significant freedom for young "writers" today is that their interests take many possible artistic forms. Some have written for both slick magazines and mimeographed periodicals, while others have worked in several literary genres out of a serious interest in the current problems and traditions of each (a procedure itself reflecting polyliteracy), in addition to freely experimenting in the other arts. Nothing about the new generation seems to awe older people more than this freedom to write (or do) anything, though this kind of lateral movement remains obviously acceptable to the young.

Arno Karlen (b. 1937), for instance, has published poetry, fiction, translations, criticism, and slick-magazine journalism, while the poet Louis Lipsitz (b. 1938) took his doctorate in political science and teaches it at universities; Jonathan Cott (b. 1942) has written poems, rock-magazine journalism, and serious criticism of film, music, and literature, in addition to producing his own radio shows about experimental music. Don L. Lee (b. 1942) has published poetry, prose, and criticism, as well as founding the Third World Press and serving as its chief editor. (Given the temper of the times, it is not surprising that many serious poets have doubled as publishers.) J. Michael Yates (b. 1938), a U.S.-born Canadian immigrant, has published short verse, two book-length poems, short stories, prose meditations, plays for both stage and radio, photographs, criticism, philosophical essays, and translations, as well as moderating a literary radio program, plus teaching at the University of British Columbia, and creating both two literary magazines and the Sono Nis Press. Alan Sondheim (b. 1943) has written essays, poetry, and

341

"conceptual art," composed modernist music for both live and electronic ensembles, played a variety of instruments, constructed his own electronic synthesizer, exhibited both sculpture and sculptural machines, and even experimented inventively in both films and video tape, bringing to each of these artistic domains certain overarching preoccupations and a consistently avant-garde sensibility. The produce of Dan Graham (b. 1942), one of the age's pioneering minds, has so far included photography, films, poetry, essays, performance pieces, situational sculpture, and indescribable things; his forthcoming works are likely to be superficially different and yet personally consistent.

It follows that many young critics write on more than one or two arts, Herbert Read being a more persuasive exemplar than Edmund Wilson. Young critics sympathetic to the avant-garde, unlike the congenital conservatives, tend also to do remarkable creative work, their criticism often revealing an intimacy unavailable to the uncreative critical mentality—J Marks, Cott, Higgins, Lucy R. Lippard, David Shapiro, Peter Schjeldahl, Robert Smithson, and Frederic Tuten. Others, such as the poet-critics Vito Acconci and Dan Graham, have felt free enough to progress out of written literature into inter-media, such as non-literary performances, which nonetheless reveal their originally poetic sources and sensibility. What the art critic Max Kozloff noted about young visual artists is also true for certain young writers: "Today they are exploring horizontally: their identity comes from their manner of working, not from the look of the work itself." The crunching difference is that, since literary establishments are more conservative in comparison to those in the visual arts, the horizontally adventurous writers have encountered far more philistinism and frustration than similarly predisposed painters and sculptors.

The opportunities intrinsic in stylistic freedom have clearly affected nearly everyone coming of cultural age in the sixties, only some of whom, nonetheless, have chosen to explore alternative kinds of literary coherence. (The liberties taken by the underground press, in both design and language, represent a more popular analogy that falls, however, strictly within a journalistic tradition.) Indeed, since the culture shaping younger sensibilities is so different from that of a decade or two ago, it should be expected that the writing most attuned to our years will measure its historical integrity and perhaps its current relevance by stylistic distance from previous work. Whereas the decadent artist regards himself at the tail end of a development, the experimentalist feels obliged to move ahead—especially beyond the practices of decadents.

"New" has, of course, become one of the cheapest terms in contemporary discussion, used, as it is, to merchandise all kinds of capitalism's dirty laundry. When most strictly applied, "new" defines works whose style and form (*not* content) are discernibly different from what has been produced before. For that reason, beginning poets are not necessarily making new or unprecedented poems which, in turn, do not necessarily come from writers just starting to publish. It is a common conservative piety to assert, along with Granville Hicks (b. 1900), that, "In literature or in music and painting, the serious practitioner masters the conventional forms before he engages in innovation," but certain successfully innovative work done by writers then less than twenty-five—Kenneth King, Dan Graham, Dick Higgins, Tom Ahern, Richard Meltzer, Ronald Tavel, bpNichol, among others—demonstrates that a prolonged apprenticeship is no longer necessary. Indeed, much that is genuinely new in literature today has been created by young writers, extending the modernist tradition of unending innovation.

Young magazine writers have also displayed a marked penchant for uncompromised discriminations plus a related tendency to regard certain institutions and situations more skeptically than their elders—not only capitalistic industry but the rock-music business and even the writing scene. Certain platitudes once thought above close examination such as "liberalism," "healthy sexuality," "femininity," are now being scrupulously exposed. If "participatory journalism," with its novelistic techniques and subjective intrusions, characterized the best work of an older generation—Gay Talese, Joan Didion, Tom Wolfe, and Dan Wakefield (all born between 1931 and 1934)—tough-minded, investigative debunking is more typical of the younger magazine writers: Renata Adler, Joe McGinniss, Julie Baumgold, Craig Karpel, Jack Newfield, Mark J. Green, David Landau, and Steven Kelman. Not only are readers' minds changed by persuasive muckraking, but so eventually are public practices and policies. Perhaps such writing reflects a rigorous

343

and persistent honesty—saying what our predecessors did not or could not—that is perhaps generational and will, one hopes, survive these ruinous times.

II

> The reason for the vast eruption of moral protest in America since the beginning of the civil-rights struggle is that people can now afford to be good—aggressively so. —Kenneth Rexroth, *The Alternative Society* (1970).

In the imaginative literature by young writers no theme seems as pervasive as the discontinous shape of perception and expression—the reluctance or inability of the writer (or the autonomous work) to pull all the amorphous material together into the neat, linear structures of traditional exposition. This preoccupation can, in practice, be as deeply embedded in the work's statement as in its style—for example, John Brockman's book-length essays on information theory and indeterminacy, as well as these opening lines from David Shapiro's "For Chagy":

The arrow wakes up Mozart odious life that sunk the Vedas
tulips where my pistol goes and reason daily prayers for the
    dead
brush and dream you to whom the ray of tallow is shining
milk the day-old Moses and revive the nationalities past yeast.

Many other poems, not just by Shapiro (who wrote a thesis on "The Meaning of Meaninglessness"), achieve an ironic relation between the semblance of coherence, if not the *sound* of significance, and the actual acoherence of his syntax. Similarly, even if a story is superficially linear, the familiarly formed narrative often functions more as an ironic convention than a revelatory structure; for it becomes apparent that the themes established at the story's end have actually informed it from the beginning. Pynchon's deservedly honored story, "Entropy" (1960), uses rather conventional surfaces to realize a metaphor for the entropic meaninglessness of the Second Law of Thermo-dynamics—a theme also evoked in a brilliant, more structurally fragmented story, "The Heat Death of the Universe" (1967), written by Pamela Zoline, an American painter (b. 1941) living in London; and Pynchon's first novel, *V.*, also exploits his early education in science to create a realized image of the quantum theory of matter. Whereas Newton and the literature of Newtonian centuries regarded both physical matter and worldly experiences as flowing linearly in a continuous predictable pattern, the writing attuned to post-Newtonian, twentieth-century physics portrays discontinuous batches of energy flowing haphazardly across space. In *V.* are portrayed both a group of related people and modern history as a whole; just as the pattern of one duplicates the structure of the other, so the picture of experience created in the novel duplicates the imagery of matter in the new physics.

Discontinuity, it should be clear, does not mean literary incoherence, for disconnected narratives achieve, usually through repetition and interweaving, their own kind of definable coherence. The author may evoke a fairly consistent vision through numerous examples, as William Burroughs does in *Naked Lunch* (1958); or the persistent failure of the narrator to find unity may paradoxically serve to unify a particular fiction, as in certain Samuel Beckett works. Some young writers have striven very earnestly for "structureless" work; but to the extent that their writing reveals any kind of particularity—either in voice, or in diction, or simply in filling space on the printed page—some kind of literary structure has emerged. As noted before, "formless art" is either a polemical paradox or an impossible contradiction in terms, for any work that can be defined—that can be characterized in any way—is by definition artistically coherent. It follows that just because a work fails to cohere in a linear fashion need not mean that it cannot be understood; instead, as recent literature accustoms readers to its particular ways of organizing expression, so they learn to comprehend this new work in entirely different ways, often appreciating dimensions and devices they would have ignored or neglected before. Furthermore, formal discontinuity as a perceptual mode is closer to both our everyday experience of abundant stimuli, as well as the marijuana-psychedelic experience that is now more prevalent than a decade ago.

Many young writers cultivate an imaginative interest in areas of experience that were either neglected, or clichéd, or rendered superficially in previous writing. The ideal of more authentic content animates young feminist writers, literary blacks, oriental-American authors, all of whom feel obliged to transcend limiting stereotypes; it also informs, in another way, the following passage from CPGraham's *ime* (1969):

Errect to the suck of Love
Errect & plunging Up
Errect, O God let Him in
Errect, O Jesus . . . Yes . . .
Errect, O come on up, up Up
Errect, o yes, yess, yesss
Errect, o do it, do it again
Errect, o take me, have me, let Yourself Out
Errect, o yes, o yess, yessss i'm Out
Erect, O softly Now, O Holy Soft, You are Soft
    for me, Soft, & i am Holy Round

Omen

This complements a continuing, unembarrassed concern with the extremes of feeling exemplified by this haunting refrain that opens Margaret Atwood's *Power Politics* (1971):

you fit into me
like a hook into an eye

a fish hook
an open eye

Or by Grandin Conover's couplet on homosexuality:

All men have guns between their legs
Some are willing to be targets.

Or by the description of an abortion in Louise Glück's "The Egg":

Past cutlery I saw
My body stretching like a tear
Along the paper.

Or in the mad obsessions of several Jerome Charyn characters or Katherine Dunn's narrators.

This interest in emotional frontiers has its artistic complement in equally extreme styles such as the hysteria of Ishmael Reed's best fiction, the obsessive scatology of Ed Sanders'

Shards of God (1970), the fragments in rectilinear space of G.S. Gravenson's *The Sweetmeat Saga* (1971), or the narrator's radically varying penmanship (photographically reproduced) in Nancy Weber's "Dear Mother and Dad" (1970). An extreme of another kind appears in Kenneth Gangemi's scrupulously uninflected novel, *Olt* (1969), whose narrator suffers a total inability to discriminate in his experiential responses:

> [In an art museum] he looked at a painting of the skeletons of American presidents on exhibit in a Chinese museum; a painting entitled *Naked Schoolgirls Bathing in a Stream*; a series of photographs showing the transformation of a five-year-old girl into a fifty-year-old derelict; a framed blueprint of the Auschwitz raping harness; a reproduction of Rembrandt's *Man Seated Reading at a Table in a Lofty Room*; an aerial photograph of Coney Island on the 4th of July; a model of a one-family tropical island, with mountain, orchard, farm, beach, and lagoon.

Implicit in the stylistic courage of young writers is the assumption that no area of human experience can remain beyond the bounds of imaginative scrutiny.

III

> Everyone who cares about poetry hopes that each young or new poet to appear on the scene may be the one to bring forth the whole magnificent potential of poetry and lay it on the page, and thus realize the promise that poetry makes in age after age but seldom succeeds in keeping. —James Dickey, "The Son, the Cave, and the Burning Bush" (1968).

A critical survey of all the literary achievements of this younger generation, needed though it is, would be impractical, if not impossible, in a book of this size and proportion. Suffice it to say that, in the course of research, I began to compile, out of pleasure in both discovery and enumeration, a directory of writers born in 1937 or afterwards—the youngsters in the community of serious writing—whose work had impressed me enough to note their names and whose talent I could certify.

Those North Americans on the following list were chosen from the hundreds whose writings I have read—the omission of certain celebrities should indicate the presence of discrimination; and behind this select group, let me conjecture, stand literally thousands who have published completed poems, fictions, and essays (or would like to do so). In advance, I should extend apologies to those whose names are misspelled either by me or by their original publisher, and to those contemporaries whose works I have missed and shall later come to admire. Nothing is more disappointing, I know, than reading a list of names that would probably include your own, if only the compiler had known about your work; but perhaps that misfortune can be turned into a source of energy and inspiration.

For the sake of convenience, the names are divided into four categories, demarcating the genres in which in my judgment each writer particularly excels, though many of them have published in more than one (and a few do other arts as well). The numerical preponderance of poets reflects several facts: that less effort is necessary to make one's mark as a poet (though truly exceptional poetry is perhaps harder to write), that new poetry magazines and small presses (and cliques) outnumber those open to fiction, and that by the middle sixties poetry seemed to replace fiction at both the frontier and the center of American literary consciousness. Though I suspect that most of their names are unfamiliar even to each other, any "critic of contemporary writing" who cannot identify works by fifteen percent of them should, perforce, retire into the Academy to lecture on people and periods already past. Anyone who has read more than a third of them should consider himself part of an ideal literary public, for the recognition that really counts comes not from a writer's elders but from his chronological peers and successors.

POETS

Vito Hannibal Acconci	Alta	Jeffrey Apter
Duane Ackerson	Johari Amini	Siah Armajani
Ai (née Florence Anthony)	Charles Amirkhanian	Dana Atchley
D. Alexander	Jon Anderson	Margaret Atwood
Dick Allen	Bruce Andrews	
Robert Allen	Lyman Andrews	Carol Bankerd

Anita Barrows
Jan Barry
Charles M. Baxter
Marvin Bell
Michael Benedikt
Bill Berkson
Lebert Bethune
Harvey Bialy
Bill Bissett
David Bissonette
Douglas Blazek
Janet Bloom
Charles Boer
Harold Bond
James Brodey
Michael Brownstein
Donald Burgy
Christopher Bursk
Gerald Butler

Robert Carande
Robert Chatain
Laura Chester
Tom Clark
Charlie Cobb
Victor Coleman
Durward Collins, Jr.
Andrei Codrescu
Grandin Conover
Conyus
Clark Coolidge
Judy Copithorne
Victor Hernandez Cruz
Tom Cuson

Philip Dacey
Ronald Dahl
Glover Davis
Robert Dawson
James Den Boer
Wally Depew
Mike Dereszynski

Joel Deutsch
Steven Dhondt
R.H.W. Dillard
Joseph Dionne
Ray DiPalma
John Ditsky
Charles Doria
John Douglas
Barbara Drake
Norman Dubie
Dennis Dunn
Stephen Dunn
Gail Dusenbery
   (née Chiarello)
Bob Dylan

Prewitt Edelman
K.S.Ernst

Larry Fagin
Doug Fetherling
Robert Flanagan
Aaron Fogel
Robert Fones
Calvin Forbes
Siv Cedering Fox
David Franks
Kathleen Fraser
Ray Freed

Geoff Gajewski
Dan Georgakas
Daniela Gioseffi
Alex Gildzen
Martin Glass
Louise Glück
Sidney Goldfarb
Joe Goncalves
John Gorham
CPGraham
Dan Graham

Donald L. Graham
Judy Grahn
Eric Grienke
Robert Grenier
Marilyn Hacker
Drummond Hadley
Walter S. Hamady
Jeffrey Hamm
James Haning
C.G. Hanslicek
Karen Hanson
Peter Harleman
William Harmon
Michael S. Harper
Barbara Harr
Phyllis Masek Harris
William J. Harris
Jim Harrison
Robert Hass
Gerald Hausman
Thomas Head
Michael Heller
David Henderson
Jan Herman
Shael Herman
Brenda Herold
Philip Hey
Ben L. Hiatt
David Hilton
Everett Hoagland
Greg Hollingshead

Lawson Fusao Inada

Emmett Jarrett
Louis Jenkins
Paulette Jiles
Gary Johnson
Erica Jong
Norman Jordan

Stephen Kaltenbach

Allan Kaplan
Stephen Michael Katcher
Allen Katzman
Martha Kearns
W. Bliem Kern
Joshua Kesselman
W. Keorapetse Kgositsile
Joseph Knapp II
Hugh Knox
John Koethe
Ted Kooser
Joseph Kosuth
Richard Krech
T. L. Kryss
Greg Kuzma

Bertrand Lachance
Michael Lally
Ann Lauterbach
Richard Lebovitz
Dennis Lee
Don L. Lee
David Lehman
Stephen Levine
D.A. Levy
Lyn Lifshin
Frank Lima
Lou Lipsitz
Ron Loewinsohn
Lynn Lonider
Richard Lourie
K. Curtis Lyle
Sandford Lyne

Eugenia Macer
Gerard Malanga
Paul Malanga
Lee Mallory
Martin Malony
Alfredo Mantilla
Aaron Marcus

Morton Marcus
Gary Margolis
Paul Mariah
Daphne Marlott
Richard Mathews
William Matthews
John Matthias
David McAleavey
Steve McCaffery
Barry McCallion
Mark McClosky
David McFadden
Bell Meissner
David Melnick
David Meltzer
Ann Menebroker
Nina Mende
Michael Mewshaw
Richard Meyers
Brown Miller
Janice Mirikitani
William Mobius
Judith Moffett
George Montgomery
John Morgan
Richard Morris
Jonathan Morse
Susan Musgrave
Edward Mycue

F. A. Nettelbeck
Joachim Neugroschel
John Newlove
bpNichol

Tom Ockerse
Tejumola Ologboni
Toby Olson
Michael Ondaatje
P.J. O'Rourke
Gregory Orr

Jim Orvino-Sorcic
Steven Osterlund
Alicia Ostriker
Maureen Owen

Ron Padgett
Edgar Paiewonsky
Doug Palmer
Basil T. Paquet
Patricia A. Parker
Rob Patton
Ellen Pearce
John Peck
Louis Phillips
Michael Joseph Phillips
Pedro Pietri
Allan Planz
Charlie Potts
Jefry Poniewaz
Jonathan Price
Norman Henry Pritchard II

George Quasha
Susan Quist

DeWayne Rail
Rochelle Ratner
Thomas Dillon Redshaw
Lou Reed
Gay Beste Reineck
Stan Rice
Stephen Richmond
Barbara Robbins
Dwight Robhs
Aldo Rostagno
Wm. Pitt Root
Martin J. Rosenblum
Gibbons Ruark
Barbara Ryder

Saint Geraud
  (né Wm. Knott)

Dennis Saleh
Aram Saroyan
Susan Fromberg Schaeffer
David Schaff
Andre Scheinman
Edwin Schlossberg
Tom Schmidt
Jeffrey Schmitt
Dennis Schmitz
Irene Schram
Andraes Schroeder
Howard Schwartz
Rainer Schulte
James Scully
James Seay
Hugh Seidman
Alan Senauke
John Shannon
David Shapiro
Susan Sherman
Stephen Shrader
Ron Silliman
Charles Simic
John Oliver Simon
Paul Simon
John Sinclair
Ted Sloane
Joel Sloman
Alan Sondheim
Roberta Spear
Sara Spencer
David Steingass
Ira Steingroot

Jane Stembridge
Judith W. Stembergh
Stephany
Frank Stanford
Terry Stokes
Lynn Strongin
Dabney Stuart
Lynn Sukenick
Andrew Suknaski
Karen Swenson
Suzanne Szlemko

Samuel Tagatac
John Taggart
James Tate
Henry S. Taylor
Lorenzo Thomas
John Thomson
John Thorpe
Richard Tillinghast
Eric Torgersen
Robert Trammell
Quincy Troupe
Frederick Turner

David Uu
Charles Upton

Alden Van Buskirk
Peter Van Toorn
Paul Vangelisti
Stephen Vincent
Julia Vinograd

Diane Wakoski
D. r. Wagner
Anne Waldman
William Donald Wandick
Karen Waring
Klyd Watkins
Lewis Warsh
Tom Weatherly
Henry Weinfield
James Welch
J.D. Whitney
Frances Whyatt
Michael Wiater
Stephen Wiest
Kathy Wiegner
Peter Wild
Mason Williams
Keith Wilson
Warren Woessner
Shawn Wong
Susan Wong
Suzanne Woods
Douglas Worth
Andrea Wyatt
Derek Wynand

Al Young
Ian Young
Karl Young
Doug Youngblood

Paul Zelevansky

FICTIONERS

Tom Ahern
Mimi Alberts
Bill Amidon
Eric Anderson
Alain Arias-Misson

Luther Askeland
Richard Astle
Charles Aukema

Willard Bain

Carolyn Banks
Russell Banks
Frederick Barthelme
Steve Barthelme
Peter S. Beagle

M.F. Beal
W. Conger Beasley, Jr.
Barry Beckham
E.M. Beekman
John Bennett, Jr.
Joan Bernott
Marie-Claire Blas
Adrianne Blue
Robert Boles
Sandra Boucher
Joe Brainard
Bonnie Bremser
Cecil Brown
Jerry Elijah Brown
Josiah Bunting
Richard Burgin
Frederick Busch

Douglas Calhoun
Steve Cannon
Roch Carrier
Terry Champagne
Jeffrey Paul Chan
Jerome Charyn
Raymond Carver
Fred Chase
Kelly Cherry
Frank Chin
Keith Cohen
Matt Cohen
George Constable
Gerald F. Conway
Gwyneth Cravens
Michael Crichton
R. Crumb

Philip Damon
Laura Dean
Ronald De Feo
Lee DeJasu
Samuel R. Delany

Michael Disend
Thomas M. Disch
Stephen Dobyns
Rejean Ducharme
Katherine Dunn

Gordon Eklund
Susan Engberg
David Evanier

Richard Fariña
Eric Felderman
Kirby Farrell
Warren Fine
Eric Fredd
David Freeman
Paul Friedman
Norman Fruchter

Kenneth Gangemi
Lawrence Garber
Merrill Joan Gerber
Madeline Gins
Elizabet Ginsberg
David Godfrey
Michael Goldberg
Gary L. Goss
G.S. Gravenson
Ronald Green
Charles Gregory
J. Spencer Grendahl
Sally Grimes
Steven Guarino

Bertha Harris
Emily Katherine Harris
Thomas Hearron
George V. Higgins
Carol Hill
William Hjortsberg
Bruce Holbrook

Fanny Howe
Bill Hutton

J. Jeffrey Jones
Rich Jorgensen

Mark Kaminsky
Bernard Kaplan
Johanna Kaplan
Arno Karlen
Robert Eaton Kelley
William Melvin Kelley
Kenneth King
Norma Klien
Arthur Knight
Henry James Korn
William Kotzwinkle
Elaine Kraf

D.L. Lamothe
Cynthia Lasky
Melody Lawrence
Ursula K. LeGuin
Alan Lelchuk
Gerald Locklin
Phillip Lopate
Peter Lord
Keith Lowe

Gwendolyn MacEwen
Alastair MacLennan
Toby MacLennan
Gail Madonia
D. Keith Mano
Edward Marcotte
Russell Marois
Bernadette Mayer
Seymour Mayne
Dan McCall
Carole S. McCauley
Mark McGarrity

Thomas McGuane
Thomas McHale
Thomas McMahon
John Mella
Durango Mendoza
Barton Midwood
William Milani
Heather Ross Miller
Gary Moore

Peter Najarian
Jay Neugeboren
Charles Newman
Alice Notley
Craig Nova

Joyce Carol Oates
Michael O'Donohue
Diane Oliver

Alexei Panshin
Raymond Patten
Lindsay Patterson
Zeese Papanikolas
George Payerle
Oscar F. Penaranda
David Plante
Donald Porter
Thomas Pynchon

David Quanman

Peter Rand

Judith Rascoe
Earl M. Rausch
Ishmael Reed
James Reston, Jr.
David Rhodes
Robert Richkin
Grace Rooney
Jesse Rosenberg
Jerry Roth
David Rounds
Edward Ruscha
Joanna Russ
Lawrence Russell

Ira Sadoff
James Sallis
Ed Sanders
Corinne Sayer
Peter Schneeman
Shirley Schoonover
Jonathan Schwartz
Chris Scott
Mitchell Sisskind
John Sladek
Ray Smith
Paul Spike
Ronald M. Spatz
Johnny Stanton
Page Stegner
Ely Stock
Robert Stone
Jonathan Stone
Philip Alston Stone

Wayne Strandlund

Stephen Taylor
Charles Texeira
Paul Theroux
Frederic Tuten
Anne Tyler
Paul Tyner

Robert Ullian

Nick C. Vaca
M. Vaughn-James
Tom Veitch
Paul Violi

Alice Walker
Jon Walsh
Nancy Weber
Eugene Wildman
Sylvia Wilkinson
Dennis Williams
Joy Williams
L. Woiwode
William Crawford Woods
Don Wulffson
Rudolph Wurlitzer

J. Michael Yates
Lawrence Yep
Raphael Yglesias

John Zeugner
Pamela Zoline

PLAYWRIGHTS

Robert Auletta
Jeriann Badanes
Jean Barbeau
Carol Bolt
Josef Bush

Lonnie Carter
N.R. Davidson, Jr.
Charles Dizenzo
David Epstein
Marc Estrin

Tom Eyen
Richard Foreman
J.E. Franklin
David French
Gary Gardner

353

Barbara Garson
Percy Granger
Donald Greaves
John Guare
Robert Head
Robert Heide
William Hoffman
Israel Horovitz
Dennis Jasudowicz
Samuel Kachigan
Arthur L. Kopit
Barry Litvack
Charles Ludlam

Terrence McNally
Murray Mednick
Ronald Milner
Meredith Monk
Daniel Moore
John Ford Noonan
Sally Ordway
John Palmer
Robert Patrick
Ronald John Pringle
Jan Quackenbush
David Rabe
Lennox Raphael

Ken Rubin
Sam Shepherd
Archie Shepp
Robert Somerfield
Ronald Tavel
Michel Tremblay
Michael Weller
Lanford Wilson
Robert Wilson
(a.k.a., "Byrd Hoffman")
Lawrence Wunderlich
Susan Yankowitz
Ron Zuber

ESSAYISTS

Erica Abeel
Renata Adler
Michael Anania
Jervis Anderson
Michael André
Walter Arnold
Linda Arking
Ti-Grace Atkinson
Peter Axthelm
Joan Baez
Jay Bail
Stephen Barney
Anne Barry
Gregory Battcock
Julie Baumgold
Fred Beauford
Don Benson
Candice Bergen
Joseph Berke
Mel Bochner
Peter Bogdanovich
Denis Bogin
Robert Boyers
Jacob Brackman

Taylor Branch
Stewart Brand
John Brockman
Frederic Brussat
Joseph Bruchac
Stuart Byron
Ellen Canterow
Walter Carlos
Ted Castle
Robert Christgau
Peter Clekak
David Cope
Regina Cornwell
Jonathan Cott
Thomas J. Cottle
Sharon Curtin
Les Daniels
Sandy Darlington
Frank Davey
Carl Davidson
Garrett DeBell
Frank Delford
Cecily Dell
David Denby
Alan Dershowitz

Morris Dickstein
Digby Diehl
Roger Ebert
David Ehrenstein
Ira Einhorn
Katherine Ellis
Nora Ephron
Thomas Faber
James Fallows
Joseph Featherstone
Terry Fenton
Andrew Field
Shulamith Firestone
Frances FitzGerald
Eric Foner
Thomas King Forcade
Michael Fried
Ken Friedman
Len Fulton
David Gancher
Fred Gardner
Marvin Garson
James Gatsby
Peter Geismar
James Gilbert

Nikki Giovanni
Ronald J. Glasser
Michael L. Glenn
Richard Goldstein
Marcus J. Grapes
Mark L. Green
Jeff Greenfield
Emmett Grogan
Richard Grossinger
Pat Gunkel
Peter Guralnick
Patti Hagen
Tom Hayden
Gerrit Henry
Geof Hewitt
Nancy Henderson
Warren Hinckle
Anthony Hiss
Abbie Hoffman
Michael Hoffman
Britt Hume
Bruce Jackson
George Jackson
Martin Jay
John Jacob
Howard Junker
Tom Kahn
Craig Karpel
Howard Kaye
Stephen Kelman
Salley Kempton
Barbara Kevles
Steven Koch
Jane Kramer
Rosalind E. Krauss
Harold Krents
James Simon Kunen
John Lahr
David Landau
Jon Landau
Joyce Lander

Jeremy Larner
D.A. Latimer
Barry Leeds
David Lenson
John Leonard
Susannah Lessard
Lucy R. Lippard
David Littlejohn
Richard Locke
Michael Lydon
Susan Lydon
George Malko
Rich Mangelsdorff
Griel Marcus
J Marks
Gary T. Marx
Joyce Maynard
Frank D. McConnell
Alfred W. McCoy
Joe McGinniss
Eric McLuhan
Richard Meltzer
Peter Michelson
Michael W. Miles
Nancy Milford
Adam David Miller
Tom Montag
Douglas Mount
Kathy Muhlerin
Jack Newfield
Huey P. Newton
Philip Nobile
Christopher Norwood
Julius Novick
Eric Oatman
S.K. Oberbeck
John O'Neal
William O'Rourke
Peter Passell
Phoebe Pettingell
Peter Plagens

Theodore K. Raab
Rubin Rabinovitz
Philip Ramey
Carter Ratcliff
Barbara Reise
Sheldon Renan
Henry S. Resnick
Lillian S. Robinson
Paul A. Robinson
Michael Rossman
John Rothchild
G.S. Rousseau
Moshe Safdie
Robert Scheff
Jonathan Schell
Peter Schjedahl
Barry Schwartz
Edward Schwartz
Jack Scott
Erich Segal
Richard Sennett
Michael Shamberg
Gail Sheehy
Walt Shepperd
Bob Singer
P. Adams Sitney
G.P. Skratz
Harry Smith
Philip Raymond Smith
Robert Smithson
Ann Snitow
Robert Somma
Norman Spinrad
George Stade
Peter Stafford
Peter Steinfels
James Stoller
William Stott
Meredith Tax
Michael Thelwell
Michael Thomas

Hunter Thompson
William Irwin Thompson
James Tipton
James Toback
Lucian Truscott IV
David Walley

Edmund O. Ward
Paul Warshow
Paul Weaver
Steve Weissman
Ron Welburn
Ellen Willis

Judy Willis
Langdon Winner
Charles Wuorinen
Jud Yalkut
Gene Youngblood
Richard Zarro

The New Poetries

I

Art is constantly making itself; its definition is in the future. Criticism cannot therefore be a single develop- ing theory; it must be partisan and polemical in order to join art in asserting what art is to become. —Harold Rosenberg, *The Tradition of the New* (1960).

This is the sum and sum again for the publishing situation. Plain it is and has always been and must be to anyone that the best is untimely as well as rare, new and therefore difficult of recognition, without immediate general interest (any more than a tomato was until prejudice had been knocked down), there- fore dependent on discerning support (without expec- tation of money benefit) from the able; scantily saleable—and without attraction for the book trade, while wonders are advertised. And it is at the same time true that the only thing of worth in writing is this difficult, priceless thing that refreshes the whole field, which it enters, perenially, when it will, the new. —William Carlos Williams, "The Somnambulists" (1929).

"New" has become such a disreputable term in discourse about recent American poetry that anyone under thirty-five is initially reluctant to use it. There are "new" anthologies with sections devoted not only to "black poetry," "women poets," and "young poets" but also to "protest poetry" and "poetry of survival," although examples collected under these author- determined or content-determined rubrics are scarcely new with respect to poetry in general or even to their parochial cate- gories. Unless the word "new" is used to refer particularly to form and style, it becomes a platitude. This debasement of critical language, mostly in the interest of exploiting the prestige of the avant-garde without delivering the goods, regrettably obscures the emergence of genuinely new poetries.

Indeed, some innovative work is so different from traditional poetry that conservative mentalities are apt to question whether it can be called "poetry" at all; the truth, illustrated repeatedly in the history of innovative literature, is that radically new work upon its first appearance is usually put down as "not poetry" or "not art." (The most prominent recent example is Ginsberg's "Howl.") This charge is generally as ignorant as the similarly conservative contention of the new art's "formlessness," even though any sort of definable coherence (as in the following examples) establishes the existence of artistic selection and form. In my judgment, poetry is any verbal creation that descends from accepted poetry or more closely resembles accepted poetry than anything else. It is perilous to forget Marianne Moore's contention, radical in its time, that her own pieces are poetry because she finds no other classification more appropriate. Once again, in judgments of evaluation, only the good ones count.

These new poetries move, by definition, decidedly beyond the old poetries which in America cluster around several definable milestones. One is that tradition of lyricism which runs from Yeats through early Pound through Theodore Roethke, who was, in my opinion, the single greatest American poet of the early post-World War II period. Lyricism's more recent heirs include the poetries of nature perception (Bly, Dickey), of urban commentary (David Ignatow, Harvey Shapiro), of personal confession (middle Lowell, late Sylvia Plath), and more freely cadenced dark expressionism (early Ginsberg, Lamantia, LeRoi Jones). A second tradition which deals with alternative kinds of poetic coherence runs from Pound of the *Cantos* through Charles Olson into the "New York School" of John Ashbery, Frank O'Hara, and their self-congratulatory and egregiously opaque descendants, as well as the post-Black Mountain school. This tradition includes all poetries based upon isolated notations elliptically laid out in rectilinear space (exemplifying Olson's "composition by field") or upon verbal pastiche with its collage-like penchants for striking juxtaposition and leaps in rhythm and diction. American literary magazines nowadays are filled with derivatives, some more eclectic than others, of these two dominant traditions.

A third sort of old new poetry, considerably less influential than the others, consists of physically separate words and images (or photographs), which are usually the work of two artists in collaboration, but have sometimes been done, as in the examples of William Blake and Kenneth Patchen, by one man alone. A fourth milestone is the "prose poem," developed most brilliantly by early-modern Frenchmen, which customarily consists of a few strikingly crafted, highly "poetic" sentences. Truly new poetry moves beyond such typically contemporary concerns as associational syntax, jaggedly irregular rhythms, rhetorical elisions, imagistic repetition, pointed pastiche, and personal voice (whose most appropriate medium is the essay or the letter), along with transcending the subjects and sentiments (and egotisms) typical of those techniques. It moves well beyond the current practice of Lowell, Ginsberg, Dickey, Creeley, Bly—all of whom are frequently imitated in "creative writing" courses. Nonetheless, the works described below selectively reflect certain modern precedents, at the same time as they collectively enhance the great twentieth-century theme of expanding the language of human communication. For, as Mayakovsky formulated it, there is no truly revolutionary poetry without a revolutionary form. Should these examples seem initially incomprehensible, one reason is that they are formally different rather than intrinsically difficult; and that difference may also account for why they may initially seem "unpoetic." Many of them resemble the classics of modernism because they challenge and hopefully refashion our habitual ways of poetic reading.

There is not one kind of new poetry but several which collectively display clear steps beyond previous work. These several directions can in turn be divided into those that emphasize the basic materials of poetry and works that miscegenate them with other arts and concerns. The purist preoccupations of poetry include special kinds of diction (the vocabulary reflected in the selection of individual words) and unusual ways of putting words together; so that either new languages or new syntaxes can be a measure of innovation. In his poem "One Talk One" (1967), Jan Herman draws upon the vocabulary of the medical sciences, shrewdly weaving a lingo previously unknown to poetry:

energy systems gone/requires no plumbing
pulse amplitude continuous

> eliminates the need for arterial cutdowns
> the nursing word station set
> *"like a bilumen tube to which a stomach has been fastened"*
> the required function of each machine the same

His lines realize an encompassing diction that successfully transcends the collage methods actually used in the work's composition.

The Canadian poet Bill Bisset has developed a personal orthography that, along with other devices, poetically transforms simple statements:

> an whn yu cum
> an whn yu cum an whn
> yu cum an whn yu cum
> an whn yu cum an
> whn yu cum an
> whn yu cum
> an whn yu
> cum an
> whn
> yu
> cum

CPGraham mixes coined words with familiar ones:

> Heroin is the nymphomaniacish
> Orgaming in the veins

These examples echo Mayakovsky's dictum: "Neologisms are obligatory in writing poetry."

Rather than evolve new systems of syntax as James Joyce did in *Finnegans Wake*, American counter-syntactical poets strive to eschew the old ways of putting words together. One successful device is horizontal minimalism—one word to a line—that repudiates the function of syntax by giving each word (except the two articles and "of") equal weight in poetic exposition:

> kids
> bounding
> down
> from
> rocks

hit
the
shore
forcefully
and
then
run
the
length
of
it
    —Frank Samperi, "Intaglio" (1973).

Several works in Kenneth Gangemi's initial collection, *Lydia,* are unpunctuated, simplistically constructed lists whose parts are nonetheless skillfully (which is to say poetically) selected; his poem entitled "National Parks" begins:

Big Bend
Bryce Canyon

Crater Lake

Everglades

and continues uninflected in alphabetical order through "Yosemite" down to "Zion," all the chosen names being poetically evocative to varying (and idiosyncratic) degrees. Gangemi's form and taste enable him to realize, paradoxically, highly individual poems with a minimum of self-generated words.

The most impressive of Dick Higgins' poems, many of which are collected in *Foew&ombwhnw* (1969), favor the permutational organization of poetry's materials as one alternative to worn-out associational forms. A work entitled "empty streets" (1967) represents an elementary version of this compositional principle, permuting three separate phrases into three different pairs:

many boxes
many rooms
many sounds

many boxes
many sounds

> many rooms
> many sounds
>
> many boxes
> many rooms

Higgins' "Thrice Seven" (1968, also reprinted in *Foew&-ombwhnw*) is, thanks to its unusual sub-structures, one of the few recent long poems in English to avoid any formal echoes of the *Cantos*.

Pedro Pietri, a Puerto Rican poet (b. 1944) living in New York, has also worked in permutational forms as in "Prologue for Ode to Road Runner (1969)" which reads in part:

> train A town down
> down A train down
> A downtown train
> A train downtown

And so have such older poets as Jerome Rothenberg and Emmett Williams, along with Donald Burgy, a younger "conceptual artist" whose "Time Exchange #1" reads in its entirety:

> Put your then in someone's now
> Take someone's then in your now
> Put your now in someone's then
> Take someone's now in your then.

Back in the middle sixties, John Giorno introduced his remarkable experiments in repetition and line-breaking which demonstrated an old poetic truth—that varying placement can give different meanings to the same words:

> It is
> there
> It is there
> because
> we think
> it is
> there
> because we think
> it is there,
> and it is
> not

there
and it is not there
when
we do not
think
at all
when we do not think
at all.

Though stunning at first, particularly for its exploitation of mundane materials, this device becomes dulled by repetition. Nearly all of Giorno's poems express the same structural theme (while revealing morbid obsessions), and nothing else of his has been comparably distinguished. Another, more adventurous pioneer in this vein, Jackson Mac Low (b. 1921), has been experimenting for over twenty years with a variety of radically alternative structures, some of which have been more effective than others; but since most of his work remains unpublished or scattered through little magazines, it is hard to generalize about it.

Other Dick Higgins poems draw upon his experience in both Cagean musical and mixed-means theatrical composition to create an aleatory structure in which the reader may vary the poem's parts to his choice; the whole of the poet's inversely titled "New Song in the Old Style" (1967) remains, however, artistically superior to any of its comparatively prosaic realizations:

              (check one)
         ------speak
         ------dance
When I ------fall in love
         ------grow up
         ------grow old

                   (check one)
              ------I'm going to be
              ------it'll be with

                        (check one)
                   ------an apple.
                   ------a lover.

-----a smile.

-----you.

Higgins has also contributed to another new form, which is less definite and less realized so far, though still distinct, that I call suggestive poetry, to use that adjective in an especially Elizabethan sense of goading a response. In this strain of poetry, an imperative statement intends to initiate an unusual process of imaginative contemplation that is rather romantic and inevitably idiosyncratic. Some of this verges upon what I call Inferential Art—where little is made or said, though much is implied. Take, for instance, Stephen M. Katcher's classically enigmatic:

The reuse of this sentence is forbidden.

Or Higgins' "Danger Music No. Twelve (March 1962)" which reads in its entirety:

Write a thousand symphonies.

The text gains poetically from the sense that the commandment—not ten but a thousand is clearly impossible by normal means. A more concise example (that depends nonetheless upon unlimited generality) is his "Danger Music No. Thirteen":

Choose.

It should be noted that actually following the poet's instructions introduces a non-poetic dimension quite different from the strictly poetic experience of just the statement itself.

Perhaps the easiest ways to overcome the old forms of poetic organization are through vertical reductionism or the kind of one-line poems written by George Brecht which customarily are not writ large but set in mundane type:

o is at least one egg

The only precedent I know in American poetry for this quality of poetic compression appears in several poems that the noted critic Yvor Winters, of all people, wrote in the early twenties, such as "Aspen Song" which reads in its entirety:

The summer holds me here.

364

More extreme forms of poetic reductionism include Robert Lax's great long poem, *Black and White* (1966), whose total vocabulary consists of only three different words and an ampersand; Gangemi's "Guatemala," which reads in its entirety, "Quetzal!"; and the minimal manipulations of Aram Saroyan whose most memorable single poem runs:

eyeye

II

> My structures are reductive. Syntax—the systems of articulation, connection and relation between words that give linear discourse its quality of extended meaning—is simply removed. . . . What is happening is a reversal of the normal reading experience. When the cumulative process of linear understanding is frustrated, the mind turns back toward the unitary experience of words as structure. . . . My experiments invite you to regard words as an object—or more exactly, as an organism, with patterns of existing that are specific to itself, inexplicable and marvelous.
> —Clark Coolidge, as quoted in Tom Clark, *John's Heart* (1972).

None of the younger experimental poets has been as various, intelligent, and prolific as Clark Coolidge (b. 1939) who also edited one of the few genuinely avant-garde magazines of the sixties, *Joglars* (1964-66), in addition to playing drums for a poetry-conscious rock group, Serpent Power. His opening book, *Flag Flutter & U.S. Electric* (1966), collected his early forays into post-Ashberyian poetic acoherence where he attempted to realize the semblance of literary coherence without using such traditional organizing devices as meter, metaphor, exposition, symbolism, consistent allusion, declarative statements, or autobiographical reference. This effort is somewhat analogous to atonality in early twentieth-century music, where the composer likewise eschewed obvious coherences based upon tonics and dominants for more subtle forms of order; but just as successful atonal music never disintegrates into disordered noise—indeed, that is a fundamental measure of artistry—poetic acoherence must consistently distinguish itself from sheer incoherence. In a statement contributed to *The Young American*

365

Poets (1968), Coolidge wrote that "Words have a universe of qualities other than those of descriptive relation: Hardness, Density, Sound-Shape, Vector-Force, & Degrees of Transparency/Opacity." His earliest poems reveal rather extraordinary linguistic sensitivities, especially regarding the selection and placement of words.

In the course of willfully avoiding the crutches upon which the old poetry depended, in addition to the esoteric vocabulary he once favored, Coolidge pursued not just varieties of acoherence but reductionism, joining Gangemi, Lax, and Knott as one of America's most superior minimalists. This is the opening stanza of "The Next":

> the in will
> over from
> as also into as
> in is
> of as as an
> in as or
> as is as as and
> as have as is

In the back sections of Coolidge's fullest retrospective, *Space* (1970), are yet more severe examples, such as an untitled poem beginning "by a I" that contains individually isolated words no more than two letters long, scattered across the space of the page (which has so far been Coolidge's primary compositional unit). These words are nonetheless related to each other—not only in terms of diction and corresponding length (both visually and verbally) but in spatial proximity; for if they resemble musical notes, to raise that analogy again, they resound not melodies but atonal constellations of similar timbre. Above that is a visual coherence that is obvious, even if unusual and essential; for if the individual words were arranged in another way, the poem would be different. Distinctions between little and too little are admittedly subtle, if not extremely fine; but sufficient experience with this kind of poetry leads me to regard this particular work among the very best in its mode. (Indeed, most other poetry seems egregiously prolix by comparison.) Incidentally, Coolidge's work also extends radically the Olsonian traditions both of "composition by field" as opposed to lines, and of emphasis upon syllables, rather than rhyme and meter.

Another Coolidge work epitomizes a different kind of poetic reductionism—the poem composed of one and only one un-malleable word which, when read aloud, continually changes not denotatively but connotatively:

> Which, which which which which—
> which which.
> Which which which which,
> which which which which.
>
> Which which which which,
> which which which which which which,
> Which which which which
> which which which which.
>
> Which which which,
> which—which which which.
> Which which which
> which which which which.

The midwestern poet Michael Joseph Phillips has also been obsessed by this form—the repetition of minimal material—along with other experimental structures; the Canadian poet Bill Bissett has used repetition, either of a key phrase written in his personal orthography ("th tempul") or even an entire sentence ("Dinahshoremeetsthocean"), which is distributed with strict regularity but without hyphens or other punctuation through a pyramid shape and then its inversion. Pedro Pietri, mentioned before, has published poems like "The Broken English Dream" which consist entirely of repeated, evocatively-organized punctuation marks whose "Spanish" forms differ from the original English.

Like all genuinely experimental artists, Coolidge accepted the challenge of an inevitable next step—extending his delicate reductionist techniques into longer works; and among the results are two of the most consequential long poems of the past decade: "A D," originally published in *Ing* (1968) and then reprinted in *Space*; and *Suite V,* which appeared in 1972 although it was composed several years before. "A D," begins in the familiar Coolidgean way with stanzas of superficially unrelated lines, but the poetic material is progressively reduced over twenty pages (thereby recapitulating Coolidge's own poetic development in a kind of formalist autobiography) until the poem's final pages contain just vertically ordered fragments of words. *Suite V* is yet more outrageously spartan, containing nothing more than pairs of three-letter words in their plural forms with one four-letter word at the top and the other at the bottom of otherwise blank pages. This poem succeeds brilliantly in my judgment, thanks in part to the consistency imposed by its severely minimal constraint; and though lacking certain virtues of Coolidge's other long poems, such as verbal variety, it clearly ranks among the most awesome works of recent literature. The best introduction to Coolidge's excellence, incidentally, is not *Space* (which suffers from tiny typography), but the third issue of *Big Sky,* a periodical edited by Bill Berkson. While much of Coolidge's work remains unpublished, the work collected in Berkson's periodical is far more various than anywhere else. The collection in *Big Sky* also displays far better than *Space* the extent of Coolidge's poetic intelligence which is revealed not through the complexity of intellectual constructions, but through the remarkable absence of stupidities. It also shows his erudition which is expressed not through allusions but through the scrupulous lack of them, signifying an implicit awareness of styles of poetry that need no longer be done.

III

Returning the word to its status as thing, and us to our senses, is the project of [the] movement. . . . Representation/emotional/intellectual messages in the arts engage attention and obscure the medium. Therefore, to maximize awareness of medium and materials, minimize the message; in poetry, minimize semantic freight. Place up front, where nobody can fail to apprehend, consonants and vowels. Appeal through typography and spacing on page—not taking left-to-right for granted, taking nothing for granted—*first of all* to eyes, ears, the kinetic sense of this momentous act of turning the page. Capture the reader with simplicity and, though one blushes to say it, with beauty. —Alicia Ostriker, "Poem Objects" (1973).

Some of these poems broach visualization and thus the other encompassing inclination of new poetry—into intermedia where words are blended with design, or music, or film, or philosophy, or theater. Since some of these language artists were originally trained in music and the visual arts, their poetry reveals radically different attitudes toward words. The first intermedium, which I have also called "word-imagery," depends primarily upon the visual enhancement of language, so that (given Pound's definition of literature as "language charged with meaning") the layout on the page endows words with poetic connotations that they would not otherwise have. Some visual poems are drawn by hand, occasional sloppiness in draftsmanship signifying their origins as "poetry" (in contrast to the technical slickness of "design"), while others depend upon stencils, rubbed-off letters, special typography, photographic enlargers, and other graphic devices. Some are multicolored while others use only black and white. Some are done with professional collaborators, though most visual poets function as their own artists, typically preferring visual solutions that "designers" would not (or could not) do. Most work primarily with rectangular pages, but a few have made paintings and sculptures. The strategies of visual poetry include imagistic distillation that is mimetic such as my own "Concentric" (1967); non-mimetic enhancement that is nonetheless memorably iconographic, such as Robert Indiana's much-reprinted and much-plagiarized "Love" (1966) or Norman Henry Pritchard's "Peace" (1970); or representational shapes filled with words as in Jonathan Price's "Ice Cream Poem" (1968). What distinguishes these examples, except the last, from most poetry is that visual and verbal perceptions are made simultaneously; so that the poem can be perceived only in its visual form.

This art is winning so many converts that it is impossible to keep track of all the talented new names; almost every issue of the few periodicals predisposed to such work presents a new "discovery." My own list of notable North American visual poets includes Gay Beste Reineck, Tom Ockerse, Bern Porter, Mary Ellen Solt, Ruth Jacoby, Adele Aldridge, Liam O'Gallagher, Aaron Marcus, Gerd Stern, Thomas Merton (just before his premature death), bpNichol, Steve McCaffery, David Uu, Jane Augustine, John Cage, Jos C. Brilliantes, Ed Schlossberg,

```
PPPPPPEEEEEEEEAAAAAACCCCCC EEEEEE
PPPPPPEEEEEEEEAAAAAACCCCCC EEEEEE
PPPPPPEEEEEEEEAAAAAACCCCCC EEEEEE
PPPPPPEEEEEEEEAAAAAACCCCCC EEEEEE
PPPPPPPPPPPPPPPPPPPPPPPPPPPPPPPPPP
PPPPPPEEEEEEEEAAAAAACCCCCC EEEEEE
PPPPPPEEEEEEEEAAAAAACCCCCC EEEEEF
PPPPPPEEEEEEEEAAAAAACCCCCC EEEEEE
PPPPPPEEEEEEEEAAAAAACCCCCC EEEEEE
EEEEEEEEEEEEEEEEEEEEEEEEEEEEEEEEE
PPPPPPEEEEEEEEAAAAAACCCCCC EEEEEE
PPPPPPEEEEEEEEAAAAAACCCCCC EEEEEE
PPPPPPEEEEEEEEAAAAAACCCCCC EEEEEE
PPPPPPEEEEEEEEAAAAAACCCCCC EEEEEE
AAAAAAAAAAAAAAAAAAAAAAAAAAAAAAAA
PPPPPPEEEEEEEEAAAAAACCCCCC EEEEEE
PPPPPPEEEEEEEEAAAAAACCCCCC EEEEEE
PPPPPPEEEEEEEEAAAAAACCCCCC EEEEEE
PPPPPPEEEEEEEEAAAAAACCCCCC EEEEEE
CCCCCCCCCCC CCCCC CCCCCCCCCCC CCCCC
PPPPPPEEEEEEEEAAAAAACCCCCC EEEEEE
PPPPPPEEEEEEEEAAAAAACCCCCC EEEEEE
PPPPPPEEEEEEEEAAAAAACCCCCC EEEEEE
PPPPPPEEEEEEEEAAAAAACCCCCC EEEEEE
EEEEEEEEEEEEE EEEEEEEEEEEEEEEEEEEE
PPPPPPEEEEEEEEAAAAAACCCCCC EEEEEE
PPPPPPEEEEEEEEAAAAAACCCCCC EEEEEE
PPPPPPEEEEEEEEAAAAAACCCCCC EEEEEE
PPPPPPEEEEEEEEAAAAAACCCCCC EEEEEE
```

ice cream
i scream
ice cream

bright
chosen
lucent
sharp

blurred
rounded off
made indefinite
The side
uneven   nubbled
curving   the image   syrup-slow
but willed   the transformation   the taste
jagged   glyceride
eating it   the memory
silent   smirched
magical, one   shimmering
moment only   insatiable

melting
accumulating,
dribbling, about
the shape itself   the cone   to drop
the texture   cardboard
a test   the surface
an admission   sticky as plastic

the recognition   immediate and
deceiving the mind   unknown
the lettering on the rim   trivial
arguing sugar crystals,   enormous
blatant, gummy, broken

licked
the patchwork grill   moist
intensifying   still
curving   firm

outline   yet
curling its   dis-
fingers   appear-
around,   ing
and down

possessing

to draw, to take
in the hand,
to crunch
its one
point

Dana Atchley, Judy Copithorne, Carol Bankerd, Carolyn Sto-loff. Some of them are better known as "painters" (and even "composers"), but their use of language, at minimum, reveals a commitment to poetry. Given all the American resistances to this art, it is scarcely surprising that much of their work so far has appeared in European magazines and that most books of their own work are self-published. "The wonderous thing here," to quote Alicia Ostriker, a lyric poet and Blake scholar, "is simply that absolute fresh experiences can emerge when the word is liberated from its context of phrase and sentence, as if some energy customarily compressed into syntactic forms could be freed like the energy locked into an atom, when that atom is split."

As one kind of poetic intermedium depends upon visualization, sound poetry, another kind, depends upon aural manipulations more typical of music, so that the words heard aloud become radically different from those on the printed page. It is true that all great poetic declamation such as Dylan Thomas' or Allen Ginsberg's reveals an attention to the musicality of poetry; but genuine sound poetry draws upon the musical techniques of rhythm, timbre, and amplitude (loudness) to a yet further degree, poetically charging the words with meanings they would not otherwise have. Customarily chanted rather than sung, this kind of poetry depends primarily upon the sounds made by comprehensible words aurally interacting with each other. A more radical strain, even closer to music, consists of linguistically incomprehensible phonetic sounds that nonetheless *resemble* language (and thus sound superficially like a foreign tongue), such as this excerpt from Armand Schwerner's on-going *The Tablets* (1969, 1971):

> min-na-ne-ne Dingir En-lil-ra mûn-na-nîb-gi-gi
> uzu-mu-a-ki dur-an-ki-ge
> Dingir nagar Dingir nagar im-mân-tag-en-zên
> mu-mud-e-ne nam-lu-galu mu-mu-e-de

The work also incorporates visualization and other innovative devices. (However, if such sounds lack even this much linguistic semblance, the result, even if verbally produced, is *not* sound poetry but abstract music and experienced as such, "concretist" rationalizations to the contrary.) Musical instruments, if used at all, are minimal, such as the single drum accompanying the angry, inflammatory words of Abiodun Oyewole, Alafia Pudim, and Omar Ben Hassen, three New York blacks calling themselves "The Last Poets," who made a spectacular long-playing record. (Words that follow a musical line are experienced as song rather than poetry.) Cage, Pritchard, Giorno, Mac Low, Higgins have all done notable sound poetry, as have such New Yorkers as W. Bliem Kern, CPGraham, and Peter Harleman, as well as Toby Lurie in Santa Barbara, David Franks in Baltimore, bpNichol in Toronto, David Uu in Vancouver, and Byron Gysin in Tangier. Other sound poets depend upon electronic tape manipulations to produce not only collage (that old-fashioned staple) but also echoes and overdubs. The composer Terry Riley has created artistic environments filled with tape-delay systems that pick up the spectator's own words which are then electronically fed back into the environment in stunningly distorted (and yet recognizable) forms. Since printed quotations are insufficient, it is hard to talk about sound poetry without listening to examples which, like so much else in avant-garde art, must be experienced to be believed; and it is unfortunate that American record companies and radio producers are far less hospitable to this new art than comparable Europeans. Another intermedium for poetry is film, and among the notable American film-makers working poetically with words are Stan Van-DerBeek, Hollis Frampton, and Paul Sharits.

Much that seems at first to be "anti-poetry" is, instead, a radically different kind of literary expression that must be regarded as "poetry" because it cannot be defined as anything else (narrow definitions of anything as indefinable by definition as "poetry" are especially ludicrous). Though echoing the neglected eccentricities of the Dada poets, the Russian futurists, e. e. cummings (rather than Pound or Eliot), the new poetries define their current separateness by a complete rejection of some (and only some) aspects of most earlier poetry. Similar to avant-garde milestones in other contemporary arts, radically new poetry tends to emphasize one dimension at the expense (or neglect) of others. If exploiting all the possible suggestiveness of language was one of poetry's traditional motives, then the radical form that I call empirical poetry echoes a central theme of modern philosophy by completely exorcising such resonances, implicitly raising the old question of whether poetry can be as "true" as physics. It strives to offer nothing more than

MARCH 31, 1966   by Dan Graham

1,000,000,000,000,000,000,000,000.00000000 miles to edge of known universe

100,000,000,000,000,000,000.00000000 miles to edge of galaxy (Milky Way)

3,573,000,000.00000000 miles to edge of solar system (Pluto)

205.00000000 miles to Washington, D.C.

2.85000000 miles to Times Square, New York City

.38600000 miles to Union Square subway stop

.11820000 miles to corner of 14th Street and First Avenue

.00367000 miles to front door of Apartment 1D, 153 First Avenue

.00000700 miles to lens of glasses

.00000098 miles to cornea from retinal wall

unadulterated, verifiable information and yet generate that language-created mystery we call "poetic." A similar esthetic motive informs much minimal sculpture such as those pieces which attempt to expunge shapes (even "abstract" ones) of their traditional suggestiveness. It is indicative that the author of the classic example of empirical poetry, Dan Graham's "March 31, 1966," was himself an early theorist of that new artistic direction. If Kenneth Gangemi's chosen facts are highly suggestive, the lines of Graham's poem remain doggedly factual, nonetheless conveying poetically an overwhelming sense of man's small scale in the cosmos. Although poetry made in this way draws upon compositional techniques that could be called "impersonal," the best examples of this style inevitably reveal, especially to a knowledgeable audience, an artistic signature that is highly personal.

Historically, minimal sculpture led to what I have elsewhere called "situational sculpture" where rather minimalistic objects are placed in ways that enhance or reflect their surrounding space, the work of art thus encompassing both the object and its situation, as well as relations between. It is assumed that apart (or once removed) from its appropriate space the sculpture is incomplete—a mere concept demanding realization. The prime poetic example of this powerful esthetic idea is Dan Graham's "Schema," originally conceived in 1966 and first published in 1967 a year or two before the flowering of situational sculpture:

(number of)	adjectives
(number of)	adverbs
(percentage of)	area not occupied by type
(percentage of)	area occupied by type
(number of)	columns
(number of)	conjunctions
(number of)	depressions of type into surface of page
(number of)	gerunds
(number of)	infinitives
(number of)	letters of alphabet
(number of)	lines
(number of)	mathematical symbols
(number of)	nouns
(number of)	numbers

(number of)	participles
(perimeter of)	page
(weight of)	paper sheet
(type)	paper stock
(thinness of)	paper stock
(number of)	prepositions
(number of)	pronouns
(number of point)	size type
(name of)	typeface
(number of)	words
(number of)	words capitalized
(number of)	words italicized
(number of)	words not capitalized
(number of)	words not italicized

The data required by the scheme should be deduced from the page on which the work is printed, the work's publisher ideally inserting the accurate information in the left-hand column of a second page in which the right-hand column of items is reprinted; that second page becomes both a self-portrait, so to speak, of itself and an individual variant of the original scheme. (The crucial point is that these variations are not determined by personal choice as in the Higgins poem, but by verifiable measurement of the physical situation in which the poem is printed.) As Graham puts it, the scheme exists "only as information, deriving its value from the specific contingencies related to its placement on the two-dimensional surface (or medium) upholding their appearance." All correctly published versions represent, therefore, a collaboration—not only between the immutable schema and the variable page on which it is printed, but also between the poet and the book's production specialist. (It would follow, therefore, that the scheme quoted before remains incomplete; for unlike suggestive poetry, but like comparable sculpture, situational work demands its realization.)

The new theatrical poetry surpasses both "dramatic readings," with performers sitting stiffly on stools, and even that archaic (and somewhat decadent) form of a one-man literary recital; for poetic performances, as I shall call them, are theatrical events in which some-time poets (that fact alone establishing an esthetic context) turn essentially poetic impulses into performances.

Vito Acconci, who began as a poet, art critic, and translator (and even took his *pro forma* M.F.A. at Iowa), developed a self-conscious disinterest in vocabulary, progressing through poems composed primarily of unfilled parentheses or of snippets found in newspapers and other public print, to poetry revealing mechanical operations in the counter-syntactical handling of words and sometimes just letters. One 350-line poem, for instance, was distributed one line per page over 350 separate sheets of papers which were then bound into 350 copies of Acconci's otherwise uniform magazine, *0 to 9.* Another work reproduced only those letters along the vertical margins of selected pages of *Roget's Thesaurus.* He then progressed to empirical lists simply itemizing events in his own experience; but by this point he realized, "There were no clues to where I wanted to go in any poetry I read."

The obvious next step led Acconci out of words into empiricist presentations of himself and his own physical processes, the themes of his performances clearly growing out of his poetic ideas. In *Performance Test* (1969), he stared at each member of the audience for fifteen seconds apiece, while *Breathing Space* (1970) consisted of nothing more than himself and another man deep-breathing into amplified microphones, thereby exposing the characteristic timbres and rhythms of that essential form of human expression (and yet suggesting nothing more than breathing). Treating himself as material whose "vocabulary" can be turned to expressive uses, Acconci has created a series of stunning, self-obsessive (if not masochistic), conceptually indefinable performances that have won him international acclaim. His post-poetic evolution was best documented not in a poetry magazine, to be sure, but a recent issue of a new art journal, *Avalanche* (Fall, 1972).

The crucial point is that just as one extreme, miscegenated possibility for 1960's painters was the rejection of painting for other forms of art (including at times the use of language), so the freedom available to the poet today includes the rejection of words for all kinds of activities that, at their best and truest, reveal their author's origins (and thus the work's context) in poetry. Pieces of this kind, like most other forms of new poetry, are also more international than earlier verse, since they offer much less resistance to the perennial problems of translation. (And some would seem to repudiate Paul Verlaine's haughty motto: "To be understood is the worst disaster.") The new poetries also tend to be less egotistical as most of them avoid self-projection and other pretenses of "sensitivity" (while the authors are themselves less egomaniacal), for its creative processes are primarily not expressionist but constructivist, as well as classically self-restrained. Most of this poetry is non-objective, to use a critical term developed in the criticism of modernist painting, as the works emphasize properties intrinsic in the art while references to outside phenomena are either implicit or unintended. Many kinds of new poetry reflect both advanced ideas in music (i.e., permutational form) and in visual art; and not only are some of its creators also proficient in nonliterary arts, but a knowledge of current concerns in those fields is partially prerequisite to contemporary poetic literacy. A final point is that the new poetries represent not "games with language," to quote a standard objection, but genuine explorations of alternative communication forms that are as linguistically meaningful as poetry has always been.

Since the new poetries described here are all but totally unknown to the larger reading public, sympathetic critics feel obliged, for now, primarily to introduce what might later be discussed with more subtlety and discrimination. These poets testify that a profound faith in what they do, the interest of intelligent Europeans, and the energy gained from hard-won artistic triumphs, as well as the radical's instinctive commitment to change, all keep their poetic adventure going. Perhaps the fate of literature's future depends, to a degree, upon the public fortunes of post-symbolic, post-expressionistic, post-collage poetries. What does not evolve is imperiled.

18 Innovations in Fictions, Dramas, Essays

I

In reply, I should like to point out that in dealing with *new* things there is a question that precedes that of good or bad. I refer to the question, "What is it?"—the question of identity. To answer this question in such a way as to distinguish between a real novelty and a fake one *is itself an evaluation,* perhaps the primary one for criticism in this revolutionary epoch when art, ideas, mass movements, keep changing their nature, so that their most familiar features are often the most misleading. —Harold Rosenberg, *The Tradition of the New* (1960).

Literature often becomes superficially or inorganically conventional. This usually happens when it follows the narrowing dialectic of a cultural elite belonging to a class which is culturally ascendant but is losing its social effectiveness. . . . The original writer in such a situation is likely to do something that will be decried by this elite as vulgar, and hailed by a later generation as turning from literary convention to experience. . . . It is difficult to think of any new and startling development in literature that has not bestowed glass slippers and pumpkin coaches on some subliterary Cinderella. —Northrop Frye, "Nature and Homer" (1958).

A myth dominant in the fifties and taught as well to its "creative" children said that everything imaginative had already been done—that Art had come to an end through the exhaustion of intrinsic possibilities; but the great truth of artistic modernism, especially reaffirmed in the late sixties, is that there need be no end to experiment and innovation in any of the arts. Genuine stylistic leaps in literature continue to be made, representing imaginative possibilities that no one has seen before, for creative motives as old as man will always generate radically unprecedented forms. Just as James Joyce's elaborately detailed portrait of one man in a metropolis—a subject typical of naturalism—eventually took a counter-naturalistic style, so the innovative fictions discussed in this chapter echo traditional fictional concerns and yet, in crucial respects, scarcely resemble ninety-nine percent of the fictions we have already known.

Not all that is new is automatically good, of course; and just as some alternative developments will prove more fertile than others, now as well as in retrospect, so certain examples of a new artistic direction are better than most, and some new styles will inevitably have a more commanding influence upon artists and discriminating audiences than others. (And weak innovations may have a subsidiary virtue of suggesting, if not directly stimulating, stronger possibilities.) Nonetheless, the crucial rule in the serious appraisal or analysis of any new art is, to repeat, that only the best examples count, for anything less than first-rate work will be as surely forgotten as the bulk of Elizabethan theater.

One measure of contemporary excellence is the capacity to inspire in the reader, especially an experienced one, that rare and humbling awe that here before one's eyes is something that is quite different from what has gone before, and yet intrinsically successful and fine. Since the aim of creation in our time is to make a crucial contribution that extends an established artistic concern, nearly all attempts to create a "masterpiece for our time" succumb to those academic rules which are honored only between snickers of embarrassment. In truth, the dynamics of artistic change undermine the masterpiece-mentality.

Literary innovations not only expand the vocabulary of human communication, but they also inspire controversy that revives what might otherwise be moribund, thus making artists aware of neglected byways in their respective traditions. In practice, distinctly new fictions usually reject or ignore the recently dominant preoccupations of literature to draw selectively upon unmined or unfashionable strains of earlier work, recording an esthetic indebtedness that may not be immediately apparent. Thanks to innovative fiction, otherwise neglected precedents such as those forged by Gertrude Stein are revived in literature's collective memory. Furthermore, new works tend to draw upon materials and structures previously considered beneath or beyond fiction, in addition to new developments in the other arts. Many of them articulate fresh social and scientific understandings, in addition to levels of consciousness that reflect, say, the influence of hallucinogenic drugs. Some of this new work is apt to be dismissed as "not-fiction," but once again it is necessary to point out that "fiction" includes any work of man that descends from fictional concerns or resembles previous fiction more than anything else. Its authors are "fictioners," to coin a necessary generic term for writers of both novels and stories (or works in between). This stylistically new literature suffers at its beginnings from a minuscule audience and critical neglect, for it is unlikely that even ten percent of the works discussed in the following pages are familiar to readers (and perhaps the editors) of the esthetically conservative reviewing media—*The New York Times Book Review, The Saturday Review,* or *The New York Review of Books.*

The milestones in contemporary fiction are those stylistic positions that, though puzzling at first, now seem increasingly easy to understand and even imitate. One is the creation of an unusual narrative voice or voices, a technique spectacularly realized in the classic fictions of William Faulkner and Ford Madox Ford, but also informing the more recent novelistic monologues of Saul Bellow, John Hawkes, and Philip Roth, as well as most of Donald Barthelme's shorter stories (nearly all of these works take as their subject the madness or "vision" of their protagonists). However, since first-person narrators no longer provide problematic reading experiences, novels conceived in this form can become best-sellers. (Indeed, creating a fictitious voice nowadays is a favorite exercise in sophisticated fiction workshops which typically teach not "how to write," but how literature has recently been written.) A second milestone appropriates the poetic-painterly technique of collage-composition and applies it to fiction either as shrewdly placed juxtapositions, as in Michel Butor's magnificent *Mobile* (1963), or through the more random "cut-up" technique of William Burroughs. Successful examples of both methods display a narrative line more various and jagged than previous fictions and, at times, a realized multiple perspective, in addition to a continuity of style and vision that transcends the sharply discontinuous surface.

383

The stories of Jorge Luis Borges and Vladimir Nabokov's *Pale Fire* epitomize a third position, defined by turning the forms and trappings of literary scholarship into ironic fiction—a style that has influenced John Barth and Ronald Sukenick, among others. Physically separate words and images constitute a fourth fictional milestone whose tradition dates back at least as far as Kenneth Patchen's *The Journal of Albion Moonlight* (1944); and both Donald Barthelme's captioned prints and R. Crumb's beloved anti-comix are still, in form as well as contents, essentially funny books, differences in motives and imagery notwithstanding. Fiction's principal new structure in the early sixties was the scrupulously flat work in which the standard inflections of narrative are eschewed as the story simply goes on and on, all of its parts, whether paragraphs or just sentences, contributing equally to the whole. Generally dealing with social absurdity, these works come to conclusions that seem intrinsically arbitrary. The major influence here was Samuel Beckett's novels, though an earlier precursor, actually concerned with something else (ostinato repetition), was Gertrude Stein's *The Making of Americans* (originally written in 1906-12). A more recent gem in this mode, Kenneth Gangemi's *Olt* (1969), portrays a certain psychopathology; yet by the seventies, this strictly flat narrative form seems more past than present, as, incidentally, are the French "new novel" explorations in phenomenal perception.

Another early classic, Joyce's *Finnegans Wake*, holds a singular position because its multi-lingual techniques continue to be widely misunderstood, rarely imitated, and never exceeded—the closest approximation being *Fa:m' Ahniesgwow* (1959), a predictably neglected and unexported polyglottal book-plus-record by the German polymathic critic Hans G. Helms; and for these reasons, among others, the *Wake* still seems the great unsurpassable achievement of literary modernism. In short, the greatest fictions of recent decades establish several definite, post-realist positions that can in turn successfully classify most other prominent works of lesser rank. When Philip Roth charged, in the early sixties, that fiction could scarcely compete as imaginative experience with the far-fetched "realities" found in American newspapers, he was really judging, it is now clear, the prosaic quality of fictional ideas and fiction-reading at that time.

The past decade also witnessed numerous experiments with

alternative forms of literary coherence such as ellipses analogous
to the associational form of post-Poundian poetry. Here is a
passage from "Idaho" (1962), a short fiction by the poet John
Ashbery:

> Carol laughed. Among other things,
>   till I've finished it. It's the reason of
> dropped into Brentano's.
>   get some of the
> a pile of these. I just grabbed one...
>   —Oh, by the way, there's a tele-
> "See?" She pointed to the table.

Between the rather crystalline fragments is implied much of the
fiction's unclear action. This elliptical technique is extended to
novelistic length in Willard Bain's *Informed Sources* (1969) and
G. S. Gravenson's far superior fiction, *The Sweetmeat Saga*
(1971), in which the fragments are splayed rectilinearly across
the manuscript page. (Both books, curiously, draw heavily upon
the elliptical language of wire services, and both depend so
much upon the typography of typewriters that their manuscripts were photographed rather than typeset for final publication—their typing incidentally revealing far more of the authorial hand than normal typography.) Other examples of
recent prose that seem acoherent represent attempts to use
words to transcend language largely for unusual perceptual
effects; but the master of this fictional motive, as well as for
much other formal invention, remains Gertrude Stein—not only
in the unabridged *The Making of Americans,* which is considerably different from the short paperback edition, but also in
Geography and Plays (1922) and her posthumously published
Painted Lace (1955), all of which serve contemporary fiction
much as Pound's *Cantos* inadvertently stands to poetry today—
as a compendium of pioneering techniques that need no longer
be done. In practice, the acknowledgment of definite milestones
makes the forging of new art not only more necessary but also
more possible, for only by knowing exactly what has already
been done can the fictionalizing artist create, or the critical
reader discern, something radically new.

Whereas poetry usually strives for concentration and stasis,
fiction, by contrast, creates a universe of circumscribed activity
which may be human or naturalistic, imagistic or merely lin-

guistic; within fictional art there is generally some kind of movement from one place to another. Precisely by containing diversity and change within an encompassing frame does fiction differ from poetry; for, as Marvin Mudrick noted, "In the beginning of poetry is the word; in the beginning of fiction is the event." For this reason, fiction has favored sequential forms, as the difference between the material on one page and its successors (and predecessors) generates the work's internal life. For instance, a single page of visual poetry might stand as a picture or a "word-image," but such frames in sequence begin to evoke a fictional world not evident in one alone. Nonetheless, a linear reading experience is not a necessary characteristic of fiction, as many innovative books like the *Wake* are best dipped into, rather than read from beginning to end. Also, certain examples of new fiction are very short, some just a single page in length, others just a single line such as this by Toby MacLennan:

> He existed as a perfect sphere and rolled
> from room to room.

For even within an isolated space can sometimes be compressed a comprehensive world of artistic activity that is ultimately more fictional than poetic. (Many of these very short stories are unfortunately published and even anthologized as "prose poems," inadvertently blurring the necessary distinction between fictional fabrication and essentially poetic expression.) By and large, these general distinctions separate nearly all literary creations, though I can think of several, such as Armand Schwerner's *The Tablets* (1969, 1971), that straddle my categories, largely by mixing poetic forms with aspirations more typical of fiction.

II

> The real technical question seems to be how to succeed not even Joyce and Kafka, but those who've succeeded Joyce and Kafka and are now in the evenings of their own careers. —John Barth, "The Literature of Exhaustion" (1967).

New fictions like new poetries can be divided into those that deal only with the traditional materials of the medium and those that intermingle with other arts. As the roots of fiction have been non-metered language and ways of structuring it into narrative forms, one sure measure of originality in fiction is luminous prose that is genuinely unlike anything written before, such as the elliptical writing of bpNichol in his *Two Novels* (1969):

> lay on his bed and gazed at the desk ties below the level he'd existed on body becoming his falling into her river joining every motion she made merely his own body entering himself loving noone but himself hating himself because his body wasn't his tho she had made her body his alive inside himself blobby mass of her breasts swaying against his chest choking mamma mamma steam rising

Or this inventive pornography from Ed Sanders' *Shards of God* (1970):

> He prayed over the sexual lubricant in the alabaster jar and swirled his cock directly into it, signaling to one of the air corps volunteers to grab her ankles as he oiled himself up like a hustler chalking a pool cue. He fucked this way, in the anklegrab position, until he heard the starter's gun, at which point he whirled about, faced the bed, and leaped up into the air toward it, executing a forward one-and-a-half somersault with a full twist and landed on all fours on the mattress, ready to grope.

Whereas Nichol and Sanders generally favor familiar vocabularies, a more obvious stylistic originality comes from the simulated Africanisms of William Melvin Kelley's *Dunfords Travels Everywheres* (1970):

> They ramparded, that reimberserking evolutionary band, toring tend, detiring waygone, until that foolephant (every litre having a flow) humpened to pass Misory Shutchill's open wide oh to be, and glanzing in, unpocked his trunk, GONG to D-chel (musically)

Or by Joycean overlappings of Kenneth King's "Print-Out" (1967):

> meanWHYle the JESTurer, danSING the E of e-MOTION, exSKULLclAIMed that ba(SICK)ly the d-REAMS are ex-CELLcenterIC, CRYPTOprogrammethODDical para-BABBLES and that the germMANIC traDICTION is RE:sPONDERsibyl for his being pHAZY on hiSTORYical phoneOMENona. It SEAMS HE FOUND doc(CURED)-meants which TESTEfy that the QUEEN HAD A HIS-TORY(ECHO)TOMY, and PERSONA-ally sHEHE'HEds HESSEtant and not very optimimiMYSITC a-BOUT the FEWture.

Critical praise of inventive language needs no more support than an extended citation; but discussions of structural innovation in fiction are more problematic in an essay this short.

Innovative art nowadays tends to be either much more or much less, in terms of quantity of information (words and/or events in space), than art has previously been; and if *Finnegans Wake* represents an epitome of linguistic abundance, creating so many words out of a rather hackneyed subject (familial conflict), the contrary motive, analogous to minimalism in painting and sculpture, endeavors to tell a story with far fewer words than before, as well as avoiding the familiar perils of standard paragraphs. Sections of Gangemi's two-page "Change" (1969), initially published in his collection of "poetry," make huge leaps with every new line (if not, at times, with every new word), typically compressing great hunks of narrative experience into succinct notations:

> White face and red whiskers
> Red face and white whiskers

Or:

> Prophase
> Metaphase
> Anaphase
> Telophase

All of his short, uninflected lists vividly illustrate the fiction's announced subject. Bill Knott's "No-Act Play" (1971) tells a less definable story in a few physically separate lines, while my own "Milestones in a Life" (1971) uses one word (or occasionally two) to define the important events in the life of a fictitious successful American:

0 birth
1 teeth
2 walk

It begins on the left side of the page, concluding with columns that creep to the right:

76 measles
77 death

Certain pieces superficially similar to "suggestive poetry" are closer to fiction because in only a few words they suggest a narrative action rather than a static event. An example is Steve Kaltenbach's

Perpetuate a hoax

which was first published in 1969. The pages of Emmett Williams' pioneering novel, *Sweethearts* (1967), represent another kind of minimalism, consisting only of that title word which is subject to sequential typographic variations that evoke a heterosexual relationship. Reduced fictions are not synonymous with very short stories, for example Russell Edson's very fine miniatures or the anecdotes comprising John Cage's "Indeterminacy" (1958), both of which contain conventionally structured sentences and paragraphs.

Some new fictional forms depend upon material or structures taken from outside literature. In a witty pastiche that successfully masks its collage-composition, Frederic Tuten's *The Adventures of Mao on the Long March* (1971) mixes paragraphs of conventional historical narrative with fictitious incidents such as Greta Garbo propositioning Mao, and such extrinsic material as verbatim (but unidentified) quotations from a variety of literary sources (Hawthorne, Melville, Wilde, Jack London, Marx-Engels). Exploiting not only nonfictional materials but a nonliterary structure, Jan Herman's brilliant *General Municipal Election* (1969) takes the format of an elaborate election ballot which fills the 12″ by 24″ space with fictional (and sometimes satirical) choices, while John Barth's "Frame-Tale" (1968) must be cut from the book and then folded and pasted into a Moebius strip (an endless geometrical surface) that reads, "Once upon a time there was story that began" in an interminable circle. The extended masterwork in this mode is Richard Horn's novel, *Encyclopedia* (1969), in which alphabetized notations (filled with cross-references worth following) weave an ambiguous fiction about human interrelationships, paradoxically disordering by reordering; and this novel, like many other examples of new fiction, deliberately frustrates the bourgeois habit of continuous reading. One might say that both the rectangular page and the process of turning pages are as essential to fiction as prose and narrative form; but if the reader must skip around so much, how can he tell whether he has "finished the book"?

Several writers have considered the richly suggestive idea of an imaginative work whose parts can be interchangeably ordered like cards in a pack; however, the masterpiece in this mode has yet to arrive. *Composition No. 1* (1963) by the Frenchman Marc Saporta suffers from the semblance of a linear plot that must be pieced together; and the more pages one reads, the fuller becomes one's sense of Saporta's characters. It would seem that the form of interchangeable parts is more conducive to an absolutely uninflected work, all of whose discrete sections would have equal weight within the whole. Although the materials of *Shufflebook* (1971), a juvenile by Richard Hefter and Martin Stephen Moskof, are structurally more appropriate—one side of the cards containing "and the [name of an animal]" and the other side just verbs—the combinations are invariably slick and trivial. (Like other card fictions, this one can be played alone or in conjunction with others.) The only recent novel I know whose parts, mostly a page or two in length, can be read in any order is Marvin Cohen's *A Self-Devoted Friend* (1967) which was inappropriately published as a hard-bound book. Henry James Korn's "The Pontoon Manifesto" (1970), published in conventional form in the third issue of *US*, consists of thirty-six fictional beginnings which can theoretically be read in any order (and are, appropriately, printed on cards that can be shuffled).

Another of the supremely inventive recent novels, Madeline Gins' *Word Rain* (1969), also ranks among the most difficult, dealing with the epistemological opacity of language itself. The first sign of the book's unusual concerns and its equally special humor is its extended subtitle: "(or A Discursive Introduction to the Philosophical Investigations to G,R,E,T,A,G,A,R,B,O, It Says)"; a second is the incorporation of several concerns of new fiction—special languages, expressive design, extrinsically imposed form. Perhaps the surest indication of this novel's originality was the nearly total neglect of reviewers with the exception of Hayden Carruth who sneered in *New American Review* at fictioners' "fooling away their talents in endless novelistic puzzles, a pastime which seems to have reached an ultimate reduction—I hope it's ultimate—in *Word Rain* by Madeline Gins."

"The saddest thing is that I have to use words," announces the narrator, not only echoing the opening sentence of Ford Madox Ford's fictional study of human opacity, *The Good Soldier* (1915), but also exemplifying that Gertrude Steinian paradox of using language to reveal the limitations of both language and the reading process. This last theme of linguistic opacity is reiterated in every section rather than developed in a cumulative way, suggesting that the indicatively unpaginated book is best read in snatches as opposed to straight through. That method (which is also the book's subject) is revealed through a variety of opaque styles; but some of the passages remain more illuminating, if not more definite, than others:

> Each word on the page seemed ossified. The word face was a stone. The word guess was a flint. The words a, the, in, by, up, it, were pebbles. The word laughter was marble. Run was cartilage. Shelf was bone. Talk was an oak board. See was made of quartz. The word refrigerator was enameled. The word afternoon was concrete. The word iron was iron. The word help was wrought-iron. The word old was crag. The word touch was brick. The word read was mica and I was granite.

The book's pages are also distinguished by numerous inventive displays of printed material—lists of unrelated words with dots between them, whole sides filled mostly with dashes where words might otherwise be, pseudo-logical proofs, passages in which the more mundane expressions are crossed out, an appen-

391

dix of "some of the words (temporary definitions) not included," even a photographed hand holding both sides of a printed page, and a concluding page of print-over-print which reads at its bottom: "This page contains every word in the book." *Word Rain* suffers from the perils of its theme—a linguistic resistance that prevents most readers from discovering its purposes and from entering its imaginative world. That is also a principal fault of Frederick Barthelme's comparable, though lesser effort, *War and War* (1971); but for now, Gins's work stands as a touchstone of innovative prose.

III

> Literature seems to be intermediate between music and painting; its words form rhythms which approach a musical sequence of sounds at one of its boundaries, and form patterns which approach the hieroglyphic or pictorial image at the other. The attempts to get as near to these boundaries as possible form the main body of what is called experimental writing. —Northrop Frye, "The Archetypes of Literature" (1951).

The other strain of new fiction resembles certain parts of *Word Rain* in mixing fictional concerns with materials and techniques from the other arts. Visualization is probably a more feasible kind of miscegenation than sound-fiction which only a few writers, including Norman Henry Pritchard II and W. Bliem Kern, have broached. In the other fictional intermedium, visual dimensions are not auxiliary to language as in certain Wright Morris photographic works, but entwined within the verbal material as in word-image poetry. In Nancy Weber's "Dear Mother and Dad" (1970), a rather prosaic tale of the narrator's breakdown is brilliantly enhanced by photographically reproduced handwriting that expressively changes (and thus interprets the language) in the course of the four-page story; so that without this visual dimension the fiction would be unremarkable. In Pritchard's "Hoom" (1970), two-page spreads filled entirely with "sh" are punctuated by a progressively increasing number of spreads with other kinds of wordless typographical arrangements. And "Oab," by Robert Zend, a Canadian born in Hungary, brilliantly mixes poems and prose in various typographies with even more various designs.

In Raymond Federman's masterpiece, *Double or Nothing* (1971), a form is established for each page—usually a visual shape but sometimes a grammatical device such as omitting all the verbs—and the words of his fiction fill the allotted structure. Over these individually defined pages, which reveal an unfaltering capacity for formal invention, he weaves several sustained preoccupations, including the narrator's immigration to America, his poverty, his obsessive memories, his parsimonious passion for noodles. In *Double or Nothing,* as in much other visual fiction, the page itself is the basic narrative unit, superseding the paragraph or the sentence, as the work as a whole becomes a succession of extremely distinctive, interrelated pages. No other "novel" looks like Federman's contemporary reworking of Kafka's *Amerika,* which was written fifty years before; none of the other visual fictions is quite so rich in traditional sorts of content. Reflecting this new sense of fictional unit, several otherwise less substantial recent novels incorporate reproductions of a typewritten manuscript (Earl Conrad's *Typoo* [1969]); full-page graphics (Steve Katz's *The Exagggerations of Peter Prince* [1967] and Eugene Wildman's *Nuclear Love* [1972]); and also blank pages and totally black ones, the latter two usually signifying the absence of action or an extended, otherwise undefinable pause.

Predominantly visual fictions emulate the structure of the film in the sequential development of related images with or without words; but even in totally visual stories, the narrative exposition is far more selective and concentrated than in film and so is the audience's perceptual experience and subsequent memory of the work. Many stories that are primarily or exclusively pictorial strive to implant what artists call an "after-image"—a sense of the whole that is visually embedded in the viewer's mind long after he has experienced the work; for in this process the medium of printed pages can be more selective and concentrated than film. However, since visual fictions, unlike film, cannot simulate the experience of time, much of the "story" and nearly all of its elapsed duration occurs *between* the fiction's frames.

The best of Duane Michals' wordless photographic *Sequences* (1970) is a set of six pictures collectively entitled "The Lost Shoe," the first showing a deserted urban street with the fuzzy backside of a man walking away from the camera and up the street. In the second frame he drops on the pavement a blurred object which in the third frame is seen to be a lady's shoe; and this frame, as well as the next two, suggests that he departs up the street in a great hurry. In the sixth frame the man is nowhere to be seen, while the shoe is mysteriously on fire. The realism of all the photographs starkly contrasts with the mysteriousness of the plot, while the large changes between frames accent the absolute immobility of the camera. For this last reason, the authorial perspective is as Chekhovian as both the work's title and its passive acceptance of something inexplicably forbidding; and although "The Lost Shoe" could conventionally be classified as a photographic sequence, its ultimate impact is decidedly fictional and, as fiction, is very fine and clearly new.

M. Vaughn-James, an English artist living in Canada, has produced two book-length, line-drawn narratives that superficially resemble the comics but are far more profound and difficult, depending less upon language than pictures in sequence. The first, *Elephant* (1970), seems a prelude to *The Projector* (1971), a superior work, whose 8½" by 11" pages contain rectangular images of various sizes—one, two, four, or six to a page, or one across two pages. These frames, usually devoid of words, articulate a horrifying, almost surreal vision that is finally more bookish than cinematic. *Crackers* (1969), by the Los Angeles painter Edward Ruscha, tells a story almost entirely in photographs which are set on every right-hand page, occasionally accompanied by captions on the left. Perhaps because the pictures all have the same size and each is rather closely related to both its predecessor and successor, while the textures of the photographs seem reminiscent of old movies (and the captions printed on the left echo the silents), *Crackers* seems far closer to film—one wants to flip the pages—yet it is still a book. Eleanor Antin's *100 Boots*, begun in 1970, is an epistolary serial whose parts are picture post cards which she mails once a fortnight. In each frame, 100 boots are deployed in various settings, the herd of shoes assuming a life of their own in the course of an extended narrative that will, upon its completion, hopefully be bound into a book.

Other visual fictions differ from "The Lost Shoe" by compressing all of their material into a single page—those of Lee DeJasu and Norman Ogue Mustill—or by their total abstractness, presenting just a sequence of related shapes. In Marian Zazeela's "Lines" (1969) are five pages of related meditative shapes that become more complex for four pages prior to a delicate resolution on the fifth; Jesse Reichek's *etcetera* (1965) is an unpaginated succession of abstract black and white shapes, superficially resembling Rorschach blobs, that echo and complement each other for sixty frames, all presented without any preface or explanation. The progress seems at times symbolic of a descent, but the frames remain largely loyal to their own terms of abstract narration. In this and similar pieces, "Form *is* content, content *is* form," to quote Samuel Beckett's classic remark about *Finnegans Wake,* for both of these dimensions are by necessity experienced simultaneously. And visual fiction can articulate kinds of stories and perceptions—and offer kinds of "reading" experiences—simply unavailable to prose. This is not to say that one picture is worth a thousand words—that's usually nonsense—but that kinds of statements can best be made in images alone. Though the old forms of story-telling may be "dead," the impulse to create something new remains doggedly alive, especially in those works that invent fiction twice over—not only its material but its form.

IV

"Artist" refers to a person willfully enmeshed in the dilemma of categories, who performs as if none of them existed. . . . The contemporary artist is not out to supplant recent modern art with a better kind; *he wonders what art might be.* —Allan Kaprow, "O.K." (1966).

New directions in playwrighting have moved not only beyond theatrical realism but beyond the established conventions of Broadway, off-Broadway, off-off Broadway, and regional-academic theaters. These pioneering breakthroughs can likewise be divided into those that mingle with other media, creating what I call mixed-means events, and plays that emphasize imaginative possibilities in written texts. Among the more interesting young American creators of mixed-means theater are Robert Wilson (a.k.a. "Byrd Hoffman"), Kenneth King, Dick Higgins, and Meredith Monk, all of whom have also written scenarios and/or verbal accompaniments to their conceptually innovative pieces, for literacy is incorporated into this new theater rather than, as some have charged, excluded completely from it. By emphasizing physical instructions, say, instead of dramatic dialogue, these scripts are designed to generate radically different kinds of performance that must be seen and heard to be understood, rather than merely read.

Out of this polyartistic tradition also came another kind of radical theater: performances primarily for oneself that the reader could (and should) do on his own. When set to print, scenarios for these events resemble mixed-means instructions in their emphasis upon physical directives which are ultimately reduced to a single action. An example is Dick Higgins' "Gång-sång" (1963) which reads in its entirety:

> One foot forward. Transfer weight to this foot. Bring other
> foot forward. Transfer weight to this foot. Repeat as often
> as desired.

A more complicated epitome is "Mirror" (1963) by Chieko Shiomi, a Japanese musician then living in America:

> Stand on the sandy beach with your back to the sea.
> Hold a mirror in front of your face and look into it.
> Step back to the sea and enter into the water.

Some of these scenarios verge upon suggestive poetry simply because they are not feasible, such as her "Event for the Twilight" (1963):

> Steep a piano in the water of a pool.
> Play some piece of F. Liszt on the piano.

Writing of this sort became a speciality of the Fluxus movement, a loose post-Dada collaborative with alliances abroad, whose achievements have all but totally escaped the historians of art and literature.

Those doing distinctly innovative work as "playwrights" include Ronald Tavel, whose "theater of the ridiculous" realizes an absurd vision in an extremely witty style full of obsessive punning; Jackson Mac Low, whose scripts-for-performance depend upon chance operations and other counter-syntactical structures; Michael Kirby, who has also functioned as an essen-

tial historian-critic of this kind of theater; and Richard Foreman, whose doggedly abstract scripts eschew exposition, dramatic conflict, character psychology, and other standard audi-
ence-enticements in a radical exploration of alternative kinds of
theatrical coherence. "What, you may ask, can a play be after it
has been stripped bare of these elements?" the critic P. Adams
Sitney notes of Foreman's work: "The revelation of a series of
states of being, or a single static state of being presented from a
series of slightly modified perspectives." Early texts in Foreman's highly abstract style, such as *Angelface* (1968) and *Ida-
Eyed* (1969), depended in performance upon his own director-
ial talents for their coherences of imagery and rhythm—qualities
even more evident in the mixed-means extravagance of *Elephant
Steps* (1968); but by *Total Recall* (1970) even these theatrically
appealing dimensions were eliminated in what seemed to be an
uncompromising attempt to present a viably "untheatrical"
theater.

Another step in visual literature is, of course, the creation of
not just a story but an entire book about a single subject or
upon a single theme—an essay, so to speak, about the outside
world, in contrast to the fabrications of fiction. It is not
surprising that young artists doing books of this kind tend to
practice other arts as well and that initially non-literary artists
doing various kinds of exposition should find printed pages
more appropriate than other media. In order to present his
recent work in criticism, poetry, mixed-means performance, and
drawing, Dick Higgins hit upon the idea of an imitation prayer
book with four separate columns of type. Since his four interests are respectively distributed over the four columns of
Foew&ombwhnw (1969), the concerns of one can be compared
with the others and the presentational form itself suits the
variousness of his endeavors. The technique is fundamentally
that of collage, here used more for complementariness than
stark juxtapositions. This sort of book-syntax also informs J
Marks's *Rock and Other Four-Letter Words* (1968), which brilliantly mixes a great variety of visual and printed materials over
256 pages. Between the covers of this multiple perspective upon
rock is a wealth of imaginative design, not only of individual
pages but also of pages in sequence.

Since collage, the great syntactical innovation of early modernism, remains the prime bugaboo haunting all extended literary forms, the initial achievement of Ed Ruscha's several self-published books was his avoidance of this compositional crutch. They tend to be organized as a series of photographs upon a single theme, such as gas stations in the American West or apartment houses in Southern California. *Thirty-Four Parking Lots* (1967), probably the best of them, consists of early morning aerial photographs of Los Angeles parking lots which cumulatively dramatize that city's indenture to the automobile. Imaginatively designed expositions are, needless to say, especially hard to publish nowadays unless the author is a cultural celebrity on the level of Abbie Hoffman or Jerry Rubin. Thus, many examples of this literary possibility remain unrealized and unavailable. (For that reason, too, an adventurous publisher could do some extremely opportune work in this area.)

Among the other formally inventive expositions that have recently slipped by the barricades of American publishing are Merce Cunningham's *Changes* (1969), a freely formed introduction to his own work and thought; John Cage's *Notations* (1968), which extends his incorporative esthetic to an entire book; Allan Kaprow's *Assemblage, Environments & Happenings* (1966), where the printed text follows and echoes an exposition conveyed by over a hundred shrewdly selected photographs; Iain Baxter's *A Portfolio of Piles* (1968), a witty series of unbound but numbered photographs of piled things; Hendrik Hertzberg's *One Million* (1970), an imaginatively conceived dissertation on the magnitude of large numbers; *Samaras Album* (1971), an essay in multi-media narcissism by the sculptor Lucas Samaras; and John Brockman's hypotheses on information theory's relevance to psychology, *By the Late John Brockman* (1969), plus its sequel, *37* (1970), an essay on indeterminacy, both of which have one and only one tightly written paragraph to a printed page. The truth suggested by these books, along with conceptually comparable essays (i.e., Ihab Hassan's "Paracriticism"), is that the much-touted "New Journalism" has added little art to the moribund expository genres, while artistic writers have hardly explored the possible ways of talking about extrinsic subjects.

It should be clear by now that the writings described here represent something radically new and undefined, and as yet

398

probably undefinable in literary history—a "post-Modernism," if you will; and these examples repudiate conclusively any intimations of either literature's evolutionary death or the creative mind's reported inability to compete imaginatively with the exaggerations of contemporary life. They also suggest not just a new development in American literature, but further radical possibilities for change in imaginative forms, thereby testifying to the continuing inventive capacities of literary men. This new writing surpasses as well most earlier forms of avant-garde literature, constituting an advance perhaps best defined by the critic-poet Hugh Fox in the course of distinguishing "beat" from "hip": "The Beats were still 'linear,' the Hippies are 'curvilinear,' the Beats were 'sequential,' the Hippies are 'instantaneous,' the Beats were 'natural,' the Hippies are 'electronic.' " More crucially, the expressionistic Beats emphasized authorial voice which goes masked in nearly all strains of new literature.

Most of the writers discussed in these two chapters are still underground—disaffiliated and disorganized, rarely surfacing into public print, inhabiting a culture of little magazines and small press (or self-published) books, somewhat known to each other but unrecognized by more orthodox poets and novelists, all but totally invisible to the larger reading public and then totally excluded from nearly all anthologies except their own; so that their creative adventure is, for the while at least, doomed to isolation and frustration. There is no doubt that an intelligent audience exists for this work; the success of earlier kinds of avant-garde literature—Barth, Borges, Beckett, Barthelme—demonstrates that a large literary public does appreciate innovative writing, and that fact provides reason for hope.

Since established critics ignore this literature, reputations are primarily made among fellow avant-garde artists who, in spite of inevitable conflicts and jealousies, generally acknowledge genuine achievements and advances. As in other contemporary arts, stylistic imitation implicitly becomes not only the sincerest form of flattery, but also the most honest way of bestowing artistic honor. Despite all the pressures toward cultural alienation and literary hermeticism, most of this new literature is remarkably accessible once the open-minded reader overcomes the superficial difficulties posed by anything original.

If writers coming of age in the twenties thought poetry was

king, while those in the thirties and forties were most awed by fiction (and those in the sixties by both personal journalism and poetry), it is my hunch that the next decade will be dominated by innovative literature—by writing in any genre that decidedly surpasses what has been written before.

19

The Possibility of Rejuvenation

Now just as the artists had become tired of conventions and were breaking into new and personal forms, so Miro saw the younger critics breaking through these cultural conventions. To the elders, the result would seem mere anarchy. But Miro's attitude did not want to destroy; it merely wanted to rearrange the materials. . . The old attitude was only speciously democratic. The assumption was that if you pressed your material long enough and winningly enough upon your culturable public, they would acquire it. But the material was sometimes handed down, not grown in the garden of their own appreciations. —Randolph Bourne, "The History of a Literary Radical" (1919).

More equality for some means a reduction in privilege for others, and more democracy and autonomy for some means a loss of power for others. Those who have the privilege and the power will not give them up without a struggle and will fight the demand for more equality with all the economic and political resources they can muster. —Herbert J. Gans, "The 'Equality' Revolution" (1968).

Those who make peaceful revolution impossible make violent revolution inevitable. —John F. Kennedy, in an address (1962).

"The shits are killing us" is probably Norman Mailer's most definitive contribution to the language; but the truth is that new writers are, unlike Mailer, already quite deceased or dying. The opening sections of this book documented why intelligent writing in America is coming to an end, not, to repeat, because

401

good work is no longer written—quite the contrary is true—or because a literate public no longer exists—again untrue—but because the intermediary channels between writers and their potential readers have become so clogged and corrupted. The current "crisis" of American literature has less to do with the creation of an audience, which exists, or good new work, which is also abundant, than with its dissemination and reception, which have become progressively more problematic. The possibility of communication is sabotaged not only by the blockages of literary power, but by those intellectual deficiencies that create such growing gaps between the best culture of our time and the editorial moguls, and thus the literate public. Good important writing hangs suspended in limbo, encountering more difficulty getting published especially if its author is young, independent, or unknown. Even if it gets into print, making its existence known to likely readers is an equally insurmountable obstacle. All kinds of evidence noted before suggests that one-half of the possibly great books written today go unpublished, and that one-half of those important works which do manage to get into some kind of public print go unreviewed, unnoticed, and comparatively unsold. Moreover, whole *classes* of writing are unjustly neglected with deleterious results. If that is true and if serious new and young writers are publicly dead, no matter how lively and fine their work, then intelligent writing, as we have known it, will have come to an end.

Writers are encouraged, usually by publishers, to blame this predicament upon the "goddamned reading public," but any writer who thinks his works and/or ideas are significant, and also finds them greeted with some enthusiasm, justifiably suspects that a larger audience of readers might be interested, if only his word could reach them. However, the existence of likely readers does not, because of all the hazards noted before, necessarily assure the interest of publishers, as the distance between the domains of reading and editing have steadily increased. The dominant institutions of publishing and book-publicity have become, as we have seen, more closed than open, more self-serving than discriminating, more profit-hungry than enlightened, editorially more narrow and narcissistic than adventurous, and more dead than alive. Therefore, blaming the predicament of serious writing upon an amorphous public represents, in the end, an evasion that ought to raise further suspicions.

New and young writers have made the mistake of believing that the literary system would continue to work intelligently; but since it is breaking down into impotence and ignorance, that system is ripe for radical change. All pertinent discussion of what to do must begin by acknowledging the imminent death of literature; for unless strategies for change are based upon accurate analysis, the real world of writing will remain enshrouded by fantasy and ultimately unaffected. It follows that writers or readers who remain ignorant of literary politics are apt to court continual deception. As death within life is an extreme condition, the actions required to resuscitate intelligent writing may likewise need to take similarly radical forms. The professional world that new writers inherit need not be accepted as an eternal fate, for precisely in their capacity to overcome the current predicament lies a hope for literature's future. What we do determines "American culture," which is not only passed on to our children but exported to the world.

II

> High-level fulminations—however elegantly phrased—against slavery or war can achieve nothing unless they move men closer than the fulminators to the sources of power; but similar attacks on the degradation of language and literary taste have already changed to some degree the situation they deplore *by merely existing.* —Leslie A. Fiedler, in a review (1963).

Much discussion about what constitutes "radical action" for writers neglects the fact that writing itself can be a form of action, if not that active form most conducive to the writer's particular talents and temperament; so that the most natural kind of radical action for the writer to take on behalf of his apocalyptic professional predicament is its maximum exposure in public (and even private) print. Intelligent writing is coming to an end, let me repeat, as that forbidding prophecy must be reiterated until it infiltrates the consciousness of everyone with any interest in literature, until the cry inspires a panoply of protests and proposals. These could well include the condem-

nation and documenting of improbity, hypocrisy, and ignorance; but the truth is that tasks so elementary are still perva-
sively neglected. More "whistle blowing" by people within the
trade is also very necessary, for the neglect of iniquity should
by itself be considered an indication of a failure of both
intellect and nerve—an abdication of "the responsibility of
intellectuals." It is simply insufficient for literary editors to
rationalize that "our readers would not be interested," because
serious magazines differ from commercial ones precisely in their
willingness to lead their readers. Furthermore, both editors and
writers who compromise in covering the maladies of literary
politics are likely to succumb to other pressures. Radicalizing
the consciousness of everyone involved in the literary enterprise
is just an initial step; but since the ears of America are more
likely to hear the loudest invocations, the voices of change must
resound in a chorus.

Writers must speak out and initiate actions, even assuming
risks, for the self-preservative people who fail to object to the
decimation of their colleagues will suddenly discover themselves
proscribed as well. There are, no doubt, good reasons for an
American writer's expatriation today; but in addition to being
detrimental to literary art (in contrast, say, to music and painting), escape abroad can do little to alleviate home-front demoralizations. The key question to be asked now is how can
intelligent writing (and serious writers) survive? The hard truth
is that we need not only to write literature that will be read
again and again, but to create conditions that will insure that
such works be available in order to be remembered.

Young literary radicals have been entrusted with the necessary task of morally rejuvenating a world in which so much
pretense to ethical value has been compromised by continuing
dishonesty, for the social example that the writer ideally sets is
not only political but moral. Given the literary scene's currently
compromised condition, only by relentlessly exposing selfish-
ness and eliminating deceit within the profession can literary
people again justly claim the privilege of moral leadership. "A
well-written article exposing the flaccidity of one middlebrow
magazine may well appear in another," Fiedler continues, "and
if it does not improve the former, it has, in fact, altered the
latter by virtue of its being published there." Exposure of
marital collusion, for instance, should help to prevent its recur-

404

rence, as well as instigating an ethic specifically circumscribing the appropriate commercial relations between literary wives and literary husbands. Nothing is more demoralizing than recognizing the need for change and yet being unable to generate it.

III

> Not only Abbie [Hoffman] but the present writer and hundreds like him are enormously sensitive to the irrelevance, right now, of what we used to call "literary writing" as opposed to survival expression; and I mean that last phrase in every sense, running from one's craft to one's life—they are all the same. —Seymour Krim, "Should I Assume America Is Already Dead?" (1969).

Writers also need to rebuild a sense of discrimination based upon qualitative and rationalized cultural distinctions rather than commercial or literary-political criteria, for corruption and literary politicking both cause and exploit the decline in independent discrimination. Indeed, as the open-minded, unprejudiced consideration of works of art is so inherently antagonistic to the debasement of standards, the practice (and preaching) of uncompromised judgment restores to writing its role as criticism of art and life. In realizing the ideal unity of theory and practice, the activist studies a foul situation in order to change it. "The Self must always be *identifiable* in the revolution, not overwhelmed by it," notes the anarchist philosopher Murray Bookchin; "the Self must always be *perceivable* in the revolutionary process, not submerged by it." For several reasons, therefore, young writers, like black boxers and mythical Jews, must turn resistances and disadvantages into incentives for excellence. Rather than exploit the guilt of their repression or cite their "youth" to excuse shabby work, they are obliged to be better, both as writers and as literary citizens. Only by formulating alternatives can a writer become the subject, rather than the object, of the sentence of history.

Among the necessary intellectual tasks will be the critical rewriting of recent literary history, in part not only to separate literary-political promotions from genuine achievements, but also to acknowledge the contributions of previously ignored minorities (women, small presses, etc.). Perhaps the most convenient measure of the integrity of any future cultural history will be its neglect or repudiation of the most obviously phony promotions. Indeed, literary history that fails to consider professional realities should itself be dismissed as hopelessly innocent, for any scholar aware of literary politics should question whether academia's current sense of "major fiction" in the 1920's, for example, may be based not upon disinterested literary judgment but upon the impact of publishers' promotions. In this respect, it should be assumed that just as great books go unrecognized now, if not unpublished, so were certain possibly major texts lost then. Comparably, our current awareness of "baroque music" is based upon compositions that were largely unpublished and unheard in their own time.

To new writers has fallen the urgent task of revitalizing American literary publishing, so that the culture of the book can better compete for both creative talents and the literate audience with the other communications media. Otherwise, barring war, political revolution, or other social catastrophe, all this literary deadwood is likely to remain with us for a while. Perhaps the young could change the literary scene as radically as they changed the major American universities, the pop-music business, and the tone of political protest, all of which would be quite different today if certain initiatives had not been taken. America is filled with fresh-faced, educated young people, manuscripts in hand, who could create a qualitatively different environment for writing. The issue now, as in Bourne's time, is whether the newcomers can survive.

There are also good reasons to discredit the hypocritical and smugly ignorant "intellectuals" who have given that fine word such a bad reputation, especially among the young; for the contrasting ideal should not be anti-intellectualism, non-intellectualism, or any other form of rationalized mindlessness, but simply a more rigorously knowledgeable and pertinent use of intellect. The relevance of certain ageless standards of decency and open-minded discrimination must be reiterated, just as new criteria must be posited to acknowledge historically unprecedented situations and artistic styles. Pointed polemic is becoming a constant necessity along with hyperbolic rhetoric and what Krim calls "survival expression," all finally articulated for the sake of literature's survival.

Whereas writers have traditionally spoken for other classes of powerless and oppressed, now is the time for them to protest for the sake of themselves; for if they fail to take the radical initiative in redistributing professional power, linking their predicament to that of other exploited underlings in society, who else will speak on their behalf? Dialectically interpreted, the time is now ripe, in part because so many experienced people are disillusioned or unemployed. "Hitherto it was the mission of philosophers to interpret the world," wrote Karl Marx in his *Theses on Feuerbach* (1845), "now it is our mission to change it." "Revolution" advocated by writers is not revolutionary unless it includes changes in the channels of communication. At stake, it cannot be forgotten, is not only the fate of communication between the best writers and the best readers but, beyond that, the spiritual health, integrity, and intelligence of a "free and democratic" culture.

This literary radicalism is, quite unlike most political protest nowadays, likely to antagonize our immediate superiors, especially our editorial employers-benefactors; and that fact merely accents the need for genuine courage—perhaps greater in depth than that recently expended on anti-Vietnam protests. The situation demands that young writers need no longer feel satisfied with tokenism nor be as polite and gentlemanly as most of them have been in asserting their interests. "It is easier for everybody," Joanna Russ noted of a comparable discrepancy, "to demand saintly purity of the oppressed than to tee off on the oppressor." They must energize the weaklings who might otherwise be unable to produce what they promise, and convert or boycott the finks, such as young editors who claim sympathy for their peers but ultimately do another generation's work. Young writers must sympathize with their compatriots in established publishing who genuinely try to shift the levers, and respect their equally genuine frustrations (along with their capacities for survival). However, those who merely say they would like to publish new writers must be clearly separated from those who actually put out their books; for ambitious talk, unlike realized action, is very, very cheap.

Establishment editors must constantly be reminded of their responsibilities to literature—that invaluable commodity that separates publishing from other, less honorific industries. "Big presses," notes Dick Higgins, "face economic problems when they try to do anything right, which, on the other hand, they must be forced to do." (What if one of the larger houses opened its gates to fifty good books a year instead of a token few? Or if several publishers made such decisions? For one thing, office morale would improve enormously. For another, that kind of radical initiative might produce spectacular success.) Nonetheless, protest-pressure is simply not enough, nor can it ever be, for such an incipiently terminal situation necessitates yet further kinds of radical activity.

The real questions to ask are whether or not you are with us? And if you think you are, what have you done or are you now doing? And if you're not, do you (or why do you) pretend that you are? The time for cordial chatter has passed. If you're not contributing to the solution, you must be a part of the problem.

IV

> I doubt if we have ever had a generation—or at least a minority of one—that has engaged itself so earnestly on the side of principled action, that valued people so dearly and possessions so little, that cared enough about our country to jeopardize their own careers within it, that wanted so desperately to lead open, honest lives and to have institutions and a society which would make such lives possible. —Martin Duberman, "On Misunderstanding Student Rebels" (1969).

The imminent death of intelligent writing demands that serious writers tighten their scattered ranks and forge a more collaborative outlook. This means in practice that no one desiring professional respect can consider himself exempt from the necessities of change, that every other similarly serious writer should be seen as a potential ally (unless his activity is unspeakably distasteful or compromised), that self-serving exclusive coteries be condemned as egomaniacal evasions, and that an awareness of collective fortunes should overcome all jealousy and opportunism (and attempts to split our ranks); for serious writers are ultimately not competitors but each other's keepers whose fates are culturally entwined. In consciousness-raising, to use the parlance of the time, we cannot afford to forget that larger concerns must put more shape upon individual behavior, because literary people are so especially prone, as Stephen Spender once pointed out, to the sin of self-interested betrayal. As the era of individual skirmishing has passed, everyone must act collectively with mutual consideration and common dispatch.

Though it is usually sage to steer clear of literary politics and cultivate one's own garden, there are times when the writer must do more. He must write for the sake not just of the world but, more specifically, of writing in general and his own professional future in particular. Non-writing activity, whether commercial or literary-political, becomes the writer's investment in creating a situation more conducive to his primary work. Given our predicament now, such actions have never been so necessary or so worthy of a busy writer's time. Just as political radicals who also write should be reminded of literary-political iniquities, so those young writers who compromise or cop out should be constantly criticized. We must avoid, nonetheless, except when provoked by white-collar mugging and the like, the kinds of behavior characteristic of literary gangsters, for among our aims is becoming better contributors to the literary community.

Symbiotically united, young writers deserve each other's respect, recognizing that collective interest is finally self-interest mutually extended. Circumstances also oblige us to be the most loyal readers of one another's work and to take our book-buying business to literary bookshops rather than department or stationery stores, for any young writer who does not buy and read his colleagues' books simply need not himself be read. Unless sympathetic cultural enterprises are appropriately supported, not only will they cease to survive, but much consciousness will remain inarticulate and the desirable changes inspiring their existence are less likely to happen.

The young writers' greatest enemies are, of course, the powers of repression and reaction, but the major antagonist within us is such a limited conception of personal destiny that any sense of collective feeling or interest is inhibited. Nothing annoys me more than the experience of explaining the predicament of intelligent writing to an ambitious young writer who nods agreeably and then demands to know exactly where he (and he alone) might get *his* stuff published or *his* plays produced. Such people can rarely be persuaded that their self-centered thinking is culturally suicidal, for rarely do they recognize how they have internalized the strictly individualistic mentality of capitalism (and the literary system). Like all discriminated minorities, we must avoid the deceits ("It's really an open scene") that will keep us competing with each other for the token plums, instead of confronting real predicaments. We must both support our genuine leaders and celebrate the honest achievement of any one of us (in part as a practical index of our own possibilities); so that the success of all *Whole Earth Catalogs* or Abbie Hoffman's *Steal This Book* should be taken as indicating the kind of circulation possible through self-publishing and self-distribution, as well as an occasion to rejoice that someone of us (that is, *me* mutually extended) has overcome the barriers. Nonetheless, the success of any one or group of us is ultimately less consequential than the fate of that enterprise in which we all have a vested interest—the possible future of intelligent writing.

One necessary collective move ought to be the creation of an organization analogous to the Artworkers Coalition whose members would be united by common "class" interests greater than esthetic and ideological differences. This organization would deal toughly and seriously with the general predicament, as well as with such strictly professional problems as governmental (and editorial) censorship, default, contractual deceit, white-collar mugging, exploitation, royalty-shaving, blacklisting, and other comparably illegitimate practices. This literary workers coalition should examine how writers might get a fairer share of subsidiary benefits, much as artists have recently established a contract that gives them a percentage of the profits gained from subsequent sales of their work. It could establish a Fair Practices Agency to deal severely with reviewer-publisher collusion, unfair or corrupt sweepstakes, advertising that is objectionable to the author, literary misuse, inaccurate accounting, inequities in remuneration, as well as general questions of legitimacy. Is it legitimate for a publisher to hire someone who previously worked as a book reviewer or an editor of a reviewing medium? Is it legitimate for a literary magazine to hire for these positions someone who currently works for a publishing house? Is it legitimate for a publishing house to found a periodical that features its own writers? Since the current writers' organizations are ineffectual about these issues, and "literary agents" serve only their clients, the coalition could also become the profession's collective bargaining representative and even its lobbyist before governmental agencies. The best antidote for despotism of any sort is the organization of a strong opposition

410

party. "What is needed," as Francis V. O'Connor wrote about the art world, "is a force at the center, capable of uniting the profession and lobbying vigorously with the art establishment."

One reason why individuals feel so impotent in confronting the bureaucracies of culture is that institutions prefer to deal with other institutions, chiefs with chiefs, rather than unaffiliated Indians. Thus, a coalition, merely by existing, would create potentialities for redistributing the leverages of power as well as overcoming the present perils of individualistic competition. "Anger turns to hate," Joanna Russ adds, "when the anger is chronic and accompanied by helplessness, and although you can bully or shame people into not showing their anger, the only way to stop the anger is to stop the hurt. The cure for hate is power—not power to hurt the hurter, but *power to make the hurter stop.*" On a more personal level, the poet-essayist Jeff Berner has advocated ending "the publisher-thought-up idea that a book or proposal should not go to more than one editor at a time. Therefore, the author waits weeks, months, even years for response to an otherwise timely vision. Why should it always be a buyer's market for anyone but best-selling authors?" The losers under the current system are not only serious writers but serious readers.

The poet-publisher Ron Silliman has speculated that groups of bona fide professionals could file "class action" suits for access to an established medium, since publishers are not exempt from the anti-trust laws. For instance, several young writers who had at least once contributed to a certain prominent magazine and whose subsequent submissions had been rejected (and not accepted by a comparable journal) might be able to sue on behalf, in Silliman's phrase, of "the censorship of all those similarly situated." Since the success of this suit would depend upon proving that apparently systematic exclusion was based upon non-qualitative criteria, complete victory would be unlikely; but one incidental benefit of a good show trial would be a detailed exposure of authority in an editorial powerhouse. (This example suggests that radical writers have scarcely explored legal leverages available to their trade.) Over two thousand German writers, it should be noted, now pay dues to a modestly titled Word Producers Union which lobbies for strictly professional benefits, such as royalties on books lent by libraries (which is probably impractical) and pensions for elder writers (who are not otherwise covered). Why is it that the newcomers in many American professions other than writing—medicine, psychotherapy, the law—have formed trade organizations more radical than their predecessors? Why is it that young writers militant on behalf of other oppressed classes have ignored their own? Why haven't American writers united in the past? It is obvious that the secondary cultural benefits of such professional action would be incalculable. A disadvantaged group, as noted before, is only as strong as its organizations.

The need for new institutions, which was strong all through the sixties, remains desperate in the seventies. New writers and editors can no longer afford to cop out of doing what must be done—the founding of innumerable new publishing houses, periodicals, reviews, professional organizations, and distribution channels in which opportunities are available and standards of intelligence and integrity are respected. None of us can afford to rest as long as good books continue to go unpublished, unreviewed, undistributed, unpurchased, unread, unappreciated—as long as adventurous and courageous enterprises face the threats of commercial failure or intellectual compromise; for inaction represents a failure of nerve. Our aim need not be to overthrow old institutions, most of which are becoming irrelevant of their own accord, but to hasten the cycle of decay and rebirth and thus the establishment of new ones of all kinds, and at all levels, to effect the necessary revolution by the most peaceful and successful means.

20

What Is
To Be Done

I

Youth must distinguish carefully between the essential duties and the nonessential, between those which make for the realization of the best common ideals, and those which make merely for the maintenance of a dogma or unchallenged superstition. By resisting the pressures that would warp, do we really best serve society; by allowing our free personality to develop, do we contribute most to the common good? —Randolph Bourne, "The Dodging of Pressures" (1913).

If we are cautious or paranoid, if we focus only on our own defense and forget the issues that made us originally rebel, our feelings will spread and weaken the morale of the people. If we keep a fighting spirit, and define the issues over and over, the people will support us as their warriors. —Tom Hayden, *Rebellion and Repression* (1969).

A magazine with six thousand readers cannot seem very powerful here, and yet . . . we must take into account what would be our moral and political condition if the impulse which such a magazine represents did not exist. —Lionel Trilling, "The Function of the Little Magazine" (1946).

All this relentless criticism and heightening of collective consciousness can only be preparatory to what undoubtedly is, and will become, the most necessary kind of action—the founding of thriving alternative institutions at every level of the literary world; for the problems described here are more amenable to a series of local political solutions than, say, to comprehensive economic-political change. (The former is also far more feasible.) Since the increase in the populace of talented, serious

413

writers has not been accompanied by an increase in the quantity and quality of outlets, the fundamental solution lies simply in the creation of good, new alternatives. In practice, with plurality comes greater freedom and fluidity. Just as it is far easier to found a new magazine than change or infiltrate an ailing one, so it is more expedient to build an alternative literary society apart from the existing decay; and so it is we, rather than others, who must create a genuinely free and democratic literary situation in which new writers are developed and justly compensated rather than exploited and ignored. Just as Randolph Bourne's colleagues had to build a new literary world over old-boy resistances, so must we create the institutions through which a new generation speaks to itself. One hates to think what might have happened to post-World War I "American writing" had they not made their necessary moves.

Though every writer fears adding yet another page to the glut of American print, that medium is still more accessible and cheaper than either film or videotape. Indeed, the traditions of personal integrity, excellence, and seriousness remain more persistent in print, which is also the most propitious medium for many kinds of expository and imaginative messages. Books and magazines are more efficient pedagogical devices than either lectures or films, as well as cheaper and more portable, while very, very little on U. S. television can change consciousness as much as a good book. Nothing is as practical as print for retrieving information; nothing is more effective at presenting, with subtlety and in detail, ideas and interpretations that must be *re*read to be fully comprehended. "Stick with print," the editor Walt Shepperd quipped, "It's safer." The autobiographies of Malcolm X and George Jackson explain why prisoners desperately want good books and how books served crucial functions in the development of personal consciousness. Otherwise, not just prisoners but young people get only those ideas of the mass media and the licensed professors; they remain mentally imprisoned.

Since American book sales, which currently exceed two-and-one-half billion dollars annually, will probably double in volume by the end of the century, publishing will remain a lucrative business; yet it seems unlikely that established publishers will serve or rescue young and imaginative writing. In spite of sporadic success, it would be predictably frustrating for anyone devoted to the causes outlined here to try to infiltrate and change the literary-industrial complex. Superficial resemblances in produce notwithstanding, it presently has less and less to do with literature. It seems possible that some of the larger firms will disintegrate under the pressure of their own contradictions; for just as conglomerated publishers will decay because of excessive pressure for profits or philistine management, so most of the remaining firms may let their trade and literary departments simply wither away, concentrating instead upon more profitable concerns like textbooks, cookbooks, and the like. "That would be good business for them," notes Dick Higgins, "and since they are businesses rather than publishers, it's just as well." What might also remain, Higgins predicts, will be pornography departments, identified as such, "which will remove the onus of serious literary pretensions from their stolid business minds." The poet-critic David Lenson advises young writers to boycott the major publishers:

> Eventually the big houses are going to be in trouble because the key writers in America will be denying them manuscripts, and they will be forced to publish garbage. City dwellers will accept this garbage as literature because it is printed by the big houses, but by and large no one will be fooled for long.

The editorial-industrial behemoths might then become distributional networks for smaller firms, much as the old Hollywood "studios" have survived as distributors for independent producers.

II

What is not illusory is the reality of the new culture of opposition. It grows out of the disintegration of the old forms, the vinyl and aerosol institutions that carry all the inane and destructive values of privatism, competition, commercialism, profitability and elitism. The new culture has yet to produce its own institutions on a mass scale; it controls none of the resources to do so. For the moment, it must be content—or discontent—to feed the swinging sections of the old system with new ideas.... —Andrew Kopkind, "Woodstock Nation" (1969).

There is no question that the situation demands, to repeat, the creation of a second literary industry different from the editorial-industrial complex, both in its devotion to better books and in its awareness of the cultural abysses that must be filled. I have in mind a network of mutually sympathetic enterprises analogous to the art film industry of the late fifties which could be open and yet discriminating enough to insure that good writing is not neglected and that intelligent readers are not insulted or ignored. "In literature, as in most of our national life," Ernest Callenbach, the editor of *Film Quarterly* once wrote me, "we need more regionalism, particularism, localism, decentralization, many small initiatives, rather than a few large ones." The new book publishers, for instance, could come in various sizes, ranging from medium-sized houses doing fifty books a year in first editions of several thousand, down to truly small presses producing "limited" editions on their own hand presses. All, regardless of size, will have closer rapport with their immediate customer-readers, and all would be wise to stay modest, avoiding the pitfalls of the biggies.

Most of these new literary publishers would also be especially receptive to young and alternative work—precisely those projects which commercial publishing is presently predisposed not to handle; for precisely in those large gaps in literary communication are commercial opportunities. Incipient classics are out there in manuscript waiting to be discovered, published, and read; and the radical activity which the literary establishments fear most of all is unestablished writers forging their own channels of communication totally outside the realm of old-boy restrictions and rewards. The composer-critic Eric Salzman, after making a comparable analysis of the contemporary-music scene, proposed the founding of "Alternative Culture Records" whose works would be "produced, cooperatively and collaboratively, by the artists themselves by and for—as part of—the new culture." Practitioners and advocates of the New Literature have a particularly herculean task, not unlike that confronting Ezra Pound and his allies fifty years before. "Artists don't address themselves to audiences," notes Edmund Carpenter. "They create audiences."

It is exhilarating to speculate what might happen if a multimillionaire were willing to lose a million dollars per year as Lamar Hunt reportedly did in the initial years of his football team (the Kansas City Chiefs); for even anticipating a loss of $5,000 per book, he could print two hundred literary titles that would otherwise have no chance of creating an audience. (And among those two hundred would probably be a few commercial winners anyway.) That kind of money, informed by aspirations conscious of quality, could generate real changes in communication and climate. However, it is lamentable that even sophisticated multimillionaires are invariably parsimonious about cultural expenditures, extravagant though they may be about other things. What if, to continue with conjectures, the government or one of the grander foundations donated a million dollars to various small presses, or even individual writers, to produce two hundred literary books? One reason why this is not impossible is that the history of both private and governmental patronage is filled with precedents for reviving dimensions of culture that are not adequately supported by the current capitalist system. The prime concern of the Federal Writer's Project of the WPA, for instance, was whether writers as a class would survive the thirties' depression—and, thus, whether writing, as both an art and a profession, lived or died. Programs like these might also be financed by the specific tax proposed by the art critic Barbara Rose: "A levy on public relations and advertising—those perversions of creativity—[that] could be used to rechannel funds into the arts." The direct granting of money is a risky investment, to be sure, because every writer or publisher given largesse won't necessarily produce something significant. Nonetheless, as the art historian Francis V. O'Connor noted in another context: "The larger the amounts expended on individuals *and* the more comprehensive the programs involved, the greater are the possibilities of reaching these artists with the greatest potential in the process of doing the most good for the money."

Another appropriate move might be the founding of an Open Press that would, like the Public Broadcasting Company, be mostly subsidized by the communications industry. In brief, the Open Press would be required to publish any extended manuscript submitted to it by writers who had submitted it elsewhere *and* had previously authored at least three commercially published books—that being a minimal criterion of professionalism for this court of last resort. One would think that big publishers would want to support this channel since it would absolve them both from valid charges of "censorship-by-rejection" and from responsibilities toward older authors who have been commercially "dropped." The Open Press would do small editions that would, ideally, be sold largely to libraries, insuring the public availability of writing that might otherwise be lost. (And if a book became especially popular, it could be commercially reprinted.) Since the Government Printing Office is already America's most prolific publisher, producing over 2000 new titles every year and issuing regular lists, it could assume this extra publishing task at minimal expense. Since the U.S. Superintendent of Documents already distributes over 150 million items every year, a few extra volumes of subsidized literature would scarcely burst its seams. As a general rule, corporations that profit from writing have a responsibility to support those non-profit ventures essential to the future of writing. Since the communications channel of book publishing and distribution is becoming as much of a public trust as the electronic media, the book industry's responsibility to both cultural quality and the First Amendment might also be subject to Federal Communications Commission scrutiny, if not regulation, from the perspective, of course, of the public good.

To deal specifically with the crisis in literature, Paul Goodman proposed that a fund be created which would "underwrite a quarterly circulation of ten thousand copies of a new little magazine for, say, three years, by which time it ought to have won its own audience or go out of business." Though each new periodical opens the editorial vise and increases the productive writer's range of discriminatory choices, only a fund larger than Goodman apparently assumes could satisfy the demands of current necessity. May everyone who reads this book, whether he be a writer or lover of good writing, feel obliged to take action—found an eclectic small press or a little magazine, if you have the competence and can scare up the resources, or join a distributional network that circulates what is not being disseminated (and won't otherwise be). The results will surely make the investment worthwhile. Just as now is the time when writers *must* do more than just write, so readers are obliged to do *more* than just read.

Neither small presses nor little magazines require great amounts of money at the beginning, nor are they necessarily run at a loss. Although a private fortune would be helpful (and

418

more of them should be turned to such high-minded uses), especially if a new publisher aims to produce opulently-beautiful books or advertise its merchandise, it is scarcely necessary. More essential to success are abundant amounts of determination, energy, and responsible hard work. Even an operation presently as large and ambitious as The Coach House Press started on far more courage than capital, while Jan Herman, himself an adventurous poet, began both *San Francisco Earthquake* and the Nova Broadcast Press on a few hundred dollars. Moreover, there is no such fate as "failure" in serious alternative publishing, as everything run with persistence, a point of view, and commercial modesty eventually forges its impact, if not at times a monetary profit. "The whole operation is inefficient, and the books are slow in coming out," testifies the poet Robert Bly, founder of the Sixties Press, "but even if a small press is managed clumsily, I don't think that makes any difference. Eventually the thousand or two thousand dollars we put into a book comes back, and then we put it into another book. A lot of money is not necessary. And readers forgive inefficiency."

It should not be forgotten that people become publishers, whether large or small, because they want to issue books they like, not because they intend to make lots of money (which can be more successfully amassed by other means); but precisely by earning money on current titles can they issue more books—ideally, those that reflect personal commitments and would not otherwise get into print. Potential small publishers should be comforted by these facts: Most major modern poets did their opening books with small presses; Sylvia Beach was a Parisian bookseller who met an Irish expatriate author in her shop and then successfully published his otherwise rejected *Ulysses*; and the four books published in 1919 by Leonard and Virginia Woolf's Hogarth Press included her own *Kew Gardens* and T.S. Eliot's *Poems*.

If a private small press, for instance, is more interested in spreading messages than creating permanent books, it can consider the cheapest means of production possible such as self-typed copy reproduced on newsprint by offset printing. In the past decade, processes of this kind became far less expensive than letterpress but still neater than mimeograph (which remains cheaper). The House of Anansi's Spiderline Editions, for instance, introduced first novels published in batches of four whose varityped unjustified columns are printed on inexpensive paper with uniform paperback covers; so that new titles are produced for far less than a thousand dollars apiece. When the first edition of $1.95 copies sells out, the novel's second printing is deservedly classier. Precisely because a fresh writer wants primarily to be read, he would rather have his work—especially his first book—appear in paperback than hardback. Furthermore, since young readers won't buy a hard-cover novel priced at $6.95 or more, even if authored by a young fictioner writing primarily for his peers, until that title goes into paperback there ought to exist softback lines devoted especially to cheaper editions of major neglected books by young writers, circulating all those otherwise lost titles to the largest possible audience. There should also be more annuals of "new writing" and comparable paperback collections of pieces already published in esoteric sources.

Thanks to methods developed and exploited by the underground press, it is also possible to print, say, 3000 eight-page newspapers for a few hundred dollars. Especially as the costs of book printing continue to rise, newsprint could well become the most appropriate medium for the mass dissemination of counter-culture literature. It is also at the nexus of cost-cutting in production that small literary publishing can best be helped by modest philanthropy. Since a primary expense in offset printing is expensive compositional and plate-making equipment, it ought to be possible for the government's cultural office, or universities, or writers' organizations to establish centers where such equipment and facilities could be used gratis, the small publisher paying only for his layout materials and the actual printing of the sheets. In short, there are technologies around for writers to exploit, as well as new knowledge, all of which make small-scale printing a less fearsome process.

Indeed, this offset equipment could be opened to individual writers as well; for as commercial publishing becomes more and more closed, it will be necessary to resort to self-publication. The means available to the individual writer can run the gamut from a professionally printed book (best done with the intermediary advice of professional "production consultants") down to stapled copies that the writer mails to his friends, as well as those sympathetic libraries that would appropriately catalog such publications and make them available to students. Xerography, notes McLuhan, enables Everyman to become his own publisher by eliminating the communications middleman. So far this last method has been particularly favored by scientists who want to announce their own professional discoveries at once, rather than suffer the hazards and delay of academic publication. (Perhaps every class in "creative writing" should close with a mimeo'd compilation of the semester's best work.) Private publishing, it should be noted, is not synonymous with a vanity press which is an agency paid by the writer to produce and distribute his work. Most vanity presses charge too much for their negligible services; and since they publish so many bad books, their imprint is more of a hindrance than a help in the marketplace. Indicatively, though most major modern poets privately published (or contributed funds to the publication of) at least one of their books, only one poet of note, A. R. Ammons, has ever resorted to a well-known vanity house.

It is my observation that experimental writers in particular aim to impress their friends and colleagues first of all; so that as unfortunate developments in mainline publishing force innovative writing to become a kind of private research, the forms of instant self-publication become the unconventional writer's most particular way for promptly getting his literary goods to a receptive audience. In dealing with my own daily mail, I customarily read such packets first; for just as the shabby appearance of a new poetry journal signifies a certain authenticity of purpose, so self-publication announces a special seriousness. "It is one of the curiosities of a new medium, a new format," notes Edmund Carpenter, "that at the moment it first appears, it's never valued, but it is believed.' Self-published books also make the most appropriate gifts a writer can give, whenever the occasion warrants.

It is also inevitable at the present time that many consequential avant-garde books are, and will continue to be, initially self-published. In the past few years alone the honor roll includes Ted Berrigan's *The Sonnets* (1964), Yoko Ono's *Grapefruit* (1964, commercially reissued in 1970 thanks to a fortunate marriage), Russell Edson's *The Brain Kitchen* (1965), Barbara Garson's *MacBird* (1965), Ed Sanders' *Peace Eye* (1965), Charles Henri Ford's *Spare Parts* (1966), Dick Higgins' *Jeffer-*

421

sons *Birthday/Postface* (1964) and *Foew&ombwhnw* (1969), Aram Saroyan's *Works* (1966) and *Aram Saroyan* (1967), J. Michael Yates' *Man in the Glass Octopus* (1968), John Giorno's *Raspberry* (1968), Jos C. Brilliantes' *Sonnets in Concrete* (1968), Vito Acconci's *Book Four* (1969), Dan Graham's *End Moments* (1969), Tom Ockerse's *T.O.P.* (1970), Don Cauble's *Three on Fire* (1971), Adele Aldridge's *Notpoems* (1972), Michael Joseph Phillips' *Concrete Sonnets* (1972), Alan Sondheim's *The Analysis of Situation* (1972), Richard Zarro's *Cosmic Telegram 777/ Ode to Madame Joy* (1972), and Victor Coleman's *America* (1972)—all of which came to my attention, even though they were predictably ignored by the "reviewing" media.

Any writer seriously considering self-publication should not forget its distinguished American tradition. Most of the greatest American writers subsidized the publication of at least one of their books—William Carlos Williams, Nathanael West, Gertrude Stein, Ezra Pound, E. A. Robinson, William James, Carl Sandburg, Stephen Crane, Henry Adams, Whitman, Poe, Hawthorne, Twain, Thoreau, Washington Irving; so did such European writers as Moravia, Lawrence, Stendhal, Blake, Byron, Paine, and even Chaucer, among many others. As the American novelist James Drought, himself a self-publisher, once concluded, "Anybody who ever had anything different to say had to shell out the labor or the sheckels himself." Bill Henderson has noted that even the original *Bartlett's Quotations* and Robert's *Rules of Order* were self-published; so were such best-sellers as Edgar Rice Burroughs' *Tarzan of the Apes* (1914), Mary Baker Eddy's *Science and Health* (1875), Henry George's *Progress and Poverty* (1879), Mark Twain's *Huckleberry Finn* (1879), and Rod McKuen's first books. Paying a printer to do it is customarily cheaper (and less troublesome) than buying a press. To paraphrase an old adage: He who pays the printer gets his tome.

Self-publication also allows extravagances in production and design that a commercial publisher would reject as too exorbitant—for example, the Cauble, Higgins, and Ockerse books mentioned before, or Lon Spiegelman's *The Fence Is Always Browner on the Other Side of the Grass* (1970) which collects his "dalinographs"; for by printing in smaller editions, the writer-publisher can expend more care (and cost) upon each book. Since commercial publishing ignores all but a few photographers, it is not surprising that many of the most important recent spine-bound photographic essays were also self-published: All of Edward Ruscha's books, including his classic *Thirty-Four Parking Lots* (1967), Ralph Gibson's *The Somnambulist* (1970), Lee Friedlander's *Self-Portrait* (1970), Alwin Scott Turner's *Photographs of Detroit People* (1970), Larry Clark's devastating portrait of drug abuse, *Tulsa* (1971), Robert Gerhart III's *Eyes at Water Level* (1971), Neil Slavin's *Portugal* (1971), Richard Link's *Fossils* (1972), Fred Escher's *Hiding* (1972), Mike Mandel's *Myself: Time Exposures* (1972). Professor Arnold Gassan self-published his book, *A Chronology of Photography* (1972), an uncommonly interesting history of photography and its relation to the other arts, as well as his earlier, more successful *Handbook for Contemporary Photography* (1971). One incidental benefit of self-publication is the photographer's complete control over the size and texture of the book's paper, its design and binding, and even the quality of photographic reproduction—all those dimensions that commercial publishers neglect or handle so stupidly. (Some of the photographic self-publishers got cut-rates from super-slick printers, otherwise specializing in corporate reports, who wanted to turn their superior technology to more artistic uses.) Also, if the work or its author ever becomes internationally renowned, the privately published "limited edition" will have a monetary value many times greater than its original cost. (A single copy of Poe's *Tamerlane and Other Poems*, initially self-published in 1827, fetched over ten grand at a recent auction.) For that reason alone, books of this kind make excellent investments where, as in other *objets d'art,* financial appreciation is one reward of a collector's prophetic taste. "Remove authority," the anarchist philosopher Paul Goodman predicted in an essay on anarchism, "and there will be self-regulation, not chaos."

It follows that perhaps every fellowship in "creative writing" should have attached an optional surplus of, say, two thousand dollars which the author could use to print 500 to a thousand copies of his finished work in case commercial publishers decline it. Such a subsidy would also enable the writer to give his work away, for that kind of distribution is ultimately less time-consuming, more satisfying, and less expensive than selling it. As Jonathan Williams of Jargon Books once noted, "I'd have many less sorrows if I'd simply given away *Jargons* for 20 years, rather than trying to merchandize them." (In Soviet Russia, which has a government-subsidized writing profession, 30,000 of the 70,000 new titles produced each year are distributed gratis.) In general, it is becoming counter-productive for American foundations, as well as frustrating for writers, to create literature that will not otherwise be communicated; and now that many American writers have enough free time to complete their literary work, foundation money could better be used to further its dissemination. As Michael Hoffman noted, "In literature, particularly, it makes little sense to subsidize advanced writers if there are not developed better ways to reach advanced readers."

All signs suggest that, unless forbidding circumstances change, the next few years will witness the rapid growth of a manuscript culture that is not unlike "Samizdat" (meaning "self-publication") in Communist countries where official censorship, analogous to commercial barriers here, keep the best and most radical writing unpublished. Indeed, if current negative developments continue, one can foresee when xerography paper may well become a more honorific publishing medium than the printed book. At that dark time, "underground" writing, circulated from hand to hand, as in contemporary Russia, will ultimately have more literary consequence than stuff issued through aboveground channels, and potentially major writers will have, for the while, predominantly underground reputations. History illustrates that publishing vehicles that at first seem unpropitious, like the paperback, often play a revolutionary role in literary dissemination. As Edmund Carpenter adds, "Restricting information makes it highly explosive, while widely disseminating information neutralizes its effects."

III

In discussing the state of reviewing with people of experience—reviewers, editors, publishers and authors—we were commonly, when illustrative anecdotes had begun to accumulate into monotony, presented with the conclusion: "But everybody knows all about it. And anyway, there is nothing you can do." In a sense everybody does know. Yet if we could print some of the choicer instances we collected, most of the readers of *Scrutiny* would have a shock.... To get this fully recognized by those

> capable of recognizing it has never been wholeheart-
> edly attempted. It is worth attempting. And there is
> certainly a public—if it can be mobilized—that will
> support criticism—if it is offered. —F.R. Leavis, "The
> Literary Racket" (1932).

The next channel in the literary system that needs to be
flushed is, of course, the media of review and publicity which
are now plagued not only by corruption and subservience to the
literary-industrial complex, but an indiscriminate neglect of
almost everything important. In practice, nothing persuades a
bookstore manager to stock a new title more than attention in
the public press; and little persuades his customers to buy (or
request) a particular title more than the good words they heard
about it or its author. However, given the current biases of these
media, likely readers simply do not hear about new literature
and young writing; and without that prior attention not even
the best of those new books will reach a fraction of their
potential audience.

If the established reviews continue to ignore alternative writing, then new book-reviewing periodicals must be founded. It is
obvious that most of them should be established outside New
York (with its pressures and provincialisms), that they should
discard the archaic rule against covering paperback originals
(thereby enabling publishers to issue original editions at reasonable prices), and that they should devote a regular column or
section to important, older books that have disappeared. A
review with small, more selective circulation than *The Times
Book Review* or even *The New York Review* could also charge
more accessible advertising rates. More reviews of small-press
publications ought to appear in the underground press which
has so far neglected this opportunity. Those writers contributing to aboveground magazines should consider it their duty
to publicize underground literary activities whenever possible
and critically justified (and a willingness to do so, at least some
of the time, should separate the truly activist young from the
poseurs). It follows that any "book review" (or cultural editor)
that continues to ignore small presses and private publications
should be publicly criticized as inimical to the future of literature. To repeat, those who profit from literature are obliged to
support those nonprofit ventures essential to the future of
intelligent writing.

Book-selling, politely called "distribution," is the most recalcitrant obstacle in the literary communications process. If a new publisher's titles are as possibly commercial as those of, say, Straight Arrow, it might be able to get a large publisher's sales force to distribute their finished books for a percentage of the gross, much as the new independent film and record producers deliver completed packages to the old companies which now do less producing than distributing. Although the distributor's salesmen are likely to be more adept at getting the books around than a new publisher would be on his own, the latter nonetheless becomes victimized by his associates' inevitably more conservative taste and traditions. Otherwise, most bookstores in America will rarely display, let alone stock, alternative literature or small publishers—at least not until the title becomes as famous as Allen Ginsberg's *Howl* or *The Whole Earth Catalog.*

Small presses could avoid such obstacles by selling most of their publications by mail, either capitalizing upon some prior interest in the authors or their works (rather than first-hand examination permissible in a bookstore) or developing a list of regular subscribers who receive new titles like magazines once a month or once every two months at a fixed price. (This kind of book publishing was more customary in eighteenth-century England.) The poet-artist Davi Det Hompson, whose work is as inventive as his name, has offered annual subscriptions to his own self-published work—$30.00 for "six mailings of plans, photographs, assemblages, and occurrences. (If you are timid, send $1.00 for an introductory packet of 14 postcards.)" The success of book clubs has made American readers more accustomed to the practice of buying books "sight unseen."

However, since books by unknown writers are not likely to inspire mail orders, these in particular must be placed in retail outlets where they may be seen and purchased. As retailers prefer to deal with a single distributor rather than innumerable small suppliers, small publishers ought to form their own distribution networks with sympathetic salesmen to deal with America's numerous college bookstores and literary/radical booksellers, if not with youth-culture miscellany shops. (And customers, in turn, must patronize these more discriminating retailers.) Unless such books are intended largely for well-to-do collectors or library borrowers, the most practicable format would be the cheapest possible paperback. A distribution system of this kind might also handle classes of literary material that the big boys neglect, such as books issued in smaller editions, visual poetry-fiction, and casettes of sound poetry. It would at least reach a select national audience that, were the book enticing enough, would communicate its enthusiasm to increasingly larger circles. At that point in the dissemination process, the more conventional bookstores might become more receptive to the new distributors' salesmen. Without the first development, however, the second is all but impossible.

One step in this direction is Michael Hoffman's high-minded Small Publishers Co., recently retitled The Book Organization, which distributes several imprints—Something Else, Corinth, and Jargon being the most famous—in exchange for several thousand dollars per year in sales, each member receiving in return all receipts above that minimum figure. Given this form of cooperative structure, Hoffman's company is best prepared to handle well-heeled publishers with rather full and active lists. Another national distributor, Light Impressions, was founded in Rochester in 1970 in response to the increasing number of self-published photographic books. As its coproprietor, Lionel Suntop, wrote me, "Light Impressions is a realistic, growing and lasting structure that can provide an umbrella for privately published work"—not only distributing the books to sympathetic retailers, including their own bookstore-gallery, but also providing photographers with advice and assistance on self-production. Extending their operation, they recently founded a European office run by a German couple, and established an Updating Service/Information Bank which forwards correspondence, publishes a newsletter, and mails "conceptual projects, manifestos, solicitations for exhibitions, etc."

On a more local level is the example of The Book People in Berkeley, an efficiently operated commune that distributes small-press titles along with more standard paperback fare; and it was, typically, the first distributor of *The Whole Earth Catalog.* With even more modest enterprise, Bernard DeBoer, resident in Nutley, New Jersey, works around the clock to distribute several dozen of America's most eminent literary quarterlies to sympathetic bookstores and magazine racks in the eastern U. S., taking a small percentage of the sales they make; and his example suggests that similarly free-lance distributional

427

arrangements for smaller presses would be feasible in any canvassable area. "Most of the bookstores that have a genuine empathy for what we do," Suntop wrote, "are promoting our books. They get excited about each new release and insist on being kept informed of each new development. Many have become personal friends."

Indeed, it ought to be possible for a new small press or even an individual writer to approach such a distributor with a finished book, much as photographers presently approach Light Impressions. Providing that the distributor wanted to handle it, he could either set a minimum sum as his fee (returning to the author/publisher all receipts above that point) or merely take a wholesaler's percentage off the gross. Given his experience and reputation, a distributor of this kind would have more leverage and experience than any individual in getting alternative books into the appropriate stores (as well as collecting unpaid debts); but especially since the distributors' outlets must sell enough copies to justify not only their own stores' continued interest, but also the distributing operation's, the remaining problems involve getting those alternative books favorably displayed and securely sold. Street-selling, of course, is the ultimate form of distribution which every writer sufficiently proud of his work should try sometime.

Another possibility would be the founding of a literary institution similar to the Film-Makers Cooperative which functions as a national library to rent small circulation films that would not otherwise be available. An analogous national literary agency would keep permanent stocks of all small-press books (and perhaps little magazines too) still in print, as well as issue regular lists of items available from which bookstores, libraries, and individuals could then directly order by mail. (Some federal funding might be appropriate here.) The Committee of Small Magazine Editors & Publishers (COSMEP), which has so far worked largely at consciousness-raising, could easily take the initiative in organizing such an institution, at least for the benefit of its own national membership. The mere existence of such a distributing agency would by itself create not only the possibility of national circulation, but also a more coherent audience for alternative literature—itself a further contribution to the consciousness-raising of American readers. Corporations

428

that already fund such nonprofit cultural intermediaries as museums might underwrite such an agency.

Every American cultural metropolis ought to have a single competently staffed bookstore that keeps a permanent stock of all literary books, both hardbacks and paperbacks, published in the prior decade by large publishers and small. This system, unlike mail order, would allow the prospective reader to browse through the book before purchasing it or discover purchasable titles that he might not notice on an alphabetical list. Such a store should be locally subsidized, if such aid is necessary, and perhaps be attached to the main branch of the public library; each store should also carry books of all kinds that are published in and for that region. (The success of the new California publishers illustrates the possibilities of primarily regional distribution.) The novelist-editor Charles Newman has proposed a larger, federally subsidized system with "six regional warehouses and 100 retail outlets" which would stock otherwise neglected literary material and be staffed largely by part-time labor—students, housewives, etc. To cope with another kind of distribution problem, the novelist R. V. Cassill has proposed another kind of repository for "The Unknown American Literature" which would contain "all aborted works, all first drafts, notebooks, sketches, lousy projections of great conceptions, and unused observations from life prepared by *all* the writers in the country, however many of them there turn out to be." And these deposits should, needless to say, be arranged and indexed for fairly efficient retrieval, while copies of this index could be distributed to university libraries and other scholarly centers.

Distribution remains such a knotty obstacle (and the nexus most susceptible to dishonesty) that I suspect that a "hip capitalist," given his demonstrated administrative and financial competence in rock music and other areas, might be able to approach these problems more imaginatively. As Craig Karpel speculated, "If he were to direct his ample energies toward identifying and developing 'communities' instead of properties—I don't even pretend to know what this would *mean* in practice. . . —the counter-culture would be better off." One of these tribal kings, Jann Wenner of *Rolling Stone,* founded Straight Arrow Books using *Rolling Stone*'s pages to promote titles (and some of his own staff to write them). Like Time-Life before it, this publisher hoped to sell these largely through the mail, but its books, as noted before, have so far failed their cultural promise.

From this and similar operations could possibly arise a stronger, more populist distributional network than those sketched in the preceding paragraphs. It is said that trade bookstore sales as such have scarcely increased since 1929, the growing volume stemming instead from such outlets as magazine stands, book clubs, mail-order, subscriptions, and the like—in other words, a steady cultivation of alternative channels; and it is my suspicion that this development in bookselling has scarcely peaked. Not only are there clearly jobs to be done, but the time is especially ripe, in part because so many experienced young people have been unemployed (and perhaps professionally radicalized) during the Nixon depression. In meeting unfulfilled needs lies capitalism's greatest opportunities.

Writers should, no doubt, be paid for their work; for in Ezra Pound's just and famous aphorism, "A nation which does not feed its best writers is a mere barbarian dung heap." His colleague T. S. Eliot concurred, "No editor with the means to make a payment can justifiably do without it." One truth lost in this era of spectacular book advances is that nearly all American writers, like nearly all American artists, earn next to nothing from their work. In the current arrangement of commercial publishing, it is assumed that the publisher will make at least a middle-class living off his work, while most writers are required to earn their livelihoods from other trades (the government and the universities doing most of the "subsidizing," as noted before), unless or until their books commercially succeed. For these reasons, many writers must struggle to find spare time to devote to their literary work. It seems at first inequitable that publishers surely eat while writers may starve; but given the fact that publishing depends upon many small suppliers (and even more numerous retail outlets), it would be hard for writers to be much better reimbursed under the present system, especially if they fail to complete their projects or their titles do not sell. In truth, neither the serious writer nor comparable artists can feasibly fix, even in their own minds, a just minimum wage for their self-initiated labor.

Writers would obviously like to receive proportionately as

430

much for work sold as a painter who customarily splits the total receipts with his gallery; however, the reason why the writer receives such comparatively small percentages—ten escalating to fifteen on hardbacks, between four and ten in paperbacks—is that, unlike the painter, he has a collaborator in production. Closer analogies in this respect are a record performer or an industrial inventor, both of whom also earn "royalties." Certain recent attempts to reduce those percentages due authors are thoroughly objectionable, though the writer who deals with minimally capitalized small publishers may need to forgo his customary advance. (Some institutions, like little magazines, cannot be feasibly milked; for like the serious writers, their publishers know that certain things are worth doing at a loss or for free.) The contractual principle of escalating royalties assumes a split in the possible profits; and since the actual production costs on a best-seller can run as low as 10 percent of the book's retail price, all writers (or their Literary Workers Coalition) should insist upon an even greater share of both the subsidiary rights (paperback leasings, book clubs, etc.) and the royalties of such success. They should also insist that their books remain in print for at least three (if not five) years, rather than be speedily flushed away. Publishers refusing to grant this and other similarly considerate provisions, like those outlined in the Authors Guild's *Your Book Contract* (1961), should be publicly exposed; for inferior terms, like pay beneath a union's minimum, ultimately jeopardizes the whole profession's livelihood. Such practices might induce the excessively profit-minded publisher to lower his office extravagances (and perhaps his artificially inflated "break-even point"), or publish 10,000 copies apiece of 100 different titles, rather than one million of a single "Big Book."

The fact that so many writers have become university teachers I take to be generally beneficent, even though most literary academics are conservative in esthetics, quiescent in literary politics, unproductive as writers, and middleclass in life-style; for, bohemian pieties about "selling out" to the contrary, it is better that university money go to writers than elsewhere. Though teaching may compromise or deplete inspiration, college jobs provide more free time for writing and editing than most other comparably remunerative positions; and universities have printing and duplicating machinery that can be turned to literary uses. Moreover, literary academicians can (and should) persuade their universities to found little magazines which usually earn back their minimal expenses with increased prestige and publicity, or literary presses like those of Wesleyan and Illinois. Since American universities, unlike the publishing industry, already comprise a decentralized system, they become the ideal sponsor of counter-East Coast alternatives. "The key role which the universities play in the present period," as Herbert Marcuse observed, "is the training of counter-cadres."

One peril of literary prosperity, however, especially in payment for non-writing, lies in undermining the ideal of decent poverty; so that impoverishment, especially if the writer is good, is less a source of pride than a cause of mutual embarrassment. (Besides, poor writers, unlike the rich, often commit the social sin of talking obsessively about money.) Nonetheless, those of us who, for one reason or another, are unable to find regular employment may need to rediscover the possibilities of poverty, avoiding that devastating American syndrome of increased living costs, if only for the sake of independence from financial needs. Exactly that kind of freedom, coupled with recognition of the writer's predicament, is the prerequisite for both truly radical activity and the capacity to work gratis, whether that free labor be writing itself and/or the editing of a necessarily radical periodical. (This kind of insufficiently self-sufficient writer, needless to say, deserves more support from literature's benefactors. Indeed, there ought to be more fellowships for writers past graduate school and yet short of qualifications for Guggenheims and the like.)

The spreading of risks and costs in collaborative ventures is also necessary now, as in cooperative publishers founded by writers who then constitute its board of editors. The poet-scientist Rodham Tulloss wrote me about creating a nationwide "network of independent cells, loosely tied for purposes of mutual criticism, sharing audiences as they are discovered":

> Each cell would have its own rules (or no rules) and would consist of a variable population numbering between 10 and 30 people. They would not begin publishing immediately, but would read to each other and criticize or discuss what was read. After a few months, a body of work will appear

ready for publication. The cell, if it survives this far, must now decide how it will publish this work. Probably an offset pamphlet (bookstores like them square-bound) will be the best format. Each cell member bears a share of the printing cost. The pamphlets are sold on the street, in local stores, at literary gatherings. The other existing cells will aid in the merchandizing of each others' publications, including those of the new cell. It is my experience that the first publication, if carefully put together and aggressively hawked, will turn a profit. By the third or fourth publications, the cell should not have to rely on its members' kicking in capital for further issues.

One conceptual advantage here is that writers become each other's salesmen, and, as the community of interrelation expands, the sales force grows. (The fear, of course, is the kind of egomania that instigates a breaking of the chains.) Thinking on more advanced and commercial levels, the British novelist B. S. Johnson has proposed that ten or so established writers form a publishing cooperative whose books would be sold largely by mail (in response to advertisements). This method, unlike the other one, could capitalize upon prior popular interest in their work. Johnson estimates that the writer-publisher, after paying the printer and his share of operating costs, would retain approximately one-half of the gross receipts; all other middlemen are thus eliminated. "What writer," Johnson notes, "would agree to the humiliating percentages now offered [10 percent to 15 percent] when he could receive larger and fairer ones?" An added advantage is that enterprises of this kind establish direct contact between writer and reader, avoiding entirely a literary-industrial complex whose powers and practices become instantly irrelevant.

I mentioned *Assembling* before as a contribution to overcoming the problem of avant-garde communication, but that was scarcely enough for me or my collaborators. What the current crisis needs is at least a hundred cooperative publications like *Assembling* at every level of skill and kind of taste, each of them ideally symbolizing the new and open literary society we should collectively build. Even they would not be sufficient, however, as ten more avant-garde publishers are also required, along with fifteen fine poetry presses, twenty-five more prominent publishers outside New York, and thirty-five of Paul Goodman's proposed little magazines, along with new reviewing media and distributional networks, all of which should be supported in every possible and honest way; but even that would not be enough. What is also required is more cohesion among new writers, though that alone would not be sufficient either, nor would attempts to restore the writer's claim or moral leadership be enough. Nothing alone will suffice this "responsibility of intellectuals"; and just as no one is excused, none among us should ever feel he has done enough, because now is a moment of unprecedented crisis. If writers fail to act now, they will discover sometime soon that even the opportunity for action is gone, and their children will inherit a yet more atrocious situation. However, were everything done and done well, and were good books also written, and were the institutions of literature rejuvenated, and the editorial-industrial complex ignored, and literary power diffused, then perhaps the traditions of intelligent writing would continue to evolve.

Bibliographies

The following listing is informal, intending primarily to cite the sources of references and quotations mentioned in the text. It is divided not by individual chapters but by groups of related chapters. Certain redundancies were eliminated by not acknowledging books and essays that were already listed under earlier chapters. Inconsistencies are the author's fault, as are omissions and errors, which will be corrected in subsequent editions if appropriate notification is sent to him care of the book's publisher.

PREFACE

Connolly, Cyril. "Interview," *Antaeus,* I/4 (Winter, 1971).

Cowley, Malcolm. *The Literary Situation,* N.Y.: Viking, 1954.

Cruse, Harold. *The Crisis of the Negro Intellectual.* N.Y.: Morrow, 1967.

Farrell, James T. *The Fate of Writing in America.* N.Y.: New Directions, 1946.

Gilbert, Stuart, ed. *The Letters of James Joyce.* N.Y.: Viking, 1956.

Hills, L. Rust, et al. "The Literary Establishment," *Esquire,* LX/1 (July, 1963).

Jacobs, Jane. "Social Uses of Power," in Elizabeth Janeway, ed. *The Writer's World.* N.Y.: McGraw-Hill, 1969.

Kostelanetz, Richard. "The Beginning of *The End of Intelligent Writing,*" *The New York Ace,* 6 (April, 1972).

Krim, Seymour. *Shake It for the World, Smartass.* N.Y.: Dial, 1970.

Leavis, F. R. *Education and the University.* London: Chatto & Windus, 1943.

Leavis, Q. D. "The Discipline of Letters: A Sociological Note," in Eric Bentley, ed. *The Importance of Scrutiny.* N.Y.: George W. Stewart, 1948.

Macdonald, Dwight. "Masscult and Midcult" N.Y.: *Partisan Review,* 1961.

Mills, C. Wright. "The Social Role of the Intellectual," *Politics,* I/3 (April, 1944). Reprinted in Mills, *Power, Politics, and People.* N.Y.: Oxford Univ. Press, 1963.

Van den Haag, Ernest. *The Jewish Mystique.* N.Y.: Stein & Day, 1969.

CHAPTERS 1-2

Allen, Donald, and Robert Creeley, eds. *The New Writing in the U.S.A.* Harmondsworth, England: Penguin, 1967.

Alter, Robert. "Sentimentalizing the Jews" (1965), "Jewish Dreams and Nightmares" (1968), *After the Tradition.* N.Y.: Dutton, 1969.

Angoff, Charles, and Meyer Levin, eds. *The Rise of Jewish-American Literature.* N.Y.: Simon & Schuster, 1970.

Arendt, Hannah. *The Origins of Totalitarianism.* N.Y.: Harcourt, Brace, 1951.

Baldwin, James. *Notes of a Native Son.* Boston: Beacon, 1955.

————. *Nobody Knows My Name.* N.Y.: Dial, 1961.

Bellow, Saul, "The Swamp of Prosperity [Philip Roth]," *Commentary,* XXVIII/1 (July, 1959).

Bradbury, John M. *The Fugitives.* Chapel Hill: Univ. of North Carolina Press, 1958.

————. *Renaissance in the South.* Chapel Hill: Univ. of North Carolina Press, 1963.

Brooks, Cleanth. *Modern Poetry and the Tradition.* Chapel Hill: Univ. of North Carolina Press, 1939.

————. *William Faulkner: The Yoknapatawpha Country.* New Haven: Yale Univ. Press, 1963.

Brooks, Van Wyck, ed. *A New England Reader.* N. Y.: Atheneum, 1962.

Brustein, Robert. "First Year at Yale: An Interview," *The Third Theatre.* N.Y.: Knopf, 1969.

Canfield, Cass. *Up and Down and Around.* N.Y.: Harper's Magazine, 1971.

Charters, Ann. *Kerouac.* San Francisco: Straight Arrow, 1973.

Chisholm, Scott. "Interview with Donald Hall," *Ironwood* I/1 (Spring, 1972).

Cohen, Elliot E., ed. *Commentary on the American Scene.* Introduction by David Riesman. N.Y.: Knopf, 1953.

Cook, Bruce. *The Beat Generation.* N.Y.: Scribner's, 1971.

Cowan, Louise. *The Fugitive Group.* Baton Rouge: Louisiana State Univ. Press, 1959.

Cowley, Malcolm. "Letter to England," *The New Republic* (Feb. 13, 1935). Reprinted in Henry Dan Piper, ed., *Think Back on Us. . . .* Carbondale: Southern Illinois Univ. Press, 1967.

Creeley, Robert. *A Quick Graph.* San Francisco: Four Seasons, 1970.

Daiches, David. "Breakthrough?" *Commentary,* XXXVIII/2 (August, 1964).

Davidson, Donald. *Southern Writers in the Modern World.* Athens: Univ. of Georgia Press, 1958.

———— *The Spyglass.* Ed. by John Tyree Fain. Nashville, TE.: Vanderbilt Univ. Press, 1963.

Fiedler, Leslie A. *Waiting for the End.* N.Y.: Stein & Day, 1964.

————. "Master of Dreams," *Collected Essays.* N.Y.: Stein & Day, 1971.

Fitzgerald, Robert. "A Memoir," in *The Collected Short Prose of James Agee.* Boston: Houghton Mifflin, 1969.

Duberman, Martin. *Black Mountain.* N.Y.: Dutton, 1971.

Geismar, Maxwell. "The Jewish Heritage in Contemporary American Fiction," *Ramparts,* II/2 (Autumn, 1963).

Guttmann, Allen. *The Jewish Writer in America.* N.Y.: Oxford Univ. Press, 1971.

Hicks, Granville. *Literary Horizons.* N.Y.: New York Univ. Press, 1970.

Holman, C. Hugh. *Three Modes of Modern Southern Fiction.* Athens: Univ. of Georgia Press, 1966.

Howard, Richard. "Reflections on a Strange Solitude," *Prose.* I/1 (Autumn, 1970).

Howe, Irving. "Black Boys and Native Sons," *A World More Attractive.* N.Y.: Horizon, 1963.

————. "Introduction," to Irving Howe and Eleazar Greenberg, eds. *A Treasury of Yiddish Stories.* N.Y.: Viking, 1954.

————. "They Took Their Stand," *New York Times Book Review* (Aug. 5, 1965).

Hubell, Jay B. *Who Are the Major American Writers?* Durham, NC: Duke Univ. Press, 1972.

Karanikas, Alexander. *Tillers of a Myth.* Madison: Univ. of Wisconsin Press, 1969.

Kazin, Alfred. "Bernard Malamud: The Magic and the Dread," *Contemporaries.* Boston: Little Brown, 1962.

————. Review of *Portnoy's Complaint, New York Review of Books* (Feb. 27, 1969).

Kherdian, David. *Six Poets of the San Francisco Renaissance: Portraits & Checklists.* Fresno, CA: Giligia, 1967.

Knowles, Horace, ed. *Gentlemen, Scholars and Scoundrels.* N.Y.: Harper & Bros., 1959.

Kostelanetz, Richard. "Militant Minorities," *Hudson Review,* XVIII/3 (Fall, 1965).

Krim, Seymour. *Views of a Nearsighted Cannoneer.* N.Y.: Excelsior, 1961.

Lett, Paul, et al. "The Foley Papers," *Mutiny,* 12 (Summer, 1963).

Lowell, Robert, et al., eds. *Randall Jarrell, 1914-1965.* N.Y.: Farrar, Straus, 1967.

Malin, Irving. *Jews and Americans.* Carbondale: Southern Illinois Univ. Press, 1965.

———, and Irwin Stark eds. *Breakthrough: A Treasury of Contemporary American-Jewish Literature.* N.Y.: McGraw-Hill, 1964.

Mencken, H.L. "The Sahara of the Bozart," *Prejudices: Second Series.* N.Y.: Knopf, 1920.

Meltzer, David, ed. *The San Francisco Poets.* N.Y.: Bantam, 1971.

Mudrick, Marvin. "Malamud, Bellow & Roth," *On Culture and Literature.* N.Y.: Horizon, 1970.

Murray, Albert. "A Clutch of Social Science Fiction Fiction," *The Omni-Americans,* N.Y.: Outerbridge, 1970.

Niebuhr, H. Richard. *The Social Sources of Denominationalism.* N.Y.: Holt, 1929.

Pechter, William S. "The Art of the Film," *Contact,* IV/3 (Oct., 1963). Reprinted in *Twenty-Four Times a Second.* N.Y.: Harper & Row, 1970.

Phillips, William, and Philip Rahv, eds. *The Partisan Reader.* N.Y.: Dial, 1946.

Podhoretz, Norman. *Doings and Undoings.* N.Y.: Farrar, Straus, 1964.

Porter, Katherine Anne, et al. "The Critics, Writers & Editors," *Book Week* (Sept. 26, 1965). Reprinted as "On Modern Fiction," in *The Collected Essays and Occasional Writings of Katherine Anne Porter.* N.Y.: Seymour Lawrence-Delacorte, 1970.

Purdy, Rob Roy, ed. *Fugitives' Reunion: Conversations at Vanderbilt.* Nashville, Tenn.: Vanderbilt Univ. Press, 1959.

Rahv, Philip. "Plain Critic and *Enfant Terrible* [Leslie A. Fiedler]," *The Myth and the Powerhouse.* N.Y.: Farrar, Straus, 1965.

Rexroth, Kenneth. *The Alternative Society.* N.Y.: Herder & Herder, 1970.

———. "San Francisco Letter," *Evergreen Review,* I/2 (1957).

Roth, Philip. "Writing about Jews," *Commentary.* XXXVI/6 (Dec., 1963).

Rubin, Louis D., Jr. *The Curious Death of the Novel.* Baton Rouge: Louisiana State Univ. Press, 1967.

——— *The Faraway Country.* Seattle: Univ. of Washington Press, 1963.

———, et al. *Recent Southern Fiction.* Macon, GA: Wesleyan College, 1960.

———, and Robert D. Jacobs, eds. *Southern Renascence.* Baltimore: Johns Hopkins, 1953.

———, eds. *South: Modern Southern Literature in Its Cultural Setting.* Garden City: Doubleday, 1961.

438

Schwartz, Leo, ed. *The Menorah Treasury.* Philadelphia: Jewish Publication Society, 1964.

Shapiro, Karl. "The Jewish Writer in America," *In Defense of Ignorance.* N.Y.: Random House, 1960.

Snow, C. P. "Which Side of the Atlantic?" In John Fischer and Robert B. Silvers, eds. *Writing in America.* New Brunswick, NJ: Rutgers Univ. Press, 1960.

Solotaroff, Theodore. "All that Cellar-Deep Jazz," *Commentary,* XXXII/4 (Oct. 1961). Reprinted in *The Red Hot Vacuum.* N.Y.: Atheneum, 1970.

_____ [Anonymously]. "A Vocal Group," in Alan Pryce-Jones, ed. *The American Imagination.* N.Y.: Atheneum, 1960.

Stewart, John D. *The Burden of Time.* Princeton: Princeton Univ. Press, 1965.

Styron, William. Introduction, *Best Short Stories from the Paris Review.* N.Y.: Dutton, 1959.

Tanner, Tony. "Saul Bellow," *Encounter,* XXIV/2 (Feb., 1965).

Tate, Allen. "The Profession of Letters in the South" (1935), "The New Provincialism" (1945), *Essays of Four Decades.* Chicago: Swallow, 1968.

_____, ed. *The Fugitives: An Anthology of Verse.* N.Y.: Harcourt, Brace, 1928.

_____, ed. *A Southern Vanguard.* N.Y.: Prentice-Hall, 1947.

_____, and John Peale Bishop, eds. *American Harvest.* N.Y.: L.B. Fischer, 1942.

_____. "The Fugitive 1922-1925: A Personal Recollection Twenty Years After," *The Princeton University Library Chronicle.* III/3 (April, 1942).

Trilling, Lionel. "Introduction," to Robert Warshow, *The Immediate Experience.* Garden City: Doubleday, 1962.

Twelve Southerners. *I'll Take My Stand.* N.Y.: Harper & Bros., 1930.

Van den Haag, Ernest. "The Jewish Cultural Establishment," *The Jewish Mystique.* N.Y.: Stein & Day, 1969.

Vidal, Gore. "Ladders to Heaven," *New World Writing,* 4 (1953). Reprinted as "Novelists and Critics of the 1940's," *Sex, Death and Money.* Boston: Little, Brown, 1968.

Warren, Robert Penn. "The Hamlet of Thomas Wolfe," *American Review,* V/2 (Sept., 1935). Reprinted in *Selected Essays.* N.Y.: Random House, 1958.

_____. "Andrew Lytle's *The Long Night:* A Rediscovery," *Southern Review,* VII/1 (Jan. 1971). Reprinted in David Madden, ed. *Rediscoveries.* N.Y.: Crown, 1971.

_____, ed. *A Southern Harvest.* Boston: Houghton Mifflin, 1937.

_____, and Albert Erskine, eds. *A New Southern Harvest.* N.Y.: Bantam, 1967.

Wasserstrom, William, ed. *Civil Liberties and the Arts.* Syracuse, N.Y.: Syracuse Univ. Press, 1964.

Weinberg, Helen. *The New Novel in America.* Ithaca, NY: Cornell Univ. Press, 1970.

Winters, Yvor, ed. *Twelve Poets of the Pacific.* N.Y.: New Directions, 1937.

CHAPTERS 3 & 4

Aaron, Daniel. *Writers on the Left.* N.Y.: Harcourt, Brace, 1961.

Adler, Renata. "Polemic and the New Reviewers," *The New Yorker* (July 4, 1964). Reprinted in *Toward a Radical Middle.* N.Y.: Random House, 1969.

Aldridge, John W. "The Writer in the University," *In Search of Heresy.* N.Y.: McGraw-Hill, 1956.

Bell, Pearl K. "American Fiction: Forgetting Ordinary Truths," *Dissent,* XX/1 (Winter, 1973).

Bellow, Saul. "World-Famous Impossibility," *The New York Times* (Dec. 6, 1970).

Brossard, Chandler, ed. *The Scene Before You.* N.Y.: Rinehart, 1955.

Conroy, Jack. "Making It and Faking It on the Seaboard 'Family' Circuit," *December,* XII/1-2 (1971).

DeMott, Benjamin. "Jewish Writers in America: A Place in the Establishment," *Commentary,* XXXI/2 (Feb., 1961).

Elliott, George P. "Who Is We?" *The Nation* (1957). Reprinted in *A Piece of Lettuce.* N.Y.: Random House, 1964.

Epstein, Jason. *The Great Chicago Conspiracy.* N.Y.: Random House, 1970.

_____. "Good Bunnies Always Obey: Books for American Children," *Commentary,* XXXV/2 (Feb., 1963).

_____ "Civilization as Process: Culture as Banal Repetition," *ALA Bulletin,* LVII/7 (July, 1963).

_____. "Living in New York," *New York Review of Books, VII/1*

Fiedler, Leslie A. "Partisan Review: Phoenix or Dodo?" (1956), "Saul Bellow" (1957), *Collected Essays.* N.Y.: Stein & Day, 1971.

Geismar, Maxwell. "Reflections on Reflections," *December,* XI/1-2 (1969).

Gilbert, James Burkhart. *Writers and Partisans.* N.Y.: Wiley, 1968.

Gilroy, Harry. "The Review of Books Is Creating Lecture Bureau," *The New York Times* (July 15, 1968).

Goodman, Walter. "On the (N.Y.) Literary Left," *Antioch Review,* XXIX/1 (Spring, 1969).

Hardwick, Elizabeth, "The Decline of Book Reviewing," *Harper's* (Nov., 1959). Reprinted in John Fischer and Robert B. Silvers, eds. *Writing in America.* New Brunswick, NJ: Rutgers Univ. Press, 1960.

———. "Fiction Chronicle [Bellow]," *Partisan Review,* XV/1 (Jan., 1948).

Hills, L. Rust. "The Dirty Little Secret of Norman Podhoretz," *Esquire,* LXIX/4 (April, 1968).

Hindus, Milton. "Jewish History in Pictures," *Commentary,* XXVIII/1 (July, 1959).

Holmes, John Clellon. *Go.* N.Y.: Ace, 1952.

———. *Nothing More to Declare.* N.Y.: Dutton, 1967.

Howe, Irving. "PR," *New York Review of Books,* I/1 (Feb., 1963).

———. " 'The New Yorker' and Hannah Arendt," *Commentary,* XXXVI/4 (Oct., 1963).

———. "The New York Intellectuals," *Commentary,* XLVI/4 (Oct., 1968). Reprinted in *Decline of the New.* N.Y.: Harcourt, Brace, 1970.

Kazin, Alfred. *Starting Out in the Thirties.* Boston: Little, Brown, 1965.

———. "Acknowledgments," *Contemporaries.* Boston: Little, Brown, 1962.

———. "My Friend Saul Bellow," *Atlantic Monthly,* CCXV/1 (Jan. 1965).

———, et al. "The Negro in American Culture" (1961). Reprinted in C.W. E. Bigsby, ed. *The Black American Writer.* Vol. I. Baltimore: Penguin, 1971.

Kadushin, Charles, et al. "How and Where To Find Intellectual Elite in the United States," *Public Opinion Quarterly* (Spring, 1971).

———. "Who Are the Elite Intellectuals?" *Public Interest,* 29 (Fall, 1972).

Kefauver, Estes. *Crime in America.* London: Gollancz, 1952.

Kizer, Carolyn, quoted by Lawrence Ferlinghetti in David Meltzer, ed. *The San Francisco Poets.* N.Y.: Ballantine, 1971.

Klein, Alexander, ed. *Dissent, Power, and Confrontation.* N.Y.: McGraw-Hill, 1972.

Kostelanetz, Richard. "Men of the Thirties," *Commonweal,* LXXXI (Dec. 3, 1965).

Kramer, Hilton. "Harold Ross's 'New Yorker,' " *Commentary,* XXVIII/2 (August, 1959).

Krim, Seymour. "Ubiquitous Mailer vs. Monolithic Me," *Shake it for the World, Smartass.* N.Y.: Dial, 1970.

———., ed. *The Beats.* Greenwich, CN: Fawcett, 1960.

Lasky, Melvin, ed. *Encounters.* N.Y.: Basic Books, 1963.

Laughlin, James, and Hayden Carruth, eds. *A New Directions Reader.* N.Y.: New Directions, 1964.

Lekachman, Robert. "The Literary Intellectuals of New York," *Social Research,* XXXII/2 (Summer, 1965).

Lipton, Lawrence. *The Holy Barbarians.* N.Y.: Grove, 1959.

London, Michael, and Robert Boyers, eds. *Robert Lowell.* N.Y.: David Lewis, 1970.

Maas, Peter. *The Valachi Papers.* N.Y.: Putnam's, 1968.

Macdonald, Dwight. "Introduction: Politics Past," *Memoirs of a Revolutionist.* N.Y.: Farrar, Straus, 1957.

———. "By Cozzens Possessed," *Commentary,* XXV/1 (Jan., 1958). Reprinted in *Against the American Grain.* N.Y.: Random House, 1960.

——— "Humor, Fantasy, and Morals," *The Griffin,* IX/2 (Feb., 1960).

——— "The New York Times, Alas," *Esquire,* LIX/4-5 (April-May, 1963).

———. "The Birds of America," *New York Review of Books.* VII/9 (Dec. 1, 1965).

Macdonald, Michael C. D. "Theatre for Ideas: The Left Faces Life," *New York,* II/20 (May 19, 1969).

Mailer, Norman. "Making It, and the Establishment," *Partisan Review,* XXXV/2 (Spring, 1969). Reprinted in *Existential Errands.* Boston: Little, Brown, 1972.

Mudrick, Marvin. "The Holy Family," *The Hudson Review,* XVII/2 (Summer, 1964). Reprinted in *On Culture and Literature.* N.Y.: Horizon, 1970.

Navasky, Victor. "Notes on Cult: or, How To Join the Intellectual Establishment," *New York Times Magazine* (March 27, 1966).

Nobile, Philip. "A Review of *The New York Review of Books,*" *Esquire,* LXXVII/4 (April, 1972).

Phillips, William, and Philip Rahv, eds. *The Partisan Reader.* Introduction by Lionel Trilling. N.Y.: Dial, 1946.

———. *The New Partisan Reader.* N.Y.: Harcourt, Brace, 1953.

———. *The Partisan Review Anthology.* N.Y.: Holt, Rinehart & Winston, 1962.

Podhoretz, Norman. *Making It.* N.Y.: Random House, 1968.

———, ed. *The Commentary Reader.* N.Y.: Atheneum, 1966.

————. Review of Lionel Trilling's *The Liberal Imagination, Scrutiny,* XVIII/1 (1951).

————. "Southern Claims," *Partisan Review,* XXI/1 (Jan.-Feb., 1954).

————. "The Adventures of Saul Bellow," *Doings and Undoings.* N.Y.: Farrar, Straus, 1964.

Rahv, Philip, "Saul Bellow's Progress," *The Myth and the Powerhouse.* N.Y.: Farrar, Straus, 1965.

————. "Delmore Schwartz: The Paradox of Precocity," *New York Review of Books,* XVII/9 (May 20, 1971).

Rosenberg, Harold. "The Herd of Independent Minds," *The Tradition of the New.* N.Y.: Horizon, 1959.

Rexroth, Kenneth. Interview in David Meltzer, ed. *The San Francisco Poets.,* N.Y.: Ballantine, 1971.

Schwartz, Delmore. "Smile and Grin, Relax and Collapse," *Partisan Review,* XVII/3 (March, 1950). Reprinted in *Selected Criticism.* Introduction by Dwight Macdonald. Chicago: Univ. of Chicago Press, 1970.

————. "Adventure in America [Augie March]," *Partisan Review,* XX/1 (Jan.-Feb., 1954).

Solomon, Barbara Probst. "Notes from New York," *Views,* 6 (Autumn, 1964).

Tate, Allen. "The New Provincialism," *Essays of Four Decades.* Chicago: Swallow, 1968.

————, and John Peale Bishop, eds. *American Harvest.* N.Y.: L.B. Fischer, 1942.

Teresa, Vincent, with Thomas C. Renner, *My Life in the Mafia.* Garden City: Doubleday, 1973.

Trilling, Diana. "The Other Night at Columbia," *Partisan Review,* XXV/2 (Spring, 1959). Reprinted in *Claremont Essays.* N.Y.: Harcourt, Brace, 1964.

————. "The Radical Moralism of Norman Mailer," *Encounter* (1962). Reprinted in Nona Balakian and Charles Simmons, eds. *The Creative Present.* Garden City, Doubleday, 1962; and in *Claremont Essays.*

Trilling, Lionel. *The Liberal Imagination.* N.Y.: Viking, 1950.

————. *Beyond Culture.* N.Y.: Viking, 1965.

————. *Mind in the Modern World.* N.Y.: Viking, 1972.

————. "A Triumph of the Comic View [Saul Bellow]," *The Griffin,* II/8 (Sept., 1953).

————. "On the Death of a Friend [Elliot E. Cohen]," *Commentary,* XXIX/2 (Feb., 1960).

Ullman, Allan. "Letter-to-the-Editor," *Esquire.* LX/1 (July, 1963).

Updike, John. *Bech: A Book.* N. Y.: Knopf. 1970.

Wrong, Dennis H. "The Case of *The New York Review,*" *Commentary,* L/5 (Nov., 1970).

CHAPTERS 5 & 6 & 7

Adler, Renata. "Polemic and the New Reviewers," *The New Yorker* (July 4, 1964). Reprinted in *Toward a Radical Middle.* N.Y.: Random House, 1969.

Alvarez, A. *Under Pressure.* Baltimore: Penguin, 1965.

Barnes, Clive. "High Noon on 44th Street," *The Dramatists Guild Quarterly* (1971).

_____. "My Life and *The Times,*" *Playbill,* X/3 (March, 1972).

Bazelon, David T. *The Paper Economy.* N.Y.: Random House, 1963.

Boorstin, Daniel. *The Image.* N.Y.: Atheneum, 1962.

Booth, Wayne. *Now Don't Try to Reason with Me.* Chicago: Univ. of Chicago Press, 1970.

Burnham, Sophy. *The Art Crowd.* N.Y.: McKay, 1973.

Cerf, Bennett, quoted in Clarence Petersen, *The Bantam Story.* N.Y.: Bantam, 1970.

Chomsky, Noam, et al. *Trials of Resistance.* N. Y.: New York Review, 1970.

Clarke, Gerald. "Checking in with Truman Capote," *Esquire,* LXXVIII/5 (Nov., 1972).

Curtis, Charlotte. "An Adventure in 'The Big Cave,' " *(MORE).* I/1 (1971).

Elliott, George P., and Richard Kostelanetz. "Communications," *Hudson Review,* XVIII/4 (Winter, 1965-6).

Epstein, Jason. *The Great Conspiracy Trial.* N.Y.: Random House, 1970.

_____. "The CIA and the Intellectuals," *New York Review of Books* (April 20, 1967).

_____. "Civilization as Process: Culture as Banal Repetition," *ALA Bulletin,* LVII/7 (July, 1963).

_____, quoted in "Random House VP Says . . .," *Media Industry Newsletter,* XXIV/18 (May 6, 1971).

Fiedler, Leslie A. "Introduction," *Collected Essays.* Vol. II. N.Y.: Stein & Day, 1971.

Friedenberg, Edgar Z. "De côte de chez Podhoretz," *New York Review of Books,* X/2 (Feb. 1, 1968).

Goldman, Eric F. *The Tragedy of Lyndon Johnson.* N.Y.: Knopf, 1968.

Goldman, William. "The Approvers," *The Season*. N.Y.: Harcourt, Brace, 1969.

Goodman, Mitchell. *The Movement Toward a New America*. N.Y.: Knopf, 1970.

Hedley, Leslie Woolf. "The McGraw-Irving Syndrome," *San Francisco Fault*, I/15 (May, 1972).

Henahan, Donal. "But Was It Stravinsky?" *New York Times* (May 7, 1972).

Hover, Julie, and Charles Kadushin. "Influential Intellectual Journals," *Change*, IV/2 (March, 1972).

Howe, Irving. "The New York Intellectuals," *Decline of the New*. N.Y.: Harcourt, Brace, 1970.

––––––. ed., *Beyond the New Left*. N.Y.: McCall, 1970.

––––––. "Letters [Kostelanetz]," *Partisan Review*, XXXVI/2 (1969).

Kadushin, Charles, et al. "How and Where To Find Intellectual Elite in the United States," *Public Opinion Quarterly* (Spring, 1971).

Kluger, Richard. "If You're a Book, Then Prove It," *Book Week*, I/48 (Aug. 9, 1964).

Kostelanetz, Richard. "Into the Pressure Cooker," *Massachusetts Review*, IX/2 (Summer, 1968).

Lasch, Christopher. "The Cultural Cold War," *The Agony of the American Left*. N.Y.: Knopf, 1968.

Lasson, Robert. "The Power of the First Word [Barbara Bannon]," *New York*, VI/7 (Feb. 12, 1973).

Leonard, John. "News, Views, Reviews," *Cultural Affairs*, 12 (Fall, 1970). Reprinted in *This Pen For Hire*. Garden City: Doubleday, 1973.

Lewis, R.W.B. "Ellison's Essays," *New York Review of Books*, III/12 (Jan. 28, 1965).

Libman, Lillian. *And Music at the Close*. N.Y.: Norton, 1972.

Lowell, Robert. "Prometheus Bound," *New York Review of Books*. IX/1 (July 13, 1967).

Lucie-Smith, Edward. "Introduction," *British Poetry Since 1945*. Harmondsworth: Penguin, 1970.

Mailer, Norman. "Ministers of Taste," *Cannibals and Christians*. N.Y.: Dial, 1966.

Maloff, Saul, et al. "The Intellectuals vs. Goldman," *Harper's* (March, 1968).

Marcus, Alan. "Delay en Route," *Genesis West*, II/5 (Fall, 1963).

Miller, Merle. "The New York Review of the Literary Establishment," *Status*, (July-Aug., 1969).

_____. "Why Norman and Jason Aren't Talking," *New York Times Magazine,* (March 26, 1972).

Morris, Willie. *North Toward Home.* Boston: Houghton Mifflin, 1967.

Mount, Douglas. "If You Have Hidden Talent and Like To Eat," *Esquire,* LXXVI/6 (Dec., 1971).

Muchnic, Helen. *Russian Writers: Notes and Essays.* N.Y.: Random House, 1971.

O'Brien, Conor Cruise. "The Writer and the Power Structure," *Book Week* (June 12, 1966).

Raskin, Jonah. "I Called Him Irving," *University Review,* 23 (April, 1972).

_____. "The Irving Howe/Times Book Review Axis Welcomes John Leonard," *Scanlan's Monthly,* I/7 (Sept., 1970).

Sheed, Wilfrid. "Making It in the Big City." *Atlantic Monthly,* CCXXI/4 (April, 1968).

Sheehy, Gail. "Reporter's Notes on Revolution," *Speed Is of the Essence.* N.Y.: Pocket Books, 1970.

Smith, Harry. "The New York Review Gives Strong Preference," *The Newsletter* (March 5, 1969).

Spender, Stephen. "The Perfectly Candid Man," *New York Review of Books,* XIV/8 (April 23, 1970).

Thomson, Virgil. *Virgil Thomson.* N.Y.: Knopf, 1966.

Vidal, Gore. "Literary Gangsters," *Commentary,* IL/3 (March, 1970).

Warshow, Robert. "Letters," *Partisan Review,* XXI/2 (March-April, 1954).

Wolfe, Tom. *Radical Chic & Mau-Mauing the Flak Catchers.* N.Y.: Farrar, Straus, 1970.

X, Malcolm, with Alex Haley. *The Autobiography.* N.Y.: Grove, 1965.

CHAPTERS 8 & 9 & 10

Albrecht, Milton C., et al, eds. *The Sociology of Art and Literature.* N.Y.: Praeger, 1970.

Allen, Donald., ed. *The New American Poetry.* N. Y.: Grove, 1960.

Aronson, James. *The Press and the Cold War.* N.Y.: Bobbs-Merrill, 1970.

Author's Guild. *Your Book Contract.* N.Y.: 1961.

Bellow, Saul. "Culture Now: Some Animadversions, Some Laughs," *Modern Occasions,* I/2 (Winter, 1971).

Bensman, Joseph, and Israel Gerver, "Art and the Mass Society," *Social Problems* (Summer, 1958).

Berman, Ronald. *America in the Sixties.* N.Y.: Free Press, 1968.

Bouton, Jim, with Leonard Shecter. *I'm Glad You Didn't Take It Personally.* N.Y.: Morrow, 1971.

Brustein, Robert. *Revolution as Theatre.* N.Y.: Liveright, 1971.

Business Week. "The Big Story in Books Is Financial" (May 16, 1970).

Canfield, Cass. *Up and Down and Around.* N.Y.: Harper's Magazine, 1971.

Cerf, Bennett. An address reprinted in Gerald Gross, ed. *Publishers on Publishing.* N.Y.: Grosset & Dunlap, 1961.

Cott, Jonathan. "Poetry," in Richard Kostelanetz, ed. *The New American Arts.* N.Y.: Horizon, 1965. Reprinted in *He Dreams What's Going On Inside His Head.* San Francisco: Straight Arrow, 1973.

Cowley, Malcolm. *The Literary Situation.* N.Y.: Viking, 1954.

_____. "How Writers Lived," in Robert Spiller, et al, eds. *The Literary History of the United States.* N.Y.: Macmillan, 1948.

Creeley, Robert. *A Quick Graph.* San Francisco: Four Seasons, 1970.

_____, and Donald Allen, eds. *The New Writing in the U.S.A.* Harmondsworth: Penguin, 1967.

Crowell, Chester. "An Interview with Lyle Stuart," *Los Angeles Free Press* (April 9, 1971).

Cushman, John. "The Literary Agent and Book Publishing," *Publishers Weekly*, CCI/15 (April 10, 1972).

Drake, Albert. "Fiction from the Small Press," *S. F. Book Review*, 24 (Oct., 1972).

Elon, Amos. *The Israelis.* N.Y.: Holt, 1971.

Escarpit, Robert. *Sociology of Literature.* Painsville, Ohio: Lake Erie College, 1965.

Fay, Stephen, et al. *Hoax: The Inside Story of the Howard Hughes-Clifford Irving Affair.* N.Y.: Viking, 1972.

Feuer, Lewis S. *The Conflict of Generations.* N.Y.: Basic, 1969.

Findlatter, Richard. *What Are Writers Worth?* London: The Society of Authors, 1963.

Foote, Timothy. "Modest Proposals from a Spent Book Reviewer," *New York* V/50 (Dec. 11, 1972).

Frank, R. B. "First Novels: Their Publishers," *Panache,* 7 (1971).

Friedrich, Otto. *Decline and Fall.* N.Y.: Harper & Row, 1970.

Fuller, Mary. "An Ad Reinhardt Monologue," *Artforum,* IX/2 (Oct., 1970).

Gilman, Richard. *The Confusion of Realms.* N.Y.: Random House, 1969.

Glaser, Milton. "Most Are Bad," *New York Times Book Review* (May 6, 1973).

Green, Mark J., et al. *The Closed Enterprise System.* N.Y.: Grossman, 1972.

Hills, Penny Chapin, and L. Rust, eds. *How We Live.* N.Y.: Macmillan, 1968.

Hoffman, Abbie. "How Clifford Irving Stole That Book," *Ramparts,* XI/4 (Oct, 1972).

Hover, Julie, and Charles Kadushin. "Influential Intellectual Journals: A Very Private Club," *Change,* IV/2 (March, 1972).

Howe, Irving. "The New York Intellectuals," *Decline of the New.* N.Y.: Harcourt, Brace, 1970.

Hughes, Langston, et al. "The Negro in American Culture," in C. W. E. Bigsby, ed. *The Black American Writer.* Vol. I: Fiction. Baltimore: Penguin, 1971.

Johnson, Curt. "My Culture Agency Problem—and Yours" *The Smith,* 11 (May, 1970).

———. "The Culture Trough," *The Nation,* CCXI/5 (Aug. 31, 1970).

Jovanovich, William. *Now Barrabas.* N.Y.: Harcourt, Brace, 1964.

Kostelanetz, Richard, ed. *The Young American Writers.* N. Y.: Funk & Wagnalls, 1967.

———, ed. *In Youth.* N.Y.: Ballantine, 1972.

———. ed. *Breakthrough Fictioneers.* W. Glover, Vt.: Something Else, 1973.

Krim, Seymour. "The Unimportant Writer" (1962), "Letter to Jack Newfield (Unmailed)" (1967), *Shake It for the World, Smartass.* N.Y.: Dial, 1970.

Lehmann-Haupt, Christopher. "Twenty 1969 Books," *New York Times* (Dec. 1, 1969).

Lessard, Susannah. "Publishing Conglomerated: When Profit Becomes Censor," *Washington Monthly.* III/5 (July, 1971).

Liebling, A.J. *The Press.* Revised ed. N.Y.: Ballantine, 1964.

Lipton, Lawrence, "Secession, 1953: The State of the Arts on the West Coast," *Intro,* II/11 (1953).

Lottman, Herbert. "The Invisible Writer," *Cultural Affairs.* 12 (Fall, 1970).

Macdonald, Dwight. "Masscult & Midcult," *Against the American Grain.* N.Y.: Random House, 1962.

———. "The New York Times, Alas," *Esquire,* LIX/4-5 (April-May, 1963).

Marinetti, Filippo. *Selected Writings.* Ed. by R. W. Flint. N.Y.: Farrar, Straus, 1972.

McCormick, Ken. "Freedom of Expression," *American PEN,* IV/4 (Fall, 1972).

Mount, Douglas. "If You Have Hidden Talent and Like To Eat," *Esquire,* LXXVI/6 (Dec., 1971).

———. "The Making of a Young Editor," *Book World* (Nov. 28, 1971).

Mudrick, Marvin. "Fiction and Truth," *Hudson Review,* XXV/1 (Spring, 1972).

Padgett, Ron, and David Shapiro, eds. *An Anthology of New York Poets.* N.Y.: Random House, 1970.

Peterson, Clarence. *The Bantam Story.* N.Y.: Bantam, 1970.

Plimpton, George, and Peter Ardery, eds. *The American Literary Anthology.* Vol. I. N.Y.: Farrar, Straus, 1968. Vol II. N.Y.: Random House, 1969. Vol. III N.Y.: Viking, 1970.

Navasky, Victor S. "Studies in Animal Behavior," *New York Times Book Review* (Feb. 25, 1973).

———. "Where Books Go When They Die," *New York Times Book Review* (March 18, 1973).

Podhoretz, Norman. *Making It.* N.Y.: Random House, 1968.

Pound, Ezra. "Summary" (1916), reprinted in Margaret Anderson, ed. *The Little Review Anthology.* N.Y.: Horizon, 1970.

Rader, Dotson. "Steal This Book," *Evergreen Review* (1972).

Rahv, Philip. "On F. R. Leavis and D. H. Lawrence," *New York Review of Books* (Sept. 26, 1968). Reprinted in *Literature and the Sixth Sense.* Boston: Houghton Mifflin, 1970.

Reinhold, Robert. "Crisis of the University Press," *New York Times Book Review* (May 7, 1972).

Rich, Alan. "Russian Roulette and the Record Racket," *New York,* IV/35 (Aug. 30, 1971).

Salzman, Eric. "A Whole New Classical Ballgame," *Stereo Review,* XXVI/3 (March, 1971).

Smith, Harry. "Special Report: The New York Times Book Review," *The Newsletter* (July 30, 1969).

———. "The New York Times Book Review (Part II)," *The Newsletter* (Dec. 8, 1971).

Snyder, Richard E. "Death of a Book," *Village Voice* (Jan 11, 1973).

Stein, Robert. *Media Power.* Boston: Houghton Mifflin, 1972.

———. " 'What Am I Bid for Lyndon Johnson?' Or How the Literary Auction Works," *New York,* IV/35 (Aug. 30, 1971).

Talese, Gay. *The Kingdom and the Power.* N.Y.: World, 1969.

Unwin, Stanley. *The Truth about Publishing.* London: Allen & Unwin, 1926.

Veitch, Tom. *Die Luis Armed Story.* Cologne, Germany: Krepenheuer & Witsch, 1970.

Westcott, Glenway. "The Sound and the Fury," *Esquire* (Sept. 1963).

Weybright, Victor. *The Making of a Publisher.* N.Y.: Reynal, 1967.

449

Weyr, Thomas. "The Making of the New York Times Book Review," *Publishers Weekly,* CCII/5 (July 31, 1972).

Wildman, Eugene, ed. *Experiments in Prose.* Chicago: Swallow, 1969.

Wilson, Edmund. "The All-Star Literary Vaudeville," *The Shores of Light.* N.Y.: Vintage, 1961.

CHAPTER 11

Adler, Renata. "Selling an Enraged Bread Pudding," *Toward a Radical Middle.* N.Y.: Random House, 1969.

Aldridge, John. *In the Country of the Young.* N.Y.: Harper's Magazine, 1970.

Barrett, William. *Time of Need.* N.Y.: Harper & Row, 1972.

Brooks, Cleanth. "Telling It Like It Is in the Tower of Babel," *Sewanee Review,* IC (1971).

Brustein, Robert. "The Playwright as Impersonator," *Seasons of Discontent.* N.Y.: Simon & Schuster, 1965.

———. "Notes from the Underground," *The Third Theatre.* N. Y.: Knopf, 1969.

———. Contribution to "Art, Culture and Conservatism," *Partisan Review,* XXXIX/3 (Summer, 1972).

Burke, Kenneth. *Counterstatement.* Chicago: Univ. of Chicago Press, 1931.

Canaday, John. *Embattled Critic.* N.Y.: Farrar, Straus, 1962.

Chase, Richard. "The Fate of the Avant-Garde," *Partisan Review,* XXIV/3 (Summer, 1957).

Davenport, Guy. Essay in *The New York Times Book Review* (Jan. 16, 1972).

DeMott, Benjamin. "Tickle-Touch Theater: A Reservation," *Supergrow.* N. Y.: Dutton, 1969.

Elliott, George. "Literary Vanguard," *Commentary,* XLII/6 (June, 1967).

Fiedler, Leslie A. *Waiting for the End.* N.Y.: Stein & Day, 1964.

———. *Collected Essays.* N.Y.: Stein & Day, 1971.

Greenberg, Clement. "Necessity of Formalism" *New Literary History,* III/1 (Autumn, 1971).

Hoffer, Eric. "Thoughts," *New York Times Magazine* (April 25, 1971).

Howe, Irving. "Introduction," *Steady Work.* N.Y.: Harcourt, Brace, 1966.

———. "The New York Intellectuals," *Decline of the New.* N.Y.: Harcourt, Brace, 1970.

———. "New Styles in Leftism," in Irving Howe, ed., *Beyond the New Left.* N. Y.: McCall's, 1970.

Kahler, Erich. *The Disintegration of Form in the Arts.* N.Y.: Braziller, 1968.

Kampf, Louis. *On Modernism.* Cambridge: M.I.T. Press, 1967.

Kazin, Alfred. "The Literary Sixties," *New York Times Book Review* (Dec. 21, 1969).

―――. "Professors Are Too Sophisticated," *Saturday Review* (May 22, 1971).

Kostelanetz, Richard. *The Theatre of Mixed Means.* N.Y.: Dial, 1968.

―――. "*Commentary* Scrutinized," *Minnesota Review,* VII/3 (Nov., 1967).

Leavis, Q. D. " 'The Discipline of Letters': A Sociological Note," *Scrutiny,* XII/1 (1943).

Marcuse, Herbert. "An Interview with Parisian Journalists," *New York Times Magazine* (Oct. 27, 1968).

Meyer, Leonard. "The End of a Renaissance," *Hudson Review,* (XVI/2 (Summer, 1963). Reprinted in *Music, the Arts, and Ideas.* Chicago: Univ. of Chicago Press, 1968.

Peyre, Henri. *The Failures of Criticism.* Rev. ed. Ithaca, NY: Cornell Univ. Press, 1967.

Podhoretz, Norman, ed. *The Commentary Reader.* N.Y.: Atheneum, 1966.

―――. "The Article as Art," *Doings and Undoings.* N.Y.: Farrar, Straus, 1964.

Pops, Martin. "The Rape of Sleeping Beauty―On Dance," *Salmagundi,* 15 (Winter, 1971).

Pound, Ezra. "Summary" (1916), in Margaret Anderson, ed. *The Little Review Anthology.* N.Y.: Horizon, 1970.

Rieff, Philip. "Fellow Teachers," *Salmagundi,* 20 (Summer-Fall, 1972).

Rosenberg, Harold. *The Anxious Object* N.Y.: Horizon, 1969.

―――. *Artworks and Packages.* N.Y.: Horizon, 1969.

―――. *The De-definition of Art.* N.Y.: Horizon, 1971.

―――. "Politics of Illusion," in Ihab Hassan, ed. *Liberations.* Middletown: Wesleyan Univ., 1971.

―――. "The Post-Art Artist," *Arts in Society,* VII/2 (1971).

Shattuck, Roger. "After the Avant-Garde," *New York Review of Books,* XIV/5 (March 12, 1970).

―――. "The Dada-Surrealist Expedition: Part II," *New York Review of Books,* VIII/10 (June 1, 1972).

Simon, John. "Fraud by Participation," *New York.* V/5 (Jan. 31, 1972).

Steiner, George. *Language and Silence.* N.Y.: Atheneum, 1967.

Styron, William. "On the Literature of Collision," *Modern Occasions,* I/2 (1971).

Sykes, Gerald. *The Perennial Avant-Garde.* Englewood Cliffs: Prentice-Hall, 1970.

Trilling, Diana. "The Other Night at Columbia," *Partisan Review,* XXVI/2 (Spring, 1959). Reprinted in *Claremont Essays.* N.Y.: Harcourt, Brace, 1964.

Trilling, Lionel. "The Function of the Little Magazine," *The Liberal Imagination.* N.Y.: Viking, 1950.

———. "Preface," *Beyond Culture.* N.Y.: Viking, 1965.

Weales, Gerald. *The Jumping-Off Place.* N.Y.: Macmillan, 1969.

Wellek, René. "The Attack on Literature," *The American Scholar,* XLII/1 (Winter, 1972-3).

CHAPTER 12

Adler, Renata. " . . . Patience for the Transition to Little Films," *A Year in the Dark.* N.Y.: Random House, 1969.

———. "Radicalism in Debacle: Palmer House," *Toward a Radical Middle,* N.Y.: Random House, 1969.

Baldwin, James. "The Black Boy Looks at the White Boy," *Nobody Knows My Name,* N.Y.: Dial, 1961.

———. "Interview with John Hall," *Transatlantic Review.* 37-8 (Nov., 1970).

Bellow, Saul. "Address," in *The Writer as Independent Spirit.* N.Y.: PEN American Center, 1968.

———. "World-Famous Impossibility," *New York Times* (Dec. 6, 1970).

Booth, Wayne. *Now Don't Try to Reason with Me.* Chicago: Univ. of Chicago Press, 1970.

Bouton, Jim. *I'm Glad You Didn't Take It Personally.* Ed. by Leonard Shecter. N.Y.: Morrow, 1972.

Brown, Cecil. *The Life and Loves of Mr. Jiveass Nigger.* N.Y.: Farrar, Straus, 1969.

Brown, Claude. *Manchild in the Promised Land.* N.Y.: Macmillan, 1965.

Brustein, Robert. "If an Artist Wants To Be Serious, [etc.] ," *New York Times Book Review* (May 9, 1971).

Elliott, George P. "Against Pornography," *Harper's* (March, 1965). Reprinted in *Conversions.* N.Y.: Dutton, 1971. Also in Theodore Solotaroff, ed. *Writers and Issues.* N.Y.: New American Library, 1969.

Epstein, Joseph. "Saul Bellow of Chicago," *New York Times Book Review* (May 9, 1971).

Feuer, Lewis. *The Conflict of Generations.* N.Y.: Basic, 1969.

Glazer, Nathan. *Remembering the Answers.* N.Y.: Basic, 1971.

Gayle, Addison, "Cultural Hegemony: The Southern White Writers and American Letters," *The Black Situation*. N.Y.: Horizon, 1970.

———, ed. *Black Aesthetic*. Garden City: Doubleday, 1971.

Giovanni, Nikki. "The True Import of Present Dialogue, Black vs. Negro," *BLACK Feeling, BLACK Talk, BLACK Judgment*. N.Y.: Morrow, 1970.

Kael, Pauline. "Trash, Art, and the Movies," *Going Steady*. Boston: Atlantic—Little, Brown, 1970.

Kopkind, Andrew. "Soul Power," *New York Review of Books,* IX/2 (Aug. 29, 1967). Reprinted in *America: The Mixed Curse*. Harmondsworth, England: Penguin, 1969.

Kostelanetz, Richard. "Marshall McLuhan" (1967) & "Herman Kahn" (1968), *Master Minds*. N.Y.: Macmillan, 1969.

Macdonald, Dwight. "Masscult & Midcult," *Against the American Grain*. N.Y.: Random House, 1962.

Major, Clarence, ed. *The New Black Poetry*. N.Y.: International, 1969.

Marcuse, Herbert. *One-Dimensional Man*. Boston: Beacon, 1964.

McCall, Dan. *The Man Says Yes.* N.Y.: Viking, 1969.

Miller, Adam David, ed. *Dice or Black Bones*. Boston: Houghton Mifflin, 1970.

Mills, C. Wright. *Power, Politics and People*. N.Y.: Oxford Univ. Press, 1963.

Murray, Albert. "James Baldwin, Protest Fiction & The Blues Tradition," in Herbert Hill, ed. *Anger and Beyond*. N.Y.: Harper & Row, 1965.

———. "The Case Histories," *The Omni-Americans*. N.Y.: Outerbridge, 1970.

Podhoretz, Norman. "The Article as Art," *Doings and Undoings*. N.Y.: Farrar, Straus, 1964.

Rahv, Philip. "A Note on Bernard Malamud," *Literature and the Sixth Sense*. Boston: Houghton Mifflin, 1969.

Reed, Ishmael, ed. *19 Necromancers from Now*. Garden City: Doubleday Anchor, 1970.

———. "Too Hot for Scanlan's," *The Nickel Review*, V/1 (April, 1971).

Rosenberg, Harold. "The Heroes of Marxist Science," *The Tradition of the New*. N.Y.: Horizon, 1959.

Roszak, Theodore. "Exploring Utopia," *The Making of a Counter-Culture*. Garden City: Doubleday Anchor, 1969.

Schaar, John H., and Sheldon S. Wolin. "Where We Are Now," *New York Review of Books*, XIV/9 (May 7, 1970).

Shapiro, Karl. *To Abolish Children*. Chicago: Quadrangle, 1968.

Simon, John. "Pseudo-Art," *Movies into Film*. N.Y.: Dial, 1971.

Sontag, Susan. *Styles of Radical Will.* N.Y.: Farrar, Straus, 1969.

Talese, Gay. "Looking for Hemingway [*Paris Review*]," *Esquire,* LX/1 (July, 1963).

Thompson, Denys. *Reading and Discrimination.* London: Chatto & Windus, 1934.

Trilling, Diana. "On the Steps of Low Library," *Commentary.* XLVI/5 (Nov., 1968).

Williams, John A. "Career by Accident," *Flashbacks.* Garden City: Doubleday Anchor, 1973.

CHAPTER 13

Adler, Renata. "Introduction," *Toward a Radical Middle.* N.Y.: Random House, 1969.

Anderson, Margaret, ed. *The Little Review Anthology.* N.Y.: Hermitage House, 1953.

Aronson, James. *The Press and the Cold War.* N.Y.: Bobbs-Merrill, 1970.

Connolly, Cyril. "Fifty Years of Little Magazines," *Art and Literature* I/1 (March, 1964).

Dudek, Louis. "The Role of Little Magazines in Canada," in Dudek and Michael Gnarowski, ed. *The Making of Modern Poetry in Canada.* Toronto: Ryerson, 1970.

Eliot, T.S.: "A Commentary," *The Criterion,* XVII/69 (July, 1938).

Eshleman, Clayton, ed. *A Caterpillar Anthology.* Garden City: Doubleday Anchor, 1971.

Fiedler, Leslie A., et al. "Little Mags/Small Presses and the Cultural Revolution," *Intrepid,* 21/2 (Winter-Spring, 1971-2).

Fulton, Len, ed. *Directory of Little Magazines & Small Presses.* Paradise, CA: Dustbooks, 1965 to the present (annually).

—————. "Anima Rising: Little Magazines in the Sixties," *American Libraries,* II/1 (Jan. 1972). Reprinted in John Gordon Burke, ed. *Print Image and Sound.* Chicago: American Library Assoc., 1972.

——, An Interview by Noel Peattie, *Sipapu,* III/2 (July, 1972).

Glessing, Robert G. *The Underground Press in America,* Bloomington, IN., Indiana Univ. Press, 1970.

Gross, Beverly. "Culture and Anarchy: Whatever Happened to Lit Magazines," *Antioch Review,* XXIX/1 (Spring, 1969).

Herring, Cherry [Arlene Croce]. "The Outer Lobby," *Ballet Review,* III/3 (1970).

Hoffman, Frederick J., et al. *The Little Magazines: A History and a Bibliography.* Princeton: Princeton Univ. Press, 1946.

Johnson, Curt, and Alvin Greenberg, eds. *Best Little Magazine Fiction, 1971.* N.Y.: N.Y. Univ. Press, 1971.

Johnson, Michael L. *The New Journalism.* Lawrence: The Univ. Press of Kansas, 1971.

Kornbluth, Jesse, ed. *Notes from the New Underground.* N.Y.: Viking, 1968.

———. "The Underground Press and How It Went," *Antioch Review,* XXIX/1 (Spring, 1969).

Kostelanetz, Richard. "Critical Writing for American Magazines: A Memoir and a Valedictory," *Works,* I/4 (Summer, 1968).

———. "The New Music," *The Yale Review,* LIX/2 (Dec., 1969).

Landesman, Jay, and Gershon Legman, eds. *The Compleat Neurotica.* N.Y.: Hacker Art Books, 1963.

Mangelsdorff, Rich. "Smallpress Rap," *The Book Review,* 17 (1970).

May, James Boyer, "Toward Print," in Len Fulton and J.B. May, eds. *Directory of Little Magazines and Small Presses.* Seventh ed. Paradise, CA: Dust Books, 1971.

McCrindle, Joseph, ed. *Stories from the Translantic Review.* N.Y.: Holt, Rinehart & Winston, 1970.

McLuhan, Marshall, and Edmund Carpenter, eds. *Explorations in Communication.* Boston: Beacon, 1960.

Morris, Richard. "Questionnaire Responses," *COSMEP Newsletter* (Special Issue, 1963).

Pollak, Felix. "Landing in Little Magazines: Capturing (?) a Trend," *Arizona Quarterly,* XIX/2 (Summer, 1963).

Putzel, Max. *The Man in the Mirror: William Marion Reedy and His Magazine.* Cambridge: Harvard Univ. Press, 1963.

Rikhoff, Jean, ed. *The Quixote Anthology.* N.Y.: Universal Library, 1961.

Rohm, Ethel Grodzins. *The Open Conspiracy.* Harrisburg, PA.: Giniger/ Stockpole, 1970.

Sanders, Ed, et al. "Ellipsing Along with—Pow? The New Journalism," *Cheetah,* I/8 (May, 1968).

Sitney, P. Adams, ed. *Film Culture Reader.* N.Y.: Praeger, 1970.

Smith, Harry. "What is COSMEP," *Small Press Review,* III/4 (1972).

Spackman, Peter, and Lee Ambrose, eds. *The Columbia University Forum.* N.Y.: Athcneum, 1968.

Swados, Harvey. "More Short Stories, Fewer Short Stories," *New York Times Book Review* (Jan. 21, 1973).

Wasserstrom, William. *The Time of the Dial.* Syracuse, NY: Syracuse Univ. Press, 1963.

———, ed. *A Dial Miscellany.* Syracuse, NY: Syracuse Univ. Press, 1963.

Whittemore, Reed. *Little Magazines.* Minneapolis: Univ. of Minnesota Press, 1963.

Weinstein, James, and David W. Eakins, eds. *For a New America.* N.Y.: Vintage, 1970.

Yates, Richard, ed. *Stories for the Sixties.* N.Y.: Bantam, 1963.

CHAPTER 14

Albright, Thomas. "New Art School: Correspondence," *Rolling Stone,* 106 (April 13, 1972).

Alta, "Like It Is," *Small Press Review,* IV/3 (1972).

Brooks, Gwendolyn, ed. *A Broadside Treasury.* Detroit: Broadside, 1971.

Brotherson, Robert. Book reviews in *Works,* II/2 (Fall-Winter, 1969).

Cerf, Bennett, quoted in Gerald Gross, ed. *Publishers on Publishing.* N.Y.: Universal Library, 1961.

Charters, Ann. *Kerouac.* San Francisco: Straight Arrow, 1973.

Collier, Peter. "For Fun and Profit in San Francisco," *New York Times Book Review* (Feb. 13, 1972).

Fiedler, Leslie A. "Which Writer Under Thirty-Five [etc.]," *Esquire,* LXXVI/4 (Oct., 1972).

Francis, Wynne. "The Little Presses," *Canadian Literature,* 33 (Summer, 1967).

Fulton, Len, ed. *Small Press Record of Books.* Paradise, CA: Dustbooks, 1969.

————. *Small Press Record of Books, 1969-72.* Second ed. Paradise, CA: Dustbooks, 1972.

————. "See Bukowski Run," *Small Press Review,* IV/4 (May, 1973).

Godrey, David & James Lorimer. "Publishing in Canada," in Robert Fulford, et al., eds. *Read Canadian.* Toronto: James Lewis & Samuel, 1972.

Harris, Mark. "Alan Swallow, 1915-66," *New York Times Book Review* (Dec. 18, 1966).

Higgins, Dick. "A Something Else Manifesto," *Manifestos.* N.Y.: Something Else, 1966.

————. "The Small Presses," *Works,* II/1 (Spring, 1969).

Hopper, John. Book reviews in *Works,* II/1 (Spring, 1969).

Jacob, John "Yer Blewze," *COSMEP Newsletter* III/6 (March, 1972).

Kherdian, David. "Poetry and the Little Press," *Ararat,* XI/2 (Spring, 1970).

Kostelanetz, Richard. "Small Presses," *Panache,* 7 (1971).

———. "Why *Assembling*," in Bill Henderson, ed. *The Publish Yourself Handbook.* Yonkers, NY: Pushcart Press, 1973.

Kreymborg, Alfred. *Troubadour.* N.Y.: Sagamore, 1957.

Krim, Seymour. "What's This Cat's Story?" *Views of a Nearsighted Cannoneer.* N.Y.: Excelsior, 1968.

Morris, Richard. "Questionnaire Responses," *COSMEP Newsletter* (Special Issue, 1973).

Mount, Douglas. "San Fran," *Publishers Weekly* (Dec. 13, 1971).

Randall, Dudley. "The Poets of Broadside Press," *Black Academy Review,* I/1 (Spring, 1970).

Rexroth, Kenneth. "Poetry in the 70's," *The Alternative Society.* N.Y.: Herder & Herder, 1970.

Seeley, John R. "Progress from Poverty?" *Liberation,* XI/5 (Aug., 1966).

Swallow, Alan. "American Publishing and the American Writer," *An Editor's Essays of Two Decades.* Denver: Swallow, 1960.

Weybright, Victor. *The Making of a Publisher.* N.Y.: Reynal, 1967.

Yates, J. Michael. "The Sono Nis Press (Autumn, 1971)," *American PEN,* III/4 (Fall, 1971).

CHAPTERS 15 & 16

(Rather than acknowledge all of the young writers' books, the following list selects titles mentioned in the text or the single most substantial books of those writers mentioned, as well as unusually comprehensive anthologies of young writers' works.)

Anania, Michael, ed. *New Poetry Anthology # 1,* Chicago: Swallow, 1970.

Anson, Peter, ed. *Canada First.* Toronto: House of Anansi, 1969.

Atwood, Margaret. *Power Politics.* Toronto: House of Anansi, 1971.

Bourne, Randolph. "Youth," *Atlantic Monthly,* 109 (April, 1912).

Brown, Cecil. "James Brown, Hoodoo and Black Culture," *Black Review No. 1.* N.Y.: Morrow, 1971.

Carroll, Paul, ed. *The Young American Poets.* Chicago: Follett, 1968.

Cauble, Don. "Doug Blazek: Not This, Not That," *Studies in the Twentieth Century,* 7 (Spring, 1971).

Charyn, Jerome. *The Tar Baby.* N.Y.: Holt, 1973.

Connolly, Cyril. *Previous Convictions.* N.Y.: Harper & Row, 1963.

Coombs, Orde, ed. *We Come as Liberators.* N.Y.: Dodd, Mead, 1970.

Delbanco, Nicholas. *Consider Sappho Burning.* N.Y.: Morrow, 1969.

Dickey, James. "The Son, the Cave, and the Burning Bush," *Sorties.* Garden City: Doubleday, 1971.

Disend, Michael. *Stomping the Goyim.* N.Y.: Croton, 1969.

Fox, Hugh. *The Living Underground.* Troy, N.Y.: Whitson, 1970.

Gangemi, Kenneth. *Olt.* N.Y.: Orion, 1969.

Gans, Herbert J. "The Racial Crisis," *People and Plans.* N.Y.: Basic, 1968.

Gerald, John Bart, and George Blecher, eds. *Survival Prose.* Indianapolis: Bobbs-Merrill, 1971.

Glück, Louise. *Firstborn.* N.Y.: World, 1968.

Gombrich, E.H. *Art and Illusion.* N.Y.: Pantheon, 1960.

Graham, Dan. *"End Moments."* N.Y.: Privately published, 1969.

Gravenson, G. S. *The Sweetmeat Saga.* N.Y.: Outerbridge, 1971.

Greinke, L. Eric., ed. *10 Michigan Poets.* Grand Rapids, MI: Pilot Press, 1972.

Hewitt, Geof, ed. *Quickly Aging Here.* Garden City: Doubleday Anchor, 1969.

Higgins, Dick. *Foew&ombwhnw.* N.Y.: Something Else, 1969.

Holland, Cecelia. "Letters," *Authors Guild Bulletin* (Dec.-Jan., 1971).

Jovanovich, William. *Now, Barrabas.* N.Y.: Harper & Row, 1964.

Kawin, Bruce. *Telling It Again and Again.* Ithaca, NY: Cornell Univ. Press, 1972.

Katz, Elia. *Armed Love.* N.Y.: Holt, 1972.

Kazin, Alfred. "Oates," *Harper's,* CCXLIII/2 (Aug., 1971).

Klonsky, Milton, ed. *Shake the Kaleidoscope.* N.Y.: Pocket, 1973.

Kostelanetz, Richard, ed. *The Young American Writers,* N.Y.: Funk & Wagnalls, 1967.

————, ed. *Seeing Through Shuck.* N.Y.: Ballantine, 1972.

————, ed. Manifestos of young writer-editors, *The American PEN,* III/4 (Fall, 1971).

Kozloff, Max. Quoted in "The New Art: It's Way, Way Out," *Newsweek* (July 29, 1968).

Krauss, Rosalind E. *Terminal Iron Works: The Sculpture of David Smith.* Cambridge: M.I.T. Press, 1971.

Lahr, John. *Up Against the Fourth Wall.* N.Y.: Grove, 1970.

Lee, Dennis, ed. *T. O. Now.* Toronto: House of Anansi, 1968.

Lippard, Lucy R. *Changing.* N.Y.: Dutton, 1971.

Malley, Jean, and Hale Tokay, eds. *Contemporaries.* N.Y.: Viking, 1972.

Matilla, Alfredo, and Iván Silén, eds. *The Puerto Rican Poets.* N.Y.: Bantam, 1972.

McCall, Dan. *The Man Says Yes.* N.Y.: Viking, 1969.

McMichael, James, and Dennis Saleh, eds. *Just What the Country Needs, Another Poetry Anthology.* Belmont, CA: Wadsworth, 1971.

Newman, Charles, and William A. Henkin, Jr., eds. *Under 30,* Bloomington, IN: Indiana Univ. Press, 1969.

Monaco, Richard, ed. *New American Poetry.* N.Y.: McGraw-Hill, 1973.

Nichol, bp. *bp.* Toronto: Coach House, 1967.

———, ed. *The Concrete Chef.* Ottawa: Oberon, 1970.

Oates, Joyce Carol. *them.* N.Y.: Vanguard, 1969.

O'Toole, Simon. *Confessions of an American Scholar.* Minneapolis: Univ.
of Minnesota Press, 1970.

Ortega y Gasset, José. *Man and Crisis.* N.Y.: Norton, 1958.

Planz, Allen. *A Night for Rioting.* Chicago: Swallow, 1969.

Pynchon, Thomas. *V.* Philadelphia: Lippincott, 1963.

——— *Gravity's Rainbow.* N.Y.: Viking, 1973.

———. "Entropy," in Richard Kostelanetz, ed. *Twelve from the Sixties.*
N.Y.: Dell, 1967.

Reed, Ishmael. *Mumbo Jumbo.* Garden City: Doubleday, 1972.

———. ed. *19 Necromancers for Now.* Garden City: Doubleday Anchor,
1970.

Rosenblum, Martin J., ed. *Brewing: 20 Milwaukee Poets.* Lyme Center,
NH: Giligia, 1972.

Russ, Joanna. "The New Misandry," *Village Voice* (Oct. 12, 1972).

Sallis, James. *A Few Last Words.* N.Y.: Macmillan, 1970.

Schreiber, Ron, ed. *31 New American Poets.* N.Y.: Hill & Wang, 1969.

Spender, Stephen. "The Young Writer, Present, Part, and Future," in A.L.
Bader, ed. *To the Young Writer.* Ann Arbor: Univ. of Michigan Press,
1965.

Veitch, Tom. *Die Luis Armed Story.* Cologne, Germany: Kiepenheuer &
Witsch, 1970.

Wakoski, Diane. *The George Washington Poems.* N.Y.: Riverrun, 1967.

Waldman, Anne, ed. *The World Anthology.* N.Y.: Bobbs-Merrill, 1971.

———, ed. *Another World.* N.Y.: Bobbs-Merrill, 1971.

Weber, Nancy. "Dear Mother and Dad," *Assembling,* 1 (1970). Also reprinted in *In Youth.* (1972).

Wilentz, Ted, and Tom Weatherly, eds. *New Black Poets.* N.Y.: Hill &
Wang, 1970.

Williams, William Carlos. "The Somnambulists," *transition,* 18 (Nov.,
1929).

Wittkower, Rudolf and Margot. *Born Under Saturn: The Character and
Conduct of Artists.* N.Y.: W.W. Norton, 1969.

Wolven, Fred, and Duane Locke, eds. *New Generation: Poetry.* Ann
Arbor, MI: Ann Arbor Review, 1971.

Yates, J. Michael, ed. *Contemporary Poetry of British Columbia.* Victoria, B. C.: Sono Nis, 1971.

Youngblood, Gene. *Expanded Cinema.* N.Y.: Dutton, 1970.

Zoline, Pamela. "The Heat Death of the Universe," in Judith Merrill, ed. *England Swings SF.* N.Y.: Ace, 1970. Also reprinted in *In Youth.*

CHAPTER 17

Acconci, Vito. *Book Four.* N.Y.: 0 to 9, 1968.

_____. Notes and an Interview, *Avalanche,* 6 (Fall, 1972).

Aldridge, Adele. *Notpoems.* Riverside, CT.: Magic Circle, 1972.

Antin, David. "Modernism and Postmodernism," *Boundary* 2, I/1 (Fall, 1972).

Bankerd, Carol. *Graphic Poems.* Princeton, NJ: Privately published, 1969.

Bissett, Bill. *nobody owns the earth.* Toronto: House of Anansi, 1971.

_____. *poems for yoshi.* Vancouver: Blewointment, 1972.

Brecht, George. Various "Fluxus" publications (c. 1965, N.Y.).

Brilliantes, Jos C. *Sonnets in Concrete.* Washington, D.C.: Privately published, 1968.

Burgy, Donald. *Art Ideas for the Year 4000.* Andover, MA: Addison Gallery of American Art, 1970.

Colombo, John Robert, ed. *New Direction in Canadian Poetry.* Toronto: Holt-Canada, 1971.

Coolidge, Clark. *Flag Flutter and U.S. Electric.* N.Y.: Lines, 1966.

_____ *Clark Coolidge.* N.Y.: Lines, 1967.

_____ *Ing.* N.Y.: Angel Hair, 1968.

_____ *Amount.* N.Y.: Adventures in Poetry, 1969.

_____ *Space.* N.Y.: Harper & Row, 1970.

_____. *The So.* N.Y.: Adventures in Poetry, 1971.

_____ *Suite V.* N.Y.: Adventures in Poetry, 1972.

_____ "The Clark Coolidge Issue," *Big Sky,* 3 (1972).

Clark, Tom, *John's Heart.* N.Y.: Grossman Goliard–Santa Fe, 1972.

Gangemi, Kenneth. *Lydia.* Los Angeles: Black Sparrow, 1970.

Giorno, John. *Balling Buddha.* N.Y.: Kulchur Foundation, 1970.

Graham, Dan. *"End Moments."* N.Y.: Privately published, 1969.

Gross, Ronald, and George Quasha, eds. *Open Poetry.* N.Y.: Simon & Schuster, 1973.

Higgins, Dick. *Jefferson's Birthday.* N.Y.: Something Else, 1964.

_____ *Foew&ombwhnw.* N.Y.: Something Else, 1969.

Hompson, Davi Det. *Davi Det Hompson.* N.Y.: Alexandre Iolas Gallery, 1970.

Indiana, Robert. *Robert Indiana.* Philadelphia: Univ. of Pa. Press, 1968.

———. *Graphics.* Notre Dame, IN: St. Mary's College, 1969.

Kaprow, Allan. "O.K.," *Manifesto.* N.Y.: Something Else, 1966.

Kostelanetz, Richard. *Visual Language.* Brooklyn, N.Y.: Assembling, 1970.

———, ed. *Imaged Words & Worded Images.* N.Y.: Outerbridge & Dienstfrey, 1970.

———. "Words and Images Artfully Entwined," *Art International,* XIV/7 (Sept. 20, 1970).

Lax, Robert. *Black & White.* N.Y.: Journeyman, 1971.

Mac Low, Jackson. *22 Light Poems.* Los Angeles: Black Sparrow, 1970.

———. *Stanzas for Iris Lezak.* West Glover, VT: Something Else, 1972.

Nichol, bp, et al. ("The Four Horsemen"). *Canadada* (ST 88760 036 0).

Ockerse, Tom. *T. O. P.* Bloomington, IN: Privately published, 1971.

O'Gallagher, Liam. *Planet Noise.* San Francisco: Nova Broadcast, 1969.

———. *The Blue Planet Notebooks.* San Francisco: X-Communications, 1972.

Ostriker, Alicia. "Poem Objects," *Partisan Review,* XL/1 (Winter, 1973).

Oyewole, Abiodum, et al. *The Last Poets* (Douglas 3).

Nichol, bp, et al. ("The Four Horsemen"). *Canadada* (ST 88760 036 0).

Pietri, Pedro. "Prologue for Ode to Road Runner," *Revista del Instituto de Estudios Puertorriqueños,* I/1 (1971).

———. "The Broken Spanish Dream," in Alfredo Matilla & Iván Silén, eds., *The Puerto Rican Poets.* N.Y.: Bantam, 1972.

Phillips, Michael Joseph. *The Concrete Book.* Milwaukee, WI: Privately published, 1971.

———. *Concrete Sonnets.* Indianapolis: Privately published, 1972.

Pritchard, Norman Henry II. *The Matrix.* Garden City: Doubleday, 1970.

———. *Eecchhooeess.* N.Y.: New York Univ. Press, 1971.

Rosenberg, Harold. *The Tradition of the New.* Second ed. N.Y.: Horizon, 1960.

Samperi, Frank. *Quadrifariam.* N.Y.: Grossman, 1973.

Saroyan, Aram. *Aram Saroyan.* N.Y.: Random House, 1968.

Schwerner, Armand. *The Tablets, I-VIII.* West Branch, IA: Cummington, 1969.

———. *The Tablets, I-XV.* N.Y.: Grossman, 1971.

Williams, William Carlos. "The Somnambulists," *transition.* 18 (Nov., 1929).

Young, La Monte, ed. *An Anthology.* Second ed. Munich: Heinar Friedrich, 1969.

CHAPTER 18

Ashbery, John. "Idaho," *The Tennis-Court Oath.* Middletown, CT: Wesleyan Univ. Press, 1962.

Bain, Willard. *Informed Sources.* Garden City: Doubleday, 1969.

Barth, John. "Frame-Tale," *Lost In the Funhouse.* Garden City: Doubleday, 1968.

Barthelme, Frederick. *War and War.* Garden City: Doubleday, 1971.

Beckett, Samuel, et al. *Our Exagmination Around His Factification.* Paris: Shakespeare & Co., 1929.

Berne, Stanley. *The Dialogues.* N.Y.: Wittenborn, 1962.

————. *The Multiple Modern Gods.* N.Y.: Wittenborn, 1964.

———— *The Unconscious Victorious.* N.Y.: Wittenborn, 1969.

Bowles, Jerry, ed. *This Book Is a Movie.* N.Y.: Delta, 1971.

Brockman, John. *By the Late John Brockman.* N.Y.: Macmillan, 1969.

————. *37.* N.Y.: Holt, Rinehart & Winston, 1970.

Cage, John. *Notations.* N.Y.: Something Else, 1968.

Carruth, Hayden. "The Writer's Situation," *New American Review,* 8 (April, 1970).

Conrad, Earl. *Typoo.* N.Y.: Paul S. Eriksson, 1969.

Cunningham, Merce. *Changes.* N.Y.: Something Else, 1969.

Depew, Wally. *Once.* Paradise, CA: Dustbooks, 1971.

Edson, Russell. *The Childhood of an Equestrian.* N.Y.: Harper & Row, 1973.

Federman, Raymond. *Double or Nothing.* Chicago: Swallow, 1971.

Fox, Hugh. *The Living Underground.* Troy, NY: Whitson, 1970.

Gangemi, Kenneth. *Lydia.* Los Angeles: Black Sparrow, 1970.

Gins, Madeline. *Word Rain.* N.Y.: Grossman, 1969.

Herman, Jan. *General Municipal Election.* San Francisco: Nova Broadcast, 1969.

Hertzberg, Hendrik. *One Million.* N.Y.: Simon & Schuster—Gemini, Smith, 1970.

Horn, Richard. *Encyclopedia.* N.Y.: Grove, 1969.

Kaprow, Allen, *Assemblage, Environments & Happenings.* N.Y.: Abrams, 1966.

Katz, Steve. *The Exagggerations of Peter Prince.* N.Y.: Holt, 1967.

Kelley, William Melvin. *Dunfords Travels Everywheres* Garden City: Doubleday, 1970.

King, Kenneth. "Print-Out," in Richard Kostelanetz, ed. *Future's Fictions.* Princeton, NJ: Panache, 1971.

Knott, Bill. "No Act Play," *Auto-Necrophilia.* Chicago: Follett, 1971.

Kostelanetz, Richard. *In the Beginning.* Somerville, MA: Abyss, 1971.

———. *Accounting.* Sacramento, CA: Poetry Newsletter, 1973.

———. "Milestones in a Life," *In Youth.* N.Y.: Ballantine, 1972.

———. ed. *Breakthrough Fictioneers.* W. Glover, VT: Something Else, 1973.

MacLennan, Toby. *1 Walked Out of 2 and Forgot It.* Millerton, NY: Something Else, 1972.

Marks, J *Rock and Other Four-Letter Words.* N.Y.: Bantam, 1968.

Michals, Duane. *Sequences.* Garden City: Doubleday, 1970.

Nichol, bp. *Two Novels.* Toronto: Coach House, 1969.

Pritchard, Norman Henry II. "Hoom," in Ishmael Reed, ed. *19 Necromancers from Now.* Garden City: Doubleday, 1970.

Reichek, Jesse. *etcetera.* N.Y.: New Directions, 1965.

Ruscha, Edward. *Twenty-Six Gasoline Stations.* Los Angeles: Edward Ruscha, 1962.

——— *Some Los Angeles Apartments.* Los Angeles: Edward Ruscha, 1965.

——— *Sunset Strip.* Los Angeles: Edward Ruscha, 1966.

———. *Thirty-Four Parking Lots.* Los Angeles: Edward Ruscha, 1967.

———. *Nine Swimming Pools.* Los Angeles: Edward Ruscha, 1968.

———. *Crackers.* Hollywood: Heavy Industry, 1969.

Sanders, Ed. *Shards of God.* N.Y.: Grove, 1970.

Samaras, Lucas. *Samaras Album.* N.Y.: Whitney Museum of American Art., 1971.

Saporta, Marc. *Composition No. 1.* N.Y.: Simon & Schuster, 1963.

Schwerner, Armand. *The Tablets, I-XV.* N.Y.: Grossman, 1971.

Shiomi, Chieko. *Events and Games.* N.Y.: Fluxus, 1964.

Stein, Gertrude. *The Making of Americans.* N.Y.: Something Else, 1966.

———. *Geography and Plays.* N. Y.: Something Else, 1968.

———. *Painted Lace.* New Haven: Yale Univ. Press, 1955.

Tuten, Frederic. *The Adventures of Mao on the Long March.* N.Y.: Kasak/Citadel, 1971.

Vaughn-James, M. *Elephant.* Toronto: New Press, 1970.

——— *The Projector.* Toronto: Coach House, 1971.

Weber, Nancy. "Dear Mother & Dad," in Richard Kostelanetz and Henry Korn, eds. *Assembling.* Brooklyn: Assembling, 1970.

Wildman, Eugene. *Nuclear Love.* Chicago: Swallow, 1972.

———, ed. *Experiments in Prose.* Chicago: Swallow, 1969.

Young, La Monte; and Marian Zazeela. *Selected Writings.* Munich: Heinar Friedrich, 1970.

Zekowski, Arlene. *Concretions.* N.Y.: Wittenborn, 1962.

————. *Abraxas.* N.Y.: Wittenborn, 1964.

————. *Seasons of the Mind.* N.Y.: Wittenborn, 1969.

Zend, Robert. "Oab," *Exile*, I/1 (1972).

CHAPTERS 19 & 20

Art Workers Newsletter. "Fair Practices Agency," II/3 (1972).

Bly, Robert. "The Sixties Press," *Works.* II/1 (Spring, 1969).

Bondy, Francois. "German Writers Rallying to Word-Producer's Union," *New York Times* (Jan. 11, 1971).

Bookchin, Murray. "Post-Scarcity Anarchy," *Anarchos* (Spring, 1969).

Bourne, Randolph. "The Dodging of Pressures," *Youth and Life.* Boston: Houghton Mifflin, 1913.

————. *History of a Literary Radical.* Ed. by Van Wyck Brooks, N.Y.: Huebsch, 1920.

Carpenter, Edmund, and Ken Heyman. *They Became What They Beheld.* N.Y.: Outerbridge, 1970.

Cassill, R.V. *In an Iron Time.* Lafayette, IN: Purdue Univ. Studies, 1969.

Diamond, Edwin, " 'Reporter Power' Takes Root," *Columbia Journalism Review* (Summer, 1970). Reprinted in Alfred Balk and James Boylan, eds. *Our Troubled Press.* Boston: Little, Brown, 1971.

Deschin, Jacob. "The Sagging Coffee Table," *35-mm Photography* (Spring, 1973).

Drought, James. "Robinson Crusoe in the American Literary Desert," *December,* X/1 (1968).

Duberman, Martin. "On Misunderstanding Student Rebels," *The Unconquered Past.* N.Y.: Random House, 1969.

Eliot, T. S. "A Commentary," *The Criterion* XVII/69 (July, 1938).

Fiedler, Leslie "A Voice in Opposition," *New York Times Book Review* (April 21, 1963).

Gans, Herbert J. "The 'Equality' Revolution," *New York Times Magazine* (Nov. 3, 1968).

Goodman, Paul, "A New Deal for the Arts," *People or Personnel.* N.Y.: Random House, 1965.

Hayden, Tom. *Rebellion and Repression.* N.Y.: Meridian, 1969.

Henderson, Bill and Nancy, eds. *The Publish Yourself Handbook.* Yonkers, NY: The Pushcart Press, 1973.

Higgins, Dick. "Something Else Press, Inc.," *Works,* II/1 (Spring, 1969).

Hoffman, Michael. "Small Publishers," *Cultural Affairs.* I/2 (Fall, 1970).

Johnson, B. S. "A Living for Writers," *The New Society* (Jan. 9, 1969).

Karpel, Craig. "Das Hip Kapital," *Esquire,* LXXIV/6 (Dec., 1970).

Kopkind, Andrew. "Woodstock Nation," *Hard Times* (Oct., 1969).

Krim, Seymour. "Should I Assume America Is Already Dead?" *Shake It for the World, Smartass.* N.Y.: Dial, 1970.

Lenson, David. "The Next Poetry: A Reach of Prophets," *S. F. Book Review*, 24 (Oct., 1972).

O.M. Collective. *The Organizer's Manual.* N.Y.: Bantam, 1971.

Marcuse, Herbert. "The Left Under Counterrevolution," *Counterrevolution and Revolt.* Boston: Beacon, 1972.

Mangione, Jerre. *The Dream and the Deal.* Boston: Little, Brown, 1972.

Nader, Ralph, et al. eds. *Whistle Blowing.* N.Y.: Grossman, 1972.

Newman, Charles. "The Uses and Abuses of Death," *Tri-Quarterly*, 26 (Winter, 1973).

Rose, Barbara. "The Big Squeeze," *New York Magazine*, V/9 (Feb. 28, 1972).

Russ, Joanna. "The New Misandry," *Village Voice* (Oct. 12, 1972).

Salzman, Eric. "A Whole New Classical Ballgame," *Stereo Review*, XXVI/3 (March, 1971).

Spender, Stephen. *World Within World.* London: Hamish Hamilton, 1951.

Stein, Robert. *Media Power.* Boston: Houghton Mifflin, 1972.

Taylor, Henry. "Vantage and Vexation of Spirit [Vanity Presses]," *Georgia Review* (Spring, 1971).

Thornton, Gene. "Personal Encounters [Self-Published Photography]," *Saturday Review—the Arts* (Dec. 2, 1972).

Trilling, Lionel. "The Function of the Little Magazine," *The Liberal Imagination.* N.Y.: Viking, 1950.

Williams, Jonathan. "The Jargon Society," *Cultural Affairs*, 12 (Fall, 1970).

ACKNOWLEDGMENTS

Every effort has been made to verify the spelling of all proper names and to trace the ownership of all copyrighted material, in addition to making full acknowledgment of the latter's use. If any error or omission has occurred, it will be corrected in subsequent editions, provided that appropriate notification is submitted in writing to the publisher.

Excerpt from "Idaho" by John Ashbery, reprinted from *The Tennis Court Oath* (1960), by permission of Wesleyan University Press.

Excerpt from "Power Politics" by Margaret Atwood, reprinted by permission of the House of Anansi Press, Toronto. Copyright © 1971 by Margaret Atwood.

"an whn yu cum" by Bill Bissett, from *pomes for yoshi* (blewointment-press).

Excerpt from "The Next" by Clark Coolidge, reprinted from *Big Sky, 3* (1972) by permission of the author. Copyright © 1972 by Clark Coolidge.

Excerpt from Kenneth Gangemi's *Lydia* (Black Sparrow, 1970), by permission of the author. Copyright © 1970 by Kenneth Gangemi.

Excerpt from *Olt* (Orion, 1969), reprinted by permission of Grossman, Publishers. Copyright © 1969 by Kenneth Gangemi.

Excerpt from Nikki Giovanni's *BLACK Feeling BLACK Talk BLACK Judgment* (Morrow, 1970), by permission of the publisher. Copyright © 1968, 1970 by Nikki Giovanni.

Poems by CPGraham, reprinted *ime* (Pym-Randall, 1969) by permission of the author. Copyright © 1969 by Courtenay Peter Graham.

"Schema" & "March 21, 1966" by Dan Graham, reprinted from *End Moments* (1969) by permission from the author. Copyright © 1967, 1968, 1969 by Dan Graham.

"Concentric" by Richard Kostelanetz, reprinted from *Visual Language* (Assembling Press, Brooklyn, N.Y. 11202), by permission of the author. Copyright © 1967, 1970 by Richard Kostelanetz.

"Milestones in a Life," reprinted from *In Youth* (Ballantine, 1972), by permission of the author. Copyright © 1971, 1972 by Richard Kostelanetz.

"Ice Cream Poem," by Jonathan Price, reprinted by permission of the author. Copyright © 1968 by Jonathan Price.

467

Index

(The following list omits the names mentioned in alphabetical order on pages 84-86, on pages 348-56, and in the bibliographies. It also neglects to index the publisher-editors in chapters 13 and 14, the "missing" writers on page 262, the intermedia poets on page 374, and the authors of self-published books on pages 421-3, unless the individuals listed in those places are also mentioned elsewhere in the book. It may still be incomplete.)

471

RICHARD KOSTELANETZ   New York, New York, May 14, 1940

Studied at Brown, Columbia, and London universities. M.A. in American History. Phi Beta Kappa.

Received Woodrow Wilson Fellowship, Fulbright Scholarship, Pulitzer Fellowship in Critical Writing, and Guggenheim Fellowship.

Published essays on various cultural subjects in periodicals both large and small, here and abroad.

Contributing editor of *The Humanist, Arts in Society, The New York Ace,* and *Lotta Poetica.*

Collected a selection of his widely reprinted profiles of American artists and intellectuals as *Master Minds* (1969).

Authored several critical books of his own and edited over a dozen more volumes of or about contemporary art, literature, criticism, and social thought.

Cofounder-compiler of *Assembling,* an annual book-length collection of "otherwise unpublishable" creative work; coproprietor, Assembling Press.

Writer-narrator-producer of television programs about art and literature.

Contributed his poems and stories to anthologies and literary journals, in addition to public exhibitions of avant-garde poetry and post-visual art around the world.

Currently completing his second collection of visual poems, *I Articulations,* and a book of Short Fictions, as well as initiating critical studies of contemporary experimental literature.

Lives in New York City, though frequently traveling to give expository lectures and "illuminated demonstrations" of his creative work.

Stands six feet tall, weighs 180 pounds, and loves especially to swim and read.

480